1-2-3® Release 2.2 Made Easy

1-2-3® Release 2.2 Made Easy

Mary Campbell

Osborne **McGraw-Hill**

Berkeley New York St. Louis San Francisco
Auckland Bogotá Hamburg London Madrid
Mexico City Milan Montreal New Delhi Panama City
Paris São Paulo Singapore Sydney
Tokyo Toronto

Osborne **McGraw-Hill**
2600 Tenth Street
Berkeley, California 94710
U.S.A.

For information on translations and book distributors outside of the
U.S.A., please write to Osborne **McGraw-Hill** at the above address.

A complete list of trademarks appears on page 505.

1-2-3® Release 2.2 Made Easy

234567890 DODO 89

ISBN 0-07-881554-1

Acquisitions Editor: Elizabeth Fisher
Technical Reviewer: Chris Noble
Copy Editor: Dana Dubrinsky
Word Processor: Judy Koplan
Composition: Bonnie Bozorg
Proofreaders: Kay Luthin, Barbara Conway
Production Supervisor: Kevin Shafer

CONTENTS
AT A GLANCE

TABLE OF CONTENTS

ACKNOWLEDGMENTS

This book is the result of the efforts of many individuals. I would like to extend my special thanks to the following individuals:

Gabrielle Lawrence, who helped with every phase of the book.

Kristy Fordham, who created all the screens and checked each exercise to ensure it produced the correct results.

Chris Noble, who took time from his busy schedule and well deserved vacation to review each chapter of the book. His insight and attention to every detail of Release 2.2 were a great help.

Liz Fisher, who managed the entire process of making this a book and helped in many ways to produce a quality product.

Ilene Shapera, who handled all the queries and helped us find the right words for quick changes at the end of sometimes long days.

Kevin Shafer, who has done his usual wonderful job with the production of the book.

Dana Dubinsky, who performed a meticulous copyediting job.

To all of those at Lotus who were such an immense help through the beta process for Release 2.2 and 3 including Susan Erabino, Chris Noble, Mary Beth Rettger, Danielle Romance, Alexandra Trevelyan, and Scott Tucker.

INTRODUCTION

1-2-3 has become such an important business tool that it seems difficult to remember what it was like to perform financial analyses without it. Although there have been many spreadsheet products from which to select, 1-2-3 has continued to offer the speed and functionality to meet the needs of the majority of spreadsheet users.

Release 2.2 has many new features that extend the usefulness of the product. For example, the new Settings Sheets provide a look at the overall selections within a given area of 1-2-3. New Search and File Link features make the product practical for applications involving many spreadsheet entries or the consolidation of information between files. A Learn feature allows you to create macros without being a programming expert. Although there are many new options from which to select, the familiar interface with the older releases of 1-2-3 will allow you to master the new features quickly.

About This Book

This book is designed to present the new Release 2.2 features in an easy-to-learn format. You will use these new features as you create practical application examples. Because you are introduced to these commands in the context of application examples, you not only will see the keystrokes used to make things happen but will learn what capabilities these features offer.

The exercises within the book are presented in a step-by- step tutorial format to guarantee your success. Knowing when to use a command is not left to chance, since you are offered detailed instructions throughout the model-building process. With the building block approach presented in this book you will find your 1-2-3 skills increasing rapidly as you move from chapter to chapter.

How This Book Is Organized

This book is divided into 13 chapters. In most cases, each chapter contains just the right number of new features to cover in a single session. The first few chapters provide the building blocks for your first model. After you have mastered these topics, you will probably want to progress through the remaining topics sequentially, leading gradually to more advanced topics. Because the models in the later chapters are self-contained, you can also work with them without first becoming familiar with the examples in earlier chapters.

Chapter 1 will get you started with the package. It explains the important features of 1-2-3's display and introduces the new help structure for the package. It also introduces the entry of numbers and labels on the worksheet. You will learn how to use the new Undo feature to protect your worksheet investment.

Chapter 2 provides an introduction to the use of formulas on the worksheet. You will learn how formulas add power to the worksheet through What-if capabilities.

Chapter 3 provides information to tailor the format of your entries to your needs. You will learn how to select currency, fixed, percent, scientific notation, date, or other cell formats on the worksheet. You will also learn how to change the width of columns to display the new formats and to use Release 2.2's efficient Column-Range option.

Chapter 4 shows you how to protect your investment in model building through the use of files that can be stored on your disk permanently. You will learn about Release 2.2's ability to create backup files, as you learn how easy it is to store and retrieve data on your disk.

Chapter 5 covers everything you need to know to copy entries that you have already made to other locations on the worksheet. In this chapter you will learn techniques for rearranging worksheet data to change models. You will also learn to use Release 2.2's new Range Search feature to locate cell entries quickly.

Chapter 6 provides explanations and examples of 1-2-3's print features. You will learn how to do everything from printing a draft of your worksheet to adding headers and other sophisticated options. Later, in Chapter 13, you will supplement the basics learned in this chapter with the new spreadsheet publishing options offered by Allways, an Add-In that ships with every copy of the Release 2.2 software.

Chapter 7 introduces you to 1-2-3's built-in functions. These are formulas that are prerecorded and stored within the package for instant access. You will learn about the different categories of functions that 1-2-3 offers and will learn to select those that meet your needs.

Chapter 8 introduces 1-2-3's graphic features, which provide tools for presenting numeric data in an understandable fashion. You will learn how to create a variety of graph types. In Chapter 13 you will learn how to supplement 1-2-3's basic graph printing features with Allways, which can print graphs without exiting from 1-2-3.

Chapter 9 covers the data management features of the package. You can use these to create a simple database. You will also find examples that show you how to sort information in the database and selectively copy information to create a quick report.

Chapter 10 focuses on the advanced built-in functions—more sophisticated than the ones in Chapter 7. With minimal work, they can add to your models the power of logic and sophisticated business calculations.

Chapter 11 expands on the basic file management features introduced in Chapter 4. The chapter teaches you how to combine several files and how to link cells between worksheets to access data. You can use these features to create consolidations for your business.

Chapter 12 examines the basics of 1-2-3 macros, including the new Learn features which make macro creation easy. You will learn how to record keystrokes for execution at a later time.

Chapter 13 introduces the powerful spreadsheet publishing Add-In, Allways. Allways allows you to use the full capabilities of your print device and to integrate text and graphics on the page.

The appendixes provide detailed installation instructions, a glossary of terms, and a complete list of @functions.

Conventions Used in This Book

Throughout this book you will be instructed to make entries in 1-2-3 models. Each of these entries will be shown in boldface. If you are already somewhat familiar with the technique being presented, scan the instructions quickly and enter only the information in boldface to perform the exercise.

The full menu command is shown in each instruction requiring a menu selection. You can choose to type the first letter of each menu option or to highlight the desired option and press ENTER.

WHY THIS BOOK
IS FOR YOU

Because you probably have a limited amount of time to spend learning 1-2-3's essential features, this book is for you. By following the instructions in this book, you will learn all of the commands that you will need for most financial models. You will quickly understand the functionality of this new product without having to cover every menu command.

Or, if you are an existing 1-2-3 user who has learned to use 1-2-3 on your own, this book offers you a quick review of some basic techniques and introduces a few advanced features. If you find you do not have the time or money for a formal class, this book allows you to learn on your own and at your own pace.

Perhaps you have been making entries in 1-2-3 models for years and feel it is time to create your own. This book will help build the confidence you need. The instructions in each exercise have been tested repeatedly to ensure accuracy and will enable you to create successful models quickly.

Whether you are a first time user of 1-2-3 or someone who needs usable information quickly, this book will provide you direct access to essential 1-2-3 procedures needed to avoid the frustration learning a complex computer product can otherwise produce.

1

WORKSHEET BASICS

You are about to enter the world of 1-2-3. This journey will give you a new way of working with everyday business problems—a way that is both efficient and flexible. Traditionally, business problems are worked out on green-bar columnar pads, commonly used by accountants and business managers to evaluate financial decisions. 1-2-3 replaces the paper versions of these worksheets by turning your computer into a large electronic version of this columnar pad.

You will learn to use 1-2-3's worksheet features to handle the same types of problems previously solved on columnar pads. Applications such as budgeting, financial planning, project cost projections, breakeven analysis, and cost planning are some of the applications you might consider. You also will learn to pattern calculations after real-world situations and lay out models representing the problem to be solved on the electronic worksheet.

The electronic sheet of paper that 1-2-3 places into your computer's memory has a structure organized to help you construct these models. The electronic worksheet is arranged into rows and columns, allowing you to enter numbers, labels, and formulas. Making these entries on 1-2-3's worksheet offers significant advantages over making them on paper. For example, once you have entered a calculation on paper, it is difficult to make a change. However, 1-2-3 provides a number of features that facilitate change. On a paper worksheet, you must update calculations every time you change a number; however, because 1-2-3 can remember calculations, it recalculates the worksheet automatically when you update a number.

In this chapter you will look at beginning and ending a worksheet session, worksheet organization, entering numbers and labels on the worksheet, correcting data-entry errors, using the new Undo feature, and accessing 1-2-3's Help features. Since the material in this chapter covers some of the basic building blocks of worksheet-model construction, you will want to master it completely before progressing to more advanced topics. Although you probably are eager to start using 1-2-3's features, you may have to complete some preliminary work first in order to get maximum knowledge from this chapter. Before you begin, assess your current knowledge of the PC and whether your copy of 1-2-3 is ready to use. If you are a new PC user, read Appendix A before proceeding. If 1-2-3 has not yet been installed on your system, complete this step from the instructions in Appendix A before proceeding. Then, once you have filled in the gaps, continue reading and working with this chapter.

LOADING 1-2-3 TO BEGIN A SESSION AND QUITTING WHEN YOU HAVE FINISHED

You cannot begin to use 1-2-3 until you have loaded it into the memory of your computer system. The procedure depends on whether you are using a floppy disk or hard disk system. Network users follow different procedures depending on where 1-2-3 has been installed and need to follow the specific instructions supplied by the network administrator for activating 1-2-3.

Starting 1-2-3 from a Hard Disk

To start 1-2-3 from a hard disk, you need to activate the directory that contains the 1-2-3 files. If you have installed the files in a directory on drive C named 123, you need to follow these steps.

1. Activate the C drive by starting (*booting*) the system from drive C.

   If your system is already on with DOS loaded but another drive is active, you can activate drive C by typing **C:**. Once drive C is active, the DOS prompt displays as C>.

2. Activate the subdirectory containing the 1-2-3 files. To activate the directory 123, type **CD \123** and press ENTER.

   If your files are in another directory, substitute the name of your directory for 123 in the entry.

3. Type **123** and press ENTER to start the 1-2-3 program.

   A Lotus copyright screen will display and after a brief delay it will be replaced by an empty worksheet screen.

Starting 1-2-3 from a Floppy Disk

To start 1-2-3 on a floppy disk system, follow these steps.

1. Place the operating system disk in drive A and turn on the system.

   The operating system will boot and is likely to respond with a prompt for the date.

2. Enter the current date in the format mm-dd-yy and press ENTER.

3. Enter the current time in the format hh:mm and press ENTER.

4. Remove the operating system disk and replace it with the 1-2-3 system disk.

5. Type **123** and press ENTER.

   The copyright screen appears briefly, followed by an empty worksheet display.

Quitting 1-2-3

When you have finished all your 1-2-3 tasks for the day, you will want to return to the operating system to work with other programs. To end your 1-2-3 session and return to the operating system, you can type **/QY** to activate 1-2-3's menu and select the Quit and Yes commands. 1-2-3 understands your entry as a request to clear memory and end the program unless there is data in memory that has not been saved. 1-2-3 keeps track of whether you have changed any cells on the worksheet and whether you have saved the worksheet after making changes. If you have not saved the changes, 1-2-3 prompts you with the message "WORKSHEET CHANGES NOT SAVED! End 1-2-3

Control panel   Mode indicator

A1:   READY

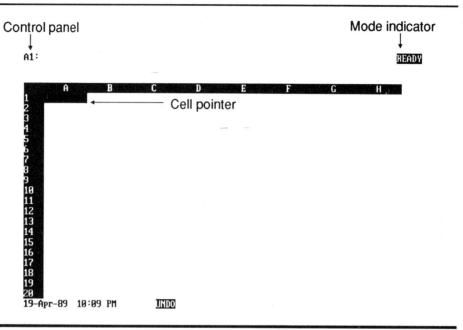

Cell pointer

19-Apr-89   10:09 PM   UNDO

FIGURE 1-1.   Left corner of worksheet visible on the screen

anyway?" and expects you to respond with **Y** or **N**. Typing **Y** causes 1-2-3 to end immediately. Once you are back at the operating system, you can run another program or enter direct operating system requests. You can start 1-2-3 again by typing **123** and pressing ENTER. If you elect to stay in 1-2-3 in response to the prompt, type **N**. 1-2-3 does not end, allowing you to save the data in memory if you wish. Also in this chapter you will learn the procedure for saving entries in the worksheet.

WORKSHEET ORGANIZATION

When you load 1-2-3 into the memory of your computer, you will see only the upper left corner of your worksheet. Your display should match the one shown in Figure 1-1 (unless someone has changed the default column width). This initial display lets you glimpse the 8 leftmost columns and the first 20 rows of the worksheet. The worksheet is much larger than it first appears. There are 256 columns in the worksheet, named A to IV. Single alphabetic letters are used first; then AA to AZ, BA to BZ, and so on. Rows are named with numbers rather than letters. Release 1A of the package has 2048

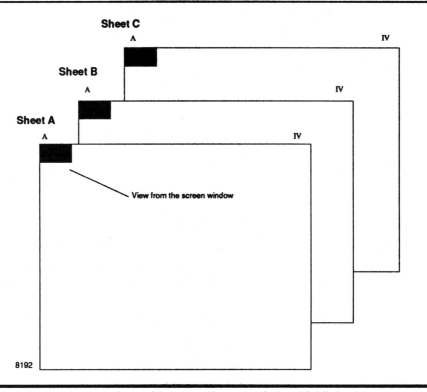

FIGURE 1-2.   Entire worksheet with the small screen window highlighted

rows; Release 2 and higher releases have 8192 rows. Figure 1-2 shows the entire worksheet, compared with the small portion that is visible when you first load the package.

The Cell Pointer

Each location on the worksheet is referred to as a *cell*. Each cell is uniquely identified by its column and row location. The column is always specified first to create cell locations such as A1, C10, IV8192, Z1025, and IJ850. A *cell pointer* always marks the current location with a small highlighted bar. In a new worksheet, such as the one in Figure 1-1, the cell pointer is located in cell A1. The location of the cell pointer is extremely important: It marks the location of the active cell, the only cell into which you can make an entry without first moving the cell pointer.

Other Important Indicators

The top three lines of the screen are called the *control panel*. You can see this panel in Figure 1-1; it is used to monitor most of your 1-2-3 activities. As you make entries on the worksheet, these entries will appear in the control panel. The panel also monitors 1-2-3's activities and tells you when 1-2-3 is ready to proceed with new activities. In addition, the control panel functions as a place keeper, letting you know your current location on the worksheet and specifics about that location.

THE TOP LINE   The top line of the control panel almost always displays the location of the cell pointer in the left corner. This location is referred to as the *cell address;* it always matches the location of the cell pointer in the lower portion of the worksheet. As you begin to make worksheet entries, you will find that this location also displays the contents of the cell, as well as any width or formatting changes that you have applied to this cell.

Figure 1-3 shows a 1-2-3 screen with $5 in cell C6. Here, the control panel tells you that the cursor is in C6, a format of currency with zero decimal places is used for the format (C0), and the column has been assigned a width of three [W3]. The last piece of information is the *contents* of the cell, represented by the 5. All these special entries will be discussed in detail in other chapters.

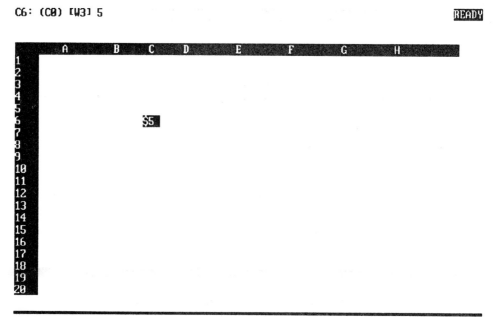

FIGURE 1-3.   Control panel entries for cell format, width, and contents

THE MODE INDICATOR   The right corner of the top line of the control panel contains a *mode indicator*. When you first load 1-2-3 this indicator will display READY, indicating that 1-2-3 is ready to respond to whatever you enter. The mode indicator can tell you either that 1-2-3 is busy with your previous request or that it is ready to do something new. It can also tell you to correct an error, point to a worksheet location, or select a menu choice. Once 1-2-3's mode indicator changes from READY to another mode, you must either follow along with 1-2-3's plans or find a way to change the indicator. Many new users become frustrated at this point, but you can avoid frustration by watching the mode indicator and staying in sync with its current mode. Table 1-1 lists all the modes you can encounter, along with their meanings. They will also be pointed out in later chapters, as new activities cause 1-2-3 mode changes.

Indicator	Meaning
EDIT	The cell entry is being edited. EDIT can be generated by 1-2-3 when your cell entry contains an error. It can also be generated by pressing F2 (EDIT) to change a cell entry.
ERROR	1-2-3 has encountered an error. The problem will be noted in the lower left corner of the screen. Press ESC to clear the Error Message, and correct the problem specified in the Error Message at the bottom of the screen.
FILES	1-2-3 wants you to select a filename to proceed. This message is also shown when you request a list of the files on your disk.
FIND	The /Data Query Find command is active.
HELP	A Help display is active.
LABEL	1-2-3 has decided that you are making a label entry.
MENU	1-2-3 is waiting for you to make a selection from the menu.
NAMES	1-2-3 is displaying a menu of range or graph names.
POINT	1-2-3 is waiting for you to point to a cell or a range. As soon as you begin to type, the POINT mode will change to the EDIT mode.
READY	1-2-3 is currently idle and is waiting for you to make a new request.
STAT	Worksheet status information is displayed.
VALUE	1-2-3 has decided that you are making a value entry.
WAIT	1-2-3 is processing your last command and cannot begin a new task until the flashing WAIT indicator changes to READY.

TABLE 1-1.   Mode Indicators

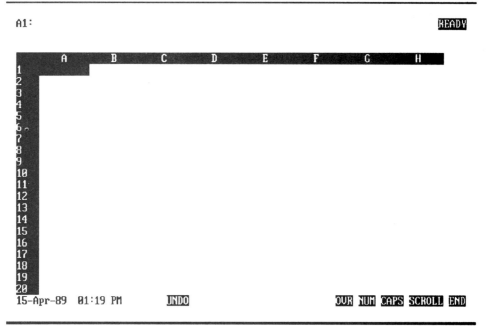

FIGURE 1-4.   Indicators in the bottom line of the display

OTHER CONTROL PANEL LINES   Lines two and three of the control panel will take on special significance as you begin to alter cell entries and use 1-2-3's features. When you use 1-2-3 commands, line two lists all your options at any point. Line three gives an explanation of each choice. The use of these lines to alter cell entries will be covered elsewhere in this chapter, and displaying options in this area is discussed in Chapter 3.

THE BOTTOM LINE OF THE SCREEN   The bottom line of the display can also provide a variety of information. Figure 1- 4 shows some of the potential entries.

In Release 2.2, the lower left corner displays the date and time unless you ask 1-2-3 to display the filename in this area. The date and time are updated constantly. If you choose to display the filename, the date and time will still display until a file is assigned a name and saved on disk. You will learn how to change Release 2.2's display for this area in Chapter 3. This area is blank in Release 1A. If an error occurs in any release, it is temporarily replaced with an Error Message, such as "Disk Full," "Printer Error," or "Disk Drive Not Ready." Whenever an Error Message displays in the lower left corner, the mode indicator displays ERROR in the upper right corner. The ERROR indicator will blink and your computer will sound a warning beep. You cannot proceed until you press the escape (ESC) key to acknowledge the error.

The area to the right of the date and time (or of the Error Message display) informs you when certain keys have been pressed. It also tells you if 1-2-3 has encountered a special situation. Five of these indicators are designed to inform you that a certain key or key sequence has been pressed. These indicators are

CAPS	This indicator is highlighted at the bottom of the screen when the CAPS LOCK key is pressed. Pressing this key causes the alphabetic keys to produce capital letters.
END	This indicates that the END key has been pressed. The END key is used to move the cursor to the end of entries in a given direction or to the end of a group of blank cells in a given direction. After using the END key, you must use an arrow key to indicate the direction. The END indicator reminds you to press an arrow key.
NUM	This indicates that the NUM LOCK key has been pressed and that you can enter numbers from the keyboard's numeric keypad. This provides an alternative to using the top row of keys.
SCROLL	This indicates that the SCROLL LOCK key has been pressed. It affects the way in which information scrolls off the screen. Without SCROLL LOCK, information scrolls off your screen one row or column at a time. With SCROLL LOCK, the entire window shifts each time you press the UP ARROW or DOWN ARROW.
OVR	OVR indicates that the INS (INSERT) key has been pressed. When editing cell entries, you will sometimes want to use the over-strike. This feature lets you enter characters that replace the characters in the original entry, rather than adding them to the original entry.

There are also five other indicators that monitor advanced features and have broader meanings. One of the most important of these is the *UNDO indicator*. When UNDO is present, you can eliminate the effect of the last command or cell entry. If you do not see UNDO at the bottom of the screen, it means that it has been disabled with the /Worksheet Global Default Other Undo Disable command and will not be able to eliminate any of the actions you take until it is again enabled. At that point it will begin keeping track of your last action in order to be able to undo it. Since Undo can only be enabled when the worksheet is blank, the current file must be saved and the worksheet erased before it is possible to enable the Undo feature. Undo is covered in more detail later in this chapter as well as in subsequent chapters that cover menu options. The other indicators will be covered as they occur elsewhere in this book.

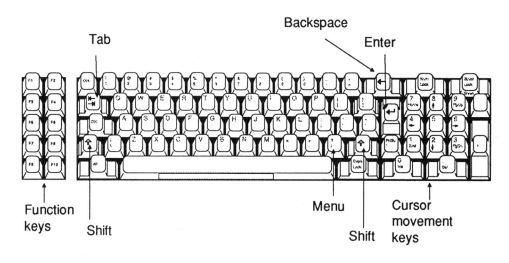

FIGURE 1-5.   The PC keyboard

MOVING AROUND
ON THE WORKSHEET

Now you are ready to learn to navigate your way around 1-2-3's worksheet in preparation for constructing models with entries in worksheet cells. You will look at the basic features as well as the more advanced options that let you travel long distances quickly.

Basic Options

You can accomplish 1-2-3's basic pointer movements with the *arrow keys*. These may be located directly on the numeric keypad keys or they may reside on separate keys, depending on the age and model of your computer system. Figures 1-5 and 1-6 show two popular keyboard configurations, with the arrow keys highlighted. Even if your keyboard is slightly different, you should find it relatively easy to locate the keys with the arrows on them. If the arrow keys on your keyboard also house other functions, be careful that the keys are set for the arrow key function. For example, on keyboards where the arrow keys reside on the numeric keypad keys, pressing NUM LOCK causes these keys to enter numbers rather than move the cell pointer. You can tell that NUM

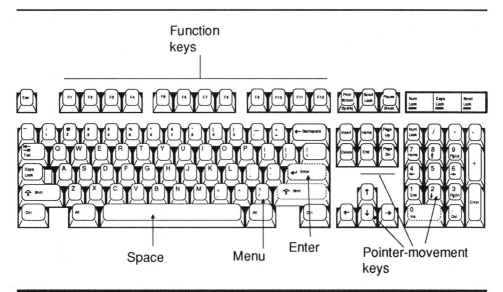

Function
keys

Space   Menu   Enter   Pointer-movement
keys

FIGURE 1-6.   IBM's enhanced keyboard

LOCK has been pressed by the NUM indicator in the bottom line of the display panel; in that case, press NUM LOCK a second time to remove the indicator from the screen before using the arrow keys to move the cell pointer.

MOVING WITH THE ARROW KEYS   Each of the arrow keys moves the cursor one cell in the direction indicated by the arrow. Your computer's keyboard will record multiple presses if you hold down a key. So if you need to use the arrow key, be careful to press it only once and release your finger if you want to move the cursor only one cell at a time. Try the following exercise with these keys to become expert in their use.

1. With your cursor in the starting A1 location, press the RIGHT ARROW once. Your cursor should now be in B1, as follows:

2. Press RIGHT ARROW a second time to move your cursor to C1.

3. Press DOWN ARROW twice to move your cursor to C3.

4. Press DOWN ARROW a few more times until your cursor reaches C20, as follows:

If you depress DOWN ARROW and move too far down the screen, row 1 will scroll off the screen. You can move your cursor back to line 20, but line 1 will not reappear until you move your cursor all the way to the top.

5. Press RIGHT ARROW until your cursor is in H20; then press it again to scroll a column off the screen as you move to I20. Your screen will look like this:

6. Press UP ARROW until your cursor is in I1; then press the LEFT ARROW until the cursor returns to A1.

7. Press LEFT ARROW again.

Unless someone has disabled 1-2-3's beep feature, you will hear a beep informing you that the cell pointer cannot be moved. You may want to practice with these keys a little more to ensure that you are comfortable with their use. You can use them to move to any worksheet location. Clearly, however, some shortcuts will be required. The arrow key method would take too long to move you to cell IV200, for example, and return to A1.

There is a variety of methods for moving the cursor more quickly. Some use special keys to make the move to a new location; others use a combination of keys. The HOME key is the quickest way to return to A1, the home position or beginning location on a worksheet. As soon as you press this key, the cell pointer moves from its current location to A1. If you have a PC style keyboard with only one key labeled HOME, you will want to be certain NUM LOCK is not shown at the bottom of the screen before pressing HOME.

PGUP AND PGDN   PGUP moves the cursor up 20 rows without moving it from its current column. Of course, this key works effectively only when the cursor is in row 21 or greater. If the cursor is in B1 and you press PGUP, 1-2-3 will beep at you and will not move the cursor at all, since the cursor is already at the top of the worksheet. If the cursor is in B5, PGUP will move it to B1; if the cursor is in B26, PGUP will move it up 20 rows to B6. PGDN does the exact opposite: It moves the cursor down by 20 rows. However, if you are fewer than 20 rows from the bottom edge of the sheet, then it will take you to the bottom.

THE END KEY   The END key can be used in combination with the arrow keys to move you to the end of the worksheet in the direction specified. When a worksheet contains data, END functions differently and moves you to the last blank cell, or to the last cell containing data in the direction you specify. END will stop at the last cell with an entry or the last blank cell, depending on whether it was resting on a blank cell or a cell containing data when you pressed it.

To use the END key and arrow combination, follow these steps.

1. Move the cell pointer to A1, then press the END key.

Verify that the END indicator has appeared in the lower right corner of the worksheet, as shown in Figure 1-7. Next, press the arrow key that specifies the direction in which you wish to move.

2. Press the RIGHT ARROW key.

The cell pointer will move to the last cell on the right, IV1.

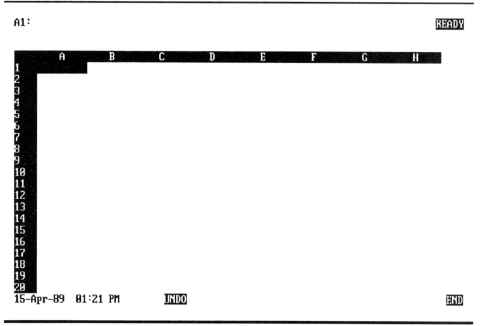

A1:   READY

15-Apr-89   01:21 PM   UNDO   END

FIGURE 1-7.   The END indicator at the bottom of the screen

3. Press END followed by the DOWN ARROW key.

   The cell pointer is now in IV2048 or IV8192, depending on whether you are using Release 1A or a higher release of 1-2-3.

Once you have placed entries on the worksheet, the END key can take on a different function. It will move the cell pointer to the last entry in the direction you indicate. Figure 1-8 shows a worksheet containing data with the cell pointer originally located in A2.

In the example shown in Figure 1-8, if you press the END key and then the DOWN ARROW key, the cell pointer will be relocated to A10, the last cell in column A that contains data. 1-2-3 places the cell pointer in this location since it is searching for the first blank cell in the specified direction. It is important that your data be entered in contiguous cells for this feature to work effectively. If you press the END key again and then the RIGHT ARROW key, the cell pointer will be relocated to E10, the last cell in row 10 that contains data.

Press the HOME key to move to A1 again, then try a quick approach to move to E10. First press the END key, then press HOME. When this sequence is used, 1-2-3 moves the cell pointer to E10, the last worksheet cell that contains an entry.

A2: 'Part_No   READY

	A	B	C	D	E	F	G	H
1								
2	Part_No	Price	Quantity		Bin	Warehouse		
3	AX-8976	4.67	100		7	15		
4	BY-8761	8.90	75		6	1		
5	CD-7865	7.75	100		8	6		
6	ER-5412	6.60	50		2	3		
7	FG-6611	12.98	65		1	4		
8	GT-8811	15.89	76		7	1		
9	MB-6512	3.56	150		5	15		
10	RT-8976	10.95	100		4	4		
11								

FIGURE 1-8.   Entries for monitoring the effect of the END key

THE CTRL KEY   The CTRL key can be used with the arrow keys to move a width of the screen to the right or left. Unlike the END key, CTRL is not pressed before the arrow key, but simultaneously. To move the cell pointer from A1 to I1, press CTRL and hold it down while pressing the RIGHT ARROW key. To move the cell pointer back to A1 again, press CTRL with the LEFT ARROW key.

THE GOTO KEY   Your last option for moving the cursor quickly is the GOTO option provided by the F5 key. To use this direct cell pointer movement, follow these steps:

1. Press F5.

2. Type **Z10** and press ENTER.
   1-2-3 immediately positions your cell pointer in Z10, regardless of the pointer's beginning location.

USING ALL THE BASIC CELL POINTER OPTIONS   The following comprehensive example uses a variety of the quick pointer movement features. It should help to reinforce your understanding of the various options. First press HOME to position your cursor in A1. Then follow this sequence of entries.

1. Press PGDN twice to position the cursor in A41.

2. Press END, followed by RIGHT ARROW, to position your cell pointer in IV41.

3. Press CTRL-LEFT ARROW twice to move two screens to the left and position your cell pointer in HY41.

4. Press END, followed by LEFT ARROW, to position the cell pointer in A41.

5. Press END, followed by UP ARROW, to position your cursor in A1.

6. Press F5, enter **S2**, and press ENTER to place your cell pointer in S2.

7. Press HOME to return your cursor to A1.

CORRECTING ERRORS

You may wonder why you are already learning about error correction when you have not yet made a single cell entry. The reason is that everyone makes at least a few mistakes, and it is impossible to predict when you will make your first one. Therefore, it is best to be prepared before you begin to explore cell entries. There are several error-correction methods. The one you use depends on whether you are still entering the entry you want to correct, or whether you have already finalized the entry by pressing ENTER or moving the cell pointer to a new location.

Fixing an Entry
Before It Is Finalized

To correct an error while making an entry into a cell, you can press BACKSPACE to delete the last character you entered. Suppose that you intend to enter "SALES" but that you omit the "E." To correct this error, try this option with the following steps.

1. Move your cursor to A1.

2. Type **SALS**, then press BACKSPACE to delete the last S.

3. Type **ES**.

Do not press any additional keys. You will use this partially completed entry in the next example.

ESC is a more dramatic way to eliminate characters. It eliminates all the characters you have typed in a cell as long as you have not finalized the entry. Try this method: Press ESC. The entire entry, SALES, will disappear and 1-2-3 will be ready to accept a new entry.

There is one more error-correction method that allows you to edit an entry while you are making it. Since it functions the same whether or not the cell entry has been finalized, it will be discussed in the next section on finalized entry-correction methods.

Fixing a Finalized Entry

You can finalize and display entries in the cells in which you want to enter them by pressing ENTER or moving the cell pointer to a new location. Once the entry is finalized in this way, you must use other methods for correcting mistakes.

RETYPING ENTRIES   One way to change a cell entry that has been finalized is to retype it. Follow these steps to create and correct finalized entries.

1. Type **SALS** in A1 and press ENTER.

    This time you will find that neither BACKSPACE nor ESC will affect the entry. One method of changing the contents of A1 is to retype your entry.

2. With the cell pointer in A1, type **SALES** and press ENTER to make the correction.

    This method gets the job done but requires a considerable amount of unnecessary typing.

EDITING A FINALIZED ENTRY   A better method, especially for longer entries, is to edit the entry and change only the mistakes. You must be in the EDIT mode to make this type of change. To place yourself in EDIT mode, press F2 (EDIT). (Later you will find that 1-2-3 sometimes automatically places you in EDIT mode when it is not happy with the cell entry you are trying to finalize.) Regardless of how you get there, once you are in EDIT mode, the entry in the cell will be placed in the second line of the control panel, just as it was when you originally entered it.

Within the EDIT mode, the special keys that you used to move the cell pointer around on the worksheet function differently. Now the RIGHT and LEFT ARROW keys move you a character to the right or left each time you press them. This allows you to position your small flashing cursor on a letter that you want to delete, or to move it where you want to make an insertion.

The HOME key also takes on a new function within the EDIT mode: It moves you to the front of the entry. If the correction you need to make occurs at the beginning of the entry, HOME moves you to that location quickly. The END key moves in the opposite direction. It places the flashing cursor at the end of the entry.

Within the entry, two different keys can be used to reverse characters. You can press BACKSPACE to delete the character to the left of the flashing cursor, or you can press DEL to delete the character above this cursor. If you type a character from the keyboard, it will be added to the right of this cursor location unless you first press INS to start the *overstrike* setting (overstrike replaces characters already in the entry). Let's try an example using each of these keys.

1. Type the characters **SELRS** in B2 and press ENTER. The screen looks like this:

2. With the cell pointer still in B2, press F2 (EDIT).

   1-2-3 will display the entry in the cell in the second line of the control panel with a small blinking cursor at the end, like this:

B2: 'SELRS   EDIT
'SELRS

3. Press BACKSPACE to move the cursor one position to the left to delete the "S." Then type **Y**.

4. Press the LEFT ARROW again to position the cursor under the "R"; then type **A**.
   Since 1-2-3 was in its default INSERT mode, the "A" was added to the left of the "R."

5. Move the cursor until it is under the "E" and press INS once to go into overstrike mode. Then type **A**. 1-2-3 will replace the "E," with the following result.

6. Press ENTER.

The entry will be finalized in the cell and INS will disappear from the edit line of the control panel. You can press INS again to toggle back to INSERT, as the opposite feature is activated each time you press it.

THE NEW UNDO FEATURE

Release 2.2 offers the new Undo feature. This new feature allows you to reverse the effect of the last menu command in most cases and can reverse the last entry you finalized. The secret to using Undo effectively is to make sure you invoke it before taking any other actions, since it can change only the last action performed.

The actual effect of Undo is to reverse the effect of the actions taken since the last time 1-2-3 was in READY mode. If you just made an entry in a cell, using Undo would reverse this entry. If you just performed an action requiring multiple steps and 1-2-3 did not return to READY mode between steps, using Undo would reverse all the steps.

In Chapter 4 you will learn about the use of Undo for reversing menu commands. For now, you can use it to eliminate your last cell entry if you see UNDO at the bottom of the screen. All that is required is pressing the ALT-F4 (UNDO) key. If you are working with Release 2.2 and do not see UNDO at the bottom of your screen, it is disabled. To enable the feature, you must first clear the worksheet from memory since Undo cannot be enabled with worksheet data in memory. If the worksheet has not been saved, you would enter /FS, type a 1- to 8-character name for the worksheet, and press ENTER to save it. You would then enter /WEY to clear memory. With the preliminary work completed, you can enter /WGDOUE and the UNDO indicator should appear. You would then put the worksheet back in memory by entering /FR, typing the name you used when saving it, and pressing ENTER. Note that earlier releases of 1-2-3 do not have the Undo feature unless you installed the Lotus HAL program.

TYPES OF
WORKSHEET ENTRIES

1-2-3 has two basic types of entries for worksheet cells: *labels* and *values*. Labels are text characters that can be used to describe numeric data you plan to place on the worksheet or to store character information. Label data can never be used in arithmetic calculations, even if it contains numbers. Value data, on the other hand, consists of either numbers or *formulas*. Formulas result in numbers but are entered as a series of calculations to be performed. The numeric digits, cell addresses, and a limited set of special symbols are the only entries that can be made in those cells categorized as value entries.

1-2-3 attempts to distinguish label entries from value entries by the first character you enter into a worksheet cell. As long as this first character is not one of the numeric digits or characters that 1-2-3 considers numeric, it will be treated as a label.

1-2-3 will generate a default label prefix for any entry it considers to be a label. If you were to enter **Sales** in a cell, 1-2-3 would treat the entry as a label because the first character in the entry is an alphabetic character. Since 1-2-3 always makes its determination from the first character, entering **15 Johnson St.** causes 1-2-3 to reject your entry when you attempt to finalize it; the first character is numeric and 1-2-3 attempts to treat the entire entry as a value. 1-2-3 is also very stubborn once it determines the type of entry it thinks you planned for a cell. The only way you can change its mind is by editing the cell contents or pressing ESC to start over. After a little practice with the label entries in your first few models, however, you will know all the tricks to put you in command of how your entries are interpreted.

Entering Labels

Label entries in 1-2-3 cells must all begin with one of the three acceptable *label prefixes*. These are a single quotation mark ('), a double quotation mark ("), or a caret (^). Each of these three symbols causes 1-2-3 to align the contents of the cell differently.

Beginning with a ' is the default option and causes the label entry to be left aligned in the cell. 1-2-3 will even generate this label prefix for you if your entry begins with an alphabetic character or a special symbol that is not considered part of the value entry options. Using the " causes the entry to be right aligned in the cell, and using the ^ symbol causes the entry to be centered. If you choose right or center justification, begin your label entry with the special symbol and follow it immediately with the text that you wish the cell to contain. If you choose to begin a label entry with a character that 1-2-3 considers to be a value, you may start your entry with one of the three label prefixes to trick the package into treating it like a label. Before starting an actual model, try each of these exercises.

1. Move your cell pointer to A1 with the arrow keys, type **AT**, and press ENTER.
   AT appears in the display of the worksheet. However, when you observe the entry in the top line of the control panel, you will notice that it reads 'AT. The reason is that 1-2-3 generated the label prefix for you. Because of this prefix, your entry should also appear as left aligned within cell A1 and will match this:

2. Use DOWN ARROW and move the cursor to A2. Type **"AT** and press ENTER. Your entry should be right aligned in the cell display.

3. Use DOWN ARROW to move to A3. Type **^AT** and press ENTER.
   The entry should be centered in the cell, as follows:

4. Use DOWN ARROW and move to A4. Type **3AT** and press ENTER.
   Notice that 1-2-3 beeps at you, will not accept this entry, and places you in EDIT mode.

5. Press HOME and add the single quotation mark at the front of the entry. Then press ENTER again.
   This time 1-2-3 accepts the entry. This is because you have asked it to treat the entry as a label, even though the first character is a number, by placing a label prefix at the front of the entry. Your worksheet should now appear like this:

6. To have a blank screen displayed, select /Worksheet Erase Yes by typing the slash (/) and the first letter of each word. This was just a practice exercise, so you can clear every thing you have entered. You will find the commands required to erase an entire worksheet on 1-2-3's menus. For now you need to take the required key sequence on faith, but you will learn all the details in a subsequent chapter.

   Now you will put your newly acquired label entry techniques to work to build the model shown in Figure 1-9. This model compares two investment properties. You could easily modify the model to compare two potential stock or bond investments, two departments, or two sales managers. All you need is information pertinent to the subjects being compared. All the entries you make in this section of the chapter will be entered as labels. These labels can be used to describe the data the model will contain and the calculations the model will perform, as well as to provide an overall description of the model's purpose so that you can see the versatility of label entries.

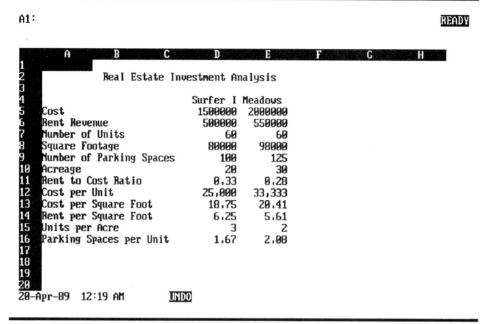

A1:   READY

	A	B	C	D	E	F	G	H
1								
2		Real Estate Investment Analysis						
3								
4				Surfer I	Meadows			
5	Cost			1500000	2000000			
6	Rent Revenue			500000	550000			
7	Number of Units			60	60			
8	Square Footage			80000	98000			
9	Number of Parking Spaces			100	125			
10	Acreage			20	30			
11	Rent to Cost Ratio			0.33	0.28			
12	Cost per Unit			25,000	33,333			
13	Cost per Square Foot			18.75	20.41			
14	Rent per Square Foot			6.25	5.61			
15	Units per Acre			3	2			
16	Parking Spaces per Unit			1.67	2.08			
17								
18								
19								
20								

20-Apr-89   12:19 AM   UNDO

FIGURE 1-9.   Real estate investment model

You will continue to build this model by adding numeric entries in the next section of this chapter; you will complete it in Chapter 2 by adding formulas. Follow these steps to create the model shell shown in Figure 1-10.

1. Move the cell pointer to A5 with the arrow keys, and type **Cost**.

   This step enters a label that describes the detail entries that will be placed in row 5. You may wonder why you are not entering the title or heading line first. Often it is easier to choose an appropriate location for titles and headings after you have positioned the detail below it. A few rows are skipped to allow for the eventual addition of a heading and entries, which is why you begin in row 5 rather than row 1.

2. Press DOWN ARROW to move to A6 and finalize your entry in cell C5.

   There are two methods for finalizing cell entries. You can use the arrow keys to move to a new location, or you can press ENTER. The DOWN ARROW is a better method: You need to position your cursor for the next entry anyway, and this approach lets you both finalize and position with a single keystroke.

3. With your cursor in A6, type **Rent Revenue** and press ENTER.

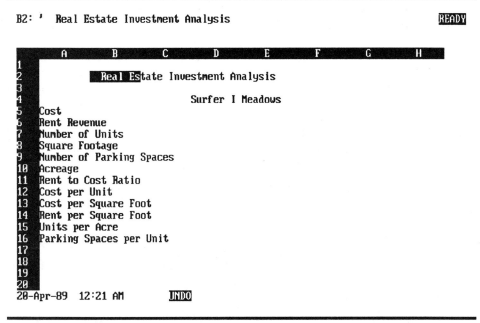

B2: ' Real Estate Investment Analysis   READY

```
          A        B        C        D        E        F        G        H
1
2                  Real Estate Investment Analysis
3
4                               Surfer I Meadows
5    Cost
6    Rent Revenue
7    Number of Units
8    Square Footage
9    Number of Parking Spaces
10   Acreage
11   Rent to Cost Ratio
12   Cost per Unit
13   Cost per Square Foot
14   Rent per Square Foot
15   Units per Acre
16   Parking Spaces per Unit
17
18
19
20
20-Apr-89  12:21 AM              UNDO
```

FIGURE 1-10.   Label entries that build the shell

This time you are using ENTER rather than the DOWN ARROW so that you can examine the label entry in the cell in which you entered it. Notice the label prefix that is automatically generated for you at the front of the entry; this was also added at the front of your last entry. This label entry is different from the last one: It is longer than the default cell width of nine characters, which means that it is too long to fit in cell A6. However, 1-2-3 borrows display space from cell B6 rather than shortening the label entry to fit in A6. Had B6 contained data, its space would not have been available; 1-2-3 then would have truncated the display to fit within the nine-character width for column A. But even though the label entry may be truncated when displayed, 1-2-3 will always retain the complete entry in memory.

This approach means that complete label entries are always available for display in the event that the cell width is increased or the cell to the right no longer contains an entry. Remember that these long label entries are always stored in the original cell where you entered them. If you choose to go back and edit the entry, you must edit this cell regardless of where the entry is displayed.

4. Move to A7 with the DOWN ARROW. Type **Number of Units** and press the DOWN ARROW again.

5. Complete the remainder of these vertical label entries by making sure that your cell pointer is in the cell specified, and type the entry shown here.

   A8   Square Footage
   A9   Number of Parking Spaces
   A10   Acreage
   A11   Rent to Cost Ratio
   A12   Cost per Unit
   A13   Cost per Square Foot
   A14   Rent per Square Foot
   A15   Units per Acre
   A16   Parking Spaces per Unit

6. Press F5, type **D4**, and press ENTER. Type **Surfer I** and finalize by pressing the RIGHT ARROW.

   This step added a column heading, which represents the name of the first apartment house you are evaluating. The F5 (GOTO) key, the quickest way to position the cell pointer, was used for this entry.

7. Type **Meadows** and press ENTER.

8. Use the UP ARROW and the LEFT ARROW to move to B2.

9. Type **Real Estate Investment Analysis** and press ENTER.

   The heading is a little too far to the left. Using C1 for the entry would not work, since it would be too far to the right. A useful method is to add a few spaces at the front of the entry to position the heading exactly as you wish.

10. With your cursor in B2, press F2 (EDIT). Then press HOME to move to the front of the entry.

11. Press the RIGHT ARROW once to move the cursor to the right of the label prefix. Press the SPACEBAR twice to add two spaces at the front. Then press ENTER.

    These extra spaces make your model look better by moving the heading toward the center.

The entry of the title should complete the label entries and lay the groundwork for the numeric data, which you will add in the next step.

Entering Numbers

Numbers are one of the two types of value entries that 1-2-3 permits. As value entries, they follow much more rigid rules than label entries. Like labels, numbers are constant at a given moment in time; they do not change as the result of arithmetic calculations. They are placed in a cell and will remain as you enter them unless you take some direct action to change them. Numbers can contain any of the numeric digits from 0 through 9. The other characters that are allowable in regular numeric entries are . + and −. The . is used to separate the whole-number portion of the entry from the decimal digits; the + indicates a positive number, and the − indicates a negative number.

Several characters can be part of a numeric entry in special situations. A % sign can be used at the end of a numeric entry to indicate a percentage, but it is not allowed in other positions within the entry. Spaces, commas, and other characters cannot be added to numeric entries except by using the formatting options, which will be covered in Chapter 3. The only exception to this rule is the use of the letter "e" (either E or e), which can be used to represent numbers in powers of 10 (referred to as *scientific notation*). For example, 3.86E−5 is .0000386. This number can also be represented as (3.86*10^ −5) or 3.86E−5. The caret symbol represents exponentiation or the power of 10 that this number is raised to. Entering 3.86*10^ −5 would be considered a formula. Although it is still a value entry, it requires operations that are not needed when entering numeric digits.

You will enter only the numbers for the constant numeric data on the worksheet. Even though numeric entries are considered constants, there is nothing to prevent you from updating any of these numbers, once they are entered, by typing a new number or editing the existing entry. For this model, the numbers you will enter are the first six entries in the column. The other entries will be the result of formulas added in the next chapter; these cells will remain blank initially. As you enter the first numeric digit in each cell, you will notice that the READY mode indicator is replaced by VALUE. The first character is all that 1-2-3 needs to determine the type of cell entry. Follow these steps.

1. Move the cell pointer to D5 with the arrow keys. Type **1500000** and press ENTER.

   Notice that you did not enter any commas or other characters. You can have 1-2-3 add them at a later time as a formatting option, if you wish. Also, notice that 1-2-3 did not add a label prefix in front of this number since it considers it a value.

2. Move the cell pointer to D6 with DOWN ARROW. Type **500000**, then press DOWN ARROW.

3. Type **60**, then press DOWN ARROW.

4. Type **80000**, then press DOWN ARROW.

5. Type **100**, then press DOWN ARROW.

6. Type **20**, then use UP ARROW and RIGHT ARROW to move to E5.

7. Complete these same entries for the Meadows building with the following entries:

E5	2000000
E6	550000
E7	60
E8	95000
E9	125
E10	30

Figure 1-11 shows the result of entering each number. Remember that it is easy to change any of the entries. You can type a new number or edit a cell. Try a few changes, following these steps.

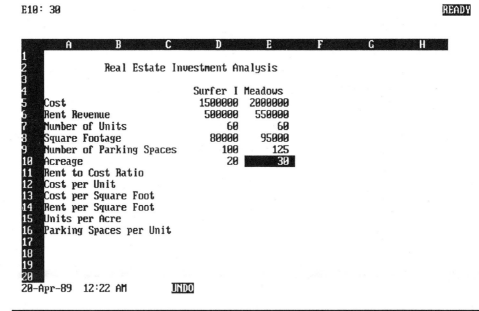

FIGURE 1-11.   Adding numbers to the shell

1. Move to E8 and press F2 (EDIT).

2. Press LEFT ARROW to move your cursor under the 5.

3. Press DEL to remove 5.

4. Type **8**.

5. Finalize your entry by pressing ENTER.

You also could have finalized with the UP or DOWN ARROW key. However, the RIGHT and LEFT ARROW keys are not options for finalizing while you are editing, since they take on the new function of moving within the cell entry. Since this is the last entry that you will make in the model, save a copy of the model to disk. The commands that handle saving files are covered in Chapter 4 in detail. For now, all you need to know is that you need a menu command in order to save a file. You must select /File Save and enter the name of the file you wish to save. If the file is already stored on the disk, you must confirm your desire to save by entering **R** for Replace. You can select each of these commands by typing the first letter of the command, but you must enter the filename in full. Select /File Save, type **REALEST**, and press ENTER.

GETTING HELP

Navigating your way around the worksheet and entering numbers and labels in worksheet cells probably has seemed quite simple. That is because you have taken everything a step at a time. As you begin to add more skills to your toolkit of 1-2-3 options, you may find that you need a quick refresher on an earlier topic. Although you can always look back to the particular chapter or to your 1-2-3 reference manual, 1-2-3's onscreen *Help facility* will often provide just the hints you need to complete your planned task. Accessing the Help feature is as easy as pressing F1 (HELP). You can do this even if you are in the middle of a task, such as entering a label in a cell. 1-2-3 will not disrupt the in-progress task; instead, it will set the task aside temporarily to let you review help information on the screen.

If you press F1 (HELP) before starting a task, 1-2-3 will display a HELP screen relating the READY mode for your selection. Assuming that you are in READY mode, try this right now and press F1. If you are using Release 2.2, your screen should match the one in Figure 1-12. (The Release 1A and 2.01 HELP screens are similar but not always exactly the same, since some Release 2.2 features are different.) To select information on any topic, just place your highlighted bar on the desired topic and press ENTER. If you choose Formulas or Numbers, additional information will be presented,

A1:   <u>**HELP**</u>

1-2-3 Help Index

<u>About 1-2-3 Help</u>	Linking Files	1-2-3 Main Menu
Cell Formats	Macro Basics	/Add-In
Cell/Range References	Macro Command Index	/Copy
Column Widths	Macro Key Names	/Data
Control Panel	Mode Indicators	/File
Entering Data	Operators	/Graph
Error Message Index	Range Basics	/Move
Formulas	Recalculation	/Print
@Function Index	Specifying Ranges	/Quit
Function Keys	Status Indicators	/Range
Keyboard Index	Task Index	/System
Learn Feature	Undo Feature	/Worksheet

To select a topic, press a pointer-movement key to highlight the topic and then
press ENTER. To return to a previous Help screen, press BACKSPACE. To leave
Help and return to the worksheet, press ESC.

24-Jul-89 02:38 PM

FIGURE 1-12.   HELP screen presented from READY mode

A1:   <u>**HELP**</u>

Types of Formulas --   1-2-3 has four types of formulas:

Numeric	Performs calculations with numbers. For example, +B5*5 multiplies 5 times the value in B5.
String	Performs calculations with strings (text enclosed in quotation marks or labels in a worksheet). For example, the formula +"Mr. "&B2 concatenates (joins together) Mr. (space) and the label in cell B2.
Logical	Performs true/false tests on numeric or string values and returns 1 (for true) or 0 (for false). For example, +A1>500 returns 1 if the value in cell A1 is greater than 500 and 0 if the value in A1 is less than or equal to 500.
@Function	Performs specific database, date and time, financial, logical, mathematical, special, statistical, or string calculations. For example, the formula @SUM(B10..F10) calculates the sum of the values entered in the range B10..F10.

<u>Entering Formulas</u>   @Function Index   Help Index
24-Jul-89 02:39 PM

FIGURE 1-13.   Requesting additional help for entering numbers

A1:   **HELP**
Salaries

LABEL Mode -- This indicator in the upper right corner of the screen means
you can enter a label. The following keys have special meanings:

ESC	Cancels entry and returns to READY mode.
BACKSPACE	Erases the character preceding the cursor.
ENTER	Completes the entry. 1-2-3 stores the label in the current cell, and returns to READY mode.
COMPOSE (ALT-F1)	Allows you to create characters not available on the keyboard.
EDIT (F2)	Switches to EDIT mode. Press again to return to LABEL mode.
← → ↑ ↓	Completes the entry and moves the cell pointer in the direction indicated by the key you pressed.

NOTE If you are trying to enter data as a label and 1-2-3 switches to VALUE
or EDIT mode, the program is probably interpreting your entry as a value.
Try preceding the entry with the label prefix ' " or ^. (For more information,
see Label Formats.)

Help Index
24-Jul-89 02:40 PM

FIGURE 1-14.   Requesting help while entering a label

such as the display in Figure 1-13. There may be additional levels of help that you can
select in the same manner, depending on the topic. When you have finished, leave
HELP mode by pressing ESC. This returns you to the 1-2-3 task where you left off. If
you request help with F1 after beginning a task, 1-2-3 provides context-sensitive help.
This is 1-2-3's best guess as to the type of help you need, based on the entries you
have made so far. Assuming that you were entering a label and wanted additional
information on 1-2-3's label-entering rules, you could press F1 before finalizing. Try
this by entering the label **Salaries** in a worksheet cell and pressing F1 before finalizing
your entry. Figure 1-14 shows the HELP screen that is presented for Release 2.2. You
still have the option of selecting help on less specific topics by choosing the Help
Index at the bottom of the screen. Figure 1-15 shows some typical topics provided by
this index.

When you have finished using the Help feature, you can press ESC again to return
to the worksheet. Everything will be exactly as you left it. 1-2-3 effectively places a
marker in your current location and records your actions up to that point before
displaying the HELP screen so that it can put things back exactly as you left them.
Even the partially completed label entry will be waiting for you to finalize it. Since
you actually do not wish to make another entry at this time, you can press ESC again
to eliminate it.

```
A1:                                                                        HELP

Printer error -- You aborted a /Print Printer Go command by pressing CTRL-BREAK,
 or your printer cannot receive or print information.  Check the printer for
 for problems such as loose cables, jammed paper, no power, or being off-line.
 If necessary, refer to your printer manual.

No print range specified -- You selected /Print [Printer or File] Go without
 specifying a print range to print.  Select /Print [Printer or File] Range to
 tell 1-2-3 what to print before you select /Print [Printer or File] Go.

No printer driver loaded -- No printer driver was added to the current driver
 set.  Use Install to add your printer to the current driver set.  For
 information on using Install, see Chapters 3 and 4 of "Setting Up 1-2-3."

No text printer driver loaded -- You selected /Worksheet Global Default Printer
 Name without a text printer driver in the current driver set.  Use Install
 to add your text printer driver(s) to the current driver set.  For more
 information on using Install, see Chapters 3 and 4 of "Setting Up 1-2-3."

Error Message Index                                            Help Index
Printer error
```

FIGURE 1-15.   Looking at the Help Index

1-2-3 can assist you when you encounter an error message. Just press F1 (HELP), select the Help Index, and choose Error Message to see an explanation of each message, as well as actions that you can take to correct the error.

REVIEW EXERCISE

You have had a chance to look at the basic entry features for numbers and labels. Before starting on formula entries covered in the next chapter, you can put your new skills to work entering some basic information about a company's assets. Figure 1-16 shows the completed entries.

1. If your worksheet contains entries, enter /**WEY** to select Worksheet Erase Yes from the menu and clear the screen.

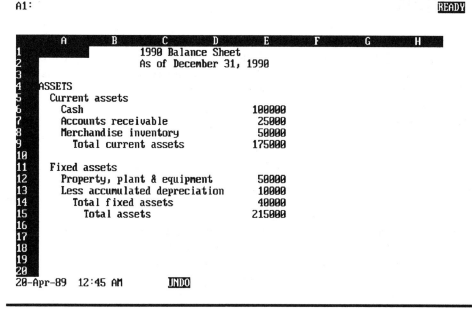

A1:   READY

	A	B	C	D	E	F	G	H
1			1990 Balance Sheet					
2			As of December 31, 1990					
3								
4	ASSETS							
5	Current assets							
6	Cash				100000			
7	Accounts receivable				25000			
8	Merchandise inventory				50000			
9	Total current assets				175000			
10								
11	Fixed assets							
12	Property, plant & equipment				50000			
13	Less accumulated depreciation				10000			
14	Total fixed assets				40000			
15	Total assets				215000			
16								
17								
18								
19								
20								

20-Apr-89 12:45 AM   UNDO

FIGURE 1-16. Entries to record a company's assets

2. Use the RIGHT ARROW key to move to C1 and place the first heading entry in the cell.

   Hint: Since the entry begins with a number and contains label characters, you will want to type a label indicator first like '. Complete the entries in C2 and A4.

3. Complete the remaining label entries as shown in cells A5..A15.

   Hint: Use the SPACEBAR to add two spaces for each new level of indentation.

4. Use the arrow keys to move to E5 and complete the numeric entries shown.

5. Save the worksheet by entering /**FS**, typing **ASSETS**, and pressing ENTER.

6. To erase your screen and begin a new model enter /**WEY**.

REVIEW

- To start 1-2-3, you must first load the operating system into the memory of your computer. With a hard disk system, all you need to do is turn the system on with drive A empty. Next activate the 1-2-3 directory. For example, if 1-2-3 is stored in the 123 directory, you would type **CD \123** and press ENTER, then type **123**

Key	Meaning
UP ARROW	Moves the cell pointer up one cell.
DOWN ARROW	Moves the cell pointer down one cell.
RIGHT ARROW	Moves the cell pointer one cell to the right in READY mode. In EDIT mode, moves one character to the right.
LEFT ARROW	Moves the cell pointer one cell to the left. In EDIT mode, moves the cell pointer one character to the left.
CTRL-LEFT ARROW	Moves one screen to the left.
CTRL-RIGHT ARROW	Moves one screen to the right.
PGUP	Moves up one screen.
PGDN	Moves down one screen.
END	Causes the arrow key pressed next to move the cell pointer to the last blank cell or the cell containing the last contiguous entry in the direction specified. When pressed with EDIT mode in effect, takes you to the end of the entry.
HOME	Moves the cell pointer to A1. When EDIT mode is in effect, places the cursor at the front of your entry. When pressed following END, moves the cell pointer to the last cell on the spreadsheet that contains an entry.
ESC	Eliminates an entry that is not finalized. Exits from the 1-2-3 Help feature. When pressed repeatedly allows you to escape from a menu selection made in error.
F1 (HELP)	Activates the 1-2-3 Help feature.
F2 (EDIT)	Places you in EDIT mode to allow the correction of entries without retyping. The arrow keys, HOME, and END all function differently when EDIT mode is in effect.
F5 (GOTO)	When followed by typing a cell address and pressing ENTER, moves the cell pointer to the address specified.
ALT-F4 (UNDO)	When no intervening actions have occurred, eliminates the last cell entry finalized. Can also eliminate the effect of most menu commands.

TABLE 1-2.   Special Keys

and press ENTER to begin the program. On a floppy disk system, you must place the operating system disk in drive A before turning the system on. After the operating system starts, respond to its prompts for date and time entries, remove the operating system disk, put the 1-2-3 system disk in the drive, type **123**, and press ENTER.

- The highlight that marks your place on the worksheet is called the cell pointer. Use the keys in Table 1-2 to move it around. The control panel at the top of the screen provides valuable information about 1-2-3. Look at the upper right corner of the screen to see the mode indicator and determine 1-2-3's current mode. Look at the upper left of the screen to see the current cell's contents, format, and width.

- The bottom line of the screen displays the date and time or filename. It also displays indicators for several keys and other options that can tell you what to expect from 1-2-3.

- Correcting worksheet entries will depend on whether or not they were finalized. One set of techniques works for active entries and another set is most useful for the ones that were not finalized. The Undo feature can eliminate an entry just finalized or reverse the result of a 1-2-3 command if Undo is enabled. Just press ALT-F4 (UNDO) to use it.

- Cells can be empty or contain labels or values. Labels are treated as characters by 1-2-3. Depending on the label prefix, they may be left aligned ('), right aligned ("), or centered (^). One type of value is a number. You can use the digits 0 through 9 or special symbols like . + and − in number entries.

- To save the current worksheet enter /**FS**, type a name of not more than eight characters with no spaces, and press ENTER. If there is a file with that name on the disk, you can type **R** if you wish to replace the existing file with the current worksheet.

- To access 1-2-3's Help feature, press F1 (HELP).

- To erase the current worksheet without saving it, enter /**WEY**.

- To quit 1-2-3, enter /**QY**. If you have not saved your worksheet, you need to enter another **Y** to confirm that you want to quit.

2

DEFINING YOUR CALCULATIONS

Calculations are an important part of many of the business tasks that you perform. Some calculations are simple. If you get a 10% discount when you purchase from a given vendor, it takes no great effort to calculate your savings. And it is simple to calculate the total number of employees in your group if the headcount increases by five. In fact, these calculations are so easy that you can compute them without even writing them down.

However, not all computations are this simple. For example, if you want to determine the most economic quantity to order for each item in your inventory, you will need to perform a much more complex calculation, one that is difficult to compute without writing it down. Even when you do write complex computations on paper, mistakes are easy to make. And if conditions change slightly, the numbers in your computations are likely to change as well, requiring you to redo the calculations.

Evaluating a *series* of conditions could cause you to spend a considerable amount of time redoing calculations.

1-2-3 provides an easy-to-use solution, one that eliminates the need for you to perform calculations yourself. You simply define for 1-2-3 the calculations you wish to perform, and it handles the computations. To do this you must determine each step in the computational process and record these instructions in a cell on 1-2-3's worksheet. These recorded instructions for handling calculations are known as formulas. Once these formulas are entered, 1-2-3 will handle all the work required for computing your results.

The process of entering these formulas is really quite simple and not too different from the way you entered numbers and labels in Chapter 1. These formulas will tell 1-2-3 what data to operate on and which of the operators will be used. A sample formula for profit might be Sales–Cost of Goods Sold; a sample formula for net payable on an invoice might be Amount– (Amount∗Purchase Discount).

This chapter will show you how to enter any of these formulas, using references to the worksheet cells that contain your data. This feature is very powerful; it allows you to reuse applications even when significant changes occur. This flexibility makes formulas such a valuable addition to your worksheet models.

In this chapter, you will look at all the features provided by 1-2-3 to handle your calculations. You will find that they have wide applicability: The same methods are used to calculate interest expense, budget projections, salary increases, and any other calculation. In addition to the basics, you will also explore 1-2-3's full set of features for building more complex formulas, including the string formulas (which manipulate text data rather than numeric values).

FORMULA BASICS

Formulas, like the numbers you entered in Chapter 1, are value entries. Unlike numbers, however, they produce results that vary, depending on the entries they reference. This variability makes formulas the backbone of spreadsheet features: It allows you to make *what-if projections* based on changing entries on your worksheet. You can update the formula results without changing the formula itself. The only requirement is new entries for the variables referenced by the formula.

The Basic Rules of Entry

To enter a formula in a cell, you must define for 1-2-3 the location of the variables involved and the operations you wish performed on them. 1-2-3 supports three types of formulas: arithmetic formulas, logical formulas, and in Release 2 and higher, text or string formulas. A few general rules apply to all formulas and some special conventions will be observed for the special types of formulas. The special rules will be discussed when each type of formula is discussed, but the general guidelines will be given here.

The first and perhaps most important rule is that the first character in a formula entry must always come from the following list of value characters:

+ − (@ # $. 0 1 2 3 4 5 6 7 8 9

The second rule is that formulas cannot contain extraneous spaces except within names or text. As you type the examples presented, be especially careful not to separate the formula components with spaces. The third and last rule pertains to the length limitation for a formula: As with other cell entries, it cannot exceed 240 characters in Release 2.2. Unless you are building some really complex calculations, this last rule is not likely to impose a restriction.

ARITHMETIC FORMULAS

Arithmetic formulas are nothing more than instructions for certain operations: addition (+); subtraction (−); multiplication (∗); division (/); and exponentiation (^), which represents raising a number to a specific power, such as 3 cubed or 2 squared. These are the same types of operations you can compute by hand or with a calculator. When you record these formulas on the worksheet, you can build the formula with the arithmetic operators and references to the numbers contained in other worksheet cells. The result of the calculation will be determined by the current value of the worksheet cell referenced. You can see the advantage of recording these formulas on a worksheet more clearly when you wish to change one of the numbers. All you need to do is change the number in the referenced cell. Since the formula has already been entered and tested, it will be available on a permanent basis. Anytime you wish the same set of calculations to be performed, you can enter the numbers involved without having to reenter the formula; the sequence of required calculations will be stored on the worksheet in the cell that contains the formula.

Entering Simple Arithmetic Formulas

1-2-3's formulas can be entered with numeric constants, as in 4∗5 or 3+2. However, numeric constants within formulas are limiting: You would have to change formulas as conditions change. A better method is to store these constants in a worksheet cell.

When you wish to use this value in a formula, you can use its cell address within the formula. Then, if the value changes, you need only enter a new number where it is stored; the formula will use it automatically. Using cell addresses in formulas requires one additional rule: Since cell addresses begin with non-numeric characters, an entry's initial alphabetic character (for example, A2+B3) will cause it to be treated as a label entry.

This means that an entry like this would appear in the worksheet cell just as you typed it, rather than performing any calculations. Try this with the following entries.

1. Move the cell pointer to A2, type **3**, and press ENTER.

2. Move the cell pointer to B3, type **2**, and press ENTER.

3. Move the cell pointer to D2, type **A2+B3**, and press ENTER.
   No calculation is performed for you. 1-2-3 decided that the cell entry was a label, since its first character was alphabetic. This approach, which does not perform any calculations, produces the following display:

Several of the numeric characters can be used to begin a formula. The + is a logical choice as a character to add to the front of the formula: It requires only one keystroke and will not affect the contents of A2. Try this new entry to see the results: Type **+A2+B3** in D2.

This time, 1-2-3 interpreted your entry as a formula and computed the result of adding the current contents of A2 to the current contents of B3. Since A2 contains a 3 and B2 contains a 2, the formula you entered displays a 5 in D2, as follows:

When you point to D2, you still see the formula you entered in the control panel. If, later on, you decided to change A2 to 10, the result displayed in D2 would change to a 12 as evidence that the formula was still doing its assigned task.

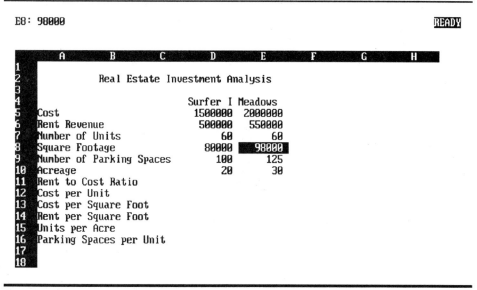

E8: 90000   READY

	A	B	C	D	E	F	G	H
1								
2			Real Estate Investment Analysis					
3								
4				Surfer I	Meadows			
5	Cost			1500000	2000000			
6	Rent Revenue			500000	550000			
7	Number of Units			60	60			
8	Square Footage			80000	98000			
9	Number of Parking Spaces			100	125			
10	Acreage			20	30			
11	Rent to Cost Ratio							
12	Cost per Unit							
13	Cost per Square Foot							
14	Rent per Square Foot							
15	Units per Acre							
16	Parking Spaces per Unit							
17								
18								

FIGURE 2-1.   Real estate model from Chapter 1

When you enter formulas using their cell addresses, 1-2-3 is not fussy and will accept either upper- or lowercase. The formula +A2*AB3 is equivalent to +a2*ab3 or +a2*Ab3 and computes the same results.

Adding Formulas to The Real Estate Model

You will use your new formula techniques to add the formulas to the real estate investment model that you started in Chapter 1. If the model is still in the memory of your computer, you are ready to begin. If you have just started a new 1-2-3 session and wish to recall your copy of the model from your disk, type **/FRREALEST** and press ENTER. The model shown in Figure 2-1 should be displayed on your screen in preparation for adding the formulas.

The first formula you need to enter is the *rent-to-cost ratio*. You compute this ratio by dividing the rent by the cost. Each investment will be evaluated separately; you will enter the computations for Surfer I first. Follow these instructions to add the formulas.

1. Move the cell pointer to D11.

    This is an appropriate location for the first Surfer I calculation.

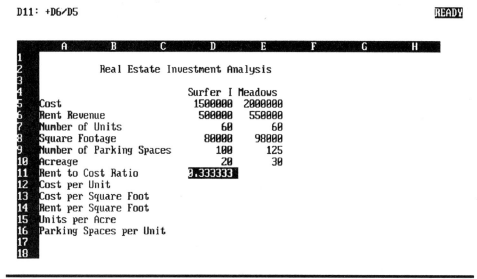

D11: +D6/D5   READY

	A	B	C	D	E	F	G	H
1								
2			Real Estate Investment Analysis					
3								
4				Surfer I	Meadows			
5	Cost			1500000	2000000			
6	Rent Revenue			500000	550000			
7	Number of Units			60	60			
8	Square Footage			80000	98000			
9	Number of Parking Spaces			100	125			
10	Acreage			20	30			
11	Rent to Cost Ratio			0.333333				
12	Cost per Unit							
13	Cost per Square Foot							
14	Rent per Square Foot							
15	Units per Acre							
16	Parking Spaces per Unit							
17								
18								

FIGURE 2-2.   Formula entered in D11

2. Type **+D6/D5** and press ENTER.

    Since the rent revenue for this property is stored in D6 and the cost is in D5, the formula will calculate the ratio you need. Your result should appear like the one in Figure 2-2, with the formula you entered displayed in the control panel and the result of the calculation shown in the cell.

    The next computation is *cost per unit*. This calculation splits the total cost evenly across all units to give you an estimate of what one unit costs.

3. Move the cell pointer to D12 with the DOWN ARROW key. Type **+D5/D7**. This formula divides the cost by the number of units. The next formula will allocate the cost on a square-footage basis.

4. Move the cell pointer to D13 with the DOWN ARROW key. Note that moving down a cell after typing the formula finalizes your entry and positions you for your next entry. Then type **+D5/D8** and press the DOWN ARROW key.

    The remaining three formulas for Surfer I follow the same pattern.

5. Type **+D6/D8** and press DOWN ARROW.

6. Type **+D7/D10** and press DOWN ARROW.

7. Type **+D9/D7** and press ENTER.

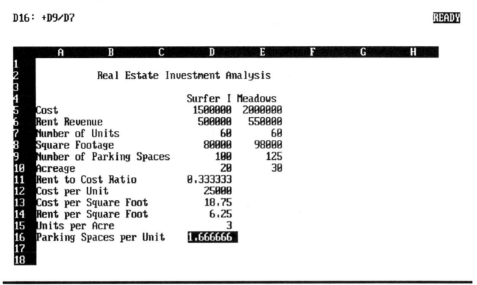

D16: +D9/D7   READY

	A	B	C	D	E	F	G	H
1								
2		Real Estate Investment Analysis						
3								
4				Surfer I	Meadows			
5	Cost			1500000	2000000			
6	Rent Revenue			500000	550000			
7	Number of Units			60	60			
8	Square Footage			80000	98000			
9	Number of Parking Spaces			100	125			
10	Acreage			20	30			
11	Rent to Cost Ratio			0.333333				
12	Cost per Unit			25000				
13	Cost per Square Foot			18.75				
14	Rent per Square Foot			6.25				
15	Units per Acre			3				
16	Parking Spaces per Unit			1.666666				
17								
18								

FIGURE 2-3.   All of the formulas entered for Surfer I

This completes the entries for Surfer I and produces the results shown in Figure 2-3.

Subsequently, you will learn techniques for copying formulas like these to other locations rather than reentering a set of similar formulas for the Meadows property. For now you need practice with formula entry, and the second set of formulas lets you look at another formula-entry method.

Entering Arithmetic Formulas With the Point Method

The formulas in the last section were all built by typing both the arithmetic operators and the cell addresses they referenced. This method works fine if you are an average typist and if all the referenced cells are within view on the worksheet. However, if neither of these conditions is true, typing the formulas may lead to a higher error rate than necessary. 1-2-3 provides a second method of formula entry, which can reduce the error rate. With this method, you type only the arithmetic operators, and you select the cell references by using the arrow keys to position the cell pointer on the cell you wish to reference. 1-2-3 adds the cell address to the formula being built in the control panel and changes the mode indicator from VALUE to POINT. This method provides visual verification that you are selecting the correct cell and eliminates the problems of typing mistakes. Follow these steps to add the first formula for the Meadows property using the pointing method of formula entry.

1. Move your cell pointer to E11, then type +.

   You can use the + on the key next to the pointer movement keys or the one over the =.

2. Next move your cell pointer to E6.

   This will cause the cell address to appear in your control panel like this:

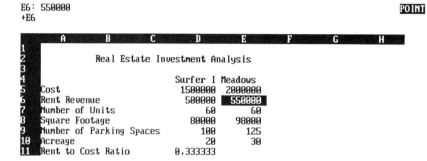

Note that the indicator in the upper right corner of the screen has changed to POINT.

3. Type /.

   Notice that the cell pointer returns to the cell where the formula is being recorded.

4. Move your cell pointer to E5. Your control panel will now contain the complete formula, as follows:

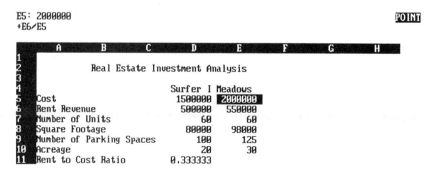

5. Press ENTER to finalize the formula.
    The following result will appear.

E11: +E6/E5   READY

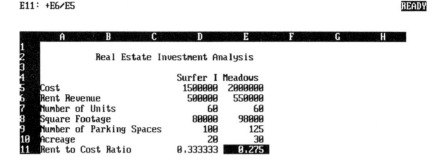

Completing the Meadows Formulas

The remaining Meadows formulas can be completed by using the pointing method, following these steps.

1. Move your cell pointer to E12 and type +. Then point to E5 with the UP ARROW and type /. Next point to E7 and press ENTER.

2. Move your cell pointer to E13 and type +. Point to E5 with the UP ARROW and type /. Point to E8 and press ENTER.

3. To enter the formula for rent per square foot, begin by moving the cell pointer to E14 and typing +. Use the UP ARROW to move to E6. Then type /, move to E8, and press ENTER.

4. Move the cell pointer to E15 and type +. Use the UP ARROW to move to E7. Type /, then move to E10 and press ENTER.

5. Move the cell pointer to E16 and type +. Use the UP ARROW to point to the number of parking spaces in E9. Then type /, move to the number of units in E7, and press ENTER. The completed model is shown in Figure 2-4.

You will notice that ENTER was used to finalize each of the formulas. If you had attempted to finalize by pressing an arrow key, the last reference in the cell would have been changed by this movement of the cell pointer. With the pointing method of

E16: +E9/E7   READY

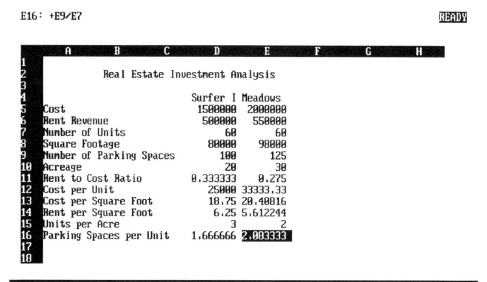

FIGURE 2-4.   Remaining formulas entered for Meadows

formula construction, ENTER will always be your only way of finalizing a formula. Other than the differences in the entry method, these two sets of formulas will perform identically. Once a formula has been entered, it is not possible to determine which entry method was chosen since the results are the same.

Using Your Formulas
To Perform a What-if Analysis

Now that you have entered the basic formulas, your investment analysis model is complete. This kind of model will help you compare the two properties; in addition, it can assist you in your negotiations. You might feel that the price of one unit has more flexibility than the other; or perhaps the seller might be willing to add additional parking spaces or to include vacant land that is adjacent to the apartment complex. All these factors can change your evaluation of the properties. If you were performing your computations manually, each of the possibilities would require a new set of calculations and be time-consuming. But now that you have automated the calculations, each option requires only that you enter a new number on the worksheet to have the package perform a new comparison immediately.

Let's look at how easy it is to evaluate each change in conditions. Suppose that you were able to negotiate a new price of $1,600,000 for the Meadows building. To add the updated data to your model, follow these steps.

1. Move the cell pointer to E5.

2. Press F2 (EDIT) to enter EDIT mode.

3. Press HOME to move to the beginning of the entry.

4. Delete the first two digits by pressing DEL twice.

5. Type **16** to replace the digits you just eliminated.

6. Press ENTER to finalize your entry.

    After entering these new entries, you will find that the results of formula calculations have been updated. They indicate that the rent-to-cost ratio and the cost per unit for the two properties are much closer than you might have thought.

Use the same process to add the updates for the Surfer I building. If you feel that the owners will agree to add 50 more parking spaces and include another 15 acres of land at the same purchase price, you will want to make the following changes.

1. Move the cell pointer to D9.

2. Type **150** and press ENTER.

3. Move the cell pointer to D10.

4. Type **35** and press ENTER.

Rather than editing the original entries, you retyped the new figures this time. You will have to evaluate each situation to see which is the quickest method. For very short entries like these last two, it is often just as easy to type the new entries.

As these last entries show, what-if analysis is quite simple once you have the formulas entered. The results of the most recent changes are shown in Figure 2-5. You could easily use these techniques to evaluate potential changes in purchase price or other options with only a minimal investment in time.

Now that you have updated your model with formulas and the results of what-if analysis, you will want to save the updated copy on disk to reflect the current status

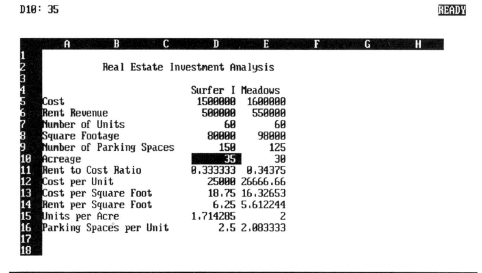

D10: 35   READY

	A	B	C	D	E	F	G	H
1								
2		Real Estate Investment Analysis						
3								
4				Surfer I	Meadows			
5	Cost			1500000	1600000			
6	Rent Revenue			500000	550000			
7	Number of Units			60	60			
8	Square Footage			80000	98000			
9	Number of Parking Spaces			150	125			
10	Acreage			35	30			
11	Rent to Cost Ratio			0.333333	0.34375			
12	Cost per Unit			25000	26666.66			
13	Cost per Square Foot			18.75	16.32653			
14	Rent per Square Foot			6.25	5.612244			
15	Units per Acre			1.714285	2			
16	Parking Spaces per Unit			2.5	2.083333			
17								
18								

FIGURE 2-5.   Changing the acreage to see the formula results updated

of the worksheet. Enter **/FS** and press ENTER. You did not have to type the filename this time, since it was saved previously. To ensure that the copy on disk is replaced with the current copy in memory, take one additional step: When 1-2-3's prompt message asks if you wish to cancel the request, replace the copy on disk, or backup the file saving the old copy with a .BAK extension and the current model with a .WK1 extension and enter **R** to replace the file.

Using Some of the Other Arithmetic Operations

The model you just completed used only the division operation in all the formulas. Now let's look at another calculation that uses other operators to perform the computations. Erase the real estate calculations—you have saved them to your disk. Enter **/WEY**.

Now you will use the blank worksheet to lay out a model that computes an employee's gross pay, given an hourly rate of pay and regular and overtime hours worked. 1-2-3 does not assign the same priority to each of the arithmetic operators. You can use this to your advantage in constructing this formula. 1-2-3 evaluates formulas from left to right but it completes all the multiplication and division operations before coming back through the formula to perform addition and subtraction. Use a multiplication process to calculate regular pay, and then use another multiplication process to calculate overtime pay before adding the results of the two operations. 1-2-3 will automatically do the two operations in this sequence, due to their priorities. Priorities will be covered in greater detail elsewhere in this chapter, along with a solution for altering the normal priority sequence. Keep this model simple for now: Enter just the basic information for one employee following these steps.

1. With the cell pointer in A1, type **Employee** and press the RIGHT ARROW.

2. Type **"Hours** and press RIGHT ARROW.

3. Type **"Rate** and press RIGHT ARROW.

4. Type **"O. Hrs** and press RIGHT ARROW.
   Use an alphabetic "O" in your entry or 1-2-3 will not let you finalize it without the quotation marks.

5. Type **"Gross Pay** and press ENTER. Notice that the " symbol was used at the beginning of the label entry. As you recall from Chapter 1, the " symbol causes 1-2-3 to right-align the label entry in the worksheet cell. This means that the column labels will line up with the first value in the database.

6. Move the cell pointer to A2 with the HOME and DOWN ARROW keys and type **J. Smith**. Then press RIGHT ARROW.

7. Type **40** and press RIGHT ARROW.

8. Type **3.75** and press RIGHT ARROW.

9. Type **10** and press RIGHT ARROW. Your entries should appear like this:

E2: `READY`

	A	B	C	D	E	F	G	H
1	Employee	Hours	Rate	O. Hrs	Gross Pay			
2	J. Smith	40	3.75	10				

The next formula must calculate gross pay by multiplying regular hours by the rate of pay, then multiplying overtime hours times 1.5 times the rate of pay. The result of these two multiplication operators will be added to obtain the gross pay. This sounds complicated but can be represented succinctly in the formula.

10. Type **+B2*C2+D2*1.5*C2** and press ENTER to have 1-2-3 compute these results:

E2: +B2*C2+D2*1.5*C2   READY

	A	B	C	D	E	F	G	H
1	Employee	Hours	Rate	O. Hrs	Gross Pay			
2	J. Smith	40	3.75	10	206.25			

You could add still more employees to this model, but for now, save it by entering **/FSPAY** and pressing ENTER. You can always retrieve it again after you have learned how to duplicate formulas in Chapter 5. For the time being, continue to look at other types of formulas. Clear the entries from your worksheet by entering **/WEY**.

USING LOGICAL FORMULAS

Logical formulas are used to compare two or more worksheet values. They use the logical operators = for equal, <> for not equal, > for greater than, >= for greater than or equal to, < for less than, and <= for less than or equal to. Logical formulas can be entered with the same methods used for arithmetic formulas, but unlike arithmetic formulas, they do not calculate numeric results. Instead, they produce a result of either a zero or a one, depending on whether the condition that was evaluated is true or false. If the condition is true, 1 will be returned; if the condition is false, 0 will be returned. For example, if D4 contains a 5, the logical expression +D4<3 will return 0, since the condition is false. This capability can be used to evaluate a series of complex decisions or influence results in other parts of the worksheet.

If an expression contains both logical operators and arithmetic operators, the expression containing the arithmetic operators will be evaluated first. For example, the logical expression +D4*2>50 will be evaluated by first multiplying the current value in D4 by 2 and then performing the comparison.

Creating a Model To Calculate Commissions

One application of logical operators in a spreadsheet might be the calculation of a commission bonus. In your example, sales personnel are paid a quarterly bonus, which includes a regular sales commission and a bonus paid for meeting sales quotas. The regular commission is computed as 10% of total sales. The bonus is calculated by

D14: +C10+C11   READY

	A	B	C	D	E	F	G	H
1		Commission Calculation						
2								
3								
4	Employee:		John Smith		Quotas Met			
5	Sales Product 1:		66000		1			
6	Sales Product 2:		35000		0			
7	Sales Product 3:		9000		0			
8			110000		1			
9								
10	Commission:		11000					
11	Bonus:		1000					
12								
13								
14	Total Commission Plus Bonus			12000				
15								
16								

FIGURE 2-6. Commission model

product. A bonus of $1000 is paid for each product for which the sales quota is met. A salesperson could thus gain $3000 by meeting quotas for three products.

Look at the steps required to build the commission model shown in Figure 2-6. First, follow these directions to add the labels that are required.

1. Move the cell pointer to B1, type **Commission Calculation**, and press ENTER.

2. Move the cell pointer to A4, type **Employee:**, and press the DOWN ARROW key.

3. Type **Sales Product 1:** and press the DOWN ARROW key.

4. Type **Sales Product 2:** and press the DOWN ARROW key.

5. Type **Sales Product 3:** and press the DOWN ARROW key three times to place the cell pointer in A10.

6. Type **Commission:** and press the DOWN ARROW key.

7. Type **Bonus:** and press the DOWN ARROW key three times to place the cell pointer in A14.

8. Type **Total Commission Plus Bonus** and press ENTER.

Notice that a colon (:) has not been added at the end. This is for convenience since you do not wish the entry to display beyond column C. It means you do not have to widen the column to show more than the default of nine characters.

9. Use F5 (GOTO), type **C4**, and press ENTER. Type **John Smith** and press the DOWN ARROW key to finalize the entry of the name of the employee for whom you will be calculating commissions.

10. Type **66000** and press the DOWN ARROW key. Type **35000** and press the DOWN ARROW key. Type **9000**.

11. Position the cell pointer in E4 and type **Quotas Met**. Then press the DOWN ARROW key.

Adding Formulas to
The Commission Model

The number and label entries for this model are now complete. Your model should match the one shown in Figure 2-7. At this point, it is time to add the formulas for calculating the regular and bonus commission. For the purpose of computing the bonus, assume that the quota is $50,000 per product. Use the following steps to enter the logical formulas for determining whether the sales quota in each category was met.

1. Type +C5>50000 and press the DOWN ARROW.

This formula will produce a 1 if the Product 1 quota is met and a 0 if it is not.

2. Type +C6>50000 and press the DOWN ARROW.

3. Type +C7>50000 and press the DOWN ARROW.

4. Total the number of quotas met by adding the result of each of the logical formulas—type **+E5+E6+E7** and press ENTER.

In Chapter 7 you will learn a shortcut method for summing entries, but for now you will use simple addition.

5. Total the sales of all three products in the same fashion—move the cell pointer to C8, type +C5+C6+C7, and press the DOWN ARROW two times.

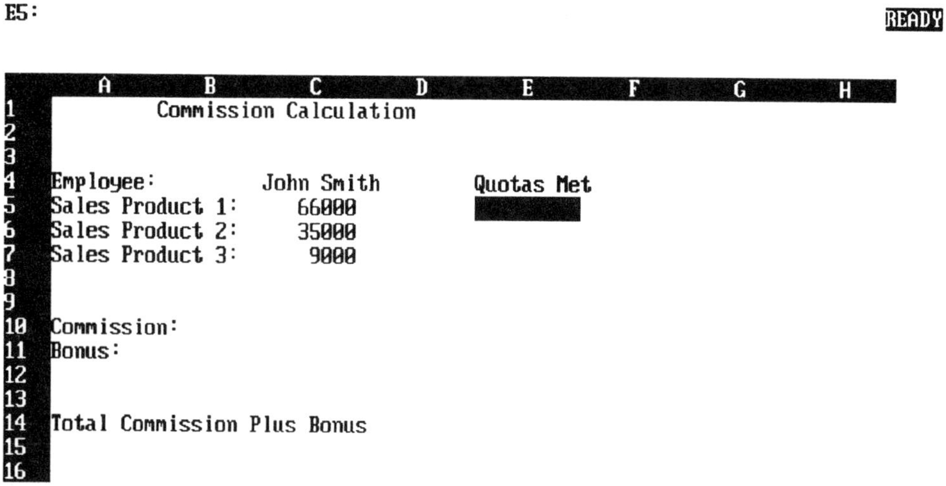

E5:   READY

```
      A        B        C        D        E        F        G        H
1               Commission Calculation
2
3
4    Employee:          John Smith      Quotas Met
5    Sales Product 1:     66000
6    Sales Product 2:     35000
7    Sales Product 3:      9000
8
9
10   Commission:
11   Bonus:
12
13
14   Total Commission Plus Bonus
15
16
```

FIGURE 2-7.   Labels and numbers for the commission model entered

6. Enter the formula for commission in C10 by typing +C8*.1 and pressing DOWN
   ARROW.

7. Type +E8*1000 and press ENTER.
   This lets you calculate the bonus commission by multiplying the number of
   quotas met by 1000.

8. Position the cell pointer in D14, type +C10+C11, and press ENTER.

Your completed model should now match the one shown at the beginning of this
section, Figure 2-6. The logical formulas it contains will respond to changes in the
model's data. Let's try a few.

1. Move the cell pointer to C7.

2. Type 73000 and press ENTER.
   You will find that a new commission plus the bonus figure of $19,400 is
   calculated immediately, as shown in Figure 2-8. The result does not display
   the dollar sign or comma; you will learn how to make 1-2-3 add them in the
   next chapter.

C7: 73000   READY

```
        A        B          C          D        E        F        G        H
1                   Commission Calculation
2
3
4   Employee:              John Smith       Quotas Met
5   Sales Product 1:          66000             1
6   Sales Product 2:          35000             0
7   Sales Product 3:          73000             1
8                            174000             2
9
10  Commission:               17400
11  Bonus:                     2000
12
13
14  Total Commission Plus Bonus      19400
15
16
```

FIGURE 2-8. Calculations after logical formulas for quotas are entered

Using Compound Operators

1-2-3 also has three *compound operators* that can be used with logical formulas. These operators are either used to negate an expression or to join two different expressions. The *negation operator* #NOT# has priority over the two compound operators, #AND# and #OR#. When the compound operator #AND# is used to join two logical expressions, both expressions must be true for the compound formula to return a *true value*. If the two expressions are joined by #OR#, either one can be true for the condition to return a true value.

You can add a second condition to your commission calculation by using the compound operators. Let's say that bonus commissions require a minimum of six months of service in addition to the minimum sales level for a product. Revise the model to allow for this new condition by following these steps.

1. Move the cell pointer to A9, type **Months in Job:**, and press the RIGHT ARROW key twice.

2. Type **4** and press ENTER.

3. Move the cell pointer to E5.

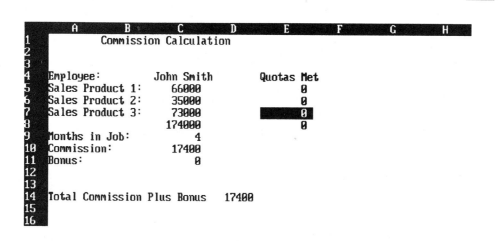

E7: +C7>50000#AND#C9>6   READY

FIGURE 2-9.   Using a complex logical formula to test two conditions

4. Press F2 (EDIT), type **#AND#C9>6**, and then press the DOWN ARROW key.

5. Use the same procedure outlined in step 4 to revise the formulas in E6 and E7.
   You will find that the bonus commission in Figure 2-9 is now zero, since the employee has been on the job fewer than six months.

6. Move the cell pointer to C9 and type **8**. Then press ENTER to see the bonus commission calculated again.

7. Enter **/FSCOMM** and press ENTER to save this worksheet to disk.

8. Enter **/WEY** to erase memory.

USING STRING FORMULAS

String formulas were added to 1-2-3 with the introduction of Release 2. Although they do not perform formula calculations as arithmetic formulas do, they enable character strings to be joined together to create headings or other data elements for the worksheet. String formulas use only one operator, the ampersand (&). This operator can be used to join variables containing character strings or string constants. For example, +"John"&"Smith" will result in JohnSmith; +"John"&" "&"Smith" will result in John Smith; and +A1&A2&A3 will result in abc if A1 contains an "a," A2 contains a "b," and A3 contains a "c." As with the other types of formulas, with string formulas you can either type the complete formula or point to the cell addresses referenced and have 1-2-3 place them in the formula for you.

   Use the string formula feature to build a part number. In this model, separate data elements provide all the different components of the All Parts, Inc., part number structure. The warehouse location, bin number, product type, and vendor are all combined to create a part number. Follow these steps to enter the data for the model.

1. Enter the worksheet heading by moving the cell pointer to B3, then typing **All Parts, Inc. Inventory Listing**, and pressing ENTER.

2. Move the cell pointer to A5, type **Location**, and press the RIGHT ARROW.

3. Type **Bin** and press RIGHT ARROW.

4. Type **Type** and press RIGHT ARROW.

5. Type **Vendor** and press RIGHT ARROW.

6. Type **Part No** and press ENTER.

7. Move the cell pointer to A6, type **'5**, and press the RIGHT ARROW.

   The single quotation mark is required since string formulas can only join label entries. Using the single quote ensures that the 5 is stored as a label.

8. Type **'12** and press RIGHT ARROW.

9. Type **AX** and press RIGHT ARROW.

10. Type **CN** and press RIGHT ARROW.

11. Verify that the cell pointer is in E6, type **+C6&"−"&D6&A6&B6**, and press ENTER.

    The part number for the first item will appear as follows.

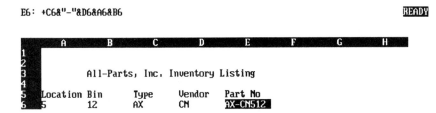

For practice, you may wish to enter the data and the required string formula to build the several additional part numbers. Like the other formula types, changing the values for any of the variables will immediately change the results produced by the string formula. Once you have completed your entries, you can save the model by entering /**FS** from the menu, typing **PARTNO**, and pressing ENTER. To clear the screen enter /**WEY**.

The advantage of the part number display in the last example would occur if the model contained information on additional parts as well as fields to the right that were also important to view. Using the string formula to build the part number, you could move the cell pointer to the right and view the other data without losing track of the part number, as follows:

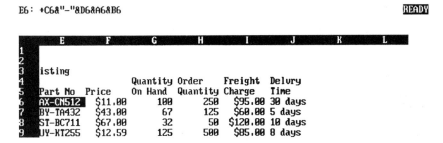

The full power of 1-2-3's string formulas will be realized when you learn to combine the string concatenation features with special string functions that can extract a portion of a string entry. These special string functions can be used for complex combinations and are an excellent tool for correcting data-entry errors. Special string functions will be covered in Chapter 10.

When more than one operator is used in a formula, it is important to know which operation 1-2-3 will perform first. This table shows the priority order for each operation that 1-2-3 can perform. If more than one operator has the same priority, they will be evaluated from left to right.

Priority	Operator	Operation Performed
8	( )	Parentheses to override priorities
7	^	Exponentiation
6	+ −	Positive and negative indicators
5	/ *	Division and multiplication
4	+ −	Addition and subtraction
3	= <>	Logical operators
	< >	
	<= >=	
2	#NOT#	Complex not indicator
1	#AND#	Complex and, complex or, and the
	#OR#	string operator
	&	

TABLE 2-1.   Operation Priorities

PERFORMING MORE COMPLEX CALCULATIONS

When 1-2-3 encounters more than one operator in a formula, it does not use a left-to-right order to compute the result. Instead, it evaluates the formula based on a set priority order for each of the operators. As you begin to build more complex formulas, you will see how important it is to understand 1-2-3's priorities in order to achieve the desired effects.

Table 2-1 shows the order of priority for each of the operators. You will notice that the parentheses are at the top of the list. This indicates that any expression enclosed within them will be evaluated first. The other operators that may cause confusion are the + and − symbols shown in levels 6 and 4. The first set represents the positive or negative sign of a value. For instance, −5*3 indicates that the five is a negative number, which should be multiplied by a positive three. On the other hand, in the expression 5−4*2 the minus symbol represents subtraction and has a lower priority than the multiplication operation, which will be carried out first.

A short example will demonstrate this clearly. Suppose you wish to add the total number of pounds of books in a shipment by combining the 10-pound weight of the books ordered with 3 pounds of stationery items and then multiplying the total weight by the per-pound shipping rate of 25 cents. You would not get the correct result if you entered 10+3*.25, since 1-2-3 would perform the multiplication first and calculate 10 plus 0.75, totaling 10.75 rather than the 3.25 you expected. To make 1-2-3 perform the calculation your way, you need to enter the data as (10+3)*.25. 1-2-3 will evaluate the expression within the parentheses first and carry out the multiplication second, resulting in the desired answer of 3.25.

Let's look at another salary model to demonstrate the importance of the priority of operations and how you can control it with parentheses. This model will project a single employee's salary based on his or her current salary, the increase percent you choose to give the employee, and the month of the increase. Since a lengthy formula is required, you will perform only the computation for one employee. However, you will want to save it and add employees once you have learned how to copy entries from one cell to another.

To enter the data for the salary computation model, follow these steps.

1. Type the following entries in the worksheet cells specified:

A2:	Name
B1:	'1989
B2:	Salary
C1:	Increase
C2:	Month
D1:	Increase
D2:	Percent
E1:	'1990
E2:	Salary

    This completes the entry of the column labels and produces these results:

E2: 'Salary   READY

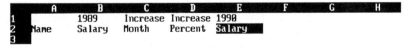

2. Type **J. Brown** in A3 and press ENTER.

3. Move the cell pointer to B3, type **35900**, and press ENTER.

    To look at the effect of giving the increase in month 5, you would need to enter a new number in C3. Try this now.

E3: ((B3/12)*(C3-1))+((B3/12)*(1+D3)*(12-(C3-1)))   `READY`

	A	B	C	D	E	F	G	H
1		1989	Increase	Increase	1990			
2	Name	Salary	Month	Percent	Salary			
3	J. Brown	35900	5	0.06	37336			

FIGURE 2-10.   Projecting next year's salary

4. Move the cell pointer to C3, type **5** in C3, and press ENTER.

5. Type **.06** in D3 and press ENTER.
   This latest entry represents the amount of the increase.

The last step is the most complicated: The formula must compute the current monthly salary and multiply it by the number of months that the individual will continue to receive this salary. The result of this first computation must then be added to the figure computed for the amount paid at the new salary level. The total dollars paid at the new salary level are computed by multiplying the current monthly salary by 100% plus the increase percentage by the number of months that the individual will receive the increased salary amount. Predictably, after such a lengthy explanation, the formula is quite long when it is recorded in the worksheet cell. Figure 2-10 shows this formula. An explanation of each of the component parts follows.

(B3/12)	Represents the annual salary divided by 12 to compute the monthly salary
(C3–1)	The month of the increase minus one or the number of months the employee receives his or her current salary
(1+D3)	Indicates that the employee will receive 100% of his or her existing salary plus an increase represented by a decimal fraction in D3
12– (C3–1)	The number of months that the employee receives the increased salary amount

6. Combining all these, enter the following formula in E3:

((B3/12)*(C3–1))+((B3/12)*(1+D3)*(12–(C3–1)))

Type carefully and give yourself a pat on the back if you manage to complete the entire entry successfully on your first attempt. If you do make a few mistakes, you can always edit your entry to make the necessary corrections. If your mistakes are serious enough, 1-2-3 will even take care of placing you in EDIT mode without requiring you to press the F2 (EDIT) key.

A few extra parentheses have been added to the formula expression to make it more readable. For example, the result would be the same if the parentheses were omitted from around (B3/12) since multiplication and division have the same priority. Using an extra pair of parentheses does not change the value of the expression as long as it does not change the order of operations. Feel free to add parentheses in this manner whenever they improve the readability of the formula without altering it. In this example, you have entered the data for only one employee, but this model could be expanded easily.

In a subsequent chapter, you will use the model to add employees; but for now, save a copy of it to disk by entering /**FSSALARY** and pressing ENTER.

USING NAMES RATHER THAN CELL ADDRESSES IN FORMULAS

Meaningful names are often easier to remember than cell addresses. If you have sales stored in B10 and a discount rate in Z2, it will be easier to remember the name of the type of information you have stored than the cell addresses, especially when you have a model with many items of data. 1-2-3 provides a way for you to name the data stored in worksheet cells. Although you will not want to make this extra effort for every model, it can be especially helpful in some situations. Before learning how to assign names to your data, you will need to learn about 1-2-3 ranges.

Range Basics

In 1-2-3, a *range* is a group of one or more cells that form a contiguous rectangle. You can use ranges in 1-2-3 to tell the package to take the same action on each of the cells in the group. When used in this way, they can provide a substantial time-savings over making separate requests to change each cell in the group. You will see more about the use of ranges in this way in Chapter 3. For now, you will want to learn the essentials that allow you to use ranges to assign names to individual worksheet cells.

Cell references are expressed by stating the column location, followed by the row location, as in A10 or C4. Since a range can include a rectangular area of cells, a range address is always expressed as two separate cell addresses set apart by a period. The typical method used to describe a range is to state first the upper left cell in the range, then use a period as a separator and supply the lower right cell in the range as in A1.B10 or C3.G20. Although you need to type only one period as a separator, 1-2-3 always converts it to two and would show these ranges as A1..B10 and C3..G20. You can assign a name to any range so that you can refer to the range by the name rather than by its cell addresses.

Elsewhere in the book, you will look at applications for applying names to ranges that include more than one cell. For now, you need to assign range names only to individual cells, since the formulas you have used thus far operate on only one cell at a time. Even though you are interested in naming one cell, you still need to refer to that cell as a range rather than attempt to use its individual cell address. This is because the command that you are using is designed to accept range addresses rather than cell addresses. The proper way of expressing a range consisting of one cell is to use the cell address for both the beginning and the end of the range. When A1 is treated as a range, the range address is expressed as A1..A1.

Naming a Range

You need to use a command from 1-2-3's menu in order to name the range. You will learn more about the various menu options in Chapter 3, but for now all you need to do is use a slash whenever you need to invoke the menu and type the first letter of the commands that you need to execute. The complicated salary formula entered in Figure 2-10 is a good place to try out the benefits of *range names*.

As you name each of the cells in the model, you are limited to 15 characters for your range name. Each range name must be unique and can refer to only one cell if you want to use it in the types of formulas entered thus far. 1-2-3 does not distinguish between upper- and lowercase and displays all range names in uppercase when you see them in formulas.

To name the three cells used in computing the 1990 salary figure for J. Brown, follow these steps.

1. Move the cell pointer to B3 as shown here:

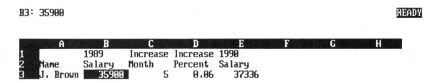

```
B3: 35900                                                          READY

         A        B        C        D        E        F        G        H
1                 1989     Increase Increase 1990
2       Name      Salary   Month    Percent  Salary
3       J. Brown  35900         5     0.06    37336
```

2. Type / to invoke the menu. Type **R** to select the Range command. Type **N** to select the Name option from the Range menu. Type **C** to select Create from the Name menu. Your screen will look like this:

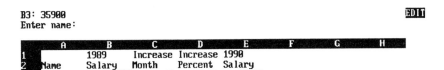

3. Type **89_salary** and press ENTER.

4. Press ENTER a second time to accept 1-2-3's suggested range designation of the current cell.

   If you forget to position the cell pointer before requesting the /Range Name Create command, 1-2-3 suggests a different range address. You can replace its suggestion by typing your own in the format B3.B3.

5. Move the cell pointer to C3, enter /**RNC** followed by **inc_mo**, and press ENTER twice.

   Again, the keystrokes /RNC are requesting an action through 1-2-3's menus. You will learn more about these menus in Chapter 3.

6. Move the cell pointer to D3, enter /**RNC** followed by **inc_%**, and press ENTER twice.

7. Move the cell pointer to E3.

   Your formula should now display like this:

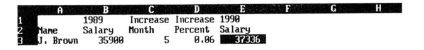

Although it is still a complex formula, it is a little easier to understand when you do not need to make the mental comparison between cell address and cell contents for each entry in the formula. If you want the range names available the next time you use a model, you must save it after assigning the range names. When you edit a cell with the F2 (EDIT) key that contains range names in the formula, the edit line displays the cell addresses rather than the range names shown in the top line. Your display will look like this:

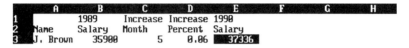

Press ENTER to finalize the entry and return to READY mode.

Although the range names are practical in this small example, they are not a good solution in all models. If you expand this model to show the salary computations for a department of 100 individuals, with each individual shown on a different row, range names would be impractical since you would need to assign a unique range name to the entries in each of the rows. In this situation, it is best to continue to use cell addresses in your formulas since it would be impractical to assign 300 unique range names to the model. On the other hand, a model containing a financial statement that is to be used in the preparation of ratios would be a good application for the assignment of range names, as similar data items are not repeated and the use of the range names would make the formulas much more readable.

Using Range Names
When Building Formulas

The last example showed you how a formula changes to display range addresses once they have been assigned. You can also assign a name to a cell before you reference it in a formula. This will allow you to specify the name with the F3 (NAME) key when building a formula. To try an example, save the model currently in memory by selecting /File Save, pressing ENTER to select Salary, and typing **R** to replace the copy on disk with the model currently in memory. Then select /Worksheet Erase Yes to clear memory. Follow these steps to try the new approach.

1. Make the following entries:

    A2   Cost
    A3   Accumulated Depreciation
    A4   Book Value
    D2   5000
    D3   1000

2. Move the cell pointer to D2 and select /Range Name Create by typing the first letter in each word after typing the slash (/).

3. Type **cost** and press ENTER twice.

4. Move the cell pointer to D3 and select /Range Name Create.

5. Type **accumulated dep** and press ENTER twice.
   Note that you are limited to 15 characters.

6. Move the cell pointer to D4. Type +, then press the F3 (NAME) key. Your display will look like this:

7. Move the highlight to COST and press ENTER.

8. Type –, then press F3 (NAME). Press ENTER with the highlight on ACCUMU-LATED DEP. Your display will look like this:

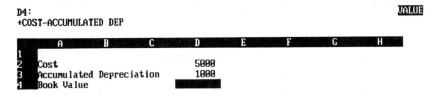

9. Press ENTER to finalize the formula entry. Your display will look like this:

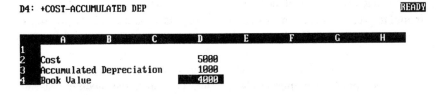

Deleting Range Names

You can delete range names that you no longer need. The command to eliminate them is also on the /Range Name menu that you have been using to create them. When you eliminate a range name, you do not eliminate the worksheet data with the range name. The formulas with references to the deleted range names revert to displaying the cell address rather than its name. To delete the range name ACCUMULATED DEP from the previous example, follow these steps.

1. Select /Range Name Delete.

2. Highlight ACCUMULATED DEP and press ENTER.
   When you move the highlight to D4, the formula will no longer display the deleted range name and will look like this:

D4: +COST-D3   READY

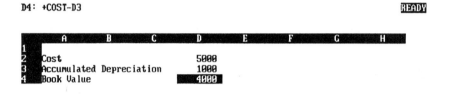

REVIEW EXERCISE

Formulas are the building blocks of all 1-2-3 models. With a little practice in formula entry, you will soon begin to think of yourself as a model construction expert. Before beginning to practice on your own application, you can try the model shown in Figure 2-11. This model allows you to compute the cost of another type of construction project when you look at the cost of adding a deck to your house as a weekend project. You can estimate the amount of each supply that you will need and enter the unit cost of each item after checking at the nearest lumber supply yard. The model shows you the total cost of the project. If you revise your estimate, you can change the number of units required for any item. If you decide to shop around for the lowest price, you also may want to revise some of the unit costs shown in the model. You also can revise the model to prepare cost estimates for other projects. You can follow this sequence in creating the model after entering /**WEY** to erase any existing entries from the screen.

1. Using Figure 2-11 as a guide, enter the description of the model in C2. Enter the column headings in C4, E4, and G4. Enter the labels representing the required supplies in A5 through A8.

A1:   READY

	A	B	C	D	E	F	G	H
1								
2			Cost estimate for deck construction					
3								
4			Unit Cost		Number Units		Total Item Cost	
5	Box nails		0.79		10		7.9	
6	Railing - 10'		4.6		40		184	
7	Decking - 12'		1.29		400		516	
8	Support posts		8.5		20		170	

FIGURE 2-11.   A model for creating construction estimates

2. Enter the unit cost figures in C5 through C8.

   Note that even though you enter .79, 1-2-3 displays the entry as 0.79. Also, an entry of 4.60 displays as 4.6. In Chapter 3 you will learn how to improve the appearance of these model entries.

3. Enter the units in E5 through E8.

4. Enter the formulas for the total cost of each item in G5 through G8.

   Hint: You can compute the formula for the total cost of the nails by entering +C5*E5. The other formulas are similar but refer to entries on different rows.

5. Place the label **TOTAL CONSTRUCTION COST** in C10, then enter the formula to compute it in G10.

   Hint: You can add each of the entries in G5 through G8 to compute the proper total and your formula will look like +G5+G6+G7+G8.

```
G10:  +TOT$_NAILS+TOT$_RAILING+TOT$_DECKING+TOT$_POSTS                    READY
```

```
        A       B       C       D       E       F       G       H
1
2                       Cost estimate for deck construction
3
4                       Unit Cost       Number Units    Total Item Cost
5   Box nails             0.79             10               7.9
6   Railing - 10'         4.6              40               184
7   Decking - 12'         1.29            400               516
8   Support posts         8.5              20               170
9
10                      TOTAL CONSTRUCTION COST                877.9
```

FIGURE 2-12.   Formula showing range names

6. Although naming the cells used in the model may not be required to understand the formula, name each of the entries in G5 through G8 for practice with naming cells.

   Hint: Use the /Range Name Create command.

   Be sure to choose unique and meaningful names.

   Hint: You might use names like TOT$_NAILS, TOT$_RAILING, TOT$_DECKING, and TOT$_POSTS.

   If you use the suggested range names and then move the cell pointer to G10, your formula will display as shown at the top of the model in Figure 2-12.

7. Save the model as CONSTRCT.

   Hint: Use the /File Save command.

REVIEW

- Formulas allow you to define computations that you want 1-2-3 to perform with the contents of worksheet cells.

- Formulas must always start with a value character and cannot exceed 240 characters.

- Arithmetic formulas are the most popular type of 1-2-3 formulas since they support typical business calculations like computing purchase discounts, invoice extensions, and sales projections. They use operators for addition (+), subtraction (−), multiplication (∗), division (/), and exponentiation (^).

- String formulas use only one operator, the ampersand (&), which allows you to join two character strings.

- Logical formulas use the logical operators equal to (=), not equal to (<>), less than (<), less than or equal to (<=), greater than (>), and greater than or equal to (>=).

- All formula operators do not have the same priority. You can use parentheses to raise the priority of an operation since 1-2-3 evaluates entries in parentheses first. Table 2-1 lists the normal priority sequence of the operators.

- A range name can be assigned to any cell on the worksheet. Formulas referencing this cell automatically display the range name in the formula. To access an existing range name when building a formula, use the F3 (NAME) key and select it from the list presented.

- A range name that is no longer needed can be deleted without deleting the data in the referenced cell. After the range name is deleted, the formula displays the cell address rather than the range name.

Commands and Keys

Entry	Action
/FR	Accesses /File Retrieve to allow you to read a file from disk into memory
/RNC	Allows you to name a worksheet cell with /Range Name Create
/RND	Allows you to delete a range name with /Range Name Delete
/WEY	Invokes /Worksheet Erase and responds with Yes to clear memory
F3 (NAME)	Allows you to access a list of range names

CHANGING THE WORKSHEET APPEARANCE

Up to this point, you have accepted 1-2-3's choices for how to present your entries. You have used the package's *default* for the format in which the data has been displayed. It is great to have this default available; it lets you build a model that produces completely accurate results without having to concern yourself with how your entries should be displayed. But it is also great to know that 1-2-3 provides a set of powerful formatting options and other commands that let you change the default settings affecting the display of your entries. There are commands that let you select a new display format for all the values on the worksheet, or change the format for the value entries in a small section of the worksheet. Other 1-2-3 commands allow you to affect the alignment of labels, either before or after you enter them. Still other commands let you change the number of characters that can be displayed in a column or hide certain columns from view. In this chapter, you will look at examples using each of these techniques. You will find that each of these 1-2-3 commands is easy to use and provides significant improvements in the appearance of your worksheet models. First, let's address how you access these commands, since they can be accessed only when 1-2-3's menu is on the screen.

1-2-3's MENUS

1-2-3's menu system is designed to make 1-2-3's commands easy to access and remember. Only one keystroke is needed to access the menu system, and Lotus has chosen words that represent their function in building the menu. Each menu option also includes a description of the tasks that it can accomplish for you. This descriptive information will make it easier for you to select the correct command as you are learning the package.

Activating the Menu

1-2-3's menu is activated by pressing the slash key (/) from READY mode. This key is located on the lower right side of your keyboard near the SHIFT key. If the mode indicator currently reads WAIT, POINT, ERROR, or something other than READY, it means that 1-2-3 will not be ready to accept your request. If you type a slash when 1-2-3 is not ready to respond, the menu will not appear onscreen. Instead, in most cases, 1-2-3 will make a beeping noise to let you know that it cannot process your request to view the main menu selections. If 1-2-3 is in EDIT mode when you enter the slash, 1-2-3 adds the slash to the current entry. You must take an action to return the indicator to READY before entering the slash. This action may be completing the entry you have already started, waiting for 1-2-3 to finish its current task, or pressing ESC to acknowledge that you saw an Error Message.

The Menu Structure

You will want to examine the menu structure that 1-2-3 presents. Type / to activate the menu and produce this display:

```
A1:                                                              MENU
Worksheet  Range  Copy  Move  File  Print  Graph  Data  System  Add-In  Quit
Global  Insert  Delete  Column  Erase  Titles  Window  Status  Page  Learn
          A         B         C         D        E        F        G        H
1
2
```

Notice that the mode indicator also changes to MENU (it will remain this way as long as one of 1-2-3's menus is displayed on the screen). The second and third lines in the control panel are devoted to the menu display. The second line in the control panel shows the various menu choices; the line beneath it provides an explanation of the types of tasks performable by the currently highlighted selection in the top row.

Currently, 1-2-3's main menu is on the screen. It is called the *main menu* because all selections must start at this point. By selecting one of the options in this display, you often are shown a submenu of choices. These allow you to refine your choice. Most of the main menu entries provide many options. You may be given as many as six levels of menus to select from before you get to your final choice. You need not be concerned with the complexity of the menus, however. The options are organized logically; with a little practice, it is easy to decide which path to select at any point.

The third line of the control panel describes each of the menu choices onscreen. Its purpose is to help guide you in making a selection. And if you make an inappropriate choice, there is an easy way to retreat and start fresh down the path to the exact command you are seeking. Again, do not be discouraged by the complexity; you will not need to learn all the menu commands. You can accomplish 90% of your work using only a small percentage of the total menu. The other commands are there to provide sophisticated options for 1-2-3's power users.

Before you examine any one particular menu choice in further detail, take a quick look at each of the main menu selections to get an overview of the types of features each of them provides. Each main menu choice and the category of tasks it performs is listed here.

Menu Selection	Type of Task Handled
Worksheet	Think of the Worksheet menu anytime you wish to make a change that will affect the worksheet. Options include globally setting the format of value entries in the worksheet cells, inserting and deleting worksheet rows or columns, and erasing the entire worksheet.
Range	Think of the Range menu when the changes you wish to make are less extensive and will affect only a section of the worksheet. Options in the Range menu include formatting a section of the worksheet, assigning a name to a group of worksheet cells, and erasing a section of the worksheet.
Copy	Use the Copy selection whenever you wish to duplicate the information from one group of worksheet cells to another group of cells. With this menu choice, you do not have to select from additional submenus. You need only specify which cells you need to copy and where you want them copied to.

Menu Selection	Type of Task Handled
Move	Move is similar to Copy, but it relocates data rather than copying it. Choose Move whenever this is the task you wish to perform. As with Copy, Move requires you to respond to its prompts rather than select from additional submenus.
File	Consider selecting File whenever you wish to perform tasks that relate to saving or retrieving data stored on the disk. Options include saving a file, retrieving a file, and listing the directory of the current disk drive.
Print	Use the Print selection whenever you wish to obtain a hard copy of the worksheet that is currently in memory.
Graph	Graph is the option to select when you wish to create a graphic representation of data stored on the worksheet. Some of the options include defining the type of graph you wish to create, defining the data to be shown on the graph, and viewing the graph that is currently defined.
Data	The Data commands are a special category that provides data-management features along with some special arithmetic features. The two most frequently used options under Data are the Sort option, which allows you to resequence your data, and the Query option, which allows you to locate and extract specific information from your model.
System	The System option provides access to the basic DOS operating system commands without having to exit to 1-2-3.
Add-In	The Add-In menu options were added to Release 2.2's menu to make it easy to work with add-in programs. With the submenu options presented with this selection, you can attach, detach, and invoke add-in programs.
Quit	Quit exits 1-2-3 without saving the worksheet currently in memory. Use this selection only when you have completed your 1-2- 3 session and already saved your work.

Each of these main menu selections will be discussed in more detail as you proceed through this book. Next, you will look at how you can select the options from 1-2-3's menus.

Making Selections

You can select an option in any menu that is displayed by typing the first letter of the menu selection, using either upper- or lowercase. In other words, to select the first option, Worksheet, you can type **w** or **W**. If you type a letter that is not used on the menu, 1-2-3 will beep at you and will not respond until you enter a valid menu selection.

A second way to make your selection is to use the LEFT or RIGHT ARROW key and move the highlighted bar (cursor) to the menu item you want and then press ENTER. This latter approach is preferred while you are learning the menu, since it causes 1-2-3 to display a description of the command you are about to choose in the third line of the control panel. If after reading this description you decide it is not the correct selection, you can continue to move to new selections until the desired description is displayed. No action will be taken until you activate a menu choice by pressing ENTER.

Sometimes just pointing to a menu selection will cause you to change your mind. In that case, move the cursor to the Quit selection. The description will tell you to use it to end your current 1-2-3 session. Since you do not want to end the current session, reading this description should convince you not to select Quit.

Often a series of menu selections is needed to complete a task with 1-2-3. Each selection helps to refine the description of your needs to 1-2-3 and selects an option lower in 1-2-3's menu hierarchy. You can think of your selection as creating command sentences with a word selected from each level of the menu hierarchy that further refines the meaning of your command. After making your first selection, you may need to choose from a submenu of additional choices to make your request clearer. A selection from the submenu may complete the process or it may invoke yet another menu level for your selection. With Release 2.2, some of 1-2-3's submenu selections also display a settings sheet showing the current entries and selections for each option in the menu.

If you think of the process as building a command sentence, you might choose File from the main menu to tell 1-2-3 that the command you want to enter involves files. You might choose Save from the File submenu to refine the file operation. Finally, you might enter **REALEST** to complete your command sentence by supplying the name under which 1-2-3 should save the file.

Try a few selections so you can see how the process works.

1. Type / to activate the menu.

2. Select Worksheet by typing **W** or by pressing ENTER, since the cursor is already positioned on that selection.

   This is the menu that will appear:

```
A1:                                                                     MENU
Global  Insert  Delete  Column  Erase  Titles  Window  Status  Page  Learn
Format  Label-Prefix  Column-Width  Recalculation  Protection  Default  Zero
          A        B        C        D        E        F        G        H
1
2
```

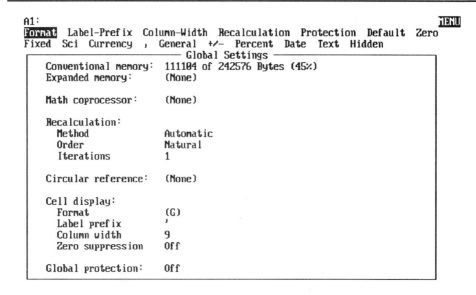

FIGURE 3-1.   The Global menu and Global Settings sheet

This menu shows all the options you have for affecting the worksheet. Press ENTER to select Global from the submenu that is presented. When you select Global, a third-level menu is presented, which should match the entries at the top of Figure 3-1. You will notice that Release 2.2 displays a *settings sheet* in the worksheet area as soon as you select Global. This sheet shows you the current setting for each Global option. Any changes made through options in the Global menu will be reflected in this sheet immediately.

Since you are just examining the menu structure, do not make any additional selections at this time. Instead, examine the methods for backing out of menu selections to return to the previous menu and eventually to the READY mode. This is useful when you accidentally make an incorrect menu selection and want to back out of it to make a new choice.

The ESC key is used to back out of one level of menu selection. Try this key to see how it works.

1. Press ESC once.

    The menu of worksheet selections returns to the screen.

2. Press ESC again.

    The main menu appears with this second press.

3. Press ESC a third time.

   The READY mode indicator appears. If you had made four menu selections, you would have had to press ESC four times to return to READY mode. An easier way to return to READY mode is to press the CTRL-BREAK key combination. That is, hold down the CTRL key while you press the BREAK or SCROLL LOCK key and then release both keys. Regardless of the number of menu selections you have made, you will immediately be taken out of the MENU mode and placed back in the READY mode.

CHANGING THE FORMAT
OF VALUE ENTRIES

The default format that 1-2-3 uses for all value entries is called the *General format*. It is somewhat unusual in that it does not provide consistent formats for all entries. The display it provides is affected by the size of the number that is entered in the cell. Some numbers display as they are entered, while others are altered to have a leading zero added or so they can be rounded to a number of decimal digits that will fit in the cell width you have selected. The General format also suppresses trailing zeros after the decimal point; if you enter them, they will not appear in the display.

Very large and very small numbers are displayed in *Scientific format*, which means that exponential notation will be used. *Exponential notation* is a method of representing a number in abbreviated form by including the power of 10 that the number should be raised to. If 100550000 is entered in a cell when the General format is in effect, 1-2-3 will use scientific notation to display it as 1.0E+8.

General format handles a wide variety of formats but often results in a display whose results have varying numbers of decimal places. This makes it less than desirable for many business models because of the inconsistencies in the display of decimal numbers. You encountered the inconsistencies in its decimal display with the investment model in Chapter 2. However, this inconsistency does not mean that General format is useless; it provides an ideal format in many situations.

General format is useful when you want to minimize the space used to display very large or very small numbers. Scientific notation ensures that these numbers will be shown in a minimum of space and that the conversion will be handled for you automatically if required. It simply is not the display to use when you need to control the number of decimal places shown.

Formatting Options

There are many alternatives to the General display format. 1-2-3 provides a wide range of formatting options that allow you to display your data with everything from dollar

Format	Cell Entry	Display
Fixed	5678	5678.00
2 decimal places	−123.45	−123.45
Scientific	5678	5.68E+03
2 decimal places	−123.45	−1.23E+02
Currency	5678	$5,678.00
2 decimal places	−123.45	($123.45)
,(Comma)	5678	5,678
2 decimal places	−123.45	(123.45)
General	5678	5678
	−123.45	−123.45
+/−	4	++++
	3	− − −
	0	.
Percent	5	500%
	.1	10%
Date (D1)	31679	24-Sep-86
Time (T1)	.5	12:00:00 PM
Text	+A2*A3	+A2*A3
Hidden	35000	

TABLE 3-1.   1-2-3's Format Options

signs and commas to percent symbols. You can even specify the number of decimal places for most of the formats. The specific formats supported by 1-2-3 and their effect on worksheet entries are shown in Table 3-1. You will apply some of these formats to models you have already created.

Scope of the Formatting Change

You can also choose how extensive an impact you want a particular format command to have by formatting the entire worksheet or a range of cells in one area of the worksheet. First, you will examine the procedure for changing the default format for a section of the worksheet.

FIGURE 3-2.   Invalid and valid ranges

CHANGING THE FORMAT FOR A RANGE OF CELLS   Everything you have accomplished with 1-2-3 so far has focused on individual cells. However, 1-2-3 also allows you to work with any contiguous rectangle of cells, called a range, to accomplish tasks such as formatting. You were introduced to ranges in Chapter 2 when you assigned names to ranges consisting of a single cell reference. Figure 3-2 shows groups of cells that are valid ranges as well as some groups that are not. The groups on the left are invalid ranges because they do not form one contiguous rectangle. The cell groups on the right are valid ranges because they form a contiguous group. As long as this rule is met, the range can be as large as you wish or as small as one cell.

You can use several methods to specify cell ranges. You can type them in like a cell address or highlight them with the cell pointer. Any two diagonally opposite corners can be used to specify the range as long as they are separated by one or more decimal points. For example, the range of cells shown in the following illustration can be specified as B4.C8, B4..C8, B8.C4, B8..C4, C8.B4, C8..B4, C4.B8, or C4..B8.

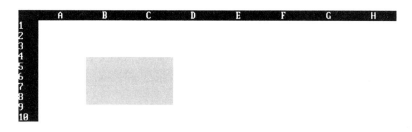

The most common way to specify a range is to use the upper leftmost cell first and the lower rightmost cell last. Also, since 1-2-3 will supply the second period, you might as well save a keystroke and just type B4.C8. If you plan to specify a range by highlighting it, you can save yourself some time by positioning the cell pointer in the upper leftmost corner of the range before beginning.

Retrieve your investment model by typing **/FRREALEST** and pressing ENTER. The model should match the one shown in Figure 3-3. To try out the range specifications as you add some formats to this model, follow these steps:

1. Move the cell pointer to D13, the upper leftmost cell in the range you will format.

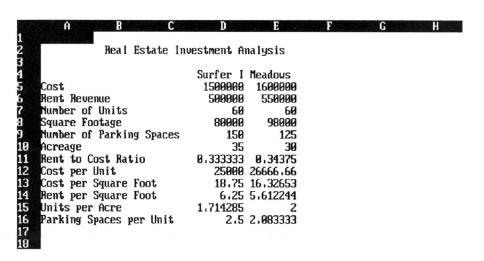

FIGURE 3-3. Real estate investment model created in Chapter 2

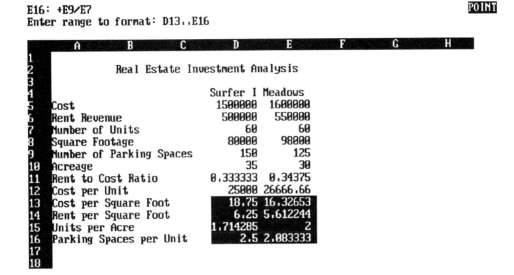

E16: +E9/E7   POINT
Enter range to format: D13..E16

```
        A        B        C        D        E       F       G       H
1
2              Real Estate Investment Analysis
3
4                                 Surfer I Meadows
5  Cost                            1500000  1600000
6  Rent Revenue                     500000   550000
7  Number of Units                      60       60
8  Square Footage                    80000    98000
9  Number of Parking Spaces            150      125
10 Acreage                              35       30
11 Rent to Cost Ratio             0.333333  0.34375
12 Cost per Unit                     25000 26666.66
13 Cost per Square Foot             18.75 16.32653
14 Rent per Square Foot              6.25 5.612244
15 Units per Acre                 1.714285        2
16 Parking Spaces per Unit            2.5 2.083333
17
18
```

FIGURE 3-4.   Highlighting a range to be formatted

2. Type / to activate the menu.

3. Use RIGHT ARROW to move the cursor to the menu option Range and press ENTER.

4. Press ENTER to select the Format option that is currently highlighted.

5. Select the Fixed format option by typing **F**.

6. Press ENTER to select the default of two decimal places.

7. Use RIGHT ARROW and DOWN ARROW to position the cell pointer in E16, highlighting the entire area to be formatted as shown in Figure 3-4. Then press ENTER.

   The format should immediately change to two decimal places for each of the entries in this section and match the display in Figure 3-5. The other range that needs to be formatted is D11..E11. This time you will not position the cell pointer first so that you can experience the extra steps involved.

D13: (F2) +D5/D8   READY

```
         A          B          C          D          E          F          G          H
1
2                        Real Estate Investment Analysis
3
4                                          Surfer I Meadows
5     Cost                                 1500000    1600000
6     Rent Revenue                          500000     550000
7     Number of Units                           60         60
8     Square Footage                         80000      98000
9     Number of Parking Spaces                 150        125
10    Acreage                                   35         30
11    Rent to Cost Ratio                  0.333333    0.34375
12    Cost per Unit                          25000   26666.66
13    Cost per Square Foot                   18.75      16.33
14    Rent per Square Foot                    6.25       5.61
15    Units per Acre                          1.71       2.00
16    Parking Spaces per Unit                 2.50       2.08
17
18
```

Figure 3-5.   Result of Format operation

8. Select /Range Format Fixed and press ENTER.

   This command sequence will accept the default of two decimal places. You cannot expand the range at this point, as it has the incorrect beginning location. You must first free the beginning of the range.

9. Press ESC. Now you will find that you can move the cell pointer to D11 without altering a range specification.

10. Type . (period).

    This will anchor the beginning of the range again.

11. Expand the range by moving the cell pointer to E11, and then press ENTER to finalize the range selection.

If you move the cell pointer to any cell that has been formatted with a Range command, you can tell the format that has been assigned to the cell, even if it is empty. This information is displayed as a single character representing the format type in the control panel. Table 3-2 presents examples of some of the commonly used format abbreviations. These format specifications are enclosed within parentheses and placed

Abbreviation	Format in Effect
(P2)	Percent with two decimal places
(T)	Text to display formulas as they are entered
(G)	General
(C0)	Currency with zero decimal places
(, 2)	Comma with two decimal places
(D1)	Date format 1
(D6)	Time format 1
(H)	Hidden format

TABLE 3-2.   Examples of Format Abbreviations

immediately after the cell address, as in the following cell, which is formatted as Text, causing the formula entry to display rather than the result of the formula:

A3: (T) +A1+A2   READY

For formats that allow you to specify the number of decimal places, a numeric digit follows, as shown here:

A1: (C2) 3   READY

The model still is not presented in the optimal format. The numbers in the cells at the top would be easier to read if they had commas inserted after the thousands position. There are two formats that will add these commas. One is referred to as the *Comma format* (,); the other is the *Currency format*. The only difference between the two is whether a dollar sign is inserted at the front of the entry. Either of these two formats could be added with another range request, but since the cells that you wish to change include all the remaining value entries on the worksheet, you will use the Global formatting option covered in the next section.

MAKING A GLOBAL FORMAT CHANGE   When you wish to alter the format of the entire worksheet or even most of it, a *Global format* change is the ideal solution.

D11: (F2) +D6/D5   READY

```
        A        B        C        D        E        F        G        H
 1
 2              Real Estate Investment Analysis
 3
 4                              Surfer I Meadows
 5   Cost                      ******************
 6   Rent Revenue               500,000  550,000
 7   Number of Units                 60       60
 8   Square Footage              80,000   90,000
 9   Number of Parking Spaces       150      125
10   Acreage                         35       30
11   Rent to Cost Ratio            0.33     0.34
12   Cost per Unit               25,000   26,667
13   Cost per Square Foot         18.75    16.33
14   Rent per Square Foot          6.25     5.61
15   Units per Acre                1.71     2.00
16   Parking Spaces per Unit       2.50     2.08
17
18
```

FIGURE 3-6.   Column width too narrow for the format selected

A Global format change alters the default format for every cell on the worksheet, including both cells with entries and cells that are currently empty. As long as the worksheet cells have not had their formats altered with /Range Format commands, the new default format will take effect. For an empty cell, this format will be used as soon as a value entry is placed in the cell. The Global formatting option is especially useful when most of the worksheet is formatted with the same option. You can choose a Global format that meets the requirement for most of the cells, and then go back and format the exceptions with a /Range Format command.

To alter the Global format for the model, follow these steps:

1. Type / to activate the menu.

2. Press ENTER to select the Worksheet option.

3. Press ENTER to select the Global option.

4. Press ENTER to select the Format option.

5. Type , to select the Comma format.

D11: (F2) +D6/D5   READY

```
        A           B           C           D           E           F           G
1
2              Real Estate Investment Analysis
3
4                                      Surfer I  Meadows
5   Cost                               1,500,000 1,600,000
6   Rent Revenue                         500,000   550,000
7   Number of Units                           60        60
8   Square Footage                        80,000    98,000
9   Number of Parking Spaces                 150       125
10  Acreage                                   35        30
11  Rent to Cost Ratio                      0.33      0.34
12  Cost per Unit                         25,000    26,667
13  Cost per Square Foot                   18.75     16.33
14  Rent per Square Foot                    6.25      5.61
15  Units per Acre                          1.71      2.00
16  Parking Spaces per Unit                 2.50      2.08
17
18
```

FIGURE 3-7.   Global width changed to 10

6. Type **0** to specify zero decimal places, and press ENTER to finalize this entry.

    The display will change to match the one in Figure 3-6. Everything looks fine except that the two cost figures are now displayed as asterisks. The values that were stored there are still in memory and are only replaced by the asterisks to indicate that once the new formats are used, the numeric values in these cells require more space than the column width allows. You can correct this quickly by increasing the Global width. This command will be explained later in the chapter; for now, the command will be entered as shown.

7. Type **/WGC10** and press ENTER.

    The columns will be widened to ten characters, producing the display shown in Figure 3-7. The columns are now wide enough to display the cost figures with commas.

CHECKING A FORMAT SETTING   If you move the cell pointer to one of the cells that has been formatted with the Global option, you will notice that there is no format code in the control panel. Only Range Formats will display in the control panel. To check the Global format setting, you have to check the worksheet's status. The

```
D11: (F2) +D6/D5                                                      STAT
Press any key to continue...
```

```
┌─────────────────── Global Settings ───────────────────────┐
│  Conventional memory: 110212 of 242576 Bytes (45%)         │
│  Expanded memory:     (None)                               │
│                                                            │
│  Math coprocessor:    (None)                               │
│                                                            │
│  Recalculation:                                            │
│    Method             Automatic                            │
│    Order              Natural                              │
│    Iterations         1                                    │
│                                                            │
│  Circular reference:  (None)                               │
│                                                            │
│  Cell display:                                             │
│    Format             (,0)                                 │
│    Label prefix       '                                    │
│    Column width       10                                   │
│    Zero suppression   Off                                  │
│                                                            │
│  Global protection:   Off                                  │
└────────────────────────────────────────────────────────────┘
```

FIGURE 3-8.   Worksheet Status screen

Worksheet Status screen provides information on all the worksheet default settings. Check it now by following these directions:

1. Enter **/W** to select the Worksheet menu.

2. Type **S** to display the status.

    Your screen will look like the one in Figure 3-8. Notice that the indicator has changed to STAT. Do not be concerned if your screen is slightly different. The status screen for Release 1A is different, and the amounts of conventional and standard memory installed vary from system to system. If you look at the format, you should see (,0).

3. Press any key.

    This last step will return you to the worksheet and READY mode.

You can use the Format option to look at the formulas within worksheet cells by using a display format of Text. This means that you can review all the formulas at once rather than having to move the cell pointer to each cell and view the control panel to see the formula. The *Text format* displays formulas in the cells where you entered them rather than showing the result of the formulas within the cell. To make this change, you must use both the Global format change and a /Range Format change. The Global change will alter the default setting for all worksheet cells; however, since Range Formats take priority, some of the cells will ignore the default. This means that you must reset the format of these cells with the /Range Format command before the cells use the default setting.

Before beginning, replace the copy of the investment model on disk with the formatted copy now in memory.

1. Type /**FS** and press ENTER.

2. A prompt message will display. Type **R** in response. This will replace the file on disk. It is important to save the file at this time because the reformatting process used to view the formulas will eliminate the Fixed and Comma formats that you wish to retain permanently.

   Since you are becoming familiar with menu selections, from now on you will be given only the entries that you should make for each exercise. Directions will no longer tell you to point to a selection and press ENTER or type the first letter of the selection. You can use whatever method you prefer, as long as you enter the menu selections specified.

3. Select /Worksheet Global Format to get to the Global Format menu or press ENTER as each menu is presented until you are looking at the menu that provides format options.

4. Select Text as the format option.

5. Move the cell pointer to D11 and select /Range Format Reset to reset the Range Format to the Global default.

6. Move the cell pointer to E16 and press ENTER to view a display of the formulas like the one in Figure 3-9.

Since the formulas in this particular model are short, you can view the complete formula within each cell. If the formulas were longer, you would need to widen the columns to see the entire formula. In the next section, you will learn all about tailoring the column width to meet your particular needs.

CHANGING WORKSHEET COLUMNS

You have examined some of the changes you can make to the appearance of individual entries in cells. There are also several commands that allow you to make changes to

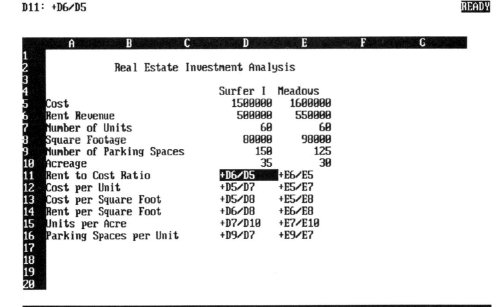

FIGURE 3-9.   Formula display

one or more columns at one time. 1-2-3 provides options that let you determine the width you wish to use for columns. In Release 2.2 you can change the width of a range of columns with one command. If you have Release 2 or higher, you can also hide or display columns on your worksheet.

Altering Column Widths

The default width of columns is nine when you begin a new 1-2-3 worksheet. This is adequate for values displayed with the General format; often, however, it is not wide enough when you want to display numbers with commas, dollar signs, and decimal places or some labels and most of the formulas you wish to display with the Text format option. At other times, the opposite might be true. Even though you may have a column that never contains more than one character, the full width of nine is always reserved for the column. If you could make some columns narrower, you might be able to view a few more columns on the screen. 1-2-3 will let you handle both types of changes by altering the column width. In fact, it even lets you choose whether to change the width of all the columns at once or alter the width of a single column.

A11: [W25] 'Rent to Cost Ratio   POINT
Enter column width (1..240): 25

```
                  A              B        C        D        E
 1
 2                            Real Estate Investment Analysis
 3
 4                                              Surfer I  Meadows
 5    Cost                                     1,500,000 1,600,000
 6    Rent Revenue                               500,000   550,000
 7    Number of Units                                 60        60
 8    Square Footage                              80,000    90,000
 9    Number of Parking Spaces                       150       125
10    Acreage                                         35        30
11    Rent to Cost Ratio                            0.33      0.34
12    Cost per Unit                               25,000    26,667
13    Cost per Square Foot                         18.75     16.33
14    Rent per Square Foot                          6.25      5.61
15    Units per Acre                                1.71      2.00
16    Parking Spaces per Unit                       2.50      2.08
17
18
19
20
```

FIGURE 3-10.   Column A widened to 25

CHANGING THE WIDTH OF ONE COLUMN   The ability to alter the width of individual columns lets you tailor your display to meet your exact needs. This is the preferred approach when you only have a few columns to change, since columns are neither wider nor narrower than the requirements of your data. Any change you make for a single column will take precedence over the Global default column width setting that you establish. This means that you can make both types of changes to your worksheet.

The investment model created in Chapter 2 provides an opportunity for changing a column width. Follow these steps for making the changes:

1. Select /File Retrieve REALEST and press ENTER.

2. Move the cell pointer to column A.
    Notice the list of long label entries in that column. It extends beyond the boundaries of column A and borrows space from column B. You can widen column A so that the entries will completely fit within the column.

3. Select /Worksheet Column Set-Width.

A1: [W20]   READY

	A	B	C	D	E
1		May 1990 Sales Contest Winners			
2					
3		Cars	Trucks	RV's	Office
4	John Larson	20	14	2	Grand Rapids, Michigan
5	Mary Ann Smithfield	32	3	3	Detroit, Michigan
6	Larry Hawkins	18	28	4	Cleveland, Ohio
7	Nancy Cline	18	32	5	Baltimore, Maryland
8					

FIGURE 3-11.   Sales contest winners

4. Press the RIGHT ARROW until column A is wide enough to display the entire entry, as in Figure 3-10. A width of 25 is a good selection.

5. Press ENTER.

This finalizes the width change. Column A will remain at a width of 25 unless you make another change. Adjusting the width of this column makes it clear where the data is entered. Adjusting the column width can also be important in Release 2 if you ever print a copy of the worksheet to a disk file. Release 2 will write data to disk only if the data fits within the column in which it was entered.

CHANGING THE WIDTH OF A RANGE OF COLUMNS   Release 2.2 allows you to alter the width of a range of columns. 1-2-3 changes the width of the range of columns with a single command, but the changes are applied to the individual columns just as if you had changed each one individually with the /Worksheet Column Set-Width command. This means that these settings will override any changes made with the /Worksheet Global Column-Width command.

You can enter the data in Figure 3-11 exactly as shown to begin trying this command. Note that the heading in row 1 in actually entered as a long label in B1. Also, the name entries in column A are truncated when you originally enter them. The full names will appear again later when the column width is altered. After completing the entries, follow these steps:

B1: [W7] 'May 1990 Sales Contest Winners   READY

```
               A             B      C      D           E                  F
1                        May 1990 Sales Contest Winners
2
3                       Cars   Trucks RV's   Office
4  John Larson            20     14     2 Grand Rapids, Michigan
5  Mary Ann Smithfield    32      3     3 Detroit, Michigan
6  Larry Hawkins          18     28     4 Cleveland, Ohio
7  Nancy Cline            10     32     5 Baltimore, Maryland
8
9
```

FIGURE 3-12.   Model after the /Worksheet Column Column-Range command was used on columns B through D

1. Move the cell pointer to A1.

2. Select /Worksheet Column Set-Width.

3. Type **20** and press ENTER.

    This changes the column width for column A to 20.

4. Position the cell pointer in column B.

5. Select /Worksheet Column Column-Range Set-Width.

6. Press the RIGHT ARROW key twice to expand the range to include columns C and D, and press ENTER.

7. Press the LEFT ARROW twice to shrink the width to 7.

8. Press ENTER.

    The result of steps 4 through 8 is to change the width of the three columns with one command sequence. Your revised model will match Figure 3-12.

9. Save this model as VEHICLES by selecting /File Save, typing **VEHICLES**, and pressing ENTER.

A1:   READY

	A	B	C	D	E	F	G	H
1			Employees Hired By Month					
2								
3		Jan	Feb	Mar	Apr	May	Jne	Jly
4	Region 1	1	7	7	6	0	3	8
5	Region 2	4	3	8	6	4	6	9
6	Region 3	5	0	5	6	8	5	6
7	Region 4	6	7	4	6	4	2	0
8	Region 5	2	3	0	9	0	6	8
9	Region 6	9	3	7	8	4	4	4
10	Region 7	4	5	2	8	8	8	5
11	Region 8	5	3	3	7	6	2	2
12	Region 9	3	0	0	6	8	9	2

FIGURE 3-13.   New employees by month

CHANGING THE WIDTH OF ALL THE COLUMNS   For certain models, all the column widths need to be altered. One possibility is using the /Worksheet Column Column-Range command, but this command covers only the range you define, whereas the Global option changes the entire worksheet, making model expansion for similar entries easy. If you have a model like the one in Figure 3-13 and wish to narrow the column width, it is also tedious to make this change a column at a time, making the /Worksheet Global Column-Width option the method of choice.

Since each entry under the "Month" heading is so small, it is better to narrow the columns and view all the months on the screen at once. The /Worksheet Global Column-Width command can make this change for you easily: Only one command is required to change all the columns. After entering the command sequence, you can type the new width or use the LEFT ARROW key to make the width narrower by one each time you press it. When you have adjusted the column to the desired width, you need only press ENTER to finalize the current selection. These entries will alter the preceding report so that all the months can be viewed. Follow these steps to make this change.

A4: 'Region 1   READY

	A	B	C	D	E	F	G	H	I	J	K	L	M	N
1				Employees Hired By Month										
2														
3		Jan	Feb	Mar	Apr	May	Jne	Jly	Aug	Spt	Oct	Nov	Dec	
4	Regio	1	7	7	6	0	3	8	6	7	3	6	7	
5	Regio	4	3	8	6	4	6	9	2	8	6	5	5	
6	Regio	5	0	5	6	8	5	6	5	0	1	5	1	
7	Regio	6	7	4	6	4	2	0	9	5	8	8	0	
8	Regio	2	3	0	9	0	6	8	5	3	4	5	8	
9	Regio	9	3	7	8	4	4	4	8	2	1	6	6	
10	Regio	4	5	2	8	8	8	5	6	5	1	1	8	
11	Regio	5	3	3	7	6	2	2	0	6	1	7	6	
12	Regio	3	8	8	6	8	9	2	0	7	9	3	1	

FIGURE 3-14. Column width narrowed globally

1. Select /Worksheet Global Column-Width.

2. Enter **5** for the width. Press ENTER. This produces the results shown in Figure 3-14.

The only problem with this display is that column A has also become smaller and will not display the region numbers. To fix this problem, do the following:

1. Move the cell pointer to column A.

2. Select /Worksheet Column Set-Width, type **9**, and press ENTER.
   This change to an individual column width fixes the problem and produces the result shown in Figure 3-15.

A /Worksheet Global Column-Width change can also be used to make all the columns wider. This is often useful when you are displaying the model as text to view its formulas. If all the formulas are approximately the same length, you may want to widen the column width to accommodate the longest formula entry.

A4: [W9] 'Region 1   **READY**

	A	B	C	D	E	F	G	H	I	J	K	L	M
1				Employees Hired By Month									
2													
3		Jan	Feb	Mar	Apr	May	Jne	Jly	Aug	Spt	Oct	Nov	Dec
4	Region 1	1	7	7	6	0	3	0	6	7	3	6	7
5	Region 2	4	3	0	6	4	6	9	2	0	6	5	5
6	Region 3	5	0	5	6	0	5	6	5	0	1	5	1
7	Region 4	6	7	4	6	4	2	0	9	5	0	0	0
8	Region 5	2	3	0	9	0	6	0	5	3	4	5	0
9	Region 6	9	3	7	0	4	4	4	0	2	1	6	6
10	Region 7	4	5	2	0	0	0	5	6	5	1	1	0
11	Region 8	5	3	3	7	6	2	2	0	6	1	7	6
12	Region 9	3	0	0	6	0	9	2	0	7	9	3	1

FIGURE 3-15.   Individual column change overrides Global change

If you want to check the default column width, you cannot point to one of the cells and see it displayed. The width is displayed in the control panel only when the change has been made to a single column with the /Worksheet Column Set-Width command. You must give the same status instruction used to check the format by selecting /Worksheet Status. Remember that you can always change this default; or, if you prefer, you can use the /Worksheet Column command to alter the width of one column.

Inserting and Deleting Columns

No matter how thoroughly you plan your worksheet applications, sometimes you need to make substantial changes to a worksheet model. You might need to add an employee to a model, delete accounts that are no longer used, or add some blank space to make the worksheet more readable. 1-2-3 will accommodate each of these needs by means of commands that let you insert or delete blank rows or columns in the worksheet.

INSERTING ROWS AND COLUMNS   You can insert blank rows and columns at any location in the worksheet you choose. Before beginning your request, tell 1-2-3

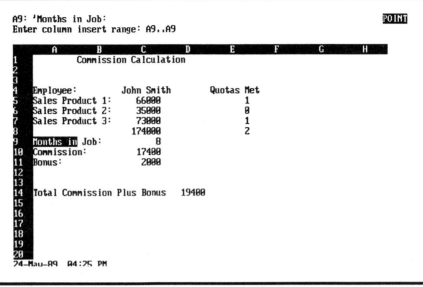

```
A9: 'Months in Job:                                          POINT
Enter column insert range: A9..A9

          A       B        C        D       E        F       G       H
1                   Commission Calculation
2
3
4        Employee:          John Smith        Quotas Met
5        Sales Product 1:      66000              1
6        Sales Product 2:      35000              0
7        Sales Product 3:      73000              1
8                             174000              2
9        Months in Job:           8
10       Commission:          17400
11       Bonus:                2000
12
13
14       Total Commission Plus Bonus    19400
15
16
17
18
19
20
         24-May-89   04:25 PM
```

FIGURE 3-16.   Inserting a column

where to place the blank rows or columns by positioning the cell pointer. If you will be adding rows to the worksheet, they will be placed above the cell pointer's location. If you will be adding columns, they will be placed to the left of the cell pointer. Once you make the request to insert rows or columns, you cannot alter the site where they will be placed. If you realize that you forgot to position the cell pointer, your only option is to press ESC to return to READY mode, move the cell pointer, and start the process over again.

When 1-2-3 inserts rows into a worksheet, the cell addresses of the data below this location are changed. It is as though 1-2-3 pushes the data down on the worksheet to make room for the new blank rows. Under normal circumstances, 1-2-3 automatically adjusts all the formulas that reference this data. The same is true for data that resides to the right of the location where columns were inserted.

The insert command is invoked by selecting /Worksheet Insert Rows. 1-2-3 prompts you for the number of rows to insert but does not use a straightforward question such as "How many rows would you like to add?" Instead, it asks for the range where you want the insertion to occur. It does not use this range to control the placement of the insertion, only to control the number of rows to insert. If you specify a range that includes three rows, three rows will be inserted. If you specify a range of one row, only one row will be inserted. Seeing this in action will clarify the way it works.

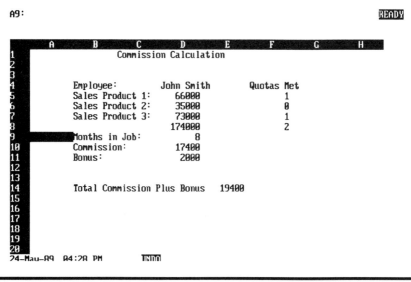

A9:   READY

	A	B	C	D	E	F	G	H
1			Commission Calculation					
2								
3								
4		Employee:		John Smith		Quotas Met		
5		Sales Product 1:		66000		1		
6		Sales Product 2:		35000		0		
7		Sales Product 3:		73000		1		
8				174000		2		
9		Months in Job:		8				
10		Commission:		17400				
11		Bonus:		2000				
12								
13								
14		Total Commission Plus Bonus		19400				
15								
16								
17								
18								
19								
20								

24-Mau-89   04:28 PM   UNDO

FIGURE 3-17.   New column added for column A

Let's add a few blank rows to the commission calculations you created in Chapter 2. Follow these steps to complete the changes:

1. Select /File Retrieve.

2. Type **COMM** and press ENTER.

3. Move the cell pointer to C8.
   Notice that the formula that totals sales is entered as +C5+C6+C7. Look at this formula again after inserting a column, and notice how 1-2-3 has automatically adjusted it for you.

4. Position the cell pointer in A9 (anywhere in column A would work just as well).

5. Select /Worksheet Insert Column to produce the display in Figure 3-16.

6. Press ENTER to restrict the insertion to one column. Figure 3-17 shows the results. If you move the cell pointer to D8, you will find that the formula has been changed and the formula for summing sales now reads +D5+D6+D7 to reflect its new location in the worksheet.

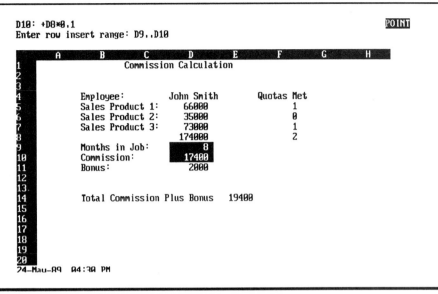

D10: +D8*0.1   POINT
Enter row insert range: D9..D10

        A   B   C   D   E   F   G   H
1   Commission Calculation
2
3
4   Employee: John Smith   Quotas Met
5   Sales Product 1:   66000   1
6   Sales Product 2:   35000   0
7   Sales Product 3:   73000   1
8   174000   2
9   Months in Job: 8
10   Commission: 17400
11   Bonus: 2000
12
13
14   Total Commission Plus Bonus   19400
15
16
17
18
19
20
24-May-89   04:30 PM

FIGURE 3-18.   Inserting a row

Inserting rows is just as easy. Let's insert two blank rows above the section that begins with Months in Job, to separate the sections of the model.

1. Move the cell pointer to D9 (any place in row 9 would work just as well).

2. Select /Worksheet Insert Rows and expand the range to include two rows as shown in Figure 3-18.

3. Press ENTER.
   You will find that two blank rows have been added, producing the results shown in Figure 3-19. Notice that the addition of some blank space on the side and between the two sections makes the model more appealing.

4. Save these changes by selecting /File Save, pressing ENTER, and typing **R**.

Hiding and Displaying Columns

Release 2 added a new feature to 1-2-3 that allows you to conceal columns from view on the display screen temporarily. The data in these columns is not altered in any way

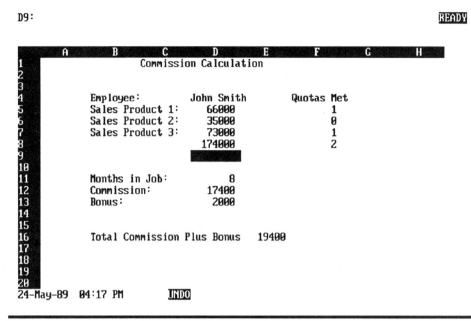

D9:   READY

	A	B	C	D	E	F	G	H
			Commission Calculation					

```
1                   Commission Calculation
2
3
4          Employee:        John Smith    Quotas Met
5          Sales Product 1:    66000            1
6          Sales Product 2:    35000            0
7          Sales Product 3:    73000            1
8                            174000            2
9
10
11         Months in Job:          8
12         Commission:         17400
13         Bonus:               2000
14
15
16         Total Commission Plus Bonus    19400
17
18
19
20
24-May-89   04:17 PM          UNDO
```

FIGURE 3-19.   Two new rows added

and can be displayed again at any time with the entry of another command. This feature is particularly useful if you are working with sensitive information such as salary data and do not wish it to be visible onscreen, in plain view of anyone who walks by your PC.

Use an expansion of the salary data you entered in Chapter 2 to take a look at how this feature works. The data for several employees is shown in Figure 3-20.

If you wanted to correct misspellings in the name entries, you might want to temporarily remove the salary information from the screen. This can be accomplished by following these steps:

1. Select /File Retrieve.

2. Type **SALARY** and press ENTER.

3. Select /Worksheet Column Hide.

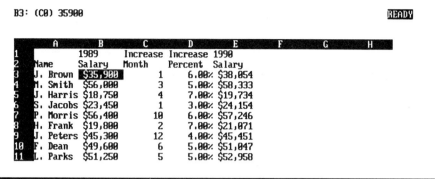

FIGURE 3-20.   Model displaying salary data

4. Point to column C as shown in Figure 3-21, and press ENTER.

   Your model will not match this exactly as you have only one row of salary entries. You will be able to see the column disappear from view.

5. Select /Worksheet Column Hide.

6. Move to column E.

7. Press ENTER.

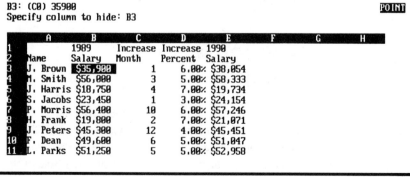

FIGURE 3-21.   Hiding a column

A3: 'J. Brown   READY

```
           A       C        D       F       G       H       I       J
        1         Increase Increase
        2 Name    Month    Percent
        3 J. Brown     1     6.00%
        4 M. Smith     3     5.00%
        5 J. Harris    4     7.00%
        6 S. Jacobs    1     3.00%
        7 P. Morris   10     6.00%
        8 H. Frank     2     7.00%
        9 J. Peters   12     4.00%
       10 F. Dean      6     5.00%
       11 L. Parks     5     5.00%
```

FIGURE 3-22.   Columns B and E hidden

The result is a worksheet with both salary columns temporarily hidden as shown in Figure 3-22. To bring these columns back into view, another set of menu entries is required.

8. Select /Worksheet Column Display.

9. Point to column B and press ENTER.

Notice that all the hidden columns are marked with an asterisk. Another command sequence is required to restore the other salary column if you select one column at a time. Your other option to affect both columns is to specify a range of columns to display.

10. Select /Worksheet Column Display, point to column E, and press ENTER.

CHANGING THE ALIGNMENT OF LABEL ENTRIES

You already learned one method for changing the alignment for a label in Chapter 2 when you entered a few of the labels by beginning them with a " symbol. This method works; but if you have a large number of labels to enter, it is time-consuming. It also requires you to edit the entries and replace the label indicator at the front of the label if you want to change its alignment. Fortunately, there are several alternatives that can be real timesavers. One option allows you to change the alignment of labels that are currently on the worksheet; the other changes the default for the current worksheet so that any new labels you enter will use the new alignment setting.

Changing Previously Entered Labels

Two methods for altering the alignment of labels are already recorded on the worksheet. You can use the EDIT method, or you can use a Range command that alters the label alignment of the rows in the range. The EDIT method follows these simple rules for editing the entry in any cell.

1. Move the cell pointer to the cell whose alignment you wish to change.

2. Press F2 (EDIT), followed by HOME, to move to the front of the entry.

3. Press the DEL key to eliminate this label indicator. Then type the indicator that corresponds to the type of alignment you want to use and press ENTER.

The second method requires less work; many cell indicators can be changed with a single command. In this case, the command is /Range Label. When you select this command, it presents the following menu:

You can choose the type of alignment you want and specify the range of entries that is affected. The major differences between this approach and a Global change are the scope of the change and the fact that the /Range Label-Prefix command affects only the cells that contain entries. Empty cells do not retain this information. If you subsequently place entries in these empty cells, the entries will be aligned in accordance with the default label prefix. To check this default, select /Worksheet Status to view the by-now-quite-familiar display screen.

Look at the effect of altering the alignment of the labels in this example:

1. Move your cell pointer to B1.

2. Type **Jan** and press the RIGHT ARROW key.

3. Type **Feb** and press the RIGHT ARROW key.

4. Type **Mar** and press the RIGHT ARROW key.

5. Continue making these entries until you enter **Aug** in H1.

6. Move the cell pointer to A1.
   Your display should look like this:

A1: 'Jan   READY

The labels are currently left-aligned in accordance with the default.

7. Select /Range Label Right.

8. Use the RIGHT ARROW key to move to H1 and press ENTER.
   Each of the entries in row 1 is now right-aligned in its cell, although subsequent entries in these cells would not be affected.

9. Select /Worksheet Erase Yes to erase this example.

Changing Alignment on a Global Basis Before Making Entries

If you change the default label alignment, any new entries you make on the spreadsheet will use this setting. Existing entries will not be affected. This option is especially useful when you wish to enter a series of column headings or other information with a different alignment. You can alter the default alignment without concern for the data already on the worksheet, then make your entries and change the alignment back to its original setting, if you wish.

Let's enter some month names as column headings, using center alignment to see how this might work.

1. Select /Worksheet Global Label-Prefix Center.

2. Move the cell pointer to B2 and type **Jan**. Then press the RIGHT ARROW key.

3. Enter **Feb** and press the RIGHT ARROW key.

4. Continue entering the month abbreviations across until you have entered **July** in H2.
   Each of your entries will be center-aligned in its cell, as follows:

H2: ^July

Each entry has a caret symbol at the front of the entry, automatically generated by 1-2-3.

ERASING WORKSHEET DATA

You have learned how to change worksheet entries and completely replace them with other data. However, there are times when you will want to eliminate the entries completely; they may be mistakes or old data that is no longer required. Whatever your reason for wanting to eliminate them, 1-2-3 provides a quick solution. 1-2-3 does not even care what type of entry the cell contains; it erases labels, numbers, and formulas with equal ease. The most common way to eliminate data is to erase a range of cells. This will eliminate all their contents. A second approach is more extensive and thus more dangerous, since it eliminates all the entries on the entire worksheet.

To erase a range of cell entries, the easiest approach is to move the cell pointer to the upper leftmost cell you wish to erase and select /Range Erase. In response to the prompt, move the cell pointer to the lower right corner of the range you wish to erase and then press ENTER. This eliminates not only the cell entry but also any label prefix assigned to the cell with a Range command. Formats assigned with a Range command are retained when the cell contents are erased and will be applied to any new entries placed in the cell.

The following data shows two entries that were made on the worksheet and finalized.

B1: 'x

Pressing ESC will not help you eliminate either entry; both have been finalized. To eliminate the "x" that was entered in error, do the following:

1. Place the cell pointer in B1.

2. Select /Range Erase.

3. Press ENTER to erase the single cell entry.

A /Worksheet Erase command packs much more destructive capability, since it eliminates everything from the worksheet. It is useful mainly if you make a complete mess and want to erase it. In that case, you can select /Worksheet Erase Yes to effectively remove the entire worksheet from memory and start over with your entries on a blank worksheet.

UNDOING APPEARANCE CHANGES

You have looked at 1-2-3's Undo feature for eliminating an entry from a worksheet cell, but Undo has even more power than the ability to eliminate an entry. When the Undo feature is enabled, 1-2-3 keeps track of all the activities that occur from the time that 1-2-3 is in READY mode until the next time it is in READY mode. As long as these activities involve only the current worksheet or its settings, it can be undone. External activities like printing or writing a file to a disk cannot be undone. If you retrieve a file, format a range, or alter the width of a range of columns, 1-2-3 will be able to undo these actions as long as the Undo feature is enabled and you invoke it before performing any new activities. Once you invoke another command or make a new entry, that action is the latest action and is the work that will be undone when you press the ALT-F4 (UNDO) key.

If you press the ALT-F4 (UNDO) key repeatedly, it will toggle the effect of your last action, first eliminating it and then restoring it again. If you change the width of a column and press ALT-F4 (UNDO), 1-2-3 will eliminate the change in the column width. Pressing it again restores the column width change just completed. Pressing it again removes it, and so on for an unlimited number of iterations. You can use this feature to toggle the effect of a number in a cell as you evaluate the results from two different possibilities.

When Undo is enabled, UNDO will appear in the bottom line of your screen. If you do not see UNDO but want the feature's safety net to protect you from mistakes like erasing the wrong range or erasing the worksheet, check to make sure your worksheet is empty, then enable it by selecting /Worksheet Global Default Other Undo Enable. The UNDO indicator will appear at the bottom of the screen. Later, if you want to disable it, you can enter the same command sequence except for the last step, where you choose Disable rather than Enable. Since Undo does require extra memory to be able to undo an action, you may not be able to keep it enabled on very large worksheets.

To see how the Undo feature can help you, first check to make sure it is enabled and then follow these steps:

1. Retrieve the VEHICLES file created earlier in the chapter by selecting /File Retrieve, typing **VEHICLES,** and pressing ENTER.

2. Move the cell pointer to column B. Select /Worksheet Column Column-Range Set-Width, highlight columns B through D by using the RIGHT ARROW, and press ENTER; then type **20** and press ENTER.

    Notice that the columns become much wider.

3. Press ALT-F4 (UNDO).

    The columns return to the width they had before you executed the last command.

4. Select /Worksheet Erase Yes.

    1-2-3 clears the screen and the model is removed from memory.

5. Press the ALT-F4 (UNDO) key to have 1-2-3 restore the worksheet in memory.

6. Press ALT-F4 (UNDO) again to have 1-2-3 erase the worksheet again.

    The Undo feature functions as a toggle switch, alternately removing the effect of your last action and then restoring it again.

REVIEW EXERCISE

You can practice some of the techniques covered in this chapter by completing the price update model shown in Figure 3-23.

1. Enter the labels in column A exactly as shown.

    Hint: Use /Worksheet Column Set-Width to widen column A to accommodate your entries.

2. Enter the labels in row 2.

    Hint: Use a label indicator in front of the year entries to make them align with the price entries below them.

3. Enter the number shown in columns B and C.

    Hint: The first percent entry is entered as .0515.

4. Format the cells in columns B through D appropriately.

    Hint: you might use /Worksheet Global Format Currency 2 and then /Range Format Percent 2 for the entries in column C.

B1: [W10] "1989   READY

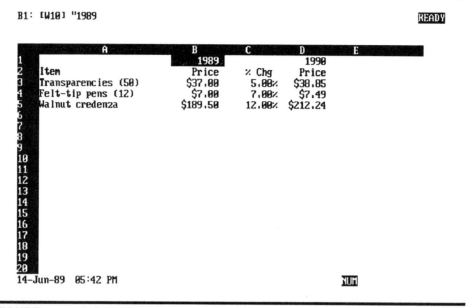

FIGURE 3-23.   Price update model

5. Change the width of columns B through D to 10.

6. Change the alignment of the entries in B1..D2 to right-aligned.
    Hint: Use the /Range Label command.

7. Enter the formulas for the price changes for 1989.
    Hint: The formula in D3 should be +B3*(1+C3).

REVIEW

- Other than basic entries and function key options, all 1-2-3 features can be accessed with selections from a series of menus. The main menu is invoked with the / key.

- You can select an option from any menu by highlighting your selection and pressing ENTER. Typing the first letter of the menu selection functions the same way.

- You can use the ESC key to back out of the menu by one level.

- You can format numeric entries to match your needs. The /Range Format command will format a contiguous group of cells. The /Worksheet Global Format command sets the default format and will format any numeric entry not formatted with the /Range Format command. Formats established with the Range command are shown in the top line of the control panel.

- You can change the column width of one or more worksheet cells. Use the /Worksheet Global Column-Width command to change the width of any cells for which an individual width is not set. Use the /Worksheet Column command to change the width of the current column. Use the /Worksheet Column Column-Range command to change the width of a group of columns. A column width established for an individual column is shown in the top line of the control panel.

- You can insert and delete rows and columns. When you delete a row or column, you delete the contents of all the cells in the row or column.

- You can hide columns of data and redisplay them. Use this feature to remove confidential information from the worksheet area of the screen.

- You can erase a group of cells with /Range Erase and the entire worksheet with /Worksheet Erase. With Undo enabled, you can undo either of these actions with ALT-F4 (UNDO).

- Use /Worksheet Global Label-Prefix to change the alignment for entries you are about to make. Use /Range Label-Prefix to alter the alignment of existing label entries.

- You can use /Worksheet Status to review the current Global settings. With Release 2.2 you can also enter /Worksheet Global to see the settings sheet.

Commands and Keys

Entry	Action
/	Invokes the menu
ESC	Backs you out of the menu by one step
CTRL-BREAK	Backs you all the way out of the menu to READY mode no matter how many levels deep you are in the menu
/RE	/Range Erase eliminates entries from a contiguous group of worksheet cells
/RF	/Range Format allows you to change the appearance of numeric entries in a contiguous group of worksheet cells
/RL	/Range Label allows you to change the alignment of a contiguous group of label entries on a worksheet

/WCCS	/Worksheet Column Column-Range Set-Width changes the width of a contiguous group of worksheet columns
/WCS	/Worksheet Column Set-Width changes the width of the current worksheet column
/WD	/Worksheet Delete allows you to delete a contiguous group of worksheet rows or columns

Entry	Action
/WGC	/Worksheet Global Column-Width changes the width of all columns that have not been set individually with the /Worksheet Column or /Worksheet Column Column-Range command
/WGF	/Worksheet Global Format changes the format of all worksheet cells whose formats have not been set with the /Range Format command
/WI	/Worksheet Insert allows you to insert blank rows and columns on a worksheet

4

WORKING
WITH FILES

New computer users always find the concept of files a little difficult to understand. This is partly because you cannot *see* a file, the way you can see entries that you place on the worksheet. But files are really quite simple to work with. They use concepts that are very similar to those you use every day for storing written documents in your office. The main difference is that computer files are stored on a disk instead of in a drawer. In this chapter, you will learn about basic file concepts and explore the basic file commands that 1-2-3 has to offer. You will then learn about new features in Release 2 and higher that allow you to temporarily exit 1-2-3 and access the file-handling features of your computer's operating system. There are a few additional differences between Release 1A and Release 2 and higher, most of them very subtle and relating to the use of directories or the display of files stored on the disk. If you are using Release 1A, check the special information in the examples that describe some of these differences.

FILE CONCEPTS

Every day you undoubtedly work with a number of different pieces of paper. Periodically, you probably place some of these papers in file folders in a cabinet or desk drawer to make space for new information on your desktop. Then, when you want to review these papers again, you search for them in the cabinet or ask your secretary to bring you the file folder you wish to see. Assuming that you have an organized filing system, the papers you want will arrive back on your desk.

Your computer uses very similar procedures to maintain its information. Taking a look at the similarities and differences will help you understand the important role that files can play for you.

Storing Information on Disk

When you store information in your computer, you provide the machine with an organizational challenge similar to the one faced by you or your secretary. In the computer's case, the "desktop" is the RAM memory of the system; and, like your desktop, it has a limited amount of space. How much space it has available in memory will dictate how much information you can place in it at any one time. Part of this space can be used for a program such as 1-2-3; another part can be used to store a worksheet that you are building with the package. Only one worksheet can be on your computer's desktop at any one time; this keeps things organized for you. Just as you use file folders to store papers, so your computer uses disk files to store information. The computer's files are maintained on disk rather than in a cabinet. When you build a model, it will be stored in the computer's desktop—its temporary memory. You generally will want to store a copy of this model in a file on your disk before you exit 1-2-3 or start creating a second model. This storage makes it possible for the computer to recall the first model another time so that you can work on it again.

TEMPORARY NATURE OF MEMORY   When working with a computer, you need to save your model before you complete it, as 1-2-3 does not automatically maintain a permanent record of your model. As soon as you turn your system off or exit 1-2-3 (whether deliberately or accidentally), the model is lost from memory. In order to use this model again, you must already have stored a copy of it in a file on your disk. The disk provides a more permanent memory since its contents are not lost when the power is off in your computer. As long as you store the file on disk, you can retrieve a copy of the file from disk and place it in the memory of your computer system again. With Release 2.2 of 1-2-3, there is a built-in safeguard to remind you to save a copy of your models to disk. The addition of a prompt message when you attempt to exit from 1-2-3 will remind you if you have not as yet saved changes to the current worksheet.

DISK MAINTAINS ITS COPY   When you are working with data in the form of papers stored in your office files and you retrieve a copy so that you can work with it again, the file no longer contains a copy. But storing data in computer disk files works differently. Once you store a copy of a model on disk, it remains there until you take some special action to remove it from the disk. Even when you retrieve a copy of the model to place it in memory again, the original copy is maintained on the disk. This feature offers a tremendous advantage over paper storage methods: If you accidentally destroy the copy in the computer's memory, you can always retrieve another copy of the model from the disk.

Organizing the Disk Data

When you create file folders for your office, you probably have a system—even a rudimentary one—for labeling these files. One rule of your system is probably that no two folders have exactly the same label. If they did, you would have a lot of difficulty finding the papers you need once they were filed. Perhaps your system for labeling file folders is quite organized. It may include color coding or some other scheme that makes it easy to categorize your files.

Storing files on disk also uses a system. Part of this system involves rigid rules you must follow; there is also room for some flexibility, however, so that you can personalize the system to suit your needs. You need not be concerned with the specifics of how the data is stored on disk. Your only concern is the rules that you need to follow when working with these files, especially those rules that center around the names you use for your files and the location of these files when they are stored.

FILENAMES   Before you can store a file on your disk, you must determine what to name it. Since the naming process follows particular, although somewhat flexible, rules, first review the options before considering the mechanics for storing the file.

Each file on a disk must have a unique name. This *filename* will consist of from one to eight characters. You can create a name using the alphabetic characters, numeric digits, and some of the special symbols. Since it can be difficult to remember which symbols are permissible and which are not, it is best to limit your use of special symbols to the _ (underline symbol). This symbol is particularly useful as a separator in a filename. For example, the name Sales_89 might be used to store the sales data for 1989. Be aware that spaces are not allowed in 1-2-3 filenames; Sales 89 would not be a valid name. Although Release 2.2 will accept a numeric digit in the first position, you may want to avoid an initial numeric character for later upward compatibility.

Although there is no flexibility in the rules already discussed, you can assign the eight allowable characters any way you like. It is best to develop some consistent rules for naming your data, as consistency can help you determine a file's contents when you see the filename later on. If you are storing sales data for a number of years, keeping one year's worth of data in each file, you could use the method already described and create names such as Sales_89 and Sales_90. You could also use names such as 89_Sales or Sls1989. It really does not matter what pattern you select for your names. What is important is that once you decide on a naming pattern, you apply it consistently for each file that you create. It is not a good strategy to name files 87_Sales, Sales_88, Sls_1989, and Sales90; this pattern is too inconsistent. You can enter filenames in either uppercase or lowercase letters, or even a combination of the two. Regardless of which type of entry you make, it will be translated into uppercase. All filenames are stored in uppercase on the disk.

You can also add *filename extensions*. These are one to three optional characters that you add to the end of a filename. They too can be entered in upper- or lowercase. They are separated from a filename by a period. For example, in Sales_89.WK1, the filename extension is .WK1. These extensions can be used to categorize files or to provide an extra three characters of description. Some programs automatically add extensions for you. 1-2-3 does this. Table 4-1 shows some of the most common filename extensions that you will encounter and the types of files they are used for.

If you are working with Release 1.0 or 1A, the extension .WKS is added to the filename every time you save a file. With Release 2 and higher, the extension that is

Filename Extension	Use
.WK1	Worksheet files in Release 2
.WK3	Worksheet in Release 3 format. Must be saved as .WK1 file to use in Release 2.2
.WKS	Worksheet files in Release 1A
.PIC	1-2-3 graph files
.PRN	Print files
.DRV	1-2-3 driver files
.COM or .EXE	Executable program files
.BAT	DOS batch files
.BAK	Backup files for Release 2.2 and 3.0
.ENC	Release 3.0 and Allways for printer files.
.ALL	Allways extensions

TABLE 4-1.   Common Filename Extensions

added is .WK1. With Release 2.2 and 3.0 you can create a backup copy of a worksheet file with the extension .BAK. 1-2-3 has other filenames that it uses when data other than models are stored in files. In Chapter 8 of this book, you will learn that you can create a graph on the screen and save a copy of this graphic image on disk. These files are automatically assigned the filename extension .PIC. You will also learn that you can print a copy of your model to the printer, or to the disk if you prefer. When you print to the disk, the print output is stored in a file with the extension .PRN. You do not need to memorize this information; 1-2-3 handles it all for you. You only need to realize what these extensions are when you want to work directly with the data stored on your disk, using commands from your operating system. These filename extensions appear when you use operating system commands. They could cause confusion if you were not at least aware that 1-2-3 was creating them and using them to distinguish different types of files.

LOCATION OF YOUR DATA

Files can be stored on either hard or floppy disks. The lower-cost hard disks, thanks to today's technology, are a popular storage medium for business computer systems. A floppy disk holds from 360,000 to over 1,440,000 characters, depending on whether you are using the standard double-sided, double-density disks or the new high-density disks. Today's typical hard disk installed in a computer system has a capacity of over 20,000,000 characters of information.

When new files are added to floppy disks, their names are added to a directory on the disk that keeps track of every file on the disk. Although you could use a single directory to maintain a hard disk, such a directory could become so lengthy that it would be difficult to work with. This would be like having a single index to catalog a whole library of reference volumes; it would take a long time to read. More likely, each book in the collection has its own index. Some books may even have chapter outlines that can be referenced for contents.

To lessen the burden of the main disk index, you can set up *subdirectories* for your hard disk. Subdirectories function as a second-level index to group files that are related. You can create these groupings on any basis you like, including for each individual who uses the system, for each application category on the system, or by application program. In all cases, common files such as DOS utilities normally are maintained in the *root directory* (the main directory on the disk). When subdirectories are added, their names are placed in the root directory; however, the names of the files they contain are kept in the subdirectory, not in the root directory. Subdirectories are organized in a hierarchical structure, as shown in Figure 4-1. Here, the entries in the main directory include two references to subdirectories. These subdirectories must be created through commands in your operating system. Although 1-2-3 cannot create the directories, it will use whichever directory is current on the hard disk, and it gives you commands that let you activate another directory.

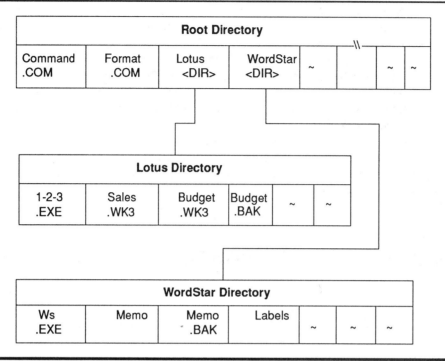

FIGURE 4-1.   Directory and subdirectories

1-2-3 always assumes that you want to work with files on the current or default directory. This means that if you are content to use the current directory, you do not need to specify it when saving your data. However, if you want to use a different disk drive or a directory other than the current default, you must either change the default or enter the file location along with the filename (depending on which release of 1-2-3 you are using). You will look at both of these possibilities in the next section.

1-2-3 FILE COMMANDS

You can use commands on 1-2-3's menu to handle your file-management tasks. There are menu selections for saving your data into disk files and retrieving copies of these files to place in memory. 1-2-3 has grouped each of the file-management commands under the File selection in the main menu. You bring this menu to your screen by selecting /File. The following will appear:

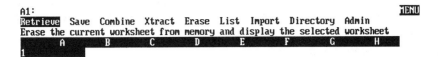

You will have an opportunity to try many of these commands in the following sections.

File Save

1-2-3 does not save your files automatically. It is your responsibility to save the data you enter in memory. It is best to do this periodically; do not wait until you are ending your 1-2-3 session before you save data for the first time. A good guideline is to save every 20 to 30 minutes. If you save with that frequency, you can never lose more than 20 to 30 minutes of your work, even if the power goes off unexpectedly.

SAVING THE FIRST TIME You use a slightly different procedure to save your data the first time. Since you have never saved the data before, you need to enter a filename to identify your data on the disk. If you are saving onto floppy disks, you also need to ensure that a formatted disk is placed in the current drive. At this point, make a few entries on the current screen and then save the data.

1. Erase memory by selecting /Worksheet Erase Yes.

2. Move the cell pointer to B2 and type **Qtr1**. Press the RIGHT ARROW key. Type **Qtr2** through **Qtr4** in C2 through E2, as follows:

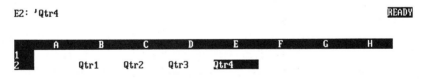

3. Select /File Save to produce the following display:

The exact appearance of your screen will depend on which drive you are using as the default and the names of the files you have already stored on this drive.

4. Type **QTRSALES** and press ENTER to supply the name to use when storing your data.

> After you have completed the last entry, the disk drive light will activate momentarily while your data is being written to disk. When the file has been placed on the disk, the indicator light will change from its WAIT status back to READY. At this point, you can continue to work on this model or start a new one, since you know that this one has been saved to the disk. For now, you will want to make some additions to this model to see how the process differs for subsequent saves.

SUBSEQUENT SAVES   Each time you save a model that is already on the disk, you have the option of replacing the copy on the disk with the information that is currently stored in memory, of entering a new name, or in Release 2.2 of creating a backup file. If you have saved the model previously, 1-2-3's default will be to save the model under this name. Make the following changes to the model and save the model again with these steps:

1. Move the cell pointer to A3 and type **Sales**. Press DOWN ARROW. Type **Expenses** in A4 and **Profit** in A5.

2. Select /File Save. 1-2-3 will present this display:

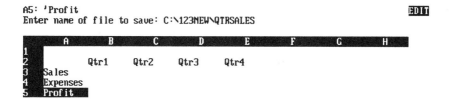

> Notice that 1-2-3 is suggesting that the file be saved under the same name you used previously. If you are working with Release 1A, your display will be slightly different, as Release 1A does not display the drive and directory.

3. Press ENTER. 1-2-3 will present this menu:

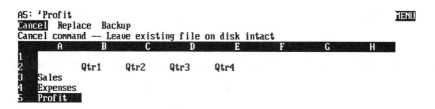

1-2-3 is asking if you wish to cancel the save request, replace the copy of the model stored on disk with the current contents of memory, or backup the original file using the same filename but a new filename extension for the original file and the same filename with a .WK1 extension for the current contents of memory.

4. Select Replace. 1-2-3 will save the updated model under the name you used previously.

If you want to save a model under a new name, 1-2-3 makes this possible. When 1-2-3 suggests that you use the original name, all you need to do is type a new name. Then, when you press ENTER, the file will be saved under the new name. This feature is especially useful when you need to create two similar copies of a model. You can create identical entries on both files, then save the model under two different names before entering the changes on the duplicate file.

If you are working with Release 2 or higher, you can save a file to a directory other than the current one. To do this, specify the directory you want when you use /File Save. If 1-2-3 suggests that you use C:\LOTUS\QTRSALES but you wish to use A:SALES, when 1-2-3 presents its suggestion, do the following:

1. Press ESC.

2. Press ESC two more times to remove the entire suggestion. The first ESC removes the filename, the second the extension, and the third the drive and directory.

3. Type the complete *pathname,* which includes the drive, directory, and filename (A:SALES for this example).

MAKING A BACKUP COPY OF THE WORKSHEET   Sometimes when you revise a document, you keep the previous version of the document in the file cabinet along with the current version. For example, if you revise a budget projection, you may keep the previous projection until after the budget meeting for comparison purposes. You can refer to the previous copy in the event that you want to revert to any of the old projections or as a backup in case you lose the later copy. Release 2.2 offers the same feature for your worksheet files. The third choice in the /File Save command that does not appear in other releases is Backup. When you select this option, 1-2-3 renames the worksheet file stored on disk with a .WK1 extension to a file with the same name but with a .BAK extension. Then 1-2-3 saves the current worksheet using the .WK1 extension. As an example, make the following changes to the model and save the model again with these steps.

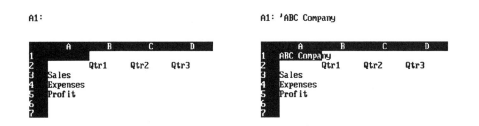

FIGURE 4-2.   Worksheet file and backup file

1. Move the cell pointer to A1 and type **ABC Company**. Press ENTER.

2. Select /File Save. 1-2-3 suggests that the file be saved under the same name you used previously.

3. Press ENTER. 1-2-3 displays the options Save, Backup, and Replace.

4. Select Backup. 1-2-3 saves the updated model under the name you used previously. The previous version of the file is saved with a .BAK extension.

To understand what the /File Save Backup feature offers, imagine looking inside the QTRSALES.WK1 and the QTRSALES.BAK files. Their contents are shown in Figure 4-2. On the left side, the QTRSALES.BAK file does not have ABC Company in the upper left corner of the worksheet, since this file contains the worksheet as it existed after the previous save operation. On the right side, the QTRSALES.WK1 file has ABC Company in the upper left corner, since this file was created by the most recent save operation. If you ever need to use the backup version, you can use it just as you would use a normal worksheet file. Each time you backup the file, 1-2-3 replaces the .BAK file with the .WK1 file on disk; then it copies the worksheet in 1-2-3's memory to disk using the .WK1 extension. The use of the Backup option always allows you to save the current file on disk and its most recent previous version as a backup. This allows you to subsequently access either version of the model. You can also use Undo to toggle between the two files if you try it immediately after retrieving the .BAK version of the file.

File Retrieve

A *file-retrieve operation* reads a worksheet file from disk and places it in the memory of your computer. When it places the model in memory, it erases the memory's previous contents. This means that you must always save a copy of your worksheets in memory in order to retain a copy before you bring another worksheet into memory. Of course, if Undo is enabled, you can use it to eliminate a big mistake like retrieving a file before saving the current file as long as you remember to use it immediately after retrieving the file.

RETRIEVING FROM THE DEFAULT DRIVE   When you want to bring a worksheet file into memory, most of the time you will want to use the default drive since this is the same drive you have been using for data storage. If you don't take any special action, 1-2-3 assumes that this is where it should look for worksheet files and automatically displays a list of all the worksheet files on this drive. Release 2 or higher even displays the file list in alphabetic sequence to make it easy for you to find the file you want. You can press F3 (NAME) to see a full-screen listing of all the filenames. You can select a file by pointing to it with the highlighted bar 1-2-3 provides you. You can also type the name of the file from your keyboard either before or after 1-2-3 displays its list. However, one thing you cannot do is use a first-letter entry. This feature will work with all of 1-2- 3's other menus, but not with a /File Retrieve operation.

Follow these steps to retrieve the QTRSALES file from the disk in the current directory:

1. Select /File Retrieve.

   A list of filenames similar to this display will appear.

2. Use the arrow keys to move the highlighted bar through the list until it is on QTRSALES. Then press ENTER.

   If you need additional information about the files to make a selection and are using Release 2 or higher, you can press F3 before you make a selection. 1-2-3 expands the list to provide information on the size of each file and the date and time each file was created, as shown in Figure 4-3.

In Release 2.2, if you need to retrieve a backup file, you must type the filename and include the .BAK extension. For example, if you want to retrieve the backup of QTRSALES.WK1, you would enter QTRSALES.BAK for the filename to retrieve. Typing the filename is required since 1-2-3 displays only the list of files with WK as the first two letters in the filename extension.

RETRIEVING FROM ANOTHER LOCATION   Release 2 or higher lets you retrieve a file that is not on the current disk or in the current directory, but the retrieve

```
A5: 'Profit                                                      FILES
Name of file to retrieve: C:\123NEW\*.wk?
          ME2F1_11.WK1    04/15/89        13:39          2073
ME2F1_11.WK1   ME2F1_18.WK1    ME2F1_19.WK1    ME2F1_20.WK1    ME2F2_10.WK1
ME2F2_11.WK1   ME2F2_12.WK1    ME2F2_13.WK1    ME2F2_14.WK1    ME2F2_15.WK1
ME2F2_16.WK1   ME2F2_3.WK1     ME2F2_5.WK1     ME2F2_9.WK1     ME2F3_10.WK1
ME2F3_11.WK1   ME2F3_12.WK1    ME2F3_13.WK1    ME2F3_15.WK1    ME2F3_17.WK1
ME2F3_18.WK1   ME2F3_2.WK1     ME2F3_3.WK1     ME2F3_5.WK1     ME2F3_6.WK1
ME2F3_7.WK1    ME2F3_9.WK1     ME2I2_1.WK1     ME2I2_4.WK1     ME2I3_4.WK1
ME2I3_8.WK1    ME2I3_9.WK1
```

FIGURE 4-3.   Expanding the list for files to retrieve

procedure changes slightly. Release 1A does not allow you to change directories without first using the /File Directory command (discussed later in this chapter). After using this command to change the directory, you can use the standard command sequence for a file retrieve to achieve your goal.

To change the directory for a retrieve operation, you must override the default directory setting for this one activity. The difference in the process is subtle: You begin and end the same way as usual, but you change the directory in the middle.

Assuming that you have data disks that you can place in two of your drives and that the default drive is drive A, use these steps to try the procedure.

1.   Select /File Retrieve.

2.   Press ESC twice to delete the reference to the default drive and directory. The following display appears:

```
A5: 'Profit                                                      EDIT
Name of file to retrieve:
        A       B       C       D       E       F       G       H
```

3.   Type the full name of your file, including its path and directory, and press ENTER.

Determining What Files Are on Your Disk

Just as you might look at the names of the different file folders in an office file cabinet, sometimes you may wish to look through the names of the files on your disk. The /File List command will handle this type of request for you. It lets you determine what types of files you want to view, by offering this menu selection:

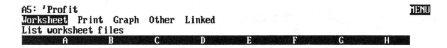

Since 1-2-3 stores worksheet, print, graph, and other types of files on the disk, these are your options when entering the command from Release 2 and above. Release 1A ignores other file types and displays only the first three selections. Linked files, available in Release 2.2, are covered in Chapter 13.

1-2-3 checks the files whose filename extension corresponds to the type of file you choose. Enter the following sequence of commands to view all the worksheet files on your disk.

1. Select /File List.

2. Select Worksheet.

3. If you have Release 2 or higher, move the highlighted bar around in the list to point to various filenames.

   As each filename is highlighted, an expanded description of the file entry appears at the top of the screen, as shown in Figure 4-4. This extra information allows you to determine the date and time for the last file update. It also lets you see the relative size of the file.

4. Press ENTER to return to READY mode.

To list files on another disk or in another directory, use the same approach described in the preceding discussion for retrieving from another disk. If you have Release 2 or higher, when you are presented with the list press ESC twice to delete the reference to the current directory and type a new drive or directory designation before pressing ENTER. For Release 1A, as always, the only way to access a different directory is to activate it by using /File Directory.

```
A5: 'Profit                                                        FILES
Enter extension of files to list: C:\123NEW\*.wk?
          ME2F1_11.WK1    04/15/89      13:39         2073
ME2F1_11.WK1    ME2F1_18.WK1    ME2F1_19.WK1    ME2F1_20.WK1    ME2F2_10.WK1
ME2F2_11.WK1    ME2F2_12.WK1    ME2F2_13.WK1    ME2F2_14.WK1    ME2F2_15.WK1
ME2F2_16.WK1    ME2F2_3.WK1     ME2F2_5.WK1     ME2F2_9.WK1     ME2F3_10.WK1
ME2F3_11.WK1    ME2F3_12.WK1    ME2F3_13.WK1    ME2F3_15.WK1    ME2F3_17.WK1
ME2F3_18.WK1    ME2F3_2.WK1     ME2F3_3.WK1     ME2F3_5.WK1     ME2F3_6.WK1
ME2F3_7.WK1     ME2F3_9.WK1     ME2I2_1.WK1     ME2I2_4.WK1     ME2I3_4.WK1
ME2I3_8.WK1     ME2I3_9.WK1
```

FIGURE 4-4.   Exploring the list of files on your disk

Removing Files from the Disk

The files that you save on your disk are retained indefinitely. In fact, 1-2-3 never eliminates any of them; it will remove a file only if you make a specific request for it to do so. The command used for eliminating files is /File Erase. To remove a file from your disk, follow these steps. (Execute them only if you have a file you wish to eliminate—these steps work!)

1. Select /File Erase.

    This produces the following display for you to select the type of file you want to erase:

The display is slightly different for Release 1A since it does not support the Other option.

2. Select Worksheet to produce a list of your worksheet files like this:

If you wish to expand this list to include file sizes and date and time stamps, press F3.

3. Use the arrow keys to position the highlighted bar on the file that you want to permanently remove from the disk, and press ENTER.

4. Select Yes to confirm that you want to delete the file.

Once you have deleted a file, there is no practical way to restore it. There are utility programs that can restore a file that has been deleted in this fashion, but they are not part of 1-2-3 and most of them require some technical expertise to use effectively. Therefore, you must be extremely cautious when removing files from the disk.

Changing the Directory

1-2-3's dependence on a *default directory*—the drive and subdirectory you are using—saves you a considerable amount of time. If you are working with a hard disk system, your data will probably be stored in a subdirectory. To work in it for a period of time, you need to be able to change to another one. A default directory means that 1-2-3 assumes that the directory you are referencing is the current default, unless you specify otherwise. If you keep this default set to the drive containing your data, you will not need to enter the directory in order to make most of your file requests. The package does provide capabilities that let you alter the directory setting. This feature means that when you want to work with worksheet files that are on the floppy disk in drive A, it will be easy to have the directory set at drive C and alter it to a floppy drive.

USING ANOTHER FLOPPY DRIVE   If you are currently working with a floppy disk-based system with two drives, your only option is to switch the other drive. If the default drive is A, you cannot keep the 1-2-3 System disk and all its help information in the drive. Rather than remove the 1-2-3 System disk from drive A, you can set the default data disk to drive B. Before beginning, make sure that the System disk is in drive A since 1-2-3 will attempt to read the current directory before allowing you to change it. Before making the change, insert a formatted disk is in drive B for data storage; 1-2-3 will check this drive as it changes the directory. To make the directory change, follow these steps:

1. Select /File Directory.

2. Enter **B:** and then press ENTER.
    When you switch drives in Release 1A, you will get an erroneous Error Message, which reads "Directory does not exist." Ignore this message. Press ENTER a second time to change the directory.

CHANGING HARD DISK DIRECTORIES   You have already seen how, if you have Release 2 or higher, you can access data on another disk or in another directory on a one-time basis with the /File Retrieve and /File Save commands. Each time you wish to use a directory other than the current one, you must enter the complete pathname for the file. The pathname includes the disk drive and an optional subdirectory along with the filename. This approach is cumbersome if you have to use information in these other locations repeatedly. A better solution is to make the other disk or directory the active one. You also use the /File Directory command to change the active directory on your hard disk. First select /File Directory. The current directory is displayed as follows:

```
A1:                                                            EDIT
Enter current directory: C:\123NEW
        A       B       C       D       E       F       G       H
1
```

In this example, the current directory is C:\123\. Next, type the new directory. If the new directory were C:\ACCT\, you would type **C:\ACCT**. The directory must already exist since 1-2-3 will not create a directory that does not already exist. With a hard disk, you can also type a drive if you want to start using one of the floppy disks for storage and retrieval.

A TEMPORARY EXIT
TO THE OPERATING SYSTEM

In Release 2 and higher, 1-2-3's System command allows you to temporarily exit from 1-2-3 to perform file-management tasks directly with the operating system. Since 1-2-3 provides a number of file-management commands in its menu structure, it is easier to use 1-2-3's menu selection when these commands are available. The DOS commands are useful for performing tasks that 1-2-3's menu does not support. Before examining how the system feature works, let's cover a few basics about your computer's operating system.

What is the Operating System?

The *operating system* that your computer uses is in some ways similar to a foreman in a production environment. A foreman manages the operation of the production line and coordinates the resources required to complete a job. The operating system in your computer is a program that manages the tasks that your computer performs and coordinates the resources required to complete a task. The operating system must always be in memory along with 1-2-3 or any other application program to ensure that these programs can access the resources of the computer system.

The operating system you will be using on your computer is MS-DOS or PC-DOS or, in the latest computers, OS/2. The letters in the OS or DOS portion of these names stand for Operating System. If you are using a program that runs only under the DOS operating system, you can run a DOS shell under OS/2 to continue to use this program. All these systems are commonly referred to as DOS.

BASIC FEATURES

Some of the basic tasks that the operating system performs are reading and writing data to and from the disk. The operating system also contains a variety of utility programs that copy files or disks, prepare disks for data storage, and check the directory of a disk. You can use these utility features before you enter a program like 1-2-3 to handle many tasks relating to file and disk information. After you place an application program like 1-2-3 into the memory of your machine, you usually can no longer access the operating system features. With Release 2 and higher of 1-2-3, Lotus has provided a temporary exit from 1-2-3 that retains all your current worksheet data in memory while you work with DOS tasks.

Types of DOS Tasks to Perform

Normally, once you are in 1-2-3 you want to forget about the operating system and enjoy the ease with which you can use 1-2-3's menu to handle tasks. But there are exceptions. One of the most important exceptions is when you want to save data on a disk and don't have a formatted disk available to save on. Without the System command, if you do not have a formatted disk available, you will lose all the data that is in memory. With the System command, you can exit temporarily and format another disk. You can then use this newly formatted disk to save your data. You can also make a copy of a file on your disk to give to another business associate: You can remain in 1-2-3, temporarily switch to DOS to complete your task, and switch back again. The steps for each of these special uses are covered in the following sections.

USING SYSTEM TO PREPARE A DISK   The DOS command for preparing a disk is FORMAT. In the following exercise, you will use this command to format a blank disk that you will place in drive A. Follow these steps to complete the exercise and return to 1-2-3.

1. Select /System.

2. If you are working with a floppy disk-based system, place the DOS disk in drive A.

3. Type **FORMAT A:** and press ENTER.

4. Place a blank disk in drive A in response to the following prompt on your screen:

   Insert a new diskette for drive A:
   and strike any key when ready

   With Release 3.0 of DOS and higher, the message will be a little different. Here, you must use ENTER to confirm that you are ready to proceed with the format operation.

```
(Type EXIT and press ENTER to return to 1-2-3)

The IBM Personal Computer DOS
Version 3.30 (C)Copyright International Business Machines Corp 1981, 1987
             (C)Copyright Microsoft Corp 1981, 1986

C>format a:
Insert new diskette for drive A:
and strike ENTER when ready

Format complete

    1457664 bytes total disk space
    1457664 bytes available on disk

Format another (Y/N)?n
C>
```

FIGURE 4-5.   Using the system feature to prepare a disk

5. Press ENTER to begin formatting.

6. Type **N** and press ENTER to indicate that you do not want to format additional disks.

7. Type **EXIT** and press ENTER to return to 1-2-3.

   A transcript of the entries for this process through step 6 is shown in Figure 4-5. Your display will look similar. However, if any bad sectors were encountered in your disk, FORMAT will skip them and notify you that it has done so with a message about the number of bad sectors excluded.

When DOS formats a disk it uses the program FORMAT.COM, which is supplied on your operating system disk. If you are working with a floppy disk system and follow the instructions in this exercise, everything will work fine. If you are working with a hard disk, the directory that contains FORMAT.COM must be the active directory when you type the format instructions. For a hard disk system where FORMAT.COM is not in the current directory, replace step 2 in the instructions with "Type **CD \.**" This changes the directory to the root directory on your hard disk where, presumably, you will have a copy of FORMAT.COM stored.

USING SYSTEM TO COPY A FILE   You can use the DOS COPY command to copy a file on your disk to another disk without leaving 1-2-3. To copy the file SALES from the disk in drive A to a formatted disk in drive B and return to your task in 1-2-3, follow these steps:

1. Select /System.

2. Place the disk containing SALES in drive A and the formatted disk in drive B.

3. Type **COPY A:SALES.WK1 B:** and press ENTER.

   The filename extension .WK1 was used in this example. If you are using Release 1A, the proper extension is .WKS. After 1-2-3 has completed the task, the screen will appear as follows:

```
(Type EXIT and press ENTER to return to 1-2-3)


The IBM Personal Computer DOS
Version 3.30 (C)Copyright International Business Machines Corp 1981, 1987
            (C)Copyright Microsoft Corp 1981, 1986

C>copy a:sales.wk1 b:
        1 File(s) copied

C>
```

4. Type **EXIT** and press ENTER.

USING SYSTEM TO CREATE A NEW DIRECTORY   You can create a new subdirectory for your hard disk without leaving 1-2-3. This option lets you create a logical section on the disk, which you can begin to use for specialized storage of worksheet data or other information. In the following example, the subdirectory will be added directly to the root directory of the disk, which is the main directory. In most cases, this is where directories should be added. Using too many levels causes confusion and makes it difficult to locate individual files. Follow these steps if you have a hard disk and wish to establish a subdirectory called BUDGET.

1. Save your current worksheet and clear memory with **/WEY**, if data from a previous task remains on your screen.

2. Select /System.

3. Type **cd ** to make the root directory active.

4. Type **md \budget** to create a subdirectory named budget.

5. Type **cd \budget** to make your new directory active.

   Figure 4-6 shows the transcript of your DOS entries on the screen up to this point.

6. Perform any DOS tasks you wish in this directory.

```
(Type EXIT and press ENTER to return to 1-2-3)

The IBM Personal Computer DOS
Version 3.30 (C)Copyright International Business Machines Corp 1981, 1987
              (C)Copyright Microsoft Corp 1981, 1986

C>cd \

C>md \budget

C>cd \budget

C>
```

FIGURE 4-6.   Creating a subdirectory

7. Type **Exit** and press ENTER to return to 1-2-3.

    Note that the current 1-2-3 directory would now be C:\123\, since 1-2-3 returned to the directory that was active before the temporary DOS exit was taken.

Returning to 1-2-3

You may have noticed in the previous examples that when you finished entering DOS commands, you returned to 1-2-3 by typing **Exit** and pressing ENTER. When you exit to DOS and return, everything is the same as it was before you entered the System request. The same worksheet will be on the screen and 1-2-3 will be ready to continue where you left off.

REVIEW EXERCISE

In the following exercise, you will practice saving and retrieving a document. Then you will try other 1-2-3 commands like /File List and System.

1. Clear any existing worksheet entries with the /Worksheet Erase Yes command.

2. Enter **Sales Report** in A1. Press DOWN ARROW twice to move to A3. Enter **Area** in A3, **East** in A4, and **West** in A5.

3. Enter **1988** in B3, **70000** in B4, and **50000** in B5.

4. Save the file using the /File Save command. Save the file as AREASALE.

5. Erase the worksheet in the computer's memory.
   Hint: Use the /Worksheet Erase command. The file that you just saved is still saved to the disk.

6. Retrieve the AREASALE worksheet using the /File Retrieve command. Highlight the filename or type **AREASALE** and press ENTER.

7. Find the file in the directories listing. Use the /File List Worksheet command. Move the highlight to your AREASALE worksheet file. Notice the date and time. Press ESC until you return to READY mode.

8. Find the file using the operating system. Use the System command to temporarily exit to DOS. Type **DIR AREASALE** and press ENTER. Find your file in the listing. If you have other files that have a filename of AREASALE with a different extension, 1-2-3 includes them in the list.

9. Type **Exit** to return to 1-2-3. Notice that the worksheet has remained in 1-2-3's memory.

10. Add new data by entering **1989** in C3, **85000** in C4, and **70000** in C5. Figure 4-7 shows the final results.

11. Save the file again with the /File Save command and replace the existing file copy with the current worksheet.

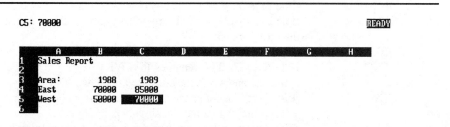

FIGURE 4-7. AREASALE worksheet

REVIEW

- Files provide permanent storage for your worksheets. You can save and retrieve worksheets to a floppy or hard disk.

- You can save a worksheet with the /File Save command. When you save a file the first time, you must provide a filename. When you save it again, 1-2-3 displays the filename to select. If you press ENTER to select the displayed filename, you must select between Cancel, Replace, and Backup (Release 2.2 only). You can also enter a new filename to save the worksheet in memory under the new filename.

- You can retrieve a worksheet with the /File Retrieve command. When you execute the /File Retrieve command in Release 2 or higher, 1-2-3 lists the files in alphabetical order that you can select.

- You can list files in a directory using the /File List command. With Release 1, you can list worksheet, graph, or print files. With Release 2 and higher, you can list worksheet, graph, print, linked, or all files.

- You can select where 1-2-3 looks for the files that you work with by using the /File Directory command. When you use this command, you can provide a new directory before pressing ENTER. With Release 1, you must change the directory before retrieving or saving a file to the new directory.

- With Release 2 and higher, you can access the DOS operating system with the System command while keeping 1-2-3 and the worksheet in the computer's memory. You can use this feature to format disks, copy files, and create subdirectories.

Commands

/FD	/File Directory allows you to change the default directory
/FE	/File Erase eliminates a copy of a file on disk
/FL	/File List displays a full screen list of all the files in the current directory or disk
/FR	/File Retrieve retrieves a file from disk and places it in memory
/FSB	/File Save Backup renames the .WK1 extension with a .BAK extension and saves the current version as .WK1
/FSC	/File Save Cancel cancels a save request without saving when 1-2-3 prompts that the file already exists
/FSR	/File Save Replace replaces the current copy on disk with the current contents of memory

5

MAKING 1-2-3 DO MOST OF YOUR WORK

Until now, you have had to enter every worksheet entry that you needed for your models. While that is similar to using a columnar pad for your entries, it does not take advantage of the productivity features offered by a package like 1-2-3. This chapter introduces some of these features. Making only a few entries, you often can complete your model by putting 1-2-3 to work.

In this chapter, you will be introduced to commands that can move worksheet data to a new location. This means that if the requirements of your application change, it will be easy to restructure the worksheet. You will also learn how to restructure data stored in a column to a row orientation and vice versa. Again, this is quite an improvement over the eraser method that manual spreadsheets provide. Finally, this chapter introduces you to a new command in Release 2.2 that allows you to search for characters in labels or formulas. This new command also offers a replace feature that you can use to modify labels and formulas quickly.

1-2-3's Copy command, also covered in this chapter, has more potential than any other command to increase your productivity with 1-2-3. You will learn the ins and outs of copying both label and formula data. You will also learn about other 1-2-3 features, such as repeating label entries and generating a series of numeric entries. Once you have mastered the copy feature, you will want to master some of the tools that can help you monitor your expanded worksheet. For example, you will learn how to control the recalculation of formulas stored on the worksheet. In addition, you will be introduced to commands for splitting your screen display into two windows and freezing certain information on the screen.

COPYING WORKSHEET DATA

Copying entries on a manual worksheet is a laborious task. To make an additional set of entries that duplicate existing ones, you must pick up your pencil and physically copy each entry that you wish to make. Naturally, duplicate entries take just as long to make as the original entries.

When you make duplicates with 1-2-3, however, this is not the case. For any entry that you wish to duplicate, you can have 1-2-3 complete most of the work for you. Just tell 1-2-3 what you want to copy and where you want it copied to. 1-2-3 does all the remaining work. It can take a column of label entries and copy it to ten new columns. It can even take a row of formulas that calculate all your sales projections for the month of January and copy it down the page to the next 11 rows, thus giving you all the calculations for February through December. Amazingly, 1-2-3 even adjusts the formulas as it copies them.

This section uses a building-block approach in covering all the Copy command features. First, it explains how to use Copy to duplicate a label entry. Then it looks a little more closely at the Copy command's inner workings, examining its ability to adjust formulas.

Copying Labels

Many situations call for the time-saving feature of copying labels. Perhaps you want to create a worksheet that uses account titles or months of the year in two different locations. Rather than typing them again, you can use the Copy command. Not only does it save you time, but it also guarantees that both sets of entries are identical. Copy is also useful when you have a number of similar entries to make. Often, you can copy your original entries and make minor editing changes in less time than it would take to type each of the complete entries.

INVOKING COPY TO DUPLICATE LABELS   Copy is somewhat different from the other menu commands you have used. It does not have a submenu like /Range Format Currency or /Worksheet Insert Rows. Instead of using a multilayered menu approach, the Copy command uses prompts. You must respond to these prompts in order to define the source location you wish to copy information from and the target location you wish to copy information to.

When you invoke Copy by selecting /Copy, this is the first prompt message you see:

1-2-3 is asking what cells you wish to copy from. Think of this "from" range as the source of information to be copied. It suggests a range that encompasses only one cell. This suggested location is always the location of the cell pointer at the time you invoke Copy. If the location that 1-2-3 suggests is acceptable, you can press ENTER. If you like the beginning of the range but wish to enlarge it to include a row or column of cell entries, you can expand it with your pointer movement keys. If you don't like the beginning of the range, you must unanchor the starting position by pressing ESC. You will then be free to move the beginning of the range. When you want to anchor it again, use the same strategy that worked with the Format commands and type a period. Of course, you will then be free to expand the range with the arrow keys. Once you have finalized the source selection, 1-2-3's interest shifts to the target location (the location the data is copied to).

The prompt message displayed by 1-2-3 Release 2 and higher for the target range looks like this:

When you request Copy, 1-2-3 again initially suggests the location of the cell pointer. The suggested location is not a range but a single cell, since you will almost always need to move the cell pointer to define the target range. And this is *all* you need to do, since it is displayed as a cell address rather than a range. You do not have to press ESC, as there is no range to unanchor. Once you select a location to start the copy, either you must press ENTER to finalize the location or modify it to represent a range. You can create a range with the standard method of typing a period and using the arrow keys to mark the end of the range. You can even press F3 (NAME) to select a worksheet range to copy to.

Release 1A presents the same information in a different format. In this case, the target range prompt appears at the right of the screen and the source range remains on the left.

Reviewing an example will help clarify how easy it is to copy a label entry. Follow these steps:

1. Move the cell pointer to A1, type **Sales - Product A**, and then press ENTER.

2. Select /Copy to generate this prompt message:

Notice that the suggestion for the source range is A1, the location of the cell pointer when you invoked the Copy command.

3. Press ENTER.

The prompt message generated next also suggests the original location of the cell pointer as the target range. However, you must change it.

4. Move the cell pointer to A2 and press ENTER to generate these results:

The new label generated is identical to the original entry, but it required far fewer keystrokes to create. Later, you will learn how to extend this productivity even further by copying to many locations with one command. For now, here are a few additional hints for the simplest copying task: copying an entry to one new location.

MODIFYING COPIED LABELS   The entry in A2 is currently identical to the original. Sometimes this situation is exactly what you need; other times, however, a slight modification might be required. If you wanted the label "Sales - Product B" in

A2, the Copy approach is still best. However, fixing the label would require these extra steps:

1. Move the cell pointer to A2.

2. Press F2 (EDIT).

3. Press the BACKSPACE key, type **B**, and press ENTER to finalize.
    The results will look like this:

Keep this possibility in mind when you look for opportunities to copy. A Copy followed by a quick edit can still be much quicker than making new entries. Since you can use this feature with numbers as well, one potential application of Copy is to generate a list of numbers with only one digit different.

Making Copy Work Smoothly   Because of the way in which 1-2-3 suggests a location for the source range, the most efficient way to work with Copy is to position your cell pointer on the cell you wish to copy before requesting the command. If more than one cell is being copied, select the upper leftmost cell in the range being copied. This strategy will allow you to expand the cell range downward and to the right, once you are prompted for the source range.

Copying Formulas

In one sense, copying formulas is no different from copying label or number entries. It is accomplished with the same Copy command. You respond to the prompts just as you do when you are copying label and number entries. With formulas, however, you need to be able to control how 1-2-3 copies the cell addresses. If you have one constant interest rate and want all formulas to refer to it, you must be able to direct 1-2-3 to carry out that instruction. On the other hand, you need a different approach if you enter a formula for January profit that subtracts the cost of goods sold in January from the sales for January and want to copy this formula to generate formulas that calculate profit for the other 11 months. You cannot calculate February's profit by subtracting the January cost-of-goods-sold figure from January sales. You need to subtract February's cost of goods sold from February sales. Fortunately, 1-2-3 can handle this type of situation as well. These different options are handled by the type of references contained in the original formula and are not an option selected after the Copy operation begins. Let's examine an example of Copy for different reference types to help clarify this.

ADDRESS TYPES   All the cell addresses you have entered in formulas thus far have contained a column name immediately followed by a row number—for example, A1, E4, IV2000. This is the cell address specification that is used most frequently with 1-2-3. This type of address is called a *relative address*. There are two additional types of addresses: *absolute* and *mixed addresses*. They are distinguished by the way they are recorded in your formulas and the way in which 1-2-3 performs a Copy operation for each of the three types. Master the differences in the three types of addresses; the type of address references you use is critical in determining how your formulas are copied to new worksheet locations.

Relative Addresses   Relative addresses are the only type of cell address covered up to this chapter. They are easy to enter in formulas, whether you use the typing or the pointing method of formula creation. When 1-2-3 records your entry, it appears to store the formula exactly as you entered it. In fact, if you move your cell pointer to any cell that holds one of the formulas you have entered, you will see the exact formula you entered in the control panel.

However, 1-2-3 remembers your instructions in a slightly different way from what it displays. If you store the formula +A1+A2 in cell A3, 1-2-3 will interpret your instructions in this way: "Add the two cells above the location that will store the result." Everything is remembered as relative direction and distances from the cell that will contain the result when your formula contains relative references.

These relative references will mean that when you copy this type of formula to another location, 1-2-3 will adjust the formula in the new locations to reflect the same relative distances and directions. For example, if you were to copy the formula stored in A3 to B3, the formula you would see in the control panel for B3 would be +B1+B2. This formula uses different cell addresses from the original, but it still records the same relative directions: "Take the value that is two cells above the cell that will contain the results and add this value to the value that is one cell above the cell that will contain the results." This adjustment is handled automatically as long as you use relative references when you build your formulas. Since you have not learned about other types of addresses yet, this should be easy.

You will build a model that allows you to practice the formula copy process. This model records profits for the current year and projects them for the next five years. The final result of your entries will look like Figure 5-1. Follow these steps to create the model:

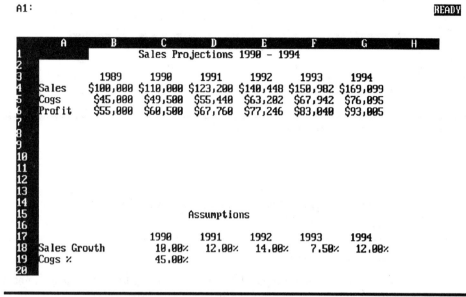

FIGURE 5-1.   Completed sales projection model

1. Select /Worksheet Erase Yes to start with a clean worksheet.

2. Move the cell pointer to C1, type **Sales Projections 1990 - 1994,** and then press ENTER.

3. Move the cell pointer to A4 and then make these entries:

A4:	Sales
A5:	Cogs
A6:	Profit
B3:	^1989
C3:	^1990
D3:	^1991
E3:	^1992
F3:	^1993
G3:	^1994

   The caret (^) symbols in front of the year entries will cause the numeric digits to be treated as labels and will center them within the cell.

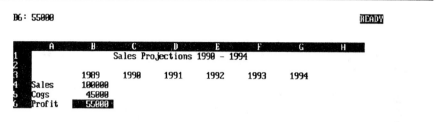

FIGURE 5-2.   Beginning sales projection model

4. Move the cell pointer to B4 and make these entries for 1989:

    B4:   100000

    B5:   45000

    B6:   55000

These entries are not computed, as they are assumed to be the actual numbers at the end of 1989. They will appear as shown in Figure 5-2.

It is time to begin thinking about how you want to project sales for the remaining years. You can use a constant growth rate that would apply to all years, or you can assume that sales will grow at varying percentages each year. Several choices abound for computing the cost of the goods sold each year. One method is to use a percentage of sales. Even if you select this method without evaluating other options, you must again decide if one percentage will be used for all years or if the percentage will vary by year. The profit calculation does not require you to make a decision, since it is always equal to sales minus the cost of goods sold. This model assumes that sales will grow at varying rates but that cost of goods sold will be the same percentage of sales each year. You must enter these assumptions before projections can be made.

5. Move the cell pointer to D15, type **Assumptions**, and press ENTER.

6. Complete these entries:

    A18:   Sales Growth

    A19:   Cogs %

    C17:   ^1990

    C18:   .1

    C19:   .45

    D17:   ^1991

    D18:   .12

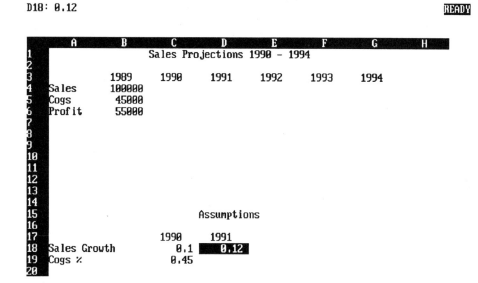

FIGURE 5-3.   Entering numbers and labels for the sales projection model

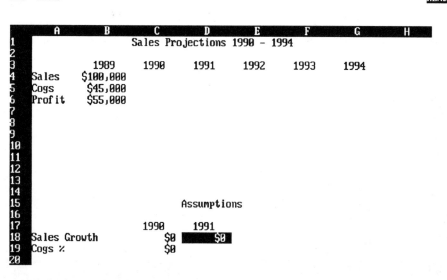

FIGURE 5-4.   Using a Global format

Your entries should look like those shown in Figure 5-3.

7. Select /Worksheet Global Format Currency. Type **0** and press ENTER. The percentages will display as zeros, like the ones in Figure 5-4.

   This instruction will set the Global format to Currency, but you will also need to use a Range Format for the percentages that will be used in the model.

8. Move the cell pointer to C18; then select /Range Format Percent and press ENTER to accept two decimal places. Use the RIGHT ARROW and DOWN ARROW keys to move the cell pointer to G19, and then press ENTER.

   The range of cells you just selected includes all the values you want formatted as percentages. It also includes a few blank cells—but they have to be included, unless you wish to apply the format with separate commands for the sales growth and cost-of-goods-sold percentage. The reformatted percentage entries are shown in Figure 5-5.

9. Move the cell pointer to C4, type **+B4*(1+C18)**, and press ENTER.

   This will compute the sales projection for 1990. Rather than typing this formula for each year, a better option is to copy it.

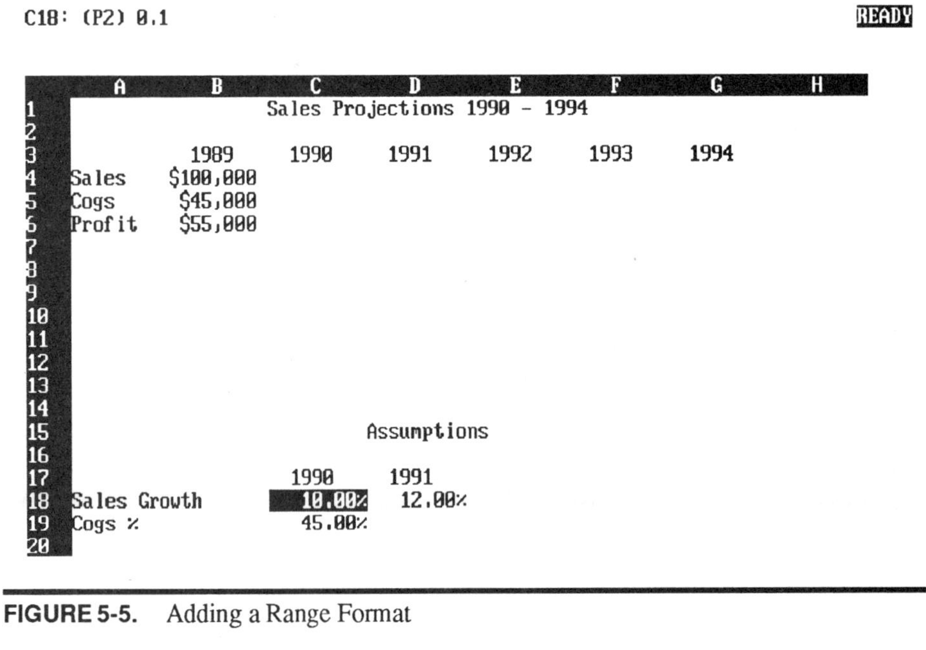

C18: (P2) 0.1   READY

```
          A         B         C         D         E         F         G         H
 1                     Sales Projections 1990 - 1994
 2
 3                   1989      1990      1991      1992      1993      1994
 4   Sales      $100,000
 5   Cogs        $45,000
 6   Profit      $55,000
 7
 8
 9
10
11
12
13
14
15                              Assumptions
16
17                             1990      1991
18   Sales Growth            10.00%    12.00%
19   Cogs %                  45.00%
20
```

FIGURE 5-5.   Adding a Range Format

10. Select /Copy. Press ENTER in response to 1-2-3's prompt message, which appears as shown in Figure 5-6.

11. Move the cell pointer to D4 and press ENTER. The cell pointer will remain in C4, which was the beginning of the source range.

12. Move the cell pointer to D4 to look at the new formula shown in Figure 5-7.
    Notice that 1-2-3 has adjusted each of the cell references to take the new location of the result into account. Each reference in the formula is the same distance and direction from the result in D4 as the original references were from C4, where the original result was computed. Before completing the copy process for sales, you will want to take a look at an absolute reference—a reference that will not be updated by a Copy operation.

Absolute Addresses   Absolute cell references are references that remain the same regardless of where the formula is copied to. The formula reference is effectively frozen in place and not allowed to change. Some special action must be taken to create these references, since they have the $ character in front of both the row and column portion of the address. $A$3 or $D$8 are examples of absolute cell references.

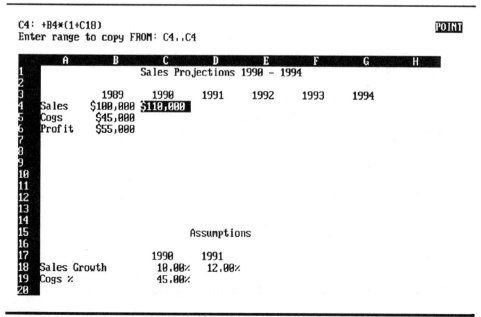

FIGURE 5-6.   Specifying the source or from range for copy

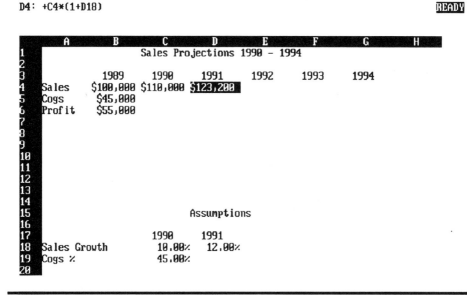

FIGURE 5-7.   The completed formula

You can create an absolute reference in one of two ways— by typing or pointing. Both parallel the creation method for relative references. If you choose to build the formula by typing, you will need to type the $ signs. If you choose to build the formula by pointing, you can press F4; 1-2-3 will then add the $ signs in front of the row and column portion of the address.

Use this approach to build the cost-of-goods-sold data, to clarify how the feature works. Follow these steps to enhance the sales projection model you were working on earlier in the chapter:

1. Move the cell pointer to C5.

2. Type +.

3. Move the cell pointer to C4 with the UP ARROW key.

4. Type *.

5. Move the cell pointer to C19 with the DOWN ARROW key.

6. Press F4 (ABS) once to add the $ signs.

C19: (P2) 0.45
+C4*$C$19

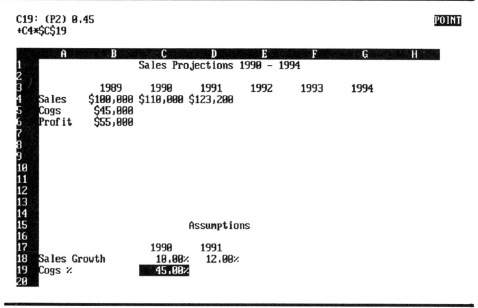

FIGURE 5-8.   Using an absolute reference

Your display should match the one in Figure 5-8. Since you are in POINT mode, you could add the $ signs with F4. If you want to type the cell address, you cannot use F4 to add them, so you will have to type them.

7. Press ENTER to complete the formula.

8. Select /Copy and press ENTER to accept C5 as the source range.

9. Move the cell pointer to D5 and press ENTER.
    If you move the cell pointer to D5, you will see that the new formula also references C19 for its cost-of-goods-sold percent, as shown in Figure 5-9.

Mixed Addresses   Mixed addresses borrow something from each of the other two types of addresses. A mixed address is "mixed" in that one part is fixed and the other part is relative. This means that either the row or the column portion of the address is fixed, but never both. During the copy process the fixed portion behaves like an absolute address, and the other portion functions like a relative address and is adjusted based on the location it is being copied to.

D5: +D4*$C$19   READY

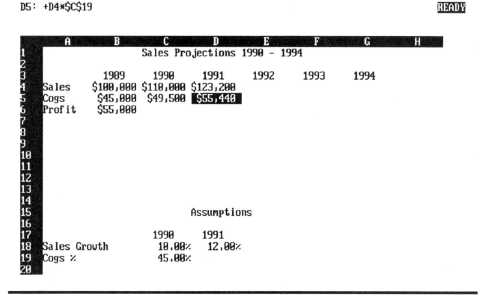

FIGURE 5-9.   Copy operation completed for the Cogs formula

A fixed address can be written like A$5 or $D7. In the first example, the column portion of the address will be adjusted as the formula is copied to different columns, yet the row portion will remain fixed if the formula is copied to other rows. In the second example, the exact opposite takes place: The column portion of the address will always remain fixed, regardless of where the formula containing it is copied. The row portion of this address will be updated when the formula is copied to a different row.

The mixed-address feature is used only if you are building complex models. Still, it is important to know that exists, in case you ever see a mixed address in a formula.

SCOPE OF COPY   You have learned how to copy a formula to a new location on the worksheet, using the exercises you have completed thus far. This is just one of the ways you can use Copy. Other options are copying the contents of one cell to many additional locations and copying many locations to many additional locations.

Copy One Entry to One New Location   You have already used this facet of the Copy operation. You used it to copy the sales and cost-of-goods-sold projections for 1990 to create the same projections for 1991. Now you will use it one more time to copy the profit calculation from 1990, but first you must enter the formula for 1990 profit and complete the assumption area. Follow these steps to add a formula for profit and then to copy the formula to one additional location.

1. Move the cell pointer to C6.

2. Type +C4– C5 and press ENTER.
   Since you wish both components of this calculation to be updated for the appropriate year when the formula is copied, both references are relative.

3. Select /Copy.

4. Press ENTER to accept the source range generated by 1-2-3.

5. Move the cell pointer to D6 with the RIGHT ARROW key and press ENTER.

6. Enter the following in the assumption area:
E17:	^1992
F17:	^1993
G17:	^1994
E18:	.14
F18:	.075
G18:	.12

   The model should look like the one in Figure 5-10. You have been making slow but steady progress in completing it. Now it is time to step up the pace and copy to more than one location at a time.

Copy One Entry to Many New Locations   1-2-3's Copy command is not restricted to the single-copy approach we have been using. By expanding the size of the target range, you can copy the entry in one cell to a range that is as large as a row or column of the worksheet. You can put this expanded version of Copy to use in completing the sales projections for the remaining years of the model. Follow these steps.

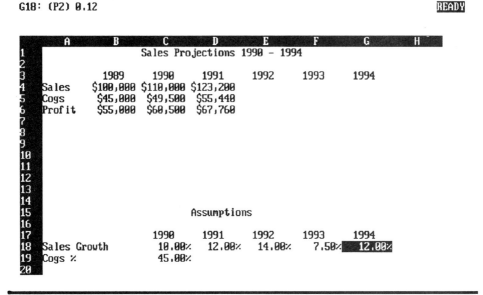

FIGURE 5-10. Profit formula added and assumptions extended

1. Move the cell pointer to D4.

2. Select /Copy and press ENTER to accept the source range.

3. Move the cell pointer to E4 in response to the prompt for the target range.

4. Type . (period).
   The period will anchor the beginning of the range and let you expand it.

5. Move the cell pointer to G4.
   The target range you are copying to is highlighted, as shown in Figure 5-11. This one command will copy the sales projection formula into E4, F4, and G4.

6. Press ENTER to produce the results shown in Figure 5-12.

Copy Many Locations to Many New Locations   You can step up the pace by copying a column or a row of formulas to many columns or many rows all in one step. To accomplish this, you must expand both the source and target ranges to include

G4:   POINT
Enter range to copy TO: E4..G4

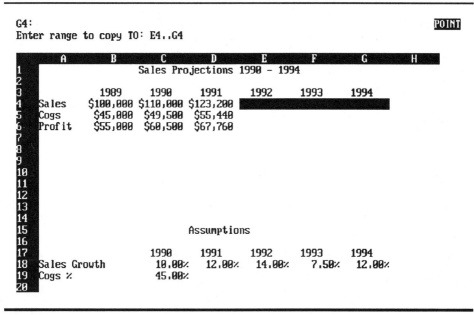

FIGURE 5-11.   Copying to a target range of more than one cell

D4: +C4*(1+D18)   READY

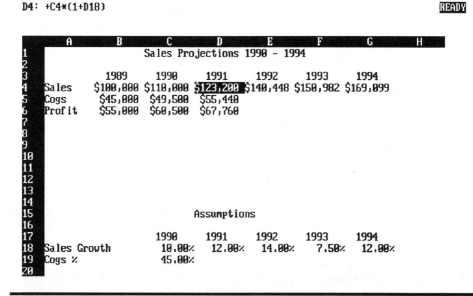

FIGURE 5-12.   Copy completed

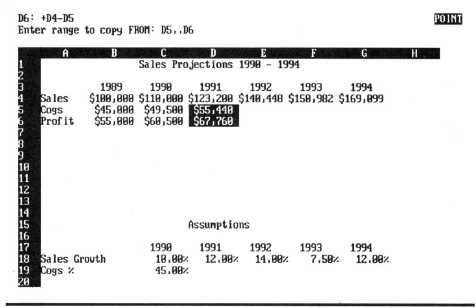

```
D6: +D4-D5                                                           POINT
Enter range to copy FROM: D5..D6

      A        B        C        D        E        F        G       H
 1                   Sales Projections 1990 - 1994
 2
 3              1989     1990     1991     1992     1993     1994
 4   Sales   $100,000 $110,000 $123,200 $140,448 $150,982 $169,099
 5   Cogs     $45,000  $49,500  $55,440
 6   Profit   $55,000  $60,500  $67,760
 7
 8
 9
10
11
12
13
14
15                            Assumptions
16
17                 1990     1991     1992     1993     1994
18   Sales Growth   10.00%   12.00%   14.00%    7.50%   12.00%
19   Cogs %         45.00%
20
```

FIGURE 5-13.   Copying a source range of more than one cell

a range of cells. You can use this approach to complete the formulas for your model. Although the column of formulas you need to copy includes only two cells, it is still a column. You will be able to copy this column of formulas to columns E, F, and G. Follow these directions to complete the Copy operation:

1. Move the cell pointer to D5.

    This location is the upper leftmost cell in the range to be copied. As long as you remember to place the cell pointer in the upper leftmost cell in the range to be copied, the copy process will be easy to follow for either rows or columns.

2. Select /Copy.

3. Expand the source range to D6 by moving the cell pointer with the DOWN ARROW key.

    The cells you are copying from should be highlighted, as shown in Figure 5-13. The location where you should place the cell pointer when expanding the source range is always the lower rightmost cell in the range to be copied.

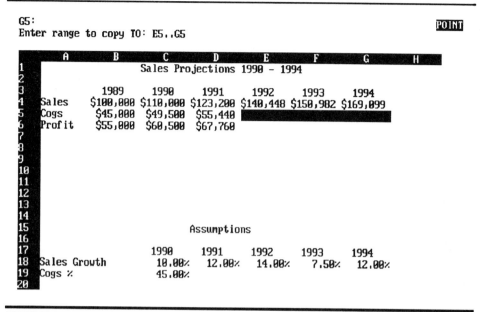

FIGURE 5-14.   Defining the target range for the copy

Again, keeping the lower rightmost cell in mind will make these directions work even when you wish to copy a row of data.

4. Press ENTER, move the cell pointer to E5, and type . (period).
   This anchors the upper leftmost cell in the target range.

5. Move the cell pointer to G5.
   You are probably thinking that G6 would have been the correct location. Since 1-2-3 already knows from your definition of the target range that you are copying a column of formulas, it only needs to know how far across the worksheet you wish to copy this column. G5 answers that question. The target cells you are copying to should be highlighted and should match the display shown in Figure 5-14.

6. Press ENTER to see the results shown in Figure 5-15.
   The procedure for copying a row of cell entries follows the same basic pattern as this example. First you must define which row of cells is in the source or from range. Next, you must tell 1-2-3 where to begin copying this row to

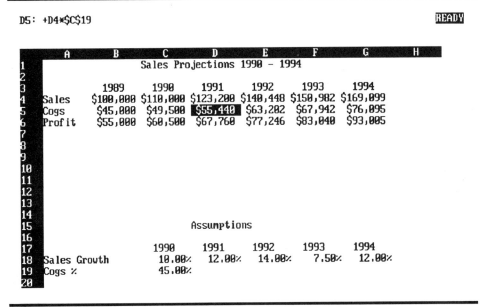

D5: +D4*$C$19   READY

	A	B	C	D	E	F	G	H
1			Sales Projections 1990 - 1994					
2								
3		1989	1990	1991	1992	1993	1994	
4	Sales	$100,000	$110,000	$123,200	$140,448	$150,982	$169,099	
5	Cogs	$45,000	$49,500	$55,440	$63,202	$67,942	$76,095	
6	Profit	$55,000	$60,500	$67,760	$77,246	$83,040	$93,005	
7								
8								
9								
10								
11								
12								
13								
14								
15				Assumptions				
16								
17			1990	1991	1992	1993	1994	
18	Sales Growth		10.00%	12.00%	14.00%	7.50%	12.00%	
19	Cogs %		45.00%					
20								

FIGURE 5-15.   Result of the Copy operation

and how far down the worksheet to copy it. Keep in mind that all these copy methods can be used just as easily for values and labels as for formula entries.

REARRANGING THE WORKSHEET

Planning is the best assurance that your completed model will both look good and meet your business needs. But even when you plan, there will be occasions when you want to rearrange the data contained in your model. 1-2-3 has commands that will reorganize the worksheet for you. This means that you do not have to reenter and erase entries the way you would with a manual version of your model. These special commands include one that can move any range of data to another range that is the same size and shape. A second command allows you to take a row of data and place it in a column or to take a column of data and place it in a row.

Moving Worksheet Data

The /Move command is used to move data in one range of the worksheet to another range. This range can be a single cell, a row of cells, a column of cells, or a rectangle with multiple rows and columns. The size and shape of the relocated data are determined by the original location of the data. This means that a row of data can only be moved to another row, not placed into a column of cells.

You can use the /Move command to relocate labels, values, and formulas. When Move relocates formulas, it adjusts the cell references in the formulas being moved to account for the new location of these formulas on the worksheet. Move also adjusts absolute references to conform to the new worksheet location.

The /Move command is very similar to the /Copy command, except that here the original location of the data is not retained. To use this command, select /Move. 1-2-3 prompts you for the source range. Just as with the /Copy command, it is easiest to specify the range if you position your cell pointer in the upper leftmost cell in the range before requesting Move. Also like the /Copy command, you can press ENTER to specify a single cell as the source or you can move the cell pointer to expand the size of the range.

After you finalize the source range with ENTER, 1-2-3 prompts you for the target range, the new location for your data. Unlike the /Copy command, Move's source range determines the size and shape of the data being moved. Therefore, all you need is a beginning location for the relocated data, which you can define by specifying the upper leftmost cell of the new area. Once you have specified the target range and finalized it with ENTER, the Move operation is complete.

You can use Move to relocate your assumptions on the current model by following these steps:

1. Move the cell pointer to A15.
    This is the upper leftmost cell in a rectangle that will include all the entries in the assumption section, including the label in row 15.

2. Select /Move.

3. Move the cell pointer to G19.
    Everything to be moved will be highlighted, as shown in Figure 5-16.

4. Press ENTER to finalize the source or from range.

5. Move the cell pointer to B22 and press ENTER.

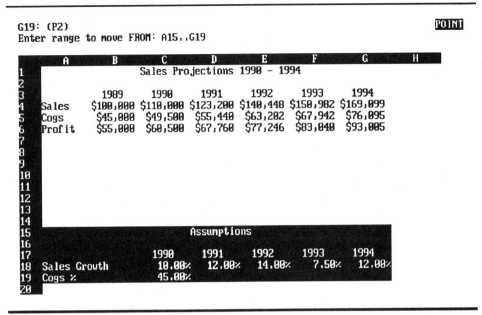

G19: (P2)   POINT
Enter range to move FROM: A15..G19

FIGURE 5-16.   Highlighting the area to move

6. Press PGDN to see where the range was moved.

   The entire range of cells containing assumption data will be relocated to B22...H26, as shown in Figure 5-17.

7. Select /File Save, type **SALESPRJ**, and press ENTER to save this worksheet.

Transposing Data

1-2-3's *transpose* features are available in Release 2 and higher. Not only do they copy data, but they also alter its orientation. Transpose places data with a row orientation into a column. Likewise, it places data with a column orientation into a row. The power of this command will become apparent the first time you need to do major restructuring of a worksheet. You will have an opportunity to try both types of transposition.

Both versions of Transpose can be used with labels and numbers. For Release 2 and 2.01, neither version should be used with formulas that contain relative references. Since the Transpose command is actually a special form of Copy, the references in the formulas will be altered as they are written to the new cells if you are using Release

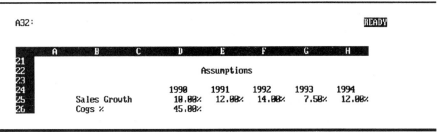

FIGURE 5-17.   Move completed

2 or 2.01. However, the data the formulas reference will still be in its original position and will cause disastrous results in the new formulas. In Release 2.2, both versions of Transpose copy the formula's values to the new locations instead of the formulas themselves. This allows you to copy the formula's results without concern for whether or not the new orientation will damage the resulting entries. The resulting copy contains values but not formulas. In all versions, the original entries remain intact, allowing you to erase either these entries or the transposed entries.

ROWS TO COLUMNS   /Range Trans (/Range Transpose for Release 2 or 2.01) makes it easy to change data that was entered in a row to a column orientation. You do not even need to tell 1-2-3 whether the data you are transposing is in a row or column. 1-2-3 can figure it out from the range that you define. All you need to do is define the data to transpose, and then specify the upper leftmost cell where you wish to place the data. The following example illustrates how this command works:

1. Select /Worksheet Erase Yes to clear the worksheet.

2. Select /Worksheet Global Column-Width, type **20**, and press ENTER.

3. Make these entries in cells B2..K2:
    B2:   Sales - Widgets
    C2:   Sales - Kites
    D2:   Sales - Wind Surfers
    E2:   Sales - Rockets
    F2:   Sales - Blocks
    G2:   Sales - Sand
    H2:   Sales - Jacks
    I2:   Sales - Rafts
    J2:   Sales - Balls
    K2:   Sales - Dolls

4. Press the HOME key.

   A few of the entries appear as follows:

A1:   `READY`

The entries are so wide that only a few are visible on the screen at once. You may decide to try a different orientation using the Transpose command.

5. Move the cell pointer to B2 and select /Range Trans (/Range Transpose for Release 2 and 2.01).

6. Select B2..K2 as the source or from range and press ENTER. This selection can be accomplished quickly with the END key, followed by the RIGHT ARROW key.

7. Move the cell pointer to A4 and press ENTER.

   This will place the entries in column A, but the original entries are still in row 2.

8. Select /Range Erase and expand the range by pressing the END key, followed by the RIGHT ARROW key, until the range reads B2..K2. Then press ENTER.

   Your screen should match the display shown in Figure 5-18.

COLUMNS TO ROWS   Transposing column data to a row is just as easy as the other way around. Try this example with the months of the year:

1. Start a new worksheet by selecting /Worksheet Erase Yes.

2. Using Figure 5-19 as your guide, enter abbreviations for each of the months in A5..A16.

3. Move the cell pointer to A5 by pressing the END key, followed by the UP ARROW key. Then select /Range Trans (/Range Transpose for Release 2 and 2.01).

4. Select the range A5..A16 and press ENTER.

5. Move the cell pointer to B3 and press ENTER.

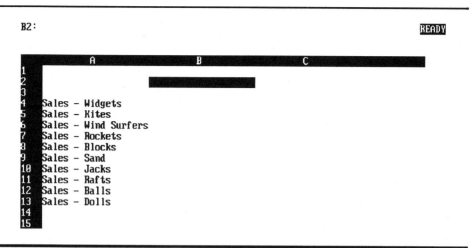

FIGURE 5-18.   Transposed data

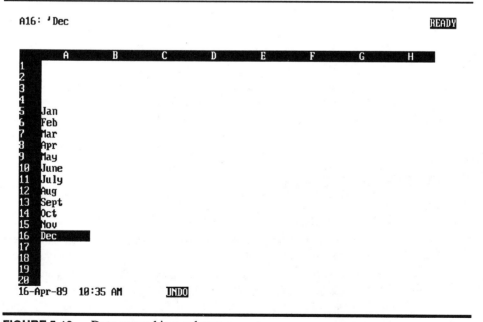

FIGURE 5-19.   Data entered in a column

A5: 'Jan   READY

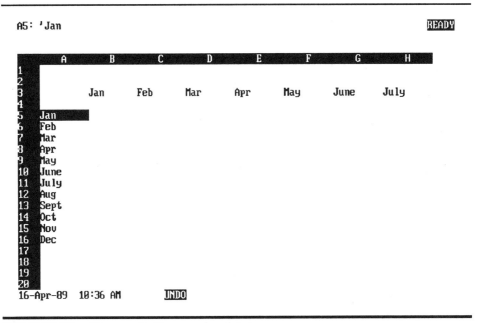

FIGURE 5-20.   The result of transposing data to a row

Although you can only see the first seven month names in Figure 5-20, the remainder have been transposed as well. The months are in the range B3..M3. The original entries will remain unless you use the /Range Erase command to remove them.

GENERATING CELL
ENTRIES

This section covers the entries that you can have 1-2-3 generate for you. The generating features are so easy to use that it is like having someone perform data entry for you free of charge. 1-2-3's *repeating label* feature can generate dividing lines and other quick entries in worksheet cells. The other feature can generate a series of numbers that have the same increment between each value in the series—for example, 1, 2, 3, 4, or 25, 50, 75, 100.

Creating Repeating Labels

You do not need a menu command to generate repeating labels. Instead, you accomplish it with the special label indicator backslash (\), followed by either a single character or a series of characters. Whichever you choose, 1-2-3 will duplicate your entry automatically to fill the complete display width of the cell and adjust the entry if you change the cell width.

You can use this feature to make a dividing line between sections of a worksheet or to create the top and bottom lines when you want to draw a box around your assumptions. Follow these steps to draw a box around the assumptions section of the worksheet:

1. Select /File Retrieve, type **SALESPRJ**, and press ENTER.

2. Move the cell pointer to A21.

3. Type * and press ENTER.
   Notice how the asterisks completely fill A21.

4. Select /Copy and press ENTER.

5. Move the cell pointer to B21, type . (period), move the cell pointer to I21, and press ENTER.

6. Move the cell pointer to A22 and type *, and then press ENTER.

7. Select /Copy and press ENTER.

8. Move the cell pointer to A23, type . (period), and then move the cell pointer to A27 and press ENTER.

9. Move the cell pointer to A21 and select /Copy.

10. Move the cell pointer to I21 with the END key, followed by the RIGHT ARROW key, and press ENTER.

11. Move the cell pointer to A28 and press ENTER.

12. Move the cell pointer to I22 and type '   *.

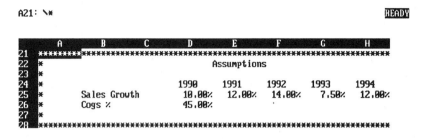

FIGURE 5-21.   Box generated with repeating labels

Leave eight spaces before the * to form the right edge of the box. Since you are entering spaces, you can omit the label indicator; 1-2-3 will automatically consider it a label and add the '.

13. Select /Copy and press ENTER.

14. Move the cell pointer to I23 and type . (period); then move the cell pointer to I27 and press ENTER.

15. Move the cell pointer to A21.

    The final result of your entries is a line of asterisks on all four sides of the assumptions. Since the display is wider than the screen width you can view only three sides of this box, as shown in Figure 5-21.

16. Select /File Save, press ENTER, and then select Replace.

17. Select /Worksheet Erase Yes.

Generating a Series
Of Numbers

It can be tedious to enter a long list of numbers. In one special situation you can assign this task to 1-2-3: when the list of numbers is a series with equal intervals. The interval can be either positive or negative, but it must be the same between every number in the series. This means that lists such as 10, 20, 30, 40; 7, 9, 11, 13, 15; 52609, 52610, 52611; and 30, 29, 28, 27 can be generated by the package. A list such as 1, 3, 7, 15

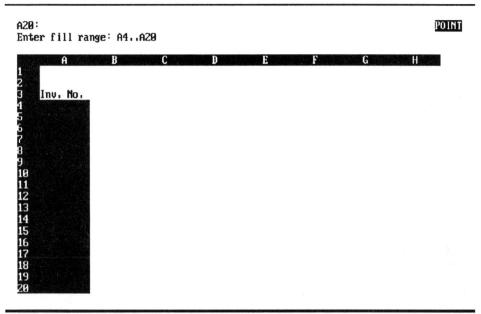

FIGURE 5-22.   Highlighting the fill range

could not be generated because the intervals between the numbers in the list are not the same.

Follow these instructions to generate a list of invoice numbers:

1. Type **Inv. No.** in A3.

2. Move the cell pointer to A4.

    This is the upper leftmost cell in the range where you will have 1-2-3 generate numbers.

3. Select /Data Fill, type ., and use the DOWN ARROW key to highlight the fill range to A20, as shown in Figure 5-22. Then press ENTER.

4. Type **57103** and press ENTER in response to the prompt for the start number.

5. Press ENTER to accept 1 for the "step" increment number.

    This is the value that is added to each value in the list to create the next entry.

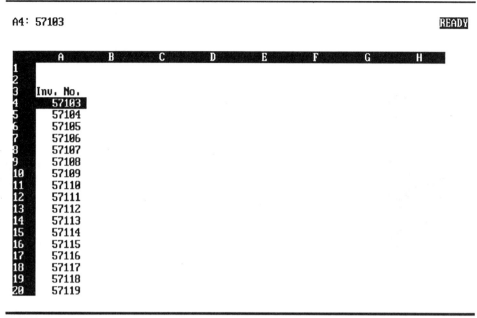

FIGURE 5-23.   Numbers generated by /Data Fill

6. Type **59000**.

    The entries in the control panel should look like this:

The stop value must always be as large as the last value in the list. This means that there are two factors that can end a list. The fill numbers stop being generated at the end of the range selected. They can also stop sooner if the stop value is not large enough to accommodate the numbers you are generating.

7. Press ENTER.

    The list of numbers generated is shown in Figure 5-23. Naturally, you can make your range larger to generate a larger list of numbers. You can also choose a horizontal range of cells and create an entry for each cell in the row.

8. Select /Worksheet Erase Yes.

WORKSHEET COMMANDS FOR EXPANDED DATA

Now that you have learned the secrets of creating these models quickly, you can create many more models as well. Some of the models you create will contain data for many months or years. You will also want to learn some of the tricks that make working with these models easier, such as controlling recalculation. This is a helpful trick, because as your models grow larger, 1-2-3 takes longer to recalculate after each of your entries. 1-2-3's speed seems quite good, compared to manual alternatives, when you do what-if analysis; but if you are entering a long list of account names or invoice numbers, it is annoying to have to wait for the program to finish recalculating. In this section you will learn how to put yourself in charge of the recalculation process.

You will also need additional tools to use for large models, since the entire model cannot be kept on the screen. And you will learn the techniques of creating a second window and freezing certain information on the screen. Both of these techniques are covered in this section.

Recalculation

1-2-3's recalculation options are accessed with the /Worksheet Global Recalculation command. This is actually three commands in one, since it lets you change three different aspects of recalculation. You can select when the worksheet will recalculate, the order in which it will recalculate formulas, and how many times it recalculates the worksheet. The latter two options are advanced features of recalculation that are seldom required. If you are curious about these, check your 1-2-3 manual. The first option affects when the recalculation occurs. This is a real time-saver that can be used with any large worksheet. Release 2.2 uses minimal recalculation, allowing 1-2-3 to recalculate only those formulas affected by a change to the worksheet. This makes Release 2.2 faster and more efficient with all your calculations. If you are using Release 2.2, you probably will not want to change recalculation to manual since it will result only in minimal time saving.

To alter the timing of recalculation for the sales projection worksheet, follow these steps:

1. Select /File Retrieve, type **SALESPRJ**, and press ENTER.

2. Select /Worksheet Global Recalculation.
   The following menu will display.

```
A35:                                                                MENU
Natural  Columnwise  Rowwise  Automatic  Manual  Iteration
Recalculate in natural order
```

The first three options in this menu refer to the order of recalculation. The last option refers to the number of times the worksheet recalculates. The other two options, Automatic and Manual, let you determine whether the package will automatically update the model after a change or whether you wish to control recalculation.

3. Select Manual.

This option means that 1-2-3 will not recalculate formulas after a worksheet change. To recalculate them you will need to press the F9 (CALC) key.

4. Move your cell pointer to C4, type **120000**, and press ENTER.

Notice that this change does not affect the results in any category, although it does turn on the CALC indicator at the bottom of your screen. This indicator warns you that changes have been made and the worksheet has not been recalculated.

5. Press F9 (CALC).

Now you will see the results of the change.

6. Change the value in C4 back to 110000 by typing **110000**.

Again, the results are not affected.

7. Press F9 (CALC).

Your display should again show the results you started with.

8. Select /Worksheet Global Recalculation Automatic.

From this point on, every worksheet entry will cause recalculation. Keep this easy-to-make change in mind; it is a great option when you have a significant amount of data to enter.

Using Windows
To Help Monitor Data

1-2-3 allows you to split the screen into two different sections and to view a different portion of the worksheet in each section. You have the option of splitting the screen vertically or horizontally. Which method to select will depend on how your worksheet is arranged and which sections you want to view. If you want to see columns in two different areas, you will split the screen vertically. If you want to view rows from two different locations, you will want to choose a horizontal split.

The command that you use to create the split is /Worksheet Window. It is different from any other 1-2-3 command you have used: it requires you to position your cell pointer before invoking it. The location of the cell pointer determines the size of the two windows, and the window size cannot be changed while the menu is active.

After invoking the /Worksheet Window command, you must select Horizontal if you want two horizontal windows. The split will be made above the cell pointer at the time the command is invoked. Selecting Vertical will draw two vertical windows, the first of which ends immediately to the left of the cell pointer's location when the command was invoked.

Once the screen is split into two windows, you can use the F6 (WINDOW) key to move to the other window. Regardless of which window you are in, F6 always takes you to the opposite window.

The Worksheet Window menu has some additional options. The only other command that is not an advanced option is Clear. This option allows you to return to a display with one window. Cell pointer position is not important when you plan to choose Clear.

Try this exercise with your sales projection model to clarify how it works. Follow these steps:

1. Press the HOME key.

2. Use the DOWN ARROW key to move the cell pointer to A10.

3. Select /Worksheet Window.
   The menu shown in Figure 5-24 will appear.

4. Select Horizontal.

5. Press F6 (WINDOW) to move the cell pointer to the lower window.

6. Move the cell pointer to A29 to view the assumptions in the lower window.
   Your screen should match the display shown in Figure 5-25.

7. Select /Worksheet Window Clear.
   The display will return to a single window.

```
A10:                                                              MENU
Horizontal  Vertical  Sync  Unsync  Clear
Split the screen horizontally at the current row
      A       B       C       D       E       F       G       H
1                  Sales Projections 1990 - 1994
2
3              1989    1990    1991    1992    1993    1994
4   Sales   $100,000 $110,000 $123,200 $140,448 $150,982 $169,099
5   Cogs     $45,000  $49,500  $55,440  $63,202  $67,942  $76,095
6   Profit   $55,000  $60,500  $67,760  $77,246  $83,040  $93,005
7
8
9
10
```

FIGURE 5-24.   Worksheet Window menu

Using Titles with
Large Worksheets

One of the problems with large worksheets is that you cannot see all the data on the
screen at one time. This problem is magnified when you move your cell pointer to the

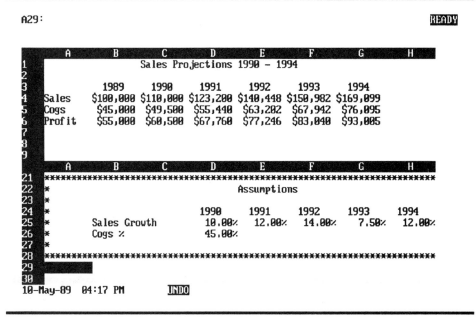

FIGURE 5-25.   Two horizontal windows

right or down and find that the labels at the left of the rows and the tops of the columns scroll off the screen. You can find yourself in a sea of numbers with no visible indication of what each of these numbers represents. The solution in 1-2-3 is to fix some of this label information on the screen.

The command that freezes label information on the screen is the /Worksheet Titles command. As with the /Worksheet Window command, the position of the cell pointer at the time you invoke this command is critical. The cell pointer location defines what information will be frozen on the screen. The command has four options: to fix titles both vertically and horizontally; to fix them vertically; to fix them horizontally; and to clear all fixed titles from the screen. This last option does not eliminate the titles themselves, but it ensures that neither vertical nor horizontal titles are frozen any longer. 1-2-3 will not let you select row titles if the cell pointer is in row 1 or column titles if the cell pointer is in column A since there would be no rows or columns selected.

If you choose to freeze vertical titles with either the Vertical or Both options, when you invoke /Worksheet Titles any columns to the left of the cell pointer will become fixed on the screen. You will not be able to move your cell pointer into these columns with the arrow keys. If you move to the right of the point where columns would normally scroll off the screen, only columns to the right of the fixed titles will scroll off the screen. The columns defined as titles will always be visible.

The situation is similar for horizontal titles, whether you choose Horizontal or Both. All rows above the cell pointer at the time /Worksheet Titles is invoked will remain frozen on the screen, even when the cell pointer moves far enough down on the worksheet to cause rows to scroll off the screen. The rows below the frozen titles can scroll off the screen, but the titles you have fixed on the screen cannot.

Looking at an example of this command with the sales projection worksheet will show you how it works. If you wanted to bring the right edge of the assumptions box into view, the left edge would scroll off the screen unless you first fixed the titles. Use these steps for fixing columns A through C:

1. Press the HOME key, and then press PGDN. Move the cell pointer to D25.

    You may think you could have just moved the cell pointer to D25, but the instructions given are the only way to ensure that you have just the desired rows and columns above and to the left of the cell pointer.

2. Select /**Worksheet Titles** to produce the display shown in Figure 5-26.

3. Select Vertical.

4. Move the cell pointer to K25 to produce the display shown in Figure 5-27. Notice that columns A, B, and C are frozen on the screen, yet columns D, E, and F scrolled off the screen.

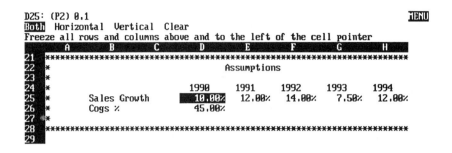

FIGURE 5-26.   Worksheet Titles menu

5. Select /Worksheet Titles Clear.

    This will unfix the titles, and columns A through C will scroll off the screen. These title-fixing features will be useful in situations where the total is at the bottom of a long column or to the right side of a long row. By fixing the titles you can check the total yet keep the corresponding labels on the screen for readability.

SEARCHING AND REPLACING WORKSHEET DATA

Once you master 1-2-3's features, you will be creating large worksheets that model your business operations. Working with larger models can make it more difficult to

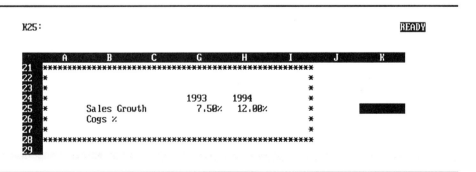

FIGURE 5-27.   Vertical titles displaying columns A, B, and C

find a particular entry as it is no longer practical to scan the model for a particular entry. If you are working with Release 2.2, you can have 1-2-3 scrutinize entries for you. 1-2-3 can match a string of characters in either labels or formulas. In addition, you can use 1-2-3's Replace option to change one or more occurrences to another set of characters. These new search-and-replace features can save you time in reviewing entries and in the editing that would be required for entries you want to change.

The /Range Search command is used for finding and replacing worksheet data. You can find text in cell formulas and labels. Since 1-2-3 can replace text as well as find it, you can use this command to correct a misspelling, change a cell address that formulas use, or find a name in a worksheet. The options for replacing text or cell addresses allow you to make all of the changes at once. If you would prefer to move a little more slowly, you can skip a matching entry, find the next matching entry to replace, or replace the current matching entry and move to the next one.

Searching Worksheet Data

1-2-3 can find text stored in formulas and labels. This feature cannot be used to search a cell that contains only numbers. Using the feature with the sales projection worksheet will show you how it works. With the SALESPRJ file in memory from the previous example, use these steps to try the /Range Search command to find the text "Sales":

1. Move the cell pointer to A1.

2. Select /Range Search. 1-2-3 prompts for the range to search.

3. Type a period to anchor one corner of the search range. Press the DOWN ARROW five times, and then press END and the RIGHT ARROW to highlight A1..G6. Press ENTER. 1-2-3 prompts for the string to search for.

    You can use either upper- or lowercase letters when typing the search string since 1-2-3 treats them as equivalent entries.

4. Type **Sales** and press ENTER. 1-2-3 prompts for where you want to look for the string. You can also type **sales** or **SALES** for the same results.

5. Select Labels. 1-2-3 will search all label cell entries for the string "Sales". 1-2-3 asks whether you want to find the string or replace the string with something else.

6. Select Find. 1-2-3 finds "Sales" in A4 (1-2-3 searches a column at a time, starting at the left most column) and creates the following display:

```
A4: 'Sales                                                         MENU
Next  Quit
Find next matching string
```

7. Select Next. 1-2-3 finds "Sales" in A3 and shows the same prompt. If you select Next, 1-2-3 will not find another "Sales" in the worksheet. 1-2-3 will beep and display an Error Message at the bottom of the screen. If you see this message, you can press ESC or ENTER to remove it and return to the READY mode.

8. Select Quit. 1-2-3 returns to the READY mode.

You can also use this command to find text in formulas. To find which cells use the 1992 sales growth in F25, you can search for a cell reference to F25 in formulas within the model by using the following steps:

1. Select /Range Search. 1-2-3 prompts for the range to search and highlights the one you selected to find "Sales".

2. Press ENTER. 1-2-3 prompts for the string to search for and displays "Sales."

3. Press ESC to remove the previous entry, type **F25**, and press ENTER.
    1-2-3 prompts to see what type of entries it should check for the string.

4. Select Formulas.
    1-2-3 asks whether you want to find the string or replace the string with something else.

5. Select Find.
    1-2-3 will search all cells containing formulas for the cell reference F25. 1-2-3 finds F25 in E4 and prompts you to determine if you want it to find the next occurrence or to quit.

6. Select Next.
    1-2-3 cannot find another formula that uses F25, so it beeps and displays this Error Message in the bottom row of the screen:

```
20
String not found
```

7. Press ESC. 1-2-3 returns to the READY mode.

Replacing Worksheet Data

If you make a few mistakes when reentering labels and formulas, the Replace option in 1-2-3's /Range Search command can handle the corrections for you. Replace not only locates your text but changes it to whatever character string you specify. You can use the SALESPRJ file and follow these steps to replace the text "Profit" with "Gross Profit":

1. Select /Range Search. 1-2-3 prompts for the range to search. It displays the range you selected for searching the worksheet earlier.

2. Press ENTER to select A1..G6. 1-2-3 prompts for the string to search for and suggests F25 from the last /Range Search command.

3. Press ESC, type **Profit**, and press ENTER.
   Since upper- and lowercase are equivalent in the search string, you can use either with identical results. 1-2-3 prompts for the type of entry within which you want to look for the string.

4. Select Labels.
   1-2-3 will search all label cell entries for the string "Profit". 1-2-3 asks whether you want to find the string or replace the string with something else.

5. Select Replace.

6. Type **Gross Profit** and press ENTER.
   1-2-3 finds "Profit" in A6 and creates the following display:

```
A6: 'Profit                                                          MENU
Replace All Next Quit
Replace string and proceed to next matching string in range
```

7. Select Replace.
   1-2-3 replaces "Profit" in A6 with "Gross Profit" and then searches for the next occurrence of "Profit". Since 1-2-3 cannot find another label that contains "Profit", 1-2-3 beeps and displays an Error Message indicating that it cannot find the search string.

8. Press ESC. 1-2-3 returns to the READY mode.

When you use the /Range Search command to replace text in formulas or labels, you must be careful about what you supply as a search string. If the text that you search for is not clearly defined, you may wind up replacing text that you did not want replaced. As an example of an unintentional replacement, suppose you want to use the sales growth rate for 1992 in 1993. One method of doing this is to replace the G25 cell reference with F25. If you use a search string of "G" and a replacement text of "F", 1-2-3 returns unexpected results since it prompts you on many unexpected matches. To show how this happens, follow these steps:

1. Select /Range Search.

     1-2-3 prompts for the range to search and highlights the one you selected in the last /Range Search command.

2. Press ENTER to accept A1..G6.

     1-2-3 prompts for the string to search for and displays "Profit."

3. Press ESC to remove the previous entry, type **G**, and press ENTER.

     1-2-3 asks where it should look for the string.

4. Select Formulas.

     1-2-3 asks whether you want to find the string or replace the string with something else.

5. Select Replace.

6. Type **F** and press ENTER.

     1-2-3 finds "G" in "Cogs" in A5 and asks whether to replace this one, replace all of them, find the next one, or quit.

7. Select All. 1-2-3 finds all occurrences of "G" in the worksheet and replaces them with "F".

     When 1-2-3 cannot find another "G," it beeps and displays an Error Message.

8. Press ESC. 1-2-3 returns to the READY mode. The screen looks like the one in Figure 5-28.

     Since the search string is not specific enough, the /Range Search command replaced every "G" in the specified range. The entries in column G will highlight the error. A better solution is to enter G25 as the search string and F25 as the replacement string. Although you must type more characters, you exclude cells that you do not want to alter.

9. Select /Worksheet Erase Yes to erase the worksheet.

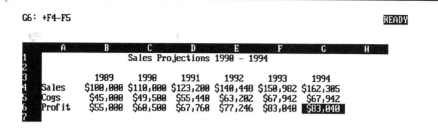

FIGURE 5-28.   Worksheet after supplying an inadequate search string

REVIEW EXERCISE

Now that you have had an opportunity to look at some of the commands that can save you time, you will want to practice with them a bit. You should pay special attention to Copy and Move since you will use these commands repeatedly in your everyday model building. Mastering them can make you a model construction expert. Follow these steps to create a model to record quarterly sales.

1. Select /Worksheet Erase Yes to clear any existing worksheet entries.

2. Place "**Qtr. 1** through "**Qtr. 4** in A3 through A6. You can refer to the model shown in Figure 5-29.

   Hint: You might enter "**Qtr1** in A3, copy the contents of A3 to A4..A6, and then edit the contents of A4..A6 so the worksheet has labels for the four quarters.

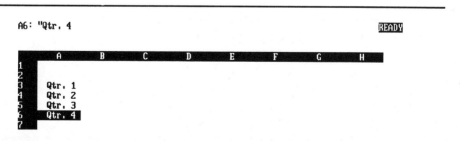

FIGURE 5-29.   Initial entries for each quarter

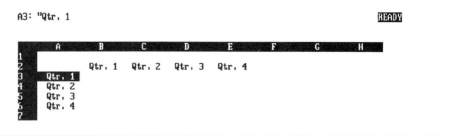

FIGURE 5-30. Transposing column entries to row entries

3. Transpose the labels from A3..A6 into column headings

   Hint: Use /Range Transpose, selecting A3..A6 as the from range and B2 as the to range. The worksheet looks like the one in Figure 5-30.

4. Erase the column entries in A3..A6.

   Hint: /Worksheet Erase will eliminate all your entries; /Range Erase is the command you need.

5. Enter **Widgets** in A3, **Things** in A4, and **Total** in A5.

6. Move "Total" from A5 to A6.

   Hint: Use /Move and select A5 as the from range and A6 as the to range.

7. Create a line with a repeating hyphen in B5 and copy the cell to C5..E5.

   Hint: Enter \— and then copy the entry with /Copy.

8. Set recalculation to manual.

   Hint: Use /Worksheet Global Recalculation Manual and remember that you will need to press F9 (CALC) when you want to see the effect of worksheet changes.

9. Enter the following numbers to these cells:

B3:	50000
C3:	60000
D3:	55000
E3:	40000
B4:	35000
C4:	55000
D4:	60000
E4:	70000

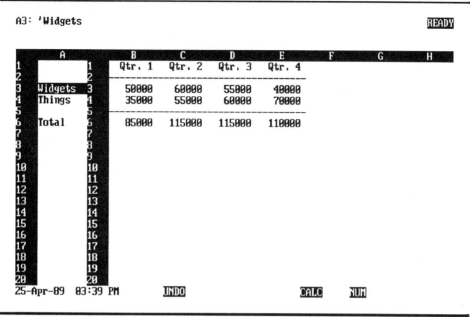

FIGURE 5-31.   Two vertical windows

10. Enter a formula in row 6 that adds the widgets and things for each quarter.
    Hint: For Qtr. 1 you can enter **+B3+B4** in B6 and then use /Copy to place the formula in other cells on this row.

11. Move the column headings from row 2 to row 1 and add a dashed line below it.
    Hint: Use /Move to relocate the column headings and then use /Copy to copy the existing line of hyphens from row 5.

12. Set recalculation to automatic to recalculate the worksheet.
    Hint: Use the /Worksheet Global Recalculation Automatic command followed by F9 (CALC). The CALC indicator at the bottom of your screen will disappear.

13. Move to B3. Create a vertical window with /Worksheet Window Vertical. The screen looks like the one in Figure 5-31. Press the F6 (WINDOW) key to switch between the two windows. Close the window with the /Worksheet Window Clear command.

E6: +E3-E4   READY

	A	B	C	D	E	F	G	H
1		Qtr. 1	Qtr. 2	Qtr. 3	Qtr. 4			
2		-------	-------	-------	-------			
3	Widgets	50000	60000	55000	40000			
4	Gizmos	35000	55000	60000	70000			
5		-------	-------	-------	-------			
6	Differenc	15000	5000	-5000	-30000			
7								

FIGURE 5-32.   Worksheet after replacing labels and formulas

14. Save the file as WIDGETS.

    The remaining steps use the /Range Search command, which is available with Release 2.2. If you are not using Release 2.2, skip these steps.

15. Replace "Things" with "Gizmos".
    Hint: Use the /Range Search command with the Replace option.

16. Replace "Total" with "Difference".
    Hint: Use the /Range Search command with the Replace option.

17. Replace the formula that adds the total widgets and gizmos for each quarter with a formula that subtracts gizmos from widgets.
    Hint: You can use /Range Search to make this change. Since it is a bit trickier than other Replace operations, each of the steps is listed for you. Press ESC and highlight the range B6..E6 as the search range. Enter **3+** for the search string. Select Formulas to search. Select Replace. Enter **3 –** as the replacement string. Select All to replace the plus sign with the minus sign. Press ESC to return to the READY mode. Including the 3 in the search and replace operation prevents the /Range Search command from prompting to see if you want to replace the plus sign at the beginning of the formula. The worksheet looks like the one in Figure 5-32.

REVIEW

- The Copy command can copy cells within a worksheet. You can copy one cell to one cell or one cell to many cells. You can also make one copy of an entire range of cells or make many copies of the same range. When you copy cells, 1-2-3 adjusts the formulas in the range depending upon whether the formulas use absolute, mixed, or relative cell addresses.

- The Move command can move cells within a worksheet. When you move cells, 1-2-3 adjusts the formulas so that all cell formulas reference the same cell contents they did before cells were moved.

- The /Range Trans command in Release 2.2 (/Range Transpose for Release 2 or 2.01) copies a range of cells and changes the cells orientation from row to column or column to row. If you transpose formulas in Release 2 or 2.01, the relative references are distorted. If you transpose formulas in Release 2.2, the command copies and transposes the values of the formulas rather than the formulas themselves.

- You can create a repeating label using the backslash (\) label prefix. The characters that you enter after the backslash are repeated for the width of the cell. This repeating label adjusts the label's width for the column's width.

- The /Data Fill command generates a series of numbers that are evenly spaced. To use this command you must provide the worksheet range that you want to fill with numbers, the number that you want to start the series with, the increment between values (positive for ascending and negative for descending), and the maximum value that can appear in the series.

- The /Worksheet Global Recalculation command determines whether 1-2-3 recalculates the worksheet whenever a worksheet entry is made or only when you press the F9 (CALC) key. For releases before 2.2, setting the recalculation to manual can increase the speed of data entry significantly.

- The /Worksheet Window command lets you create vertical and horizontal windows. These windows divide the screen so you can see two sections of your worksheet at once.

- The /Worksheet Titles command locks rows and columns on the screen display so you can always see the column or row header. The command options let you select horizontal titles (rows that always appear on the screen), vertical titles (columns that always appear on the screen), both titles (columns and rows that always appear on the screen), or clear titles (removes the titles from the screen).

- The /Range Search command, which is available in Release 2.2, can search for text in label or formula cell entries. The Replace option allows you to replace the text the command finds with different text.

Commands and Keys

Entry	Action
\	As a label prefix character, repeats the string that follows until the column width is filled
F4 (ABS)	Converts the address at the cursor's location to an absolute, mixed, or relative address

F6 (WINDOW)	Switches between the active windows
F9 (CALC)	Updates the calculations in the worksheet
/C	/Copy copies one or more cells to one or more location
/DF	/Data Fill generates a series of numbers that is a specific interval apart
/M	/Move moves one or more cells to another location
/RS	/Range Search finds or finds and replaces text in formulas and label cell entries
/RT	/Range Transpose copies one or more cells to a new location and changes the column and row orientation
/WGDRA	/Worksheet Global Default Recalculation Automatic sets 1-2-3 to recalculate the worksheet whenever an entry is made
/WGDRM	/Worksheet Global Default Recalculation Manual sets 1-2-3 to recalculate the worksheet when F9 (CALC) is pressed
/WTB	/Worksheet Titles Both freezes the rows above the cell pointer and the columns to the left of the cell pointer as worksheet titles
/WTC	/Worksheet Titles Clear clears worksheet titles created with the /WTB, /WTH, or /WTV command
/WTH	/Worksheet Titles Horizontal freezes the rows above the cell pointer as a horizontal title
/WTV	/Worksheet Titles Vertical freezes the columns to the left of the cell pointer as a vertical title
/WWC	/Worksheet Window Clear removes the window created with the /WWH or /WWV command
/WWH	/Worksheet Window Horizontal splits the screen display in half with a horizontal line, allowing you to view different sections of the worksheet
/WWV	/Worksheet Window Vertical splits the screen display in half with a vertical line, allowing you to view different sections of the worksheet

6

PRINTING YOUR WORKSHEET

Print Basics
Adding a Few Options
Special Print Options
Review Exercise
Review

In this chapter you will have an opportunity to explore 1-2-3's print features. You can use them to create a quick draft copy of your worksheet, using only a few instructions. When you are ready for a final copy, you can create a professional-looking report with a few new commands. These commands will allow you to control the print margins, access the special print options offered by your printer, and even add headers and footers to every page.

First, you will learn to use the basic print options. Then you will learn more complex print options, using the building-block approach, until you have a full set of print features that you can use. You will also have the opportunity to explore options for printing formulas and using worksheet commands to further customize your print output. Additional enhancements through the Allways package, which is available for Release 2 and higher, are covered in Chapter 13. Since this package is provided with every copy of Release 2.2 sold and offers significant new print features, you will want to explore its features as well as the print basics covered in this chapter.

PRINT BASICS

The basic print features are designed to give you quick access to a printed copy. This quick access is made possible by default values that 1-2-3 has set for options such as margins and page length. Later you will learn to override these default settings, but for now you might as well appreciate their presence; they make it easy for you to print your files.

Determining the Destination

What is the destination for 1-2-3's print features? At first the answer seems obvious. After all, if you are printing, you would expect to use the printer. But 1-2-3 offers you a choice: You can print to a printer or to a file on disk. The unexpected option of using a disk to capture print output adds considerable flexibility to the print features.

To select a destination, first access the print features by selecting /Print. This will cause the following submenu to display.

1-2-3 is asking whether to direct your output to the printer or to write it to a file. If you want to create printed hard copy immediately, choose the printer.

THE FILE OPTION   The File option is designed to let you write your print output to a file. Unlike the files that contain worksheets, this file contains print data and is referred to as an *ASCII text file*. It will automatically be assigned the filename extension .PRN. Once you have stored the information in the file you can do various things with it: print it at a later time, modify it with many word processors, and use it as input to some application programs. It is good to be aware of the printing-to-a-file special feature. However, since you will want to print to a printer most of the time, this chapter focuses on this option, giving relevant examples. Should you want to write your file to a disk, you can use any of the other options presented here.

THE PRINTER OPTION   When you select the Printer option, 1-2-3 assumes that the output device is the printer you selected when 1-2-3 was installed. As long as this printer is attached to your system and online when you tell 1-2-3 to begin printing, your print output will be sent to this device. Normally, the top or front of the printer has a series of small lights to indicate that the printer is online and ready to accept data. Verify that the printer is turned on and is online before you start to work with

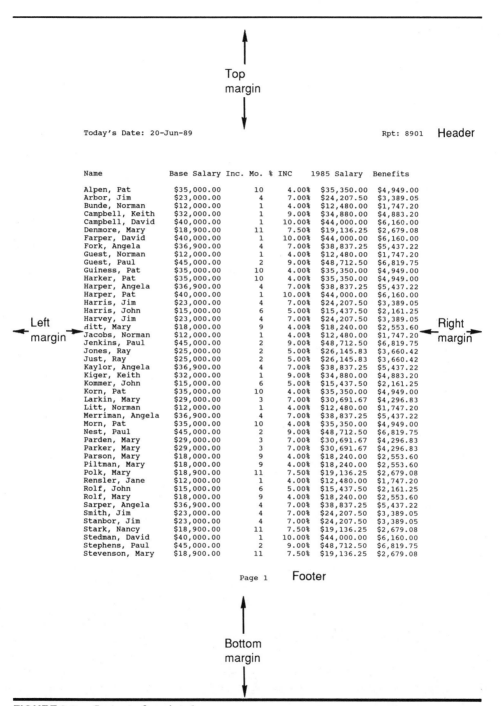

Top margin

Name	Base Salary	Inc. Mo.	% INC	1985 Salary	Benefits
Alpen, Pat	$35,000.00	10	4.00%	$35,350.00	$4,949.00
Arbor, Jim	$23,000.00	4	7.00%	$24,207.50	$3,389.05
Bunde, Norman	$12,000.00	1	4.00%	$12,480.00	$1,747.20
Campbell, Keith	$32,000.00	1	9.00%	$34,880.00	$4,883.20
Campbell, David	$40,000.00	1	10.00%	$44,000.00	$6,160.00
Denmore, Mary	$18,900.00	11	7.50%	$19,136.25	$2,679.08
Farper, David	$40,000.00	1	10.00%	$44,000.00	$6,160.00
Fork, Angela	$36,900.00	4	7.00%	$38,837.25	$5,437.22
Guest, Norman	$12,000.00	1	4.00%	$12,480.00	$1,747.20
Guest, Paul	$45,000.00	2	9.00%	$48,712.50	$6,819.75
Guiness, Pat	$35,000.00	10	4.00%	$35,350.00	$4,949.00
Harker, Pat	$35,000.00	10	4.00%	$35,350.00	$4,949.00
Harper, Angela	$36,900.00	4	7.00%	$38,837.25	$5,437.22
Harper, Pat	$40,000.00	1	10.00%	$44,000.00	$6,160.00
Harris, Jim	$23,000.00	4	7.00%	$24,207.50	$3,389.05
Harris, John	$15,000.00	6	5.00%	$15,437.50	$2,161.25
Harvey, Jim	$23,000.00	4	7.00%	$24,207.50	$3,389.05
ditt, Mary	$18,000.00	9	4.00%	$18,240.00	$2,553.60
Jacobs, Norman	$12,000.00	1	4.00%	$12,480.00	$1,747.20
Jenkins, Paul	$45,000.00	2	9.00%	$48,712.50	$6,819.75
Jones, Ray	$25,000.00	2	5.00%	$26,145.83	$3,660.42
Just, Ray	$25,000.00	2	5.00%	$26,145.83	$3,660.42
Kaylor, Angela	$36,900.00	4	7.00%	$38,837.25	$5,437.22
Kiger, Keith	$32,000.00	1	9.00%	$34,880.00	$4,883.20
Kommer, John	$15,000.00	6	5.00%	$15,437.50	$2,161.25
Korn, Pat	$35,000.00	10	4.00%	$35,350.00	$4,949.00
Larkin, Mary	$29,000.00	3	7.00%	$30,691.67	$4,296.83
Litt, Norman	$12,000.00	1	4.00%	$12,480.00	$1,747.20
Merriman, Angela	$36,900.00	4	7.00%	$38,837.25	$5,437.22
Morn, Pat	$35,000.00	10	4.00%	$35,350.00	$4,949.00
Nest, Paul	$45,000.00	2	9.00%	$48,712.50	$6,819.75
Parden, Mary	$29,000.00	3	7.00%	$30,691.67	$4,296.83
Parker, Mary	$29,000.00	3	7.00%	$30,691.67	$4,296.83
Parson, Mary	$18,000.00	9	4.00%	$18,240.00	$2,553.60
Piltman, Mary	$18,000.00	9	4.00%	$18,240.00	$2,553.60
Polk, Mary	$18,900.00	11	7.50%	$19,136.25	$2,679.08
Rensler, Jane	$12,000.00	1	4.00%	$12,480.00	$1,747.20
Rolf, John	$15,000.00	6	5.00%	$15,437.50	$2,161.25
Rolf, Mary	$18,000.00	9	4.00%	$18,240.00	$2,553.60
Sarper, Angela	$36,900.00	4	7.00%	$38,837.25	$5,437.22
Smith, Jim	$23,000.00	4	7.00%	$24,207.50	$3,389.05
Stanbor, Jim	$23,000.00	4	7.00%	$24,207.50	$3,389.05
Stark, Nancy	$18,900.00	11	7.50%	$19,136.25	$2,679.08
Stedman, David	$40,000.00	1	10.00%	$44,000.00	$6,160.00
Stephens, Paul	$45,000.00	2	9.00%	$48,712.50	$6,819.75
Stevenson, Mary	$18,900.00	11	7.50%	$19,136.25	$2,679.08

Left margin

Right margin

Bottom margin

FIGURE 6-1.   Layout of a printed page

the print commands. It is also a good idea to understand the defaults that will apply to your output before you learn about the instruction that actually starts the printing.

THE DEFAULT SETTINGS   One of the things that simplifies printing the first time you use a worksheet is the default settings that are provided for some of the print options. These defaults affect the length of a page of output and the amount of white space, or the margin, on all four sides of a printed page. The defaults also apply to the printed pages you write out to disk.

The default page that is predefined for 1-2-3 has several areas affecting the amount of data that prints on a page. The layout of a printed page defining these areas is shown in Figure 6-1. Notice that a page of output is defined as 66 lines, yet not all these lines will contain print data. Some of them are reserved for top and bottom margins. Once two lines are deducted for a top margin and two more are deducted for a bottom margin, only 62 lines will print on a page. In addition to the top and bottom margins, 1-2-3 allows three lines at both the top and bottom for a header or footer, even if you choose not to use either one. This means that of the 66 possible lines, only 56 lines will be used for printing with the default settings.

Similarly, standard print on an 8 1/2- by 11-inch sheet of paper allows 80 characters to print across the page, but the default settings will reduce this number. 1-2-3 has a default left margin setting of 4 and a default right margin setting of 76. This means that a maximum of 72 characters can print across the page if you do not modify the defaults. Initially, try the Print operation without modifying any of these defaults.

The Basic Print Options

The second level of the Print menu is the same whether you have chosen Printer or File. It is actually the main Print menu, since it is the root from which all the other print options can be selected. Figure 6-2 shows the main Print menu and the Print Settings sheet. In Release 2.2 the Print Settings sheet appears while the Print menu is active. It allows you to track all the changes that you make in the Print menu. This menu is different from any of the other menus you have used, all of which disappear as soon as you make your first selection. In contrast, the Print menu stays on your screen to allow additional selections. For this reason, it frequently is referred to as a "sticky menu." You will find it a real convenience, since most Print operations require more than one menu selection. In addition, all of the print settings that you make are listed in the settings sheet that fills the remainder of the screen. When you select an option from 1-2-3's Print menu, the settings may disappear temporarily to allow you to select cells on the worksheet. As soon as you finalize your selection, the settings sheet will reappear. As you change the settings, 1-2-3 updates the display in the Print Settings box.

```
A1:                                                                      MENU
Range Line Page Options Clear Align Go Quit
Specify a range to print
┌─────────────────────── Print Settings ───────────────────────┐
│  Destination:  Printer                                        │
│                                                               │
│  Range:                                                       │
│                                                               │
│  Header:                                                      │
│  Footer:                                                      │
│                                                               │
│  Margins:                                                     │
│    Left 4      Right 76    Top 2    Bottom 2                  │
│                                                               │
│  Borders:                                                     │
│    Columns                                                    │
│    Rows                                                       │
│                                                               │
│  Setup string:                                                │
│                                                               │
│  Page length:  66                                             │
│                                                               │
│  Format:       As-Displayed (Formatted)                       │
└───────────────────────────────────────────────────────────────┘
 25-Apr-89  05:41 PM
```

FIGURE 6-2.   Main Print menu and Print Settings sheet

Another important distinction is that 1-2-3 can remember the results of any command that affects the print setting. To have 1-2-3 remember what you want to print or any changes that you make to the print settings in a later session, first complete the definition of your print specifications, and then save the worksheet.

DEFINING THE RANGE TO PRINT   At this point you want to tell 1-2-3 how much of the worksheet you wish to print. Therefore, select the Range option from the main Print menu. The next step depends on whether the worksheet already has a print range defined. If not, just move to the beginning of the print range, type a period, and move to the end of the print range. If the worksheet was printed previously, the range address used from that time will probably still be defined.

Before you can move the cell pointer to a new beginning location, you must press ESC to unlock the beginning of the range. Whether you have printed previously or not, you can type a range reference by entering the address of the beginning of the range followed by a period and the cell address of the end of the range—for example, B3.H15. If a current range exists, 1-2-3 will immediately replace it with the range you enter; you do not need to press ESC.

The size of the range you define will affect how 1-2-3 prints your data when you request printing. If your defined range contains more data than will fit on one page, 1-2-3 will break the data into more than one page when you print. If the width of the range selected exceeds the number of characters that will print across one page, 1-2-3 will print as many columns across the first page as possible without exceeding the right margin setting. It will then break the output into more than one page. If the number of rows in the range selected exceeds the number of rows that can print on one page, 1-2-3 will generate a page break when the data prints.

To enter some data for printing and to try several options for specifying the print range, experiment with the following exercise. You could print worksheets you entered for other chapters, but you might not have one readily available. Therefore, this section offers instructions for creating employee data to be printed. You need to make quite a few entries to create this model, but it is designed to let you try each of the print options covered in this chapter without having to enter data again. You will use entries more than once to build a large file quickly. You will use the /Copy command extensively to further reduce these entry requirements.

Follow these steps to enter the model and define the print range.

1. Enter the following labels across row 1:

    A1:   SS#
    B1:   Last Name
    C1:   First Name
    D1:   Salary
    E1:   Location
    F1:   Phone
    G1:   Position
    H1:   Increase %
    I1:   '1990 Salary

2. Select /Worksheet Global Column-Width, type **11**, and press ENTER.

3. Move the cell pointer to column A, select /Worksheet Set-Width, type **13**, and press ENTER.

4. Make these entries in the cells shown:

    A2:   '516-75-8977
    B2:   Jones
    C2:   Paul
    D2:   45900
    E2:   DAL
    F2:   980
    G2:   2301

H2:	.05
I2:	+D2*(1+H2)
A3:	'541-78-6754
B3:	Parker
C3:	Mary
D3:	32100
E3:	CHI
F3:	541
G3:	1605
H3:	.04
A4:	'897-90-8769
B4:	Smith
C4:	Larry
D4:	61250
E4:	ATL
F4:	342
G4:	1402
H4:	.05
A5:	'213-78-5412
B5:	Appel
C5:	Tom
D5:	22300
E5:	BOS
F5:	219
G5:	1750
H5:	.06

5. Move the cell pointer to I2, select /Copy, and press ENTER. Move the cell pointer to I3, type . (period), move the cell pointer to I5, and press ENTER.

   This completes the first four records. You need more rows of data to get the full effect of the print features, but typing the entries would take too long. Instead, copy these entries until you have a sufficient number to print more than one page. You will, of course, have many duplicates.

6. Move the cell pointer to A2 and select /Copy. Then press END and the DOWN ARROW key, followed by END and the RIGHT ARROW key. Press ENTER to finalize the source range. Next move the cell pointer to A6 and press ENTER.

   This time you copied the first 4 rows of the worksheet to create another 4 rows. Next time you will copy the 8 existing data rows. After that you will copy the 16 entries and then the 32 entries (the number of records becomes larger each time you make a copy).

A1: [W13] 'SS#   READY

	A	B	C	D	E	F
1	SS#	Last Name	First Name	Salary	Location	Phone
2	516-75-8977	Jones	Paul	$45,900	DAL	980
3	541-78-6754	Parker	Mary	$32,100	CHI	541
4	897-90-8769	Smith	Larry	$61,250	ATL	342
5	213-78-5412	Appel	Tom	$22,300	BOS	219
6	516-75-8977	Jones	Paul	$45,900	DAL	980
7	541-78-6754	Parker	Mary	$32,100	CHI	541
8	897-90-8769	Smith	Larry	$61,250	ATL	342
9	213-78-5412	Appel	Tom	$22,300	BOS	219
10	516-75-8977	Jones	Paul	$45,900	DAL	980
11	541-78-6754	Parker	Mary	$32,100	CHI	541
12	897-90-8769	Smith	Larry	$61,250	ATL	342
13	213-78-5412	Appel	Tom	$22,300	BOS	219
14	516-75-8977	Jones	Paul	$45,900	DAL	980
15	541-78-6754	Parker	Mary	$32,100	CHI	541
16	897-90-8769	Smith	Larry	$61,250	ATL	342
17	213-78-5412	Appel	Tom	$22,300	BOS	219
18	516-75-8977	Jones	Paul	$45,900	DAL	980
19	541-78-6754	Parker	Mary	$32,100	CHI	541
20	897-90-8769	Smith	Larry	$61,250	ATL	342

FIGURE 6-3.   A look at the left side of the entries

7. Proceed with the copy by selecting /Copy. Then press END and the DOWN ARROW key, followed by END and the RIGHT ARROW key. Press ENTER, and then move the cell pointer to A10 and press ENTER.

8. Continue copying in this manner until you have entries in cells A1..I65, using the procedures described in the previous step.

9. Move the cell pointer to D2 and select /Range Format Currency 0, press ENTER, and then press END followed by the DOWN ARROW key. Press ENTER.

10. Move the cell pointer to H2 and select /Range Format Percent. Press ENTER, and then press the END key followed by the DOWN ARROW key. Press ENTER again.

11. Move the cell pointer to I2. Select /Range Format Currency. Type **0** and press ENTER. Press the END key followed by the DOWN ARROW key. Press ENTER.
    The upper portion of your entries should match what is shown in Figures 6-3 and 6-4.

G1: 'Position   READY

	G	H	I	J	K	L
1	Position	Increase %	1990 Salary			
2	2301	5.00%	$48,195			
3	1605	4.00%	$33,384			
4	1402	5.00%	$64,313			
5	1750	6.00%	$23,638			
6	2301	5.00%	$48,195			
7	1605	4.00%	$33,384			
8	1402	5.00%	$64,313			
9	1750	6.00%	$23,638			
10	2301	5.00%	$48,195			
11	1605	4.00%	$33,384			
12	1402	5.00%	$64,313			
13	1750	6.00%	$23,638			
14	2301	5.00%	$48,195			
15	1605	4.00%	$33,384			
16	1402	5.00%	$64,313			
17	1750	6.00%	$23,638			
18	2301	5.00%	$48,195			
19	1605	4.00%	$33,384			
20	1402	5.00%	$64,313			

FIGURE 6-4.   A look at the right side of the entries

12. Press the F5 (GOTO) key, type **A2**, and press ENTER to bring the left side of
    the worksheet into view on your screen.

13. Select /Print Printer Range and press the HOME key. Type . (period). Press END
    followed by HOME to highlight the range A1..I65, as shown in Figure 6-5. Press
    ENTER.
    You can use the END-HOME approach to print everything. Another method
    of moving the cell pointer to redefine the range is using the other movement
    keys, such as END-DOWN ARROW and END-RIGHT ARROW. Notice that the main
    Print menu is still in the control panel to let you make additional selections.
    Take advantage of its presence and enter the range specification a few different
    ways.

14. Select Range, press ESC to unlock the beginning of the range, and then move
    the cell pointer to B1. Type . (period) and then press the END key followed by
    the DOWN ARROW key. Press the RIGHT ARROW key twice; then press ENTER to
    select the range B1..D65.

```
I65:  (C0)  +D65*(1+H65)                                        POINT
Enter print range: A1..I65
```

	D	E	F	G	H	I
46	$45,900 DAL		980	2301	5.00%	$48,195
47	$32,100 CHI		541	1605	4.00%	$33,384
48	$61,250 ATL		342	1402	5.00%	$64,313
49	$22,300 BOS		219	1750	6.00%	$23,638
50	$45,900 DAL		980	2301	5.00%	$48,195
51	$32,100 CHI		541	1605	4.00%	$33,384
52	$61,250 ATL		342	1402	5.00%	$64,313
53	$22,300 BOS		219	1750	6.00%	$23,638
54	$45,900 DAL		980	2301	5.00%	$48,195
55	$32,100 CHI		541	1605	4.00%	$33,384
56	$61,250 ATL		342	1402	5.00%	$64,313
57	$22,300 BOS		219	1750	6.00%	$23,638
58	$45,900 DAL		980	2301	5.00%	$48,195
59	$32,100 CHI		541	1605	4.00%	$33,384
60	$61,250 ATL		342	1402	5.00%	$64,313
61	$22,300 BOS		219	1750	6.00%	$23,638
62	$45,900 DAL		980	2301	5.00%	$48,195
63	$32,100 CHI		541	1605	4.00%	$33,384
64	$61,250 ATL		342	1402	5.00%	$64,313
65	$22,300 BOS		219	1750	6.00%	$23,638

FIGURE 6-5.   Selecting a print range

15. Select Range, type **A1.I65**, and press ENTER.

    When you type the address of a replacement range, you do not have to press the ESC key first.

TELLING 1-2-3 TO BEGIN PRINTING   Once you have defined the range, simply select Go from the Print menu. Use the following step to immediately send the range you just defined to the printer:

1. Check to be sure that your printer is turned on and is online.

2. Select Go.

This will cause 1-2-3 to print the worksheet row by row and increment its internal line count with each line printed. When all the data in the defined range has been printed, 1-2-3 will return to the Print menu. The print output is shown in Figure 6-6. If you want a second copy you can select Go again, but 1-2-3 will not move to the top of a page before it starts printing again. You cannot solve this problem by paging with the formfeed or linefeed button on your computer, since 1-2-3 maintains its own line count

```
SS#            Last Name  First Name Salary      Location  Phone
516-75-8977    Jones      Paul       $45,900 DAL           980
541-78-6754    Parker     Mary       $32,100 CHI           541
897-90-8769    Smith      Larry      $61,250 ATL           342
213-78-5412    Appel      Tom        $22,300 BOS           219
516-75-8977    Jones      Paul       $45,900 DAL           980
541-78-6754    Parker     Mary       $32,100 CHI           541
897-90-8769    Smith      Larry      $61,250 ATL           342

    213-78-5412   Appel      Tom          $22,300 BOS           219
    516-75-8977   Jones      Paul         $45,900 DAL           980
    541-78-6754   Parker     Mary         $32,100 CHI           541
    897-90-8769   Smith      Larry        $61,250 ATL           342
    213-78-5412   Appel      Tom          $22,300 BOS           219
    516-75-8977   Jones      Paul         $45,900 DAL           980
    541-78-6754   Parker     Mary         $32,100 CHI           541
    897-90-8769   Smith      Larry        $61,250 ATL           342
                                          $22,300 BOS           219
```

```
    Position   Increase % 1990 Salary
        2301      5.00%    $48,195
        1605      4.00%    $33,384
        1402      5.00%    $64,313
        1750      6.00%    $23,638
        2301      5.00%    $48,195
        1605      4.00%    $33,384
        1402      5.00%    $64,313

      1750        6.00%    $23,638
      2301        5.00%    $48,195
      1605        4.00%    $33,384
      1402        5.00%    $64,313
      1750        6.00%    $23,638
      2301        5.00%    $48,195
      1605        4.00%    $33,384
                          $64,313
```

FIGURE 6-6.   Output from the Print operation

to tell it how much more space it has on a page. If you were to physically advance the paper in your printer without setting the line count to zero, the new page would only contain data part of the way down the page; the line count would increment to 66 before reaching the bottom of the page. Look at the basic control options before printing a second time. To tell 1-2-3 to begin in the second copy at the top of the page, use the instructions for advancing a page, which follow.

ADVANCING A LINE   Sometimes you want to print more than one print range. Depending on the size of each range of data, you may want to place all the ranges on a single page or place each one on a separate page. If you placed them on the same page, they would merge unless you added one or more blank lines after printing each range. 1-2-3 will do this for you when you give it the command /Print Printer Line. (Normally you need only select Line, since the Print menu is likely to be on your screen.) Each time you select Line, 1-2-3 causes the printer to advance the paper one line and add one to the internal line count.

ADVANCING A PAGE Advancing a line is fine for a small separation; but when you want data on separate pages you might have to select Line too many times to make this solution a practical one. Instead, use the command /Print Printer Page. It will quickly advance the paper to the top of the next page. Try this now: Select Page. Only Page is needed since you are already in the main Print menu.

SETTING 1-2-3'S LINE COUNT TO ZERO When the paper in your printer is set at the top of a form, you will want 1-2-3's line count to be set to zero. The command for this is Align. Try it with this entry: select Align. It looks like nothing has happened, but 1-2-3 has completed its housekeeping chore of zeroing the line count.

CLEARING THE PRINT SETTINGS The Print menu has a special command for clearing print settings from a previous operation. If you select Clear from the Print menu, these options will appear:

```
A2: [W13] '516-75-8977                                    MENU
All Range Borders Format
Return all print settings to defaults
```

The first option clears everything connected with the previous printing, and is appropriately labeled All. It sets everything back to the defaults. This means that you must define the next Print operation, just as if you had never printed before.

The second option only eliminates the definition of the print range. After executing this command, you must define a print range before printing again. If you forget, nothing will happen when you tell 1-2-3 to begin printing since there will be no default settings for the print range.

The last two options, Borders and Format, will be discussed later in this chapter along with the more advanced features they relate to. Like the other options, they eliminate any special settings that have been made and leave the worksheet as if these special features had never been invoked.

QUITTING THE PRINT MENU Since the Print menus do not disappear after you make your selections, you need a way to let 1-2-3 know you are finished selecting print options. The Quit option in the Print menu is designed to do this. Once you select

Quit you are returned to READY mode. If you are printing to a file, selecting Quit closes the .PRN file; pressing ESC also exits the Print menu and closes the .PRN file. Try it now with this command: select Quit.

SAVING YOUR PRINT SPECIFICATIONS   When the data in your worksheet data, you probably will want to produce updated copies of your report. It is easy to print a report on subsequent occasions if you have saved the worksheet file after printing. The /File Save command saves any updates to worksheet data, as well as your print settings. This means that the print range and any special settings you have entered for margins or page length will still be available the next time you need to print. You will be able to select /Print Printer Go to produce the output.

ADDING A FEW OPTIONS

You have already mastered the basics of printing. You do not need any other commands to get a printed copy of your data. But you may not be content with the appearance of your printout. If you want to improve it, the print options can assist you. You can access them by selecting Options from the main Print menu to produce this menu:

```
A2: [W13] '516-75-8977                                          MENU
Header  Footer  Margins  Borders  Setup  Pg-Length  Other  Quit
Create a header
```

This is another "sticky menu" like the main Print menu. It will stay around until you choose Quit or press ESC.

Margin Settings

To change margin settings, select Margins from the Options menu. You will be presented with a submenu that looks like this:

```
A2: [W13] '516-75-8977                                          MENU
Left  Right  Top  Bottom  None
Set left margin
```

Each option on this menu represents one of the four areas where margins can be specified. The None option, which is new to Release 2.2, removes the margin settings from the worksheet, which causes 1-2-3 to use the widest area for printing your worksheet.

Whatever values you enter for margins will change the print defaults for this one worksheet. If you save the worksheet file after making changes to the margins, the changed values will be in effect for this worksheet the next time you retrieve it. If you want to make a temporary change, don't save the worksheet after changing the margins.

The limitations placed on potential margin settings for Release 1A differ from those for Release 2 and higher. In Release 2 and higher, the limits on top and bottom margins are 0 lines to 32 lines for each of these margin choices. In Release 1A, the settings for each margin can be between 0 and 10 lines. To enter a new margin setting, select the type of margin you wish to specify; then type a new value and press ENTER.

The range of acceptable values for the right and left margins is the same for all releases of the product. You can use settings of from 0 to 240 characters for both right and left margins.

Try the following exercise with the employee data to see how margins can affect the output:

1. Select /Print Printer Options Margins.

2. Select Left, type **10**, and press ENTER.

3. Select Margins Right, type **70**, and press ENTER.

4. Select Quit.
   This Quit exits the Options menu and returns you to the main Print menu.

5. Select Go.
   You will see that one fewer column prints across the page because you have reserved more space for the right and left margins.

6. Select Page Align.

Defining Headers and Footers

Headers and *footers* are lines that appear at the top or bottom of every page of print output. Information placed in the header (at the top of a page) typically includes the date or time, an identifying report number, a report title, the preparer's name, or a page number. The most frequent entry in a footer (at the bottom of the page) is the page number.

Headers and footers can be up to 240 characters each. However, do not make them any longer than the number of characters that will fit on a page bounded by your left and right margin settings, or 1-2-3 will truncate the extra characters. For example, if you use the default left and right margin settings of 4 and 76, do not enter a header longer than 72 characters. This limit applies whether you type the header or footer at 1-2-3's prompt or store the header or footer in a cell and reference the cell. The latter method is a new Release 2.2 feature.

USING SPECIAL SYMBOLS   Two special symbols can be used anywhere in a header or footer to add special information. The @ makes 1-2-3 substitute the current system date at that location when it prints the header or footer line. The # makes 1-2-3 insert the current page number at that location in the header or footer.

Either of these special symbols can be used alone or in combination with text characters. If you wanted the words "Page Number" to appear in front of the actual page number, you would place **Page Number #** in the header. Likewise, if you wanted to label the date you could enter **Today's Date: @**.

THE THREE SECTIONS   1-2-3 allows you to define entries for the left, middle, and right sections of a header or footer. In other words, each header or footer has the potential to be divided into three sections. The sections are separated by the vertical bar symbol (|).

When you ask to enter a header by selecting /Print Printer Options Header, this is the display you will see.

```
A2: [W13] '516-75-8977                                    EDIT
Enter header:
```

Whatever you type will appear left-aligned in the header line. When you are finished entering information for the left section, type a vertical bar (|) to indicate that you would like to begin entering the center section. When you have completed the center section, type another vertical bar (|) to indicate the beginning of the entries for the right section. You can omit any section by entering the vertical bar to end the section without entering anything in it. For example, the header "||Report Number: 3405" would not place anything in the left or middle sections of the header. It would right-align "Report Number: 3405" in the header line printed at the top of every page. You can enter everything on the left side of the page by using no vertical bar characters in your header.

Try this exercise to see how adding a header can affect your output:

1. Select Options Header, type **Report No: 2350||Page #**, and press ENTER.

2. Select Quit.

3. Select Go.

4. Select Page Align.

```
Report No: 2350                                              Page 1

SS#             Last Name   First Name Salary      Location   Phone
516-75-8977     Jones       Paul          $45,900  DAL             980
541-78-6754     Parker      Mary          $32,100  CHI             541
897-90-8769     Smith       Larry         $61,250  ATL             342
213-78-5412     Appel       Tom           $22,300  BOS             219
```
```
Report No: 2350                                              Page 2

SS#             Last Name   First Name Salary      Location   Phone
541-78-6754     Parker      Mary          $32,100  CHI             541
897-90-8769     Smith       Larry         $61,250  ATL             342
213-78-5412     Appel       Tom           $22,300  BOS             219
516-77                                    $45,900  DAL             980
```

FIGURE 6-7.   Header at the top of two pages

Figure 6-7 shows the header at the top of the first two printed pages.

USING A CELL'S CONTENTS   If you are using Release 2.2, you can use the contents in a worksheet cell for the header or footer. To refer to a cell's contents, enter a backslash and the cell address or range name that you want to use for the header or footer. If you enter a range name, 1-2-3 uses the cell in the upper left corner of the range. 1-2-3 uses the cell's contents just as if you entered the cell's contents at the header or footer prompt. This means you can include the vertical bars and the two special symbols in the cell. You may want to use this new feature to select from one of several headings when you print a report. To change a heading you would simply type the cell address that contains the header that you want.

As an example, you can create the same header shown in Figure 6-7 by entering **Report No: 2350||Page #** in K1. Then from the Print Options menu you would select Header, type **\K1**, and press ENTER. If you use a cell reference to select the header or footer, the header or footer cannot contain the other special header or footer characters.

Using Borders

The labels you enter at the top and/or left side of a worksheet provide descriptive information on the first page of a printed report, but the rows of labels at the top are not repeated automatically when the rows in the worksheet continue on subsequent pages. These pages will contain data that may be meaningless without labels. Similarly, when the rows in the worksheet exceed the width of one page, only the first page will contain the columns at the left. Data further to the right will be printed on subsequent pages but will probably be meaningless without labels.

The Borders option allows you to select rows or columns that will appear at the top or left side of every page. The columns or rows you select as borders should not be included in the print range. Otherwise, this data will print twice on the first page of the report—once as part of the border and once as part of the print range.

To use the Borders option, select /Print Printer Options Borders. The following menu will display.

```
A2: [W13] '516-75-8977                                    MENU
Columns  Rows
Print border columns to the left of each print range
```

When you want to place information at the top of the worksheet on every page, choose Rows and select a range that includes at least one cell in each row you want to use. To use column information on each page, select Column and choose a range with at least one cell from every column you want to use.

You can put the Borders option to use for the employee file you started in an earlier chapter; the worksheet has more rows than will fit on one page, and the second page has no labels. Follow these steps to add the top row as a border:

1. Select Range from the main Print menu.

2. Type **A2.F65** and press ENTER.
   Notice that the row containing the labels is not included in the print range, since you will use it as a border row.

3. Select Options Borders Rows.

4. Move the cell pointer to A1 and press ENTER.

5. Select Quit.

6. Select Go followed by Page Align Clear All Quit when the printing stops.

The output contains labels at the top of both pages 1 and 2, as shown in Figure 6-8. The Clear All command eliminated all of the print settings, including the print range and borders.

```
Report No: 2350                                         Page 1


SS#            Last Name  First Name Salary     Location  Phone
516-75-8977    Jones      Paul         $45,900 DAL          980
541-78-6754    Parker     Mary         $32,100 CHI          541
897-90-8769    Smith      Larry        $61,250 ATL          342
213-78-5412    Appel      Tom          $22,300 BOS          219
   Report No: 2350                                      Page 2


   SS#          Last Name  First Name Salary     Location  Phone
   541-78-6754  Parker     Mary         $32,100 CHI          541
   897-90-8769  Smith      Larry        $61,250 ATL          342
   213-78-5412  Appel      Tom          $22,300 BOS          219
   516-              $45,900 DAL          980
```

FIGURE 6-8.   Borders option places labels on all pages

Changing the Page Length

The page length is set at a default of 66 lines for most printers. This is perfect for 8 1/2- by 11-inch paper on most printers when you are printing at 6 lines to the inch. But if you change to 8 lines to the inch or use a different size paper, you need to change the page length.

Which length to choose depends on which release of 1-2-3 you are using. Release 1A supports page lengths of any size between 20 and 100 lines. Release 2 has the same upper limit but supports a page size as small as 10 lines. Release 2.2 also has the same upper limit but supports a page size as small as 1 line.

To make a change, select /Print Printer Options Pg-Length (Page-Length in Release 1A) and type the length you want before pressing ENTER. This change in length affects only the current worksheet. If you bring a new worksheet into memory and want to use a different page length, you need to invoke the command again.

Setup Strings

Setup strings are special character sequences that you can transmit to your printer to activate special features. These special features allow you to override such standard settings as printing 6 lines per inch or using standard typeface. Depending on the features of your printer, you can access alternate fonts. Print can be 8 lines to the inch, or it can be compressed to allow more characters per inch horizontally than the standard setting of 10 or 12. If you are using Release 2 or higher, you will want to use the Allways program (discussed in Chapter 13) since it provides these customization features through menu selections. In essence, Allways has learned the setup strings for your printer; you do not need to remember them. This makes the printer's features easier to activate.

Unfortunately, print setup strings are specific to the different brands of printers. The commands that activate the features of one printer would not necessarily communicate the same information to another. The examples in this section use codes that will function for an EPSON LQ-1500, a widely used printer. Before you try any of the examples, check the manual for your printer and substitute the proper setup strings.

To add a setup string, select /Print Printer Options Setup. This display will be presented for your entry:

```
A2: [W13] '516-75-8977                                    EDIT
Enter setup string:
```

The characters you enter are generally a three-digit number preceded by a backslash. Supposing that when you look in your manual, you find that the code for compressed print is 15. In that case, type \015 and press ENTER. This print feature will be in effect for the entire worksheet when it is printed. It will also be used the next time you retrieve the file containing this worksheet, as long as you remember to save the file after entering the setup string. Also, since most printers have a memory feature, this print feature will be in effect until you turn the printer off or send a string that turns off compressed print. Keep in mind that the size of the characters affects the number that can fit across a line. If you choose an option that changes the character size, you might need to adjust your margin settings.

Try this example with the print control codes to have your printer produce compressed print:

1. Select /Print Printer Range, type **A1..I65**, and press ENTER.

2. Select Options Setup.
    You do not have to select /Print Printer again since you are already in the main Print menu.

3. Type **\015** or your control codes and press ENTER.
    You will need to substitute the proper code for your printer at this point.

4. Select Margins Right, type **132**, and press ENTER.

5. Select Quit and then Go to print, as in the example shown in Figure 6-9.

```
Report No: 2350                                                                    Page 1


SS#          Last Name  First Name Salary     Location  Phone     Position  Increase % 1990 Salary
516-75-8977  Jones      Paul       $45,900 DAL          980       2301       5.00%   $48,195
541-78-6754  Parker     Mary       $32,100 CHI          541       1605       4.00%   $33,384
897-90-8769  Smith      Larry      $61,250 ATL          342       1402       5.00%   $64,313
213-78-5412  Appel      Tom        $22,300 BOS          219       1750       6.00%   $23,638
516-75-8977  Jones      Paul       $45,900 DAL          980       2301       5.00%   $48,195
541-78-6754  Parker     Mary       $32,100 CHI          541       1605       4.00%   $33,384
897-90-8769  Smith      Larry      $61,250 ATL          342       1402       5.00%   $64,313
213-78-5412  Appel      Tom        $22,300 BOS          219       1750       6.00%   $23,638
```

FIGURE 6-9.   Using compressed print

6. Select Options Setup.

7. Type **\018** and press ENTER.
   This setup string tells the printer to suspend compressed print. You will want to check your manual for the proper string for your printer.

8. Select Quit and then Go.

9. Select Quit to exit the Print menu.
   To delete printer setup strings, select /Print Printer Clear Format. Do not use the Clear All option; it does eliminate printer setup strings, but it affects other worksheet entries as well.

SPECIAL PRINT OPTIONS

The print features you have worked with up to now are the backbone of 1-2-3's print capabilities. You will want to master them because you will use them every day to produce printed copies of all your models. A few additional print features are used less frequently but are still important. They can help you solve the occasional problems for which the regular print features offer no solution. These additional print features include special commands for printing data to a file and printing cell formulas, as well as print options that are hidden in the Worksheet menu.

Special Preparation for Writing to a File

You can write all your print output to a file by selecting /Print File rather than /Print Printer. When this is the only change you make, the file that is created is identical to the data printed to a printer. Since the file data is frequently used for a purpose other than printing, this may not be appropriate. When writing data to a file, ask yourself whether page breaks, borders, and other formatting options should be applied. If you decide that you do not want the format options included—that you want your data written to the file without regard to page breaks or any other formatting such as margins, headers, or footers— enter the following command:

/Print File Options Other Unformatted

Later, if you want to include the formatting when you print the worksheet data to your printer, you will first need to select /Print Printer Options Other Formatted to restore formatting for the worksheet.

Printing Cell Formulas

1-2-3 provides a quick way to print a list of the contents of worksheet cells. This means that what is displayed is not the result of a formula but the formula you originally entered. Other attributes of the cell, such as width and format, will also be included in the list. Cells that are blank will be excluded from the list. Since 1-2-3 prints the contents of only one cell on a line, you can see how long this list might be for even a medium-sized worksheet.

You can try this technique for a section of the current worksheet. Follow these steps:

1. Select /Print Printer Range.

2. Type **G2.I10** and press ENTER.

3. Select Options Other Cell-Formulas.

4. Select Quit to leave the Options menu, and select Go.

```
G2:  2301
H2:  (P2)  0.05
I2:  (C0)  +D2*(1+H2)
G3:  1605
H3:  (P2)  0.04
I3:  (C0)  +D3*(1+H3)
G4:  1402
H4:  (P2)  0.05
I4:  (C0)  +D4*(1+H4)
G5:  1750
H5:  (P2)  0.06
I5:  (C0)  +D5*(1+H5)
G6:  2301
H6:  (P2)  0.05
I6:  (C0)  +D6*(1+H6)
G7:  1605
H7:  (P2)  0.04
I7:  (C0)  +D7*(1+H7)
G8:  1402
H8:  (P2)  0.05
I8:  (C0)  +D8*(1+H8)
G9:  1750
H9:  (P2)  0.06
I9:  (C0)  +D9*(1+H9)
G10: 2301
H10: (P2)  0.05
I10: (C0)  +D10*(1+H10)
```

FIGURE 6-10.   Printing cell formulas

5. Select Options Other As-Displayed Quit.

   This command sequence will set the display back to the normal mode in which the printout of the worksheet matches the display you see on the screen.

6. Select Page Align Quit.

   The list produced should look like the one in Figure 6-10.

Worksheet Features To Enhance Control

The print options you have reviewed thus far have been located within the Print menu. This is exactly where you would expect to look for this type of feature. There are several additional options that can significantly affect print results, but they are activated in unexpected ways. Two of the commands are found in the worksheet menus; the other is entered directly in worksheet cells.

ADDING PAGE BREAKS   If you have Release 2 or higher, you can add a page break at any location within a worksheet to ensure that the information following the page break starts on a new page. This feature can prevent awkward breaks that can occur, for example, between the last number in a column and the total for a column. Once 1-2-3 has processed the manual page break that you insert, it will again begin processing the automatic page breaks from the location of the manual page break to the end of the document. If you do not want this, you must insert additional manual breaks to again interrupt the automatic page-processing feature.

To insert a page break in the worksheet, move your cell pointer to the leftmost cell in the print range in the row that you want to force to the top of a new page. Then select /Worksheet Page. This causes 1-2-3 to insert a blank line above the cell pointer and to place a double colon symbol (::) in the cell that contained the cell pointer. The cell pointer then moves down a line and stays on the line that contains the data it was originally with. If the double colon symbol is anywhere but at the left edge of the print range, 1-2-3 will ignore the page break request. If this symbol is at the left edge of the range and you choose a range that is more than one page across, the break will occur across all pages in the range.

If you are using Release 2 or higher, follow these steps to insert a page break in the employee listing:

1. Move the cell pointer to A25.

2. Select /Worksheet Page.
    The entries in row 25 and subsequent rows are moved down a row. The reason is that this command inserted a blank row and placed the page break symbol in the cell where the cell pointer was located when you requested the command, as shown in Figure 6-11.

3. Select /Print Printer Go.
    1-2-3 remembers your range from last time and automatically expands it by one row when you add the page break.

4. Select Page Align Quit.

ADDING SETUP STRINGS IN THE WORKSHEET   You have already seen how you can add a setup string through the Print Options menu. These setup strings activate features on your printer and stay in effect while the entire worksheet is printing. You can also embed the same setup strings within the worksheet. This approach allows you to turn setup strings on and off in different parts of a document and to use bold printing for a heading or important information.

Embedded setup strings must be in a row by themselves. Therefore, you must insert a blank row above the area where you want the setup string activated. Place the

B26: 'Appel   READY

	B	C	D	E	F	G
8	Smith	Larry	$61,250	ATL	342	1402
9	Appel	Tom	$22,300	BOS	219	1750
10	Jones	Paul	$45,900	DAL	980	2301
11	Parker	Mary	$32,100	CHI	541	1605
12	Smith	Larry	$61,250	ATL	342	1402
13	Appel	Tom	$22,300	BOS	219	1750
14	Jones	Paul	$45,900	DAL	980	2301
15	Parker	Mary	$32,100	CHI	541	1605
16	Smith	Larry	$61,250	ATL	342	1402
17	Appel	Tom	$22,300	BOS	219	1750
18	Jones	Paul	$45,900	DAL	980	2301
19	Parker	Mary	$32,100	CHI	541	1605
20	Smith	Larry	$61,250	ATL	342	1402
21	Appel	Tom	$22,300	BOS	219	1750
22	Jones	Paul	$45,900	DAL	980	2301
23	Parker	Mary	$32,100	CHI	541	1605
24	Smith	Larry	$61,250	ATL	342	1402
25	::					
26	Appel	Tom	$22,300	BOS	219	1750
27	Jones	Paul	$45,900	DAL	980	2301

FIGURE 6-11.   Inserting a page break

embedded setup string to the far left of the inserted row, and make sure that it starts with two vertical bar symbols (||). Follow these bars with the specific setup strings you want to use. Use the same format for the setup strings that you use when you add a single string through the Print Options menu. The string always starts with a backslash (\) and is followed by a three-digit number that represents an acceptable setup string for your particular printer.

Use the following instructions to boldface the heading for the employee listing. When you enter the example, substitute the setup string for your particular printer.

1. Press HOME to move to A1 in the employee worksheet.

2. Select /Worksheet Insert Row and press ENTER.

3. Type ||.

4. Continue typing \027\069 and press ENTER.

   This is the control code for boldface printing on an EPSON LQ-1500 printer. Substitute the correct control code for boldface printing on your printer; check your printer manual if you are not familiar with the codes.

```
SS#           Last Name   First Name Salary      Location   Phone
516-75-8977   Jones       Paul       $45,900 DAL            980
541-78-6754   Parker      Mary       $32,100 CHI            541
897-90-8769   Smith       Larry      $61,250 ATL            342
213-78-5412   Appel       Tom        $22,300 BOS            219
516-75-8977   Jones       Paul       $45,900 DAL            980
541-78-6754   Parker      Mary       $32,100 CHI            541
897-90-8769   Smith       Larry      $61,250 ATL            342
213-78-5412   Appel       Tom        $22,300 BOS            219
516-75-8977   Jones       Paul       $45,900 DAL            980
541-78-6754   Parker      Mary       $32,100 CHI            541
897-90-8769   Smith       Larry      $61,250 ATL            342
213-78-5412   Appel       Tom        $22,300 BOS            219
516-75-8977   Jones       Paul       $45,900 DAL            980
```

FIGURE 6-12.   Boldfacing by adding print strings to the worksheet

5. Move the cell pointer to row 3.

6. Select /Worksheet Insert Row and press ENTER.

7. Type ||\027\064 and press ENTER.
    This entry represents the two vertical bars, the backslash that starts all setup strings and the control code that indicates that you want your printer to use its default setup string again. Only the control code portion of this entry varies from printer to printer. You will need to select the correct code from your printer manual.

8. Select /Print Printer.

9. Select Range, and then type **A1.F25**.

10. Select Go.
    A portion of the output showing the highlighted entries from row 1 appears in Figure 6-12.

11. Select Page Align Quit.

HIDING COLUMNS   1-2-3's /Worksheet Column Hide command in Release 2 and higher can enhance the features of the print commands by letting you define a wide print range and hide those columns that you do not want printed. The /Print Range command allows you to define only one contiguous print range. With the Column Hide option you can effectively extend this to many separate columns of information by hiding the columns that lie between the areas you want to print.

This feature is especially advantageous when a worksheet contains confidential information. You can hide a column that contains salary information or a projected percentage increase. This allows you to create a list of employee names, locations, and phone numbers even when the salary information is in the midst of the data columns you need. The hide feature will not destroy the salary data; it merely removes the unwanted data from view temporarily. When you want to restore hidden data, use the /Worksheet Column Display command and select one or more adjacent columns that are marked by asterisks to indicate their hidden status.

If you have Release 2 or higher, follow these steps to print a copy of the employee data without the salary or social security number columns:

1. Move the cell pointer to column A.

2. Select /Worksheet Column Hide.
    The control panel asks that you specify the columns to be hidden, as shown here:

```
A2: [W13] '516-75-8977                                          POINT
Specify column to hide: A2
```

	A	B	C	D	E	F
1	SS#	Last Name	First Name	Salary	Location	Phone
2	516-75-8977	Jones	Paul	$45,900	DAL	900
3	541-78-6754	Parker	Mary	$32,100	CHI	541

3. Press ENTER to select column A.

4. Move the cell pointer to column D, where the salary information is stored.

5. Select /Worksheet Column Hide and press ENTER.

6. Select /Print Printer Clear All to remove any prior print settings.

7. Select Range, press HOME, and type . (period). Then use the RIGHT ARROW and DOWN ARROW keys until the cell pointer is in G10, and press ENTER.

8. Select Go.
    The printed report will appear like the one in Figure 6-13.

9. Select Page Align Quit.
    This command will position the paper at the top of a form, zero the line count, and exit from the Print menu, placing you back in READY mode.

```
Last Name   First Name  Location   Phone      Position
Jones       Paul        DAL           980        2301
Parker      Mary        CHI           541        1605
Smith       Larry       ATL           342        1402
Appel       Tom         BOS           219        1750
Jones       Paul        DAL           980        2301
Parker      Mary        CHI           541        1605
Smith       Larry       ATL           342        1402
Appel       Tom         BOS           219        1750
Jones       Paul        DAL           980        2301
```

FIGURE 6-13.   Hiding worksheet columns

10. Select /Worksheet Column Display and position the cell pointer in column A before pressing ENTER.

11. Select /Worksheet Column Display and select column D.
    The last two instructions prove that your original data is still intact even though it was not visible on the screen.

REVIEW EXERCISE

Rather than creating a new worksheet to practice with the print features, you can use the model created at the end of Chapter 5. You can follow these steps to test the basics as well as a few enhancement options:

1. Retrieve the SALESPRJ file that you created in Chapter 5.

2. Specify the print range as A1..I28.
    Hint: Use /Print Printer Range. Press the HOME key, type . (period), and then press END followed by HOME to highlight all of the worksheet area the file uses. Press ENTER to accept A1..I28.

3. Create a header with the date at the left preceded by "Date:" and with "Sales Forecasting Report" in the center.
    Hint: Use Options Header, enter **Date: @|Sales Forecasting Report**, and then press ENTER.

4. Add a footer with "Page:" on the right side followed by the page number.
    Hint: Select Footer, and type **||Page: #**, and press ENTER.

5. Print the worksheet.
   Hint: Be sure that your printer is turned on and is online. Then select Quit Go. This quits the Options menu and then prints your worksheet with 1-2-3's default print settings.

6. Use 1-2-3 to form-feed the paper and print the footer at the bottom of the page.
   Hint: Select Page Align Quit.

7. Add a page break in A15.
   Hint: Select /Worksheet Page to insert a page break after positioning the cell pointer in A15.

8. Hide column F.
   Hint: Use /Worksheet Column Hide.

9. Specify row 1 as a border row.
   Hint: Use /Print Printer Options Borders Rows after positioning the cell pointer in row 1. Remember to check that row 1 is not part of your print range, or it will print twice on page 1.

10. Print the worksheet again.
    Hint: Use Quit Go Page Align.

11. Clear the border setting.
    Hint: Use Clear Borders.

12. Print the cell formulas.
    Hint: Use Options Other Cell-Formulas Quit Go Page Align.

13. Set the Print Options display back to printing what is displayed on the worksheet, and then quit the Print menu.
    Hint: Use Options Other As-Displayed Quit Quit.

REVIEW

- The Print menus provide the commands and options that you use to print your worksheets. Your initial selection from the Print menu is the destination. You can print directly to the printer or to a file with a .PRN extension. Once you select a destination, 1-2-3 displays the main Print menu. Release 2.2 features a

Print Settings sheet below the Print menu to track all of your print settings as you make changes.

- To print a worksheet, you must use Range from the main Print menu to select the area of the worksheet, and then select Go. Select additional enhancements before selecting Go.

- Print settings are saved with the worksheet data.

- You can control the printer with options in the Print menus. These options include Line to advance the printer one line, Page to advance the printer to the next page, and Align to reset the line count for the printer to zero.

- 1-2-3 makes several assumptions about how it should print a worksheet. These are the default settings. They include the margins and the page length, although options under /Print Printer Options allow you to change these assumptions.

- The /Print Printer Clear command selects which of 1-2-3's print settings are removed or returned to the default setting.

- A report can contain headers and footers that appear on every page. Headers and footers can contain the "at" symbol (@) for the current date and the number sign (#) for the current page number. Vertical lines can divide the header or footer sections to left-align, center, and right-align header and footer text. With Release 2.2, you can enter a cell address or range name to use the contents of the cell referenced.

- The /Print Printer Options Borders command selects the rows and columns that appear at the top and to the left of every page. Borders allow lengthy reports to retain their identification labels.

- You can activate specific printer features by using setup strings. The /Print Printer Options Setup command activates print features for the entire printing task. Embedded setup strings activate print features for a section of the print range.

- You can prevent columns from printing by hiding them with the /Worksheet Column Hide command.

- You can document a worksheet by printing the cell formulas. Normally, 1-2-3 prints the worksheet data as it appears.

- The /Worksheet Page command inserts a page break into a worksheet. When 1-2-3 prints a worksheet with a page break, it advances to the next page when it reaches the page break.

- You can suppress the headers, footers, and page breaks when you print by using the /Print Printer Options Other Unformatted command. This option is often used to print to a file that you want to use in another computer package.

Commands

Entry	Action
/PP	/Print Printer sends print output to the printer
/PF	/Print File sends print output to a file with a .PRN extension
/PPR	/Print Printer Range selects worksheet area to print
/PPC	/Print Printer Clear removes all print settings, the range setting, the borders print settings, or the settings for margins, page length, and setup string
/PPL	/Print Printer Line advances the printer one line
/PPP	/Print Printer Page advances the printer one page
/PPA	/Print Printer Align resets 1-2-3's line count to zero
/PPG	/Print Printer Go starts printing the current selected print area
/PPQ	/Print Printer Quit exits the sticky Print menu
/PPOH	/Print Printer Options Header sets the header that appears at the top of each page
/PPOF	/Print Printer Options Footer sets the footer that appears at the bottom of each page
/PPOM	/Print Printer Options Margin sets the top, bottom, left, and right margins, or removes all margins (Release 2.2)
/PPOB	/Print Printer Options Border selects the border columns and rows
/PPOS	/Print Printer Options Setup sets the setup string
/PPOP	/Print Printer Options Pg-Length sets the page length
/PPOO	/Print Printer Options Other sets additional print formatting, such as printing the worksheet as it appears or the cell formulas, and including the headers, footers, and page breaks or suppressing them
/PPOQ	/Print Printer Options Quit exits the sticky Print Options menu
/WP	/Worksheet Page inserts a page break into a worksheet
/WCH	/Worksheet Column Hide hides worksheet columns and does not print them

7

BASIC WORKSHEET FUNCTIONS

Built-in Function Basics
A Close-up Look at Each of the Function Categories
Review Exercise
Review

Your 1-2-3 models have already shown you the importance of formulas. Formulas are actually the power behind a spreadsheet package like 1-2-3: They record your calculations and use them over and over again. But there is a problem with formulas: It takes a long time to record them, and when you are recording a long series of calculations, it is easy to make a mistake. Fortunately, 1-2-3 has built-in functions to reduce these drawbacks. These functions are prerecorded formulas that have already been verified for accuracy. All you need to do is specify which data they should operate on, each time you use them. The built-in functions also provide features that go beyond the capabilities of formulas and let you access the system date as well as calculations such as the square root and tangent.

In this chapter you will examine how 1-2-3's built-in functions are recorded on the worksheet. You will learn the syntax and the rules that provide a powerhouse of almost 90 prerecorded calculations that you can access easily. You will learn about six of the eight function categories into which all 1-2-3 functions are grouped. A seventh category includes functions that allow you to add logical capabilities to your models easily, and is covered in Chapter 8. The eighth category includes the data-management functions. These functions will be covered in Chapter 9, when data-management features are discussed. In this chapter, however, you will examine a variety of functions from the different categories and learn how to use them in application models. This chapter is longer than previous ones because it explains the many diverse functions and exposes you to some of the variety offered by these functions.

BUILT-IN FUNCTION BASICS

A few general rules apply to all functions, regardless of their type. Yet individual functions may differ from one another in terms of how they expect you to convey the data with which you want them to work. You need to know the general rules and the individual exceptions, as well as which category of function is likely to handle the task you wish to address. This section provides such information. Read it before addressing the individual function categories; it is an important first step.

General Rules

Since built-in functions are formulas, they are value entries in worksheet cells. There are several new rules that do not apply to formulas, all pertaining to the syntax of recording the different components of a function. A diagram of these components is shown in Figure 7-1. The first rule for function entry is that all functions must start with the symbol @. After entering the symbol @, you must include the special keyword that 1-2-3 uses to represent the function. This keyword is the function's name. You can enter it in either upper- or lowercase letters, but it must follow 1-2-3's spelling exactly.

RULES FOR FUNCTION ARGUMENTS   The next component within a function is the *arguments*. Arguments specify the data with which the function will work. Arguments are required by most functions, since most functions must be defined exactly in the order to be used. However, there are a few exceptions to this rule. Arguments must be enclosed within parentheses; but if the function you are using does not require arguments, you do not need to use parentheses.

When using a function that requires multiple arguments, use a comma (,) to separate the arguments. With Release 2 and higher, a semicolon (;) is an acceptable alternative. Spaces cannot be used within a function; therefore, they are not valid as separator characters. The /Worksheet Global Default Other International Punctuations command sets the argument separator, which may also include a period.

Function arguments can be provided as cell addresses, a range name that you assign to one or more cells, constants, formulas, and even other built-in functions. The examples you enter in this chapter may include some constants in functions to expedite

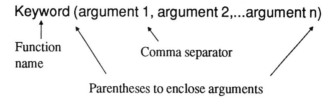

Keyword (argument 1, argument 2,...argument n)

Function
name

Comma separator

Parentheses to enclose arguments

FIGURE 7-1.   Function format

data entry. However, it is preferable to store the data needed by the function in worksheet cells and to reference those cells within the function, since a change in an argument's value will not require that you edit the function. Much variety is possible; look at these examples of the @SUM functions, which total the values you provide as arguments:

@SUM(9,4,8,7)
@SUM(A1;D3;Y6;Z10)
@SUM(Salaries,Rent_Exp,Equipment)
@SUM(A1..H4)
@SUM(A1,@SUM(B2..B3),Z2)

All five would be valid function entries, although you would need Release 2 or higher for the semicolons in the second example. As you progress through the exercises in this chapter, you will have an opportunity to use different types of arguments.

Most of the built-in functions expect value entries for arguments. Release 2 and higher have some built-in functions that require string or character data for arguments. You cannot substitute a type of data for an argument that is different from what 1-2-3 is expecting. For example, if you use 1-2-3's @SUM function, you will need to provide value entries as arguments. @SUM will add these together to produce a total. If you substitute label entries for the arguments, @SUM will return an error.

DIFFERENT TYPES OF FUNCTION ARGUMENTS   Different functions require different arguments and use them in different ways. The three basic types of functions are those that require no arguments, those that expect a list of arguments in any sequence, and those that require a specific number of arguments in a specific order.

Examples of functions that require no arguments are @RAND, @NA, and @PI. *@RAND* is used to generate a random number and does not require any input. *@NA* is used when data is missing and you want to mark its position as not available at the current time. *@PI* is used to represent the special mathematical constant 3.14159265, which is used in geometric problem solving.

There are also a number of functions that expect a list of values for arguments. The entries in the list can be single cells or ranges of cells, and can be provided in any order you like. All the statistical functions fall within this category of argument types. For example, these two functions are equivalent:

@SUM(A1,B4,C5,D2..D10,F1,H2..M4)
@SUM(F1,H2..M4,A1,C5,D2..D10,B4)

In both cases all the individual values, as well as each of the values in the ranges, will be totaled to produce a single sum. Functions that allow this interchangeability of argument order specify "list" as their argument. For example, since @SUM accepts this type of argument, you can expect to see @SUM(list) when we discuss the syntax of this function in detail.

The last type of function argument is position dependent. Functions that require arguments in a specific order cannot have their arguments reordered without erroneous results occurring. For example, the @PMT function is designed to calculate the amount of a loan payment. The function requires three arguments: the principal, the interest, and the term of the loan. Later in the chapter you will see the functions specified like this:

@PMT(principal,interest,term of loan)

When using the function, you must provide the three arguments in this exact order.

Chapter Organization

There are seven categories of functions in 1-2-3, excluding the data management functions. The various function categories form the organizational structure of the rest of this chapter. You can use the remainder of the chapter in two ways. The preferred approach is to work through the exercises in each function category to become familiar with their use. There may be function categories that apply to your models, but unless you take an in-depth look at what they can do, you might not realize their potential. Another approach, if your time is limited, is to focus on function categories for which you have immediate use, then to come back and take a look at the other categories as you need them.

A CLOSE-UP LOOK AT EACH OF THE FUNCTION CATEGORIES

The built-in functions are grouped into categories such that the functions within a category have some similarity of purpose. This logical grouping of functions allows you to focus easily on the special requirements of a category. It can also help you increase your knowledge of new functions whose purpose might be similar to some functions you are already using. For example, if you are working with the @PMT and @FV functions from the financial category, it is wise to look closely at the other financial functions. Many of them may provide useful features in your models. Although this chapter covers only a subset of the functions, a comprehensive list of all the functions can be found at the end of Chapter 10.

As you work through this section you will find that Release 2 and higher have functions that do not occur in Release 1A. Release 2 was given a whole new category of functions for working with string data. Within individual categories, these new functions for users of Release 2 and higher are appropriately marked.

Statistical Functions

"Statistics" is a word that causes many people to be apprehensive. They recall statistics as complicated mathematical procedures from a required college math course. But 1-2-3's statistical functions need not invoke this sense of alarm. They are simple to use, and they compute the most basic statistical measures. These are computations that you perform every day without even thinking of them as "statistical." They include computations such as the average, sum, count, minimum value, and maximum value.

1-2-3's statistical functions perform their magic on lists of values. Frequently these lists are a contiguous range of cells on the worksheet. They can also be a series of individual values or a combination of a range and individual values. Blank cells can be included in the list, but all the values in the blank range will count as zeros. When a range contains multiple blank cells, 1-2-3 will ignore the cells that contain blanks.

The @COUNT function is an exception to the others in the statistical category. It counts the number of non-blank entries in the list. It can accept string values in its argument list in addition to numeric values.

You will use one model to test all the statistical functions. It will contain information on the monthly sales for all the High Profits Company salespeople in region 4, as shown in Figure 7-2. Follow these steps to create the basic model before continuing:

1. Select /Worksheet Global Format Currency. Type **0** and press ENTER.

     This command establishes a Global format for the model before you enter data. Next you will format a section of the model that requires whole numbers to be displayed without the dollar sign.

G6: [W11] @SUM(D6..F6)   READY

	A	B	C	D	E	F	G
1				High Profits Quarterly Sales Figures			
2				Region 4			
3							
4				Jan	Feb	Mar	Qtr.
5	Salesperson	District	Branch	Sales	Sales	Sales	Total
6	Jason Rye	1	1705	$95,000	$105,650	$114,785	$316,235
7	Paul Jones	3	3201	$56,780	$52,300	$48,750	$157,830
8	Mary Hart	1	1705	$89,675	$108,755	$135,400	$333,830
9	Tom Bush	2	4250	$91,555	$87,600	$92,300	$271,455
10	Gary Lowe	2	4250	$76,900	$82,600	$83,500	$243,000
11	Karen Stein	3	2950	$68,565	$76,500	$82,300	$227,365
12	Cindy Boyd	2	4590	$110,800	$153,400	$105,665	$369,865
13	Jim Rogers	1	1921	$98,000	$114,785	$114,785	$327,570
14							
15		TOTAL SALES		$688,075	$781,590	$777,485	$2,247,150
16							

FIGURE 7-2.   Using the financial functions

2. Select /Range Format Fixed. Type **0** and press ENTER. Type **B6.C13** and press ENTER.

3. Move the cell pointer to column A and select /Worksheet Column Set-Width. Press the RIGHT ARROW key four times and press ENTER.

   This action widens this column to 13 positions in preparation for the data to be entered. There is one more column to be widened. You could have entered these commands, like the formatting command, after you entered the data in the worksheet. However, if you know what your final report will look like, it is often best to perform the housekeeping tasks first.

4. Move the cell pointer to column G and select /Worksheet Column Set-Width. Press the RIGHT ARROW key twice for a width of 11 and press ENTER.

   Once you have completed the housekeeping tasks, you are ready to begin entering the data for the model. You can use the completed model in Figure 7-2 as a guide to obtaining the entries, or you can use the detailed entries in step 5.

5. Place the following entries in the worksheet cells listed:

   C1:   High Profits Quarterly Sales Figures
   D2:   Region 4
   A5:   Salesperson

A6:	Jason Rye
A7:	Paul Jones
A8:	Mary Hart
A9:	Tom Bush
A10:	Gary Lowe
A11:	Karen Stein
A12:	Cindy Boyd
A13:	Jim Rogers
B5:	District
B6:	1
B7:	3
B8:	1
B9:	2
B10:	2
B11:	3
B12:	2
B13:	1
B15:	TOTAL SALES
C5:	Branch
C6:	1705
C7:	3201
C8:	1705
C9:	4250
C10:	4250
C11:	2950
C12:	4590
C13:	1921
D4:	Jan
D5:	Sales
D6:	95800
D7:	56780
D8:	89675
D9:	91555
D10:	76900
D11:	68565
D12:	110800
D13:	98000
E4:	Feb
E5:	Sales
E6:	105650
E7:	52300

E8:	108755
E9:	87600
E10:	82600
E11:	76500
E12:	153400
E13:	114785
F4:	Mar
F5:	Sales
F6:	114785
F7:	48750
F8:	135400
F9:	92300
F10:	83500
F11:	82300
F12:	105665
F13:	114785
G4:	Qtr.
G5:	Total

6. Move the cell pointer to D4 and select /Range Label Right. Move the cell pointer to G5 and press ENTER.

Your model should match the one in Figure 7-3. You are now ready to use it in testing the statistical functions.

D4: "Jan   READY

	A	B	C	D	E	F	G
1			High Profits Quarterly Sales Figures			
2				Region 4			
3							
4				Jan	Feb	Mar	Qtr.
5	Salesperson	District	Branch	Sales	Sales	Sales	Total
6	Jason Rye	1	1705	$95,800	$105,650	$114,785	
7	Paul Jones	3	3201	$56,780	$52,300	$48,750	
8	Mary Hart	1	1705	$89,675	$108,755	$135,400	
9	Tom Bush	2	4250	$91,555	$87,600	$92,300	
10	Gary Lowe	2	4250	$76,900	$82,600	$83,500	
11	Karen Stein	3	2950	$68,565	$76,500	$82,300	
12	Cindy Boyd	2	4590	$110,800	$153,400	$105,665	
13	Jim Rogers	1	1921	$98,000	$114,785	$114,785	
14							

FIGURE 7-3.   Right-aligning the labels

D15:
@SUM(

`VALUE`

	A	B	C	D	E	F	G
				High Profits Quarterly Sales Figures			
1							
2				Region 4			
3							
4				Jan	Feb	Mar	Qtr.
5	Salesperson	District	Branch	Sales	Sales	Sales	Total
6	Jason Rye	1	1705	$95,800	$105,650	$114,785	
7	Paul Jones	3	3201	$56,780	$52,300	$48,750	
8	Mary Hart	1	1705	$89,675	$108,755	$135,400	
9	Tom Bush	2	4250	$91,555	$87,600	$92,300	
10	Gary Lowe	2	4250	$76,900	$82,600	$83,500	
11	Karen Stein	3	2950	$68,565	$76,500	$82,300	
12	Cindy Boyd	2	4590	$110,800	$153,400	$105,665	
13	Jim Rogers	1	1921	$98,000	$114,785	$114,785	
14							
15			TOTAL SALES	████████			
16							

FIGURE 7-4. Entering @SUM

@SUM   The *@SUM* function totals a list of values. The syntax for the function is @SUM(list). The list can be a range of values, a list of individual values separated by commas (the argument separator), or a combination of the two.

@SUM is one of the most frequently used functions. It easily performs the laborious task of adding all of the numbers in a range without having to enter a long formula to add each value separately. It can be used just as easily to total a row of values. As with any other formula, once you have entered it for one row or column, you can easily copy it to other locations where you have similar needs.

Using @SUM to Total Sales   You will use the @SUM function to compute the total sales in each month and the total sales for each salesperson during the quarter. Follow these steps to add the sum computations:

1. Move the cell pointer to D15 as shown in Figure 7-4 and type **@SUM(**.

2. Move the cell pointer to D6 and type **.** (period) to lock the beginning of the range in place. Then move the cell pointer to D13 to highlight all the entries, as shown in Figure 7-5.

3. Type **)** and press ENTER to display the results shown in Figure 7-6.
    You have just entered your first @SUM function using the pointing method for specifying the range. If you prefer, you can always type the range address

D13: 98000   POINT
@SUM(D6..D13)

```
         A         B        C         D         E         F         G
1                      High Profits Quarterly Sales Figures
2                                Region 4
3
4                                   Jan      Feb      Mar      Qtr.
5   Salesperson District Branch    Sales    Sales    Sales    Total
6   Jason Rye        1      1705  $95,800 $105,650 $114,785
7   Paul Jones       3      3201  $56,780  $52,300  $48,750
8   Mary Hart        1      1705  $89,675 $108,755 $135,400
9   Tom Bush         2      4250  $91,555  $87,600  $92,300
10  Gary Lowe        2      4250  $76,900  $82,600  $83,500
11  Karen Stein      3      2950  $68,565  $76,500  $82,300
12  Cindy Boyd       2      4590 $110,800 $153,400 $105,665
13  Jim Rogers       1      1921  $98,000 $114,785 $114,785
14
15             TOTAL SALES
16
```

FIGURE 7-5.   Highlighting the range

rather than pointing to it, but the pointing method helps prevent errors. As you point to the beginning of the range you want to sum, you get visual verification that this is the correct beginning location for the calculation. The same is true when you point to the end of the range, since 1-2-3 highlights everything in

D15: @SUM(D6..D13)   READY

```
         A         B        C         D         E         F         G
1                      High Profits Quarterly Sales Figures
2                                Region 4
3
4                                   Jan      Feb      Mar      Qtr.
5   Salesperson District Branch    Sales    Sales    Sales    Total
6   Jason Rye        1      1705  $95,800 $105,650 $114,785
7   Paul Jones       3      3201  $56,780  $52,300  $48,750
8   Mary Hart        1      1705  $89,675 $108,755 $135,400
9   Tom Bush         2      4250  $91,555  $87,600  $92,300
10  Gary Lowe        2      4250  $76,900  $82,600  $83,500
11  Karen Stein      3      2950  $68,565  $76,500  $82,300
12  Cindy Boyd       2      4590 $110,800 $153,400 $105,665
13  Jim Rogers       1      1921  $98,000 $114,785 $114,785
14
15             TOTAL SALES       $688,075
16
```

FIGURE 7-6.   @SUM completed

the range. Either way you choose to enter the @SUM function, this function is a lot quicker than typing +D6+D7+D8+D9+D10+D11+D12+D13—the alternate method for computing the desired result.

4. With the cell pointer in D15, select /Copy. Press ENTER. Then move the cell pointer to E15 and type . (period) before moving the cell pointer to G15 and pressing ENTER.

   This Copy command totaled all the columns for you, giving you maximum use from the one function you entered.

5. Move the cell pointer to G6. Type **@SUM(**. Move the cell pointer to D6. Type ., and then move the cell pointer to F6. Type) and press ENTER.

   This formula produced a quarterly sales figure for Jason Rye.

6. Select /Copy and press ENTER. Move the cell pointer to G7 and type .. Then move the cell pointer to G13 and press ENTER.

This last instruction copies the totals down the column so that you now have a total sales figure for each salesperson for the quarter, as in the model shown earlier in Figure 7-2.

Allowing for Expansion   The example you just completed computes the monthly sales totals correctly. But if you want to add another salesperson to the bottom of the list, you need to revise the @SUM formulas at the bottoms of the columns so they include a reference to the cell containing the figure for the new employee. You don't need to do this, however, if you insert a blank row in the middle of the sum range and enter the new data there. In that case, the new row will be included automatically since 1-2-3 will expand the range. The problem is that most of your additions are at the very top or bottom of the range and 1-2-3 does not stretch the range to include these new rows. However, you can overcome this revision requirement by entering your initial sum formula a little differently.

Leaving a blank row at the top and the bottom of the column you are summing will give you the expansion capability you need. If your original @SUM range includes a blank row at the top and bottom of the range, you can insert blank rows at the top or bottom and 1-2-3 will adjust the range for you. The blank rows do not affect the @SUM results since 1-2-3 treats them as zero. To alter the original @SUM formula and then copy it across again in preparation for adding a new salesperson, follow these steps:

1. Move the cell pointer to A6 and select /Worksheet Insert Row. Then press ENTER to produce a display like the one shown in Figure 7-7.

2. Move the cell pointer to D16 and type **@SUM(D6..D15)**. Then press ENTER.

A6: [W13]   READY

```
          A         B          C         D         E         F         G
                         High Profits Quarterly Sales Figures
                                      Region 4

                                         Jan       Feb       Mar       Qtr.
   Salesperson  District  Branch        Sales     Sales     Sales     Total

   Jason Rye              1       1705  $95,800  $105,650 $114,785  $316,235
   Paul Jones            3       3201  $56,780   $52,300  $48,750  $157,830
   Mary Hart             1       1705  $89,675 $108,755 $135,400  $333,830
   Tom Bush              2       4250  $91,555  $87,600  $92,300  $271,455
   Gary Lowe             2       4250  $76,900  $82,600  $83,500  $243,000
   Karen Stein           3       2950  $68,565  $76,500  $82,300  $227,365
   Cindy Boyd            2       4590 $110,800 $153,400 $105,665  $369,865
   Jim Rogers            1       1921  $98,000 $114,785 $114,785  $327,570

              TOTAL SALES          $688,075 $781,590 $777,485 $2,247,150
```

FIGURE 7-7.   Inserting a blank row to facilitate expansion

3. Select /Copy and press ENTER. Move the cell pointer to E16 and type .. Then move the cell pointer to G16 and press ENTER.

   These new @SUM entries will allow you to expand your entries at either the top or the bottom of the database by placing the cell pointer in either row 6 or row 15 and using /Worksheet Insert Row to add a new blank row for the new employee information.

4. Move the cell pointer to A7 and select /Worksheet Insert Row and press ENTER.

5. Make these entries to add the new salesperson:

   A7:   Jane Hunt
   B7:   2
   C7:   4590
   D7:   87650
   E7:   92300
   F7:   93415
   G7:   @SUM(D7..F7)

   Notice in Figure 7-8 that the totals for each month have been adjusted to show the new results. This means that you will be able to add new entries in any location within the data and have the formula updated for you automatically. The district and branch values in this new line are formatted as fixed with 0

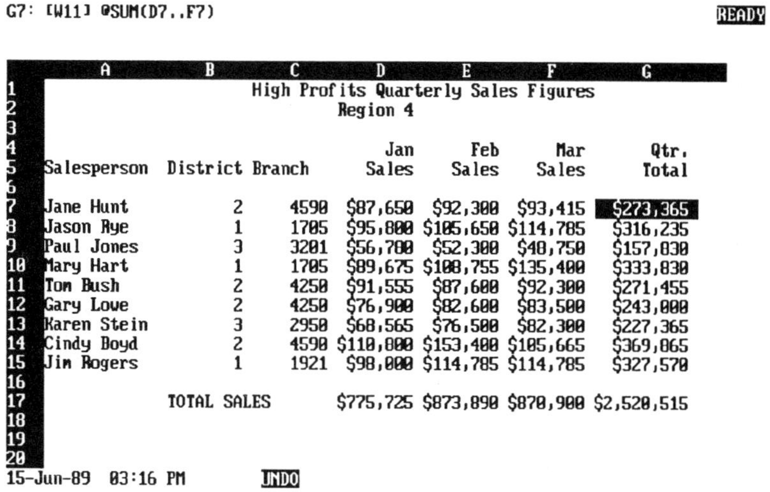

G7: [W11] @SUM(D7..F7)   READY

```
        A          B        C         D         E         F         G
1                          High Profits Quarterly Sales Figures
2                                     Region 4
3
4                                      Jan       Feb       Mar      Qtr.
5  Salesperson  District Branch       Sales     Sales     Sales    Total
6
7  Jane Hunt            2    4590   $87,650   $92,300   $93,415   $273,365
8  Jason Rye           1    1705   $95,800  $105,650  $114,785   $316,235
9  Paul Jones          3    3201   $56,700   $52,300   $40,750   $157,830
10 Mary Hart           1    1705   $89,675  $100,755  $135,400   $333,830
11 Tom Bush            2    4250   $91,555   $87,600   $92,300   $271,455
12 Gary Love           2    4250   $76,900   $82,600   $83,500   $243,000
13 Karen Stein         3    2950   $68,565   $76,500   $82,300   $227,365
14 Cindy Boyd          2    4590  $110,800  $153,400  $105,665   $369,865
15 Jim Rogers          1    1921   $98,000  $114,785  $114,785   $327,570
16
17              TOTAL SALES        $775,725  $873,890  $870,900 $2,520,515
18
19
20
```

15-Jun-89   03:16 PM   UNDO

FIGURE 7-8.   Total for the quarter

decimal place using the /Range Format command. The original ranges that were formatted did not include these cells.

6. Move the cell pointer to B7 and select /Range Format Fixed, type **0**, and press ENTER. Move the cell pointer to C7 and press ENTER. The results are shown in Figure 7-8.

@COUNT   The @COUNT function returns the number of non-blank entries in a list. Its syntax is @COUNT(list), where list can represent a range or it can represent individual cells, just as it did in the @SUM function. Unlike the other statistical functions, @COUNT does not require value entries. It can count employee names as well as entries in the sales column.

Entries that contain zero are not equivalent to blanks and will be counted. You must carefully choose which column or row of a worksheet to count since you want to select data where mandatory entries are required for each record. Otherwise, the computed count may be artificially low due to the blank values in certain fields.

Follow these steps to count the number of sales personnel for region 4 of High Profit:

1. Move the cell pointer to B18 and type '# **SALES PERSONNEL**.

2. Move the cell pointer to D18, type **@COUNT(A6.A16)**, and press ENTER.

D18: (F0) @COUNT(A6..A16)   READY

	A	B	C	D	E	F	G
1				High Profits Quarterly Sales Figures			
2				Region 4			
3							
4				Jan	Feb	Mar	Qtr.
5	Salesperson	District	Branch	Sales	Sales	Sales	Total
6							
7	Jane Hunt	2	4590	$87,650	$92,300	$93,415	$273,365
8	Jason Rye	1	1705	$95,800	$105,650	$114,785	$316,235
9	Paul Jones	3	3201	$56,780	$52,300	$48,750	$157,830
10	Mary Hart	1	1705	$89,675	$108,755	$135,400	$333,830
11	Tom Bush	2	4250	$91,555	$87,600	$92,300	$271,455
12	Gary Lowe	2	4250	$76,900	$82,600	$83,500	$243,000
13	Karen Stein	3	2950	$68,565	$76,500	$82,300	$227,365
14	Cindy Boyd	2	4590	$110,800	$153,400	$105,665	$369,865
15	Jim Rogers	1	1921	$98,000	$114,785	$114,785	$327,570
16							
17		TOTAL SALES		$775,725	$873,890	$870,900	$2,520,515
18		# SALES PERSONNEL		9			
19							

FIGURE 7-9.   Using @COUNT

The name field was chosen for counting the number of entries since it is assumed that all sales personnel have a name entry. It is possible that some salespeople who were not employed for the full quarter do not have all the months of sales data, and that counting these other fields could cause results to be lower than they should be.

3. Select /Range Format Fixed, type **0**, and press ENTER twice.
   Your model should match the display in Figure 7-9.

4. Select /File Save, type **SUMCOUNT**, and press ENTER.

The @COUNT function has widespread applicability. You can use it to count the number of loan payments that have been received. You can count the number of items in your inventory. Once you have mastered the basics you will find many worksheets where the @COUNT feature is useful.

@MIN   The *@MIN* function searches a list of values and returns the smallest value in the list. Its syntax is @MIN(list). You could use this function to find the lowest contract bid if all your bid figures were listed on a worksheet. You could also use it to find the lowest recorded temperature, the supplier with the lowest price for an item,

G19: [W11] @MIN(G6..G16)   READY

A	B	C	D	E	F	G
1			High Profits Quarterly Sales Figures			
2			Region 4			
3						
4			Jan	Feb	Mar	Qtr.
5	Salesperson	District Branch	Sales	Sales	Sales	Total
6						
7	Jane Hunt	2	4590	$87,650	$92,300	$93,415	$273,365
8	Jason Rye	1	1705	$95,800	$105,650	$114,785	$316,235
9	Paul Jones	3	3201	$56,780	$52,300	$48,750	$157,830
10	Mary Hart	1	1705	$89,675	$100,755	$135,400	$333,030
11	Tom Bush	2	4250	$91,555	$87,600	$92,300	$271,455
12	Gary Lowe	2	4250	$76,900	$82,600	$83,500	$243,000
13	Karen Stein	3	2950	$68,565	$76,500	$82,300	$227,365
14	Cindy Boyd	2	4590	$110,800	$153,400	$105,665	$369,865
15	Jim Rogers	1	1921	$98,000	$114,785	$114,785	$327,570
16						
17		TOTAL SALES		$775,725	$873,890	$870,900	$2,520,515
18		# SALES PERSONNEL	9			
19			LOWEST QTR SALES FIGURE			$157,830
20						

FIGURE 7-10.   Using @MIN

the individual who is paid the lowest salary, or in the case of the High Profit model, the lowest sales amount for a month or for the quarter.

Add a label and a calculation to show the sales for the worst performer in region 4 with these steps:

1. Move the cell pointer to D19, type **LOWEST QTR SALES FIGURE**, and move the cell pointer to G19.

2. Type **@MIN(G6.G16)** and press ENTER to produce the results shown in Figure 7-10.

You could use this low sales amount to help you establish incentive programs or minimum sales standards.

The @MIN function will ignore blank cells. Cells that contain characters are evaluated as zero and could therefore erroneously be considered the lowest value in a list. Note that the function does not highlight the entry that produced the lowest value; it only returns it. If you want to find the entry that matches the returned value, you must visually scan the values in the cells that constitute the list.

G20: [W11] @MAX(G6..G16)   READY

	A	B	C	D	E	F	G
1			High Profits Quarterly Sales Figures				
2			Region 4				
3							
4				Jan	Feb	Mar	Qtr.
5	Salesperson	District	Branch	Sales	Sales	Sales	Total
6							
7	Jane Hunt	2	4590	$87,650	$92,300	$93,415	$273,365
8	Jason Rye	1	1705	$95,800	$105,650	$114,785	$316,235
9	Paul Jones	3	3201	$56,780	$52,300	$48,750	$157,830
10	Mary Hart	1	1705	$89,675	$108,755	$135,400	$333,830
11	Tom Bush	2	4250	$91,555	$87,600	$92,300	$271,455
12	Gary Lowe	2	4250	$76,900	$82,600	$83,500	$243,000
13	Karen Stein	3	2950	$68,565	$76,500	$82,300	$227,365
14	Cindy Boyd	2	4590	$110,800	$153,400	$105,665	$369,865
15	Jim Rogers	1	1921	$98,000	$114,785	$114,785	$327,570
16							
17		TOTAL SALES		$775,725	$873,890	$870,900	$2,520,515
18		# SALES PERSONNEL		9			
19				LOWEST QTR SALES FIGURE			$157,830
20				LARGEST QTR SALES FIGURE			$369,865

FIGURE 7-11.   Using @MAX

@MAX   The *@MAX* function examines a list of values and returns the largest value in the list. It returns the exact opposite of @MIN but uses an identical syntax of @MAX(list). You could use it to find the amount sold by the top performer, the highest hourly wage or annual salary, or the highest temperature in the month of August (assuming that the worksheet contains appropriate data values for these items).

Use @MAX to determine the highest sales for the quarter by making the following entries:

1. Move the cell pointer to D20 and type **LARGEST QTR SALES FIGURE**. Then move the cell pointer to G20.

2. Type **@MAX(G6.G16)** and press ENTER.
   Like the @MIN function, @MAX ignores blank cells. It also treats labels as zeros. The results are shown in Figure 7-11.

3. Select /File Save, type **MIN_MAX**, and press ENTER.

D19: @AVG(D6..D16)   READY

	A	B	C	D	E	F	G
1			High Profits Quarterly Sales Figures				
2			Region 4				
3							
4				Jan	Feb	Mar	Qtr.
5	Salesperson	District	Branch	Sales	Sales	Sales	Total
6							
7	Jane Hunt	2	4590	$87,650	$92,300	$93,415	$273,365
8	Jason Rye	1	1705	$95,800	$105,650	$114,785	$316,235
9	Paul Jones	3	3201	$56,780	$52,300	$48,750	$157,830
10	Mary Hart	1	1705	$89,675	$108,755	$135,400	$333,830
11	Tom Bush	2	4250	$91,555	$87,600	$92,300	$271,455
12	Gary Lowe	2	4250	$76,900	$82,600	$83,500	$243,000
13	Karen Stein	3	2950	$68,565	$76,500	$82,300	$227,365
14	Cindy Boyd	2	4590	$110,800	$153,400	$105,665	$369,865
15	Jim Rogers	1	1921	$98,000	$114,785	$114,785	$327,570
16							
17		TOTAL SALES		$775,725	$873,890	$870,900	$2,520,515
18		# SALES PERSONNEL		9			
19		AVERAGE SALES		$86,192	$97,099	$96,767	$280,057
20							

FIGURE 7-12.   Using @AVG

@AVG   The @AVG function returns one value: the arithmetic average of all the values in a list. It is computed by summing all the values in the list and then dividing this sum by the number of entries in the list. @AVG is equivalent to the calculation @SUM(list)/@COUNT(list), and it uses the syntax @AVG(list).

You can use this new function to determine the average sales for each month. Follow these steps:

1. Select /File Retrieve, type **SUMCOUNT**, and press ENTER.
   This will bring the original @SUM example into memory.

2. Move the cell pointer to B19 and type **AVERAGE SALES**. Then move the cell pointer to D19.

3. Type **@AVG(D6.D16)** and press ENTER.

4. Select /Copy and press ENTER. Move the cell pointer to E19 and type .. Move the cell pointer to G19 and press ENTER.

You should now have the average for all three months and the quarter total in your model, as shown in Figure 7-12.

Date and Time Functions

Date and time information are an important part of many business decisions. Date information is needed to tell if a loan is overdue or if there is still time remaining in the discount period for an invoice. Time information can be used to calculate the service time for various tasks or to log the delivery time for various carriers. Release 1A contains functions that support the date-stamping of worksheets and the use of dates in various calculations. Release 2 and higher have time functions that allow you to time-stamp a worksheet and perform calculations that involve time differences.

WORKING WITH DATES   1-2-3 can work with dates between January 1, 1900, and December 31, 2099. A unique serial number is assigned to each date: The number for January 1, 1900, is 1 and the number for December 31, 2099, is 73050. This serial date number represents the number of days since December 31, 1899. Although representing every date in terms of its distance from December 31, 1899, may seem strange, this is what provides the date arithmetic features of the package. Since all dates have the same comparison point, you can subtract one date from another to determine how many days apart they are. If a loan is due on a date whose serial date number is 32980 and today's serial date number is 32990, then it is obvious that the loan is overdue since the serial number for the due date is lower than today's serial date number.

All of this may seem a little confusing, but 1-2-3 can reduce some of the difficulty. You will not need to calculate or enter serial date numbers. 1-2-3 does that for you with its date functions. 1-2-3 also provides a format command that formats serial date numbers so they look presentable. You can choose from a variety of date formats that are familiar to you in the Range Format menu.

Date-Stamping the Worksheet   All releases of 1-2-3 provide a way for you to put a *date stamp* on the worksheet. With Release 1A, the function you will use is *@TODAY*. This function does not require arguments; when you enter it in a worksheet cell, it always accesses the system date and displays the serial date number for the system date in the worksheet cell where you entered the function. You can use /Range Format to change the appearance of this serial date number to something more familiar. Release 2 and higher provide the identical feature, except that the function you enter is *@NOW*. You will learn some additional features of @NOW later, but for the moment the only important information about @NOW is that it enters a serial number in the worksheet cell.

The serial number contains two parts with @NOW. It consists of a whole number and a decimal fraction. The whole number represents the serial date number and the decimal fraction represents the current time. Both the date and time will be updated every time the current model is recalculated. If you save your worksheet file after entering the @NOW function, it will be available the next time you use the worksheet. Every time you boot your system, you will want to ensure that the correct date is being used so that your models can be time-stamped accurately.

You can try out this date-stamping feature with these instructions, but remember to adjust them for Release 1A by substituting @TODAY for @NOW:

1. Select /Worksheet Erase Yes.

2. Type **@NOW** and press ENTER.

   If you are using Release 2 or higher, you should see a date number display that looks something like this:

Your display will be slightly different, since it will be based on the date when you are using the worksheet. There will be an even greater difference if you are using Release 1A because the options are not the same. Once entered, this function will be updated every time the worksheet is recalculated; so if you work with the spreadsheet past midnight, you will see the date change. If you save the worksheet to disk, the next time you retrieve the worksheet an updated date will appear in the cell that contains @NOW.

3. Select /Worksheet Column Set-Width and press the RIGHT ARROW key. Then press ENTER.

   This instruction widens the display so that you can view the date and time display in this column.

4. Select /Range Format Date to produce this display:

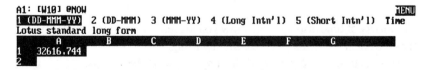

This display shows the various date-formatting options.

5. Use the RIGHT ARROW key and move to each of the menu options to view the date pattern that would be produced by selecting that option. Then select option 1 by typing **1** and pressing ENTER.

The serial date number should now be formatted with a pattern like this:

Remember that your display will look a little different, since your date is probably different from the one used for this example.

   If you include @NOW in an area of your worksheet that you normally print, you will have an automatic date stamp on every printed report you create. Since you must retrieve the worksheet in order to print it, the date will automatically be updated every time the worksheet is printed.

Time-Stamping the Worksheet   The *time-stamp* feature is accessed with the @NOW function and is only available for Release 2 and higher. The difference between using @NOW to date-stamp the worksheet and to time-stamp it is the format that you place on the result of the function. @NOW returns both a whole number and a fractional decimal. The whole number represents the number of days; the fractional decimal represents the portion of the current day that has already elapsed. If the decimal is .25, it represents a quarter of the day as having elapsed, or 6 A.M. A decimal fraction of .5 represents noon and .75 represents 6 P.M. Naturally, all the fractions between the ones listed also represent specific times within the day.

   To see these time displays as other than decimal fractions, you will need to format the entries as Time. Do this by using /Range Format Date Time, producing the following display for your selection:

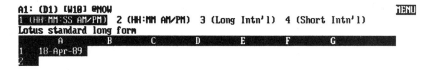

The variety of time displays will allow you to create a report that closely matches the organizational standards you are currently using.

   You can time-stamp your worksheet by following these steps:

   1. Move the cell pointer to A2, type **@NOW**, and press ENTER.

   2. Select /Range Format Date Time 2 and press ENTER.

Your display will be formatted like the following one, although the hour and minutes in the display will depend on the time of day when you make your entry.

A2: (D7) [W18] @NOW   READY

Entering Dates Many times when you work with dates, you do not want the current date. You want to record the date of hire, loan due date, or an upcoming anniversary date. 1-2-3 provides a way for you to record this date information in the worksheet. You use the *@DATE* function and supply arguments that represent the year, month, and day.

This function is the first one you have worked with where the arguments must be supplied in a specific order, as shown in this syntax:

@DATE(YR,MO,DA)

The first argument, *YR,* can be any number from 0 to 199, with 1900 represented by 0, 1989 by 89, and 2099 by 199. The month argument, *MO,* can be any number from 1 through 12. The day argument, *DA,* can be a number from 1 to 31, but it must be a valid day number for the month you select. For example, September cannot have 31 because 30 is the largest number of days in September. Since you will want the function to generate the correct serial date number for you, you must adhere exactly to the order shown for the three arguments.

You can put the @DATE function to work in a model that calculates the charges for video rentals. In this example, the charges will depend on the number of days that a patron has had the video. You will enter the customer number in column A, the video

E5: (C2) (D5-C5)*2.25   READY

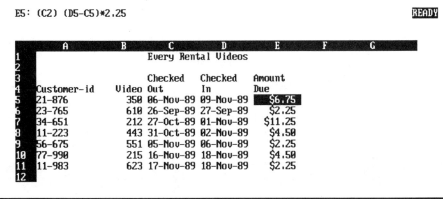

FIGURE 7-13. Result of subtracting two dates

number in column B, the date the video was checked out in column C, and the date it was returned in column D. These last two entries will be used to compute the charges. The formula you use will subtract the date when the video was checked out from the date when it was returned and multiply the number of days by $2.25. Follow these steps to make the entries and apply the formats shown in Figure 7-13.

1. Select /Worksheet Erase Yes and make these entries in the worksheet cells listed:

A4:	Customer-id
A5:	'21-876
A6:	'23-765
A7:	'34-651
A8:	'11-223
A9:	'56-675
A10:	'77-990
A11:	'11-983
B4:	Video
B5:	350
B6:	610
B7:	212
B8:	443
B9:	551
B10:	215
B11:	623
C1:	Every Rental Videos
C3:	Checked
C4:	Out
D3:	Checked
D4:	In
E3:	Amount
E4:	Due

2. Now enter these dates using the @DATE function:

C5:	@DATE(89,11,6)
C6:	@DATE(89,9,26)
C7:	@DATE(89,10,27)
C8:	@DATE(89,10,31)
C9:	@DATE(89,11,5)
C10:	@DATE(89,11,16)
C11:	@DATE(89,11,17)
D5:	@DATE(89,11,9)

D6:	@DATE(89,9,27)
D7:	@DATE(89,11,1)
D8:	@DATE(89,11,2)
D9:	@DATE(89,11,6)
D10:	@DATE(89,11,18)
D11:	@DATE(89,11,18)

3. Move the cell pointer to E5 and type **(D5-C5)∗2.25**.

   This entry is the computation for the cost of the rental. This computation is the number of days times the daily charge of $2.25. But first you must calculate the number of days by subtracting the two dates.

4. Select /Copy and press ENTER. Move the cell pointer to E6 and type **..** Then move the cell pointer to E11 and press ENTER.

5. Press HOME, and select /Worksheet Column Set-Width. Then type **16** and press ENTER.

6. Move the cell pointer to C5. Select /Range Format Date 1. Type **C5.D11** and press ENTER.

7. Select /Worksheet Column Column-Range Set-Width. Then press the RIGHT ARROW key and press ENTER to select columns C and D. Press the RIGHT ARROW key so that the dates display properly. Then press ENTER. If you are using Release 2, 2.01, or 1A, you must increase the width of each column separately.

8. Move the cell pointer to E5. Select /Range Format Currency. Press ENTER. Then type **E5.E11** and press ENTER to produce the completed model shown in Figure 7-13.

Your model is now complete. However, you may be thinking that it would be just as easy to type the date in the way you want to see it by using a label entry such as "Apr-14-88." While this solution seems reasonable, the problem is that your entry would be a label and labels cannot be used in arithmetic operations. You would not be able to subtract two dates or compare the date against the current date without converting these label entries to dates. You will learn more about this conversion process in Chapter 10. For now, use @DATE anywhere you need to record a date on the worksheet.

Extracting a Portion of a Date   There are three functions that allow you to extract part of a date. You have the choice of extracting the year, month, or day from a serial date number. The syntaxes of the three functions are

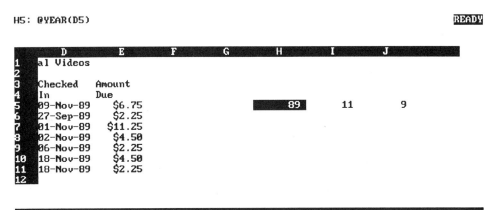

H5: @YEAR(D5)   READY

	D	E	F	G	H	I	J
1	al Videos						
2							
3	Checked	Amount					
4	In	Due					
5	09-Nov-89	$6.75			89	11	9
6	27-Sep-89	$2.25					
7	01-Nov-89	$11.25					
8	02-Nov-89	$4.50					
9	06-Nov-89	$2.25					
10	18-Nov-89	$4.50					
11	18-Nov-89	$2.25					
12							

FIGURE 7-14.   Extracting date components

@YEAR(serial date number)
@MONTH(serial date number)
@DAY(serial date number)

Try all three functions by adding new columns to the existing model for the video rentals. Follow these steps:

1. Move the cell pointer to H5. Type **@YEAR(D5)** and press ENTER.
   The year number "89" should now display in this cell.

2. Move the cell pointer to I5. Type **@MONTH(D5)** and press ENTER.
   The month number should now appear in the cell.

3. Move the cell pointer to J5. Type **@DAY(D5)** and press ENTER.
   The day number should now appear in the cell, as shown in Figure 7-14.

4. Move the cell pointer to H5, select /Copy, and press the RIGHT ARROW key twice to move the cell pointer to J5. Press ENTER. Move the cell pointer to H6 and type .. Then move the cell pointer to H11 and press ENTER.
   The model should match the data shown in Figure 7-15.

5. Press HOME. Then select /File Save, type **VIDEOS**, and press ENTER.

6. Select /Worksheet Erase Yes.

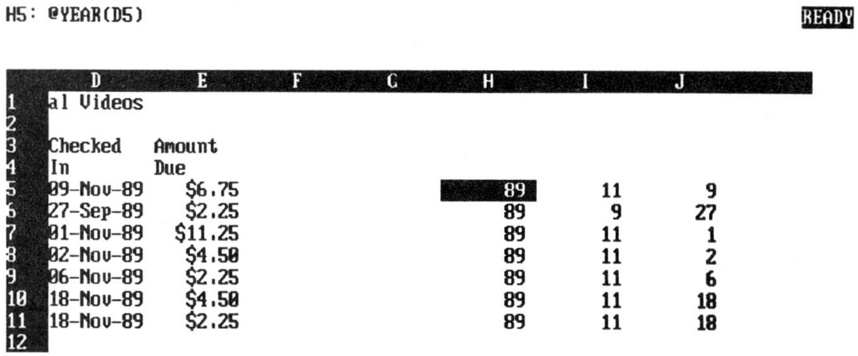

```
H5: @YEAR(D5)                                                    READY

        D          E        F        G        H        I        J
1  al Videos
2
3  Checked    Amount
4  In         Due
5  09-Nov-89   $6.75                              89       11       9
6  27-Sep-89   $2.25                              89        9      27
7  01-Nov-89  $11.25                              89       11       1
8  02-Nov-89   $4.50                              89       11       2
9  06-Nov-89   $2.25                              89       11       6
10 18-Nov-89   $4.50                              89       11      18
11 18-Nov-89   $2.25                              89       11      18
12
```

FIGURE 7-15.   Copying the date functions

Entering Times   Just as you must to use a function to enter dates, you must also use one for making time entries on the worksheet. If you enter a time representation without using the special function, you will not be able to use it in time computations. The function available in Release 2 and higher that is used to make a time entry on the worksheet is *@TIME*. This is the syntax it uses:

@TIME(hour,minute,second)

In this function, *hour* is a number between 0 and 23, with 0 representing midnight and 23 representing 11 P.M. *Minute* is a number between 0 and 59, and *second* has the same acceptable value range as *minute*.

Follow these instructions to create a worksheet that measures the time elapsed from when a vehicle is logged in for repair to when it leaves the repair shop.

1. Make these entries:

   A3:   Job
   A4:   Number
   A5:   1
   A6:   2
   A7:   3
   A8:   4
   B1:   QUICK CAR REPAIR November 12, 1989

B3:	Time
B4:	In
C4:	Repair
C5:	Tire
C6:	Brakes
C7:	Steering
C8:	Lube
D3:	Time
D4:	Out
E3:	Elapsed
E4:	Time

Your model should now look like this:

E4: 'Time   READY

```
        A         B          C          D         E         F         G         H
1                QUICK CAR REPAIR November 12, 1989
2
3  Job       Time                   Time      Elapsed
4  Number    In         Repair      Out       Time
5      1                Tire
6      2                Brakes
7      3                Steering
8      4                Lube
```

2. Move the cell pointer to B5 and select /Range Format Date Time 2. Move the cell pointer to B8 and press ENTER.

3. Move the cell pointer to D5 and select /Range Format Date Time 2. Move the cell pointer to D8 and press ENTER.

4. Move the cell pointer to E5 and select /Range Format Date Time 4. Move the cell pointer to E8 and press ENTER.

5. Type **@TIME(8,5,0)**, and press the DOWN ARROW key.
   Notice the zero entry for seconds. It is used as a place marker even when you do not have a special value to enter.

6. Type **@TIME(8,10,0)**, and press the DOWN ARROW key.

7. Type **@TIME(8,30,0)**, and press DOWN ARROW.

8. Type **@TIME(8,32,0)**, and press ENTER to produce this display:

B8: (D7) @TIME(8,32,0)   READY

```
           A        B        C         D         E        F        G        H
1                     QUICK CAR REPAIR November 12, 1989
2
3     Job      Time               Time     Elapsed
4     Number   In        Repair   Out      Time
5              1 08:05 AM Tire
6              2 08:10 AM Brakes
7              3 08:30 AM Steering
8              4 08:32 AM Lube
```

9. Complete the remaining time entries for the times the vehicles were completed by making these entries in column D:

    D5:   @TIME(9,17,0)
    D6:   @TIME(10,34,0)
    D7:   @TIME(13,18,0)
    D8:   @TIME(9,44,0)

Notice the use of a 24-hour clock representation, with the number 13 used to represent 1 P.M., as shown here:

D8: (D7) @TIME(9,44,0)   READY

```
           A        B        C         D         E        F        G        H
1                     QUICK CAR REPAIR November 12, 1989
2
3     Job      Time               Time     Elapsed
4     Number   In        Repair   Out      Time
5              1 08:05 AM Tire     09:17 AM
6              2 08:10 AM Brakes   10:34 AM
7              3 08:30 AM Steering 01:18 PM
8              4 08:32 AM Lube     09:44 AM
```

10. Move the cell pointer to E5, type **+D5–B5**, and press ENTER.

    This computes the elapsed time for the repair of the first vehicle. When you copy this formula for the remaining entries, your job will be finished.

11. Select /Copy and press ENTER. Move the cell pointer to E6 and type .. Then move the cell pointer to E8 and press ENTER to produce these results:

E5: (D9) +D5–B5   READY

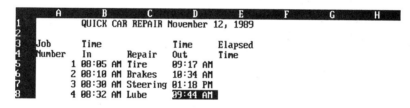

```
           A        B        C         D         E        F        G        H
1                     QUICK CAR REPAIR November 12, 1989
2
3     Job      Time               Time     Elapsed
4     Number   In        Repair   Out      Time
5              1 08:05 AM Tire     09:17 AM  01:12
6              2 08:10 AM Brakes   10:34 AM  02:24
7              3 08:30 AM Steering 01:18 PM  04:48
8              4 08:32 AM Lube     09:44 AM  01:12
```

12. Select /File Save, type **TIME**, and press ENTER.

13. Select /Worksheet Erase Yes.

Extracting Part of a Time Entry   There are three functions available in Release 2 and higher that can extract any part of a time number. They are @HOUR, @MINUTE, and @SECOND. All three use a time number as their argument, as in @HOUR(time number). Since all three follow the same pattern, you will only need to take a close look at one to understand how each of them works.

The *@HOUR* function is used whenever you wish to work with only the hour portion of a time entry. The function always returns a value between 0 and 23. You can use this function to track the delivery hour for packages if the @TIME function was used to record the time of receipt. Follow these steps to enter the information on the packages and use the @HOUR function to extract the delivery hour:

1. Complete these entries:

A1:	Time
A2:	Received
A3:	@TIME(8,4,6)
A4:	@TIME(9,11,0)
A5:	@TIME(9,30,0)
A6:	@TIME(9,45,0)
B1:	Package
B2:	Number
B3:	1761
B4:	3421
B5:	2280
B6:	7891
C2:	Recipient
C3:	B. Jones
C4:	R. Gaff
C5:	J. Bowyer
C6:	J. Kiger
D2:	Hour

2. Move the cell pointer to A3 and select /Range Format Date Time 1. Press the END key, followed by the DOWN ARROW key, and press ENTER.

3. Select /Worksheet Column Set-Width, type **14**, and press ENTER.

4. Move the cell pointer to column C and select /Worksheet Column Set-Width, type **16**, and press ENTER.

5. Move the cell pointer to D3, type **@HOUR(A3)**, and press ENTER.
   This extracts the hour number, which is 8.

6. Select /Copy and press ENTER. Move the cell pointer to D4, type ., move the
   cell pointer to D6, and press ENTER. This produces the following display:

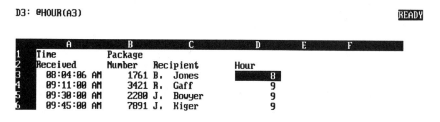

7. Select /File Save, type **HOUR**, and press ENTER.

8. Select /Worksheet Erase Yes.

String Functions

String functions are a feature that was added in Release 2. They provide a variety of
character-manipulation formulas that give you flexibility in rearranging text entries.
You can work with the entire label entry for a cell with the string functions, or with
just a part of it. The functions in this category can be real lifesavers when you have to
correct data-entry errors. You will work with abbreviated examples that correct errors
in one or two entries, but the same formula you create for one entry could be copied
down a column to correct a large portion of a worksheet. You will have the opportunity
to work with functions that change an entry from uppercase to lowercase or even
proper noun format. You will also learn how to extract one or more characters from
the beginning or the end of a character string.

When the string values you are working with are used as arguments for the string
functions, they must be enclosed in quotation marks ("). However, when these same
entries are referenced by a cell address, no quotation marks are required. For example,
the function @UPPER converts text entries to uppercase. If you want to include the
string jim smith as an argument in this function, you need to record it as @UPPER("jim
smith"). However, if you store jim smith in A5, you can write @UPPER(A5), without
quotation marks.

Some string functions produce another string as a result of the function. Other string
functions produce numeric results that are equivalent to a position number within the
string.

@UPPER   The *@UPPER* function will change all the characters to uppercase. This feature allows you to convert worksheet text data to all capital letters, if that is your preference. The syntax of the function is @UPPER(string).

Make these entries to try the function:

1. Move the cell pointer to A1, type **jim smith**, and move the cell pointer to A2.

2. Type **Bill Brown** and move the cell pointer to A3.

3. Type **JANE JONES** and move the cell pointer to B1.

4. Select /Worksheet Global Column-Width, type **12**, and press ENTER.

5. Type **@UPPER(A1)** and press ENTER.

6. Select /Copy and press ENTER. Move the cell pointer to B2, type **.**, move the cell pointer to B3, and press ENTER.

   The converted data appears like this:

```
B1: @UPPER(A1)                                                         READY

          A             B             C             D        E        F
1    jim smith     JIM SMITH
2    Bill Brown    BILL BROWN
3    JANE JONES    JANE JONES
```

@LOWER   The *@LOWER* function converts text entries to all lowercase. Regardless of whether the text is uppercase, lowercase, or in proper noun format (with the first letter capitalized), the @LOWER function produces a string that is guaranteed to be lowercase.

You can use the example you created to test the @UPPER function to test the @LOWER function. Follow these steps to add a new column to the model:

1. Move the cell pointer to C1, type **@LOWER(A1)**, and press ENTER.

2. Select /Copy and press ENTER. Move the cell pointer to C2, type **.**, move the cell pointer to C3, and press ENTER to produce this display:

```
C1: @LOWER(A1)                                                         READY

          A             B             C             D        E        F
1    jim smith     JIM SMITH     jim smith
2    Bill Brown    BILL BROWN    bill brown
3    JANE JONES    JANE JONES    jane jones
4
```

@PROPER   The *@PROPER* function converts text into the format you expect to see for proper nouns. The first letter in each word is capitalized and the remaining letters of the word are displayed in lowercase. This is another function you can use to establish consistency in the data on your worksheet. The model that was used to test the @UPPER and @LOWER functions can be used with @PROPER. Add another column to this model by following these instructions:

1. Move the cell pointer to D1, type **@PROPER(A1)**, and press ENTER.

2. Select /Copy and press ENTER. Move the cell pointer to D2, type **.**, move the cell pointer to D3, and press ENTER to produce this display:

D1: @PROPER(A1)   READY

	A	B	C	D	E	F
1	Jim smith	JIM SMITH	jim smith	Jim Smith		
2	Bill Brown	BILL BROWN	bill brown	Bill Brown		
3	JANE JONES	JANE JONES	jane jones	Jane Jones		
4						

3. Select /File Save, type **CASE**, and press ENTER.

4. Select /Worksheet Erase Yes to clear the worksheet.

@RIGHT   The *@RIGHT* function extracts one or more characters from the right of a string entry. The function has two arguments: the function you want to extract from and the number of characters to extract. The syntax of the function looks like this:

@RIGHT(string,number of characters)

Examples of this function and the results it produces are

@RIGHT("Lotus 1-2-3",5) equals 1-2-3
@RIGHT("ABC COMPANY   ",8) equals Y with seven trailing blanks

You can use this function to extract a warehouse location represented by the last three characters in every part number. Make these entries on your worksheet to see how this function works:

1. Enter the following:

    A1:   Part No.
    A2:   TY-3452-DAL
    A3:   ST-67-CHI
    A4:   JV-893-DAL
    B1:   Warehouse

2. Move the cell pointer to column A, select /Worksheet Column Set-Width, type
   12, and press ENTER.

3. Move the cell pointer to B2, type **@RIGHT(A2,3)**, and press ENTER.

4. Select /Copy, press ENTER, and move the cell pointer to B3. Type ., move the
   cell pointer to B4, and press ENTER to produce this result:

B2: @RIGHT(A2,3)   READY

The warehouse locations have been filled with the result of the @RIGHT
function. The last three characters of each part number represent the location,
which is now displayed in column B. This feature is useful if you need to create
a report that displays the warehouse locations but does not require the full
display of the part numbers. Because the warehouse location is extracted from
the longer entry, it is now much easier to focus on the information of interest.

5. Select /File Save, type **RIGHT**, and press ENTER if you want to save this model.

@LEFT   The @LEFT function removes characters from the beginning of a string.
You can use it to reference strings in separate first-name, last-name, and middle-initial
columns of the worksheet, and to combine the results of these three functions with the
string operator for concatenation (&). Concatenation will join all three into a set of
initials. Make these entries to try the @LEFT function:

1. Select /Worksheet Erase Yes.

2. Make the following entries on the worksheet:

A1:	F Name
A2:	Sally
A3:	Joe
A4:	Sam
A5:	Kim
B1:	M Init
B2:	T.
B3:	L.
B4:	P.
B5:	D.
C1:	L Name
C2:	Smith
C3:	Harris
C4:	Polk
C5:	Jackson
D1:	Initials

3. The next step involves your moving the cell pointer to D2 and then typing **@LEFT(A2,1)&@LEFT(B2,1)&@LEFT(C2,1)**. Then press ENTER to see the first set of initials displayed:

```
D2: @LEFT(A2,1)&@LEFT(B2,1)&@LEFT(C2,1)                          READY
```

	A	B	C	D	E	F	G	H
1	F Name	M Init	L Name	Initials				
2	Sally	T.	Smith	STS				
3	Joe	L.	Harris					
4	Sam	P.	Polk					
5	Kim	D.	Jackson					

In this string formula the & serves as a means of combining strings, just as a + is used with numbers.

4. Select /Copy and press ENTER. Move the cell pointer to D3, type ., and move the cell pointer to D5. Press ENTER to complete the Copy operation.

The results look like this:

```
D2: @LEFT(A2,1)&@LEFT(B2,1)&@LEFT(C2,1)                          READY
```

	A	B	C	D	E	F	G	H
1	F Name	M Init	L Name	Initials				
2	Sally	T.	Smith	STS				
3	Joe	L.	Harris	JLH				
4	Sam	P.	Polk	SPP				
5	Kim	D.	Jackson	KDJ				
6								

5. Select /File Save, type **LEFT**, and press ENTER.

@REPEAT   The *@REPEAT* function is used to duplicate a character string a specified number of times. The primary purpose of this function is to improve the appearance of the worksheet. @REPEAT can create dividing lines between the assumptions of a report and the display of the final results. In one sense, @REPEAT is similar to the backslash character (\ ) because it repeats labels. It differs in the sense that \ is restricted to filling a single cell, whereas @REPEAT can extend across many worksheet cells. In addition, @REPEAT can complete the dividing line with the entry of one function, whereas the \ character normally requires repeated entries or copying to complete its task.

If you wish, you can go back to the sales projections you entered in an earlier chapter and replace the asterisks with the backslash, using a new character sequence. For now, enter @REPEAT in a worksheet cell to see how it works. Follow these steps:

1. Move the cell pointer to A7.

2. Type **@REPEAT("+−",36)** and press ENTER.

Your display should match this:

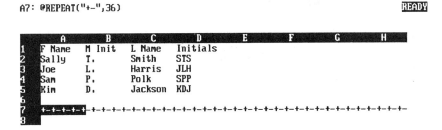

Notice that quotation marks were required in the function because a string value was placed in the function as an argument.

Math Functions

1-2-3's math functions perform both simple calculations and more complex operations suited to an engineering or manufacturing application. Rather than look at the trigonometric functions and more complex operations, you will benefit most from the general-purpose examples emphasized by the exercises in this section. You will learn how to overcome rounding problems, look at the absolute value of a number, and work with only the integer portion of a number.

@ABS   The *@ABS* function returns the positive or absolute value of a number, without regard to whether the number is positive or negative. The function is useful when you are concerned with the relative size of numbers and do not care if the number is positive or negative.

An example of this function is illustrated by the need of retail establishments to monitor cash overages and shortages in their registers. Consistent cash overages and shortages indicate a cash-control problem that should be corrected. Simply adding the overages and shortages doesn't always work: They might cancel each other out. However, examining the absolute value of the overages and shortages reveals the total amount of the differences.

Follow these instructions to set up a model for the Hot Dog House Register:

1. Select /Worksheet Erase Yes and then /Worksheet Global Format Currency. Press ENTER to accept the default of two decimal places.

2. Place these entries in worksheet cells:

A5:	Monday
A6:	Tuesday
A7:	Wednesday
A8:	Thursday
A9:	Friday
A10:	Saturday
A11:	Sunday
A13:	TOTAL DIFFERENCE FOR THE WEEK:
C1:	Hot Dog House Register
C2:	Week of November 10, 1989
C4:	Over/Under
C5:	42
C6:	−35
C7:	22.78
C8:	−57
C9:	12.58
C10:	.58
C11:	−2.10
E4:	Absolute Value

3. Move the cell pointer to E5, type **@ABS(C5)**, and press ENTER.
   This step computes the absolute value of the entry in C5.

4. Select /Copy and press ENTER. Move the cell pointer to E6, type ., move the cell pointer to E11, and press ENTER.

E13: @SUM(E5..E11)   READY

```
        A       B       C       D       E       F       G       H
1                       Hot Dog House Register
2                       Week of November 10, 1989
3
4                       Over/Under       Absolute Value
5   Monday               $42.00           $42.00
6   Tuesday             ($35.00)          $35.00
7   Wednesday            $22.70           $22.70
8   Thursday            ($57.00)          $57.00
9   Friday               $12.58           $12.58
10  Saturday             $0.58            $0.58
11  Sunday              ($2.10)           $2.10
12
13  TOTAL DIFFERENCE FOR THE WEEK:       $172.04
```

FIGURE 7-16.   Using @ABS

Once you have completed this step, all the daily cash differences have been converted to their absolute values and stored in column E.

5. Move the cell pointer to E13, type **@SUM(E5.E11)**, and press ENTER to produce the results shown in Figure 7-16.

This step computes a total of the cash differences, without regard to whether they were positive or negative, by using the absolute value of each day's total in the sum calculation. This method prevents the cash differences from partially canceling each other out and seeming like less of a problem than they actually are.

@INT   The *@INT* function lets you truncate the decimal places in a number to produce a whole number or integer. You can use it when you work with date computations in Release 2 and higher and wish to truncate the decimal fraction that represents the time portion of the current date. You can also use it when calculating the number of complete items that can be produced on a production line. To see how this function works, create a model similar to this second example.

This model will determine how many complete items can be produced from a given volume of raw material. The raw material is cowhide, and the product being produced is wallets. It has been determined that one wallet will require 0.6789 square feet of cowhide. Partially completed items will not be considered, since they cannot be shipped. It does not work to round the calculated result; the decimal fraction computed could be rounded upward and would no longer represent completed items. The only solution is to truncate the decimal portion of the number.

The @INT function that you will use when creating your model follows this syntax:

@INT(number)

Follow these steps to create your model:

1. Select /Worksheet Erase Yes and make the following entries:

A1:	Cowhide needed for 1 wallet -
A3:	Available sizes
A4:	1
A5:	5
A6:	10
A7:	15
A8:	20
A9:	25
D3:	Wallets Produced
E1:	.6789
F1:	Sq. ft.

2. Move the cell pointer to D4 and type **@INT(A4/$E$1)**.

   Notice that the argument for the @INT function is the formula A4/$E$1. This formula divides the size of the piece of raw material by the square footage requirements. The reference to the requirements of one piece is absolute; this one value will be referenced in all the calculations and should not change if this formula is copied. The second part of the formula adds the @INT function, which will cause any decimal fraction resulting from the computation to be truncated. This result will then represent the actual number of wallets that can be produced.

3. Select /Copy and press ENTER. Move the cell pointer to D5, type ., move the cell pointer to D9, and press ENTER.

   You now have the integer portion of each of the calculations, as shown here:

D4: @INT(A4/$E$1)   READY

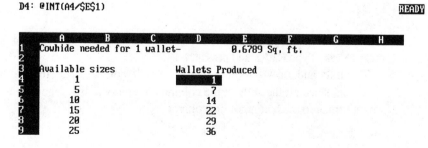

4. Select /File Save, type **INTEGER**, and press ENTER.

5. Select /Worksheet Erase Yes.

@ROUND   The *@ROUND* function actually alters the way a number is stored internally by letting you specify the number of decimal places you want. This function can solve some of the problems caused by the discrepancy between how numbers are stored and the format you use to display them. In Chapter 3 you learned that you could use the format commands (/Worksheet Global Format and /Range Format) to display numbers with a varying number of decimal places. But the problem with these changes is that the full internal accuracy is still maintained despite the change in the display appearance. The greater internal storage accuracy of the numbers being added can cause totals at the bottom of a column to appear as though they do not add properly.

Use the following steps to create a model that shows this discrepancy, and then apply the @ROUND function to the formulas in the model so that the internal accuracy is equal to the numbers that are displayed.

1. Make these entries:

A2:	Product 1 Sales
A3:	Product 2 Sales
A4:	Product 3 Sales
C1:	Price
C2:	33.3333
C3:	67.5068
C4:	3.3335
D1:	Quantity
D2:	100
D3:	50
D4:	100
E1:	Total $

2. Move the cell pointer to C2 and select /Range Format Currency, type **4**, and press ENTER. Press the END key, followed by the DOWN ARROW key, and press ENTER.

3. Move the cell pointer to E2 and select /Range Format Currency, type **0**, and press ENTER. Type **E2.E5** and press ENTER.

    The END and DOWN ARROW sequence will not work for this Format operation, since all the cells in the column are empty at this time and 1-2-3 would format to the bottom of the column.

4. Type **+C2*D2** and press ENTER.

This formula computes the total cost of the purchase. A whole number is displayed; however, a decimal fraction exists in the number stored internally because of the decimals in the price.

5. Select /Copy and press ENTER. Move the cell pointer to E3, type ., move the cell pointer to E4, and press ENTER.

6. Move the cell pointer to E5 and type **@SUM(E2.E4)**. Press ENTER to produce these results:

```
E5: (C0) @SUM(E2..E4)                                          READY
```

	A	B	C	D	E	F	G	H
1			Price	Quantity	Total $			
2	Product 1 Sales		$33.3333	100	$3,333			
3	Product 2 Sales		$67.5068	50	$3,375			
4	Product 3 Sales		$3.3335	100	$333			
5					$7,042			

The column E figures suggest that the total should be $7041, not the $7042 shown. The difference of 1 is caused by the rounding discrepancy that occurs when the total $ numbers are displayed. The @SUM function is computed from the numbers that are stored, not those that are displayed. The @ROUND function can solve this problem. But first you need to learn a little more about its syntax.

The format of the @ROUND function is

@ROUND(number to be rounded, place of rounding)

The number to be rounded can be a number, a reference to a cell that contains a number, or a formula that evaluates as a number. The place of rounding is a positive or negative number that specifies the place of rounding. Rounding to the nearest whole number uses 0 as the place of rounding. Rounding to decimal places to the right of a whole number uses positive integers for each place farther to the right. Rounding to the left of the whole-number position is represented by negative integers. Table 7-1 shows the effect of some of the rounding options on a number.

You can apply this @ROUND function to the total $ computations with these steps:

1. Move the cell pointer to E2 and press F2 (EDIT).

2. Press the HOME key to move to the front of the entry. Press DEL to delete the +.

3. Type **@ROUND(**.

Number	Rounded Number	Formula for Rounding
12345.678123	12345.6781	@ROUND($A$3,4)
	12345.68	@ROUND($A$3,2)
	12345.7	@ROUND($A$3,1)
	12346	@ROUND($A$3,0)
	12300	@ROUND($A$3,-2)
	10000	@ROUND($A$3,-4)

TABLE 7-1.   Effect of Various Rounding Options

4. Press the END key, type **,0)**, and press ENTER.

5. Select /Copy and press ENTER. Move the cell pointer to E3, type **.**, move the cell pointer to E4, and press ENTER to produce these results:

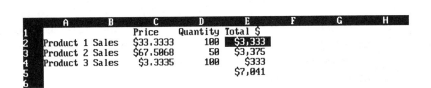

The addition of @ROUND to each formula makes the column total agree with the numbers displayed. This is because you altered the internal accuracy of each of the numbers to force it to match the display.

6. Select /File Save, type **ROUND**, and press ENTER.

7. Select /Worksheet Erase Yes.

Many worksheets will have @ROUND added to most of the formulas. To use it, follow the same procedure used in this example, making each formula an argument to the @ROUND function.

Special Functions

1-2-3's special functions are grouped together because they do not fit neatly into any of the other function categories. Some of them are used to trap error conditions. Others count the number of rows in a range or allow you to choose a value from a list of options. Still others let you examine the contents of worksheet cells closely, thus providing information about a cell's value or other attributes. For the most part, this group can be thought of as a smorgasbord of sophisticated features. Because these functions are so complex, only one of them will be introduced at this time. More sophisticated examples will be deferred until Chapter 10.

@NA   This function causes *NA* ("not available") to appear in the cell where @NA is entered. Its impact does not stop there: All worksheet cells that reference this cell will also have the value NA. There are no arguments for this function: Its syntax is @NA.

@NA is used as a flag to remind you to complete missing entries before finalizing a report. Since cells that reference this cell take on the value NA, there is no way for you to erroneously assume that a total reflects all data entries.

Create a model that uses the @NA feature to flag missing grades for an instructor. All students who miss an exam have their grade entered as @NA rather than as a test score. This means that their final grade point average will show as NA since it will reference each of the exam grades, including the one recorded as @NA. An instructor could use this model at the end of a semester to identify those students who have not yet made up missing exams. The instructor would have the option to change the missing exam grade to a 0, or to record an Incomplete for the student's final grade. Follow these steps to complete the model:

1. Make these entries to add a heading for each category and to place the students' names in the model after entering /Worksheet Column Set-Width to End pressing ENTER:

C1:	Fall Semester 1989
A3:	Student
A4:	B. Black
A5:	S. Conners
A6:	F. Dalton
A7:	G. Limmer
A8:	S. Melton
A9:	P. Stock
A10:	J. Zimmer
B3:	Exam 1
C3:	Exam 2
D3:	Exam 3
E3:	Final
F3:	Average

2. Record these grades for the first exam:

B4:	75
B5:	67
B6:	78
B7:	88
B8:	67
B9:	67
B10:	91

3. Record these entries for the second exam:

C4:	@NA
C5:	78
C6:	90
C7:	81
C8:	55
C9:	89
C10:	82

   Since B. Black did not take exam 2, @NA was recorded for that student's score. Recording NA will not give you the same effect. @NA is a value entry that will affect calculations referencing the cell. NA is a label entry and cannot be used in arithmetic calculations.

4. Record these grades for the third exam and the final exam:

D4:	82
D5:	72
D6:	89
D7:	93
D8:	40
D9:	@NA
D10:	75
E4:	88
E5:	81
E6:	92
E7:	87
E8:	60
E9:	78
E10:	89

5. Move the cell pointer to F4, type **@AVG(B4.E4)**, and press ENTER.

F4: (F1) @AVG(B4..E4)   READY

	A	B	C	D	E	F	G
1			Fall Semester 1989				
2							
3	Student	Exam 1	Exam 2	Exam 3	Final	Average	
4	B. Black	75	NA	82	88	NA	
5	S. Conners	67	78	72	81	74.5	
6	F. Dalton	78	90	89	92	87.3	
7	G. Limmer	88	81	93	87	87.3	
8	S. Melton	67	55	40	60	55.5	
9	P. Stock	67	89	NA	78	NA	
10	J. Zimmer	91	82	75	89	84.3	
11							
12							

FIGURE 7-17.   Using @NA

6. Enter /Range Format Fixed 1 and press ENTER.

7. Select /Copy and press ENTER. Move the cell pointer to F5, type ., move the cell pointer to F10, and press ENTER.

    The results are shown in Figure 7-17. Notice that the averages for B. Black and P. Stock display as NA. These averages are not available because one of the values needed to compute them is missing.

8. Select /File Save, type **NA**, and press ENTER.

9. Select /Worksheet Erase Yes.

Financial Functions

1-2-3 provides an entire category of functions to use in investment calculations and other calculations concerned with the time value of money. You can use these financial functions to monitor loans, annuities, and cash flows over periods of time. With Release 2 and higher, some depreciation calculations are also included in these financial functions. You can quickly compare various financial alternatives since you can rely on the function to supply the correct formulas. As with the other functions, all you need to supply are arguments to tailor the calculations to your exact needs.

    When you use financial functions, it is very important that all the arguments and the result use the same unit of time. For example, a function to compute the amount of a loan payment will require you to decide whether you want to calculate the payment amount on a yearly, quarterly, or monthly basis. Once you decide on one of these or on some other unit of time, you must apply it consistently across all arguments. If you choose to compute a monthly payment amount, the interest rate must be expressed as a monthly rate. Likewise, the term should be expressed as a number of months. You will work with three of the built-in functions in this section.

@DDB   The *@DDB* function, available in Release 2 and higher, computes the depreciation expense for a specific period using the double declining balance method. The format of the function is

@DDB(cost,salvage,life,period)

Cost is the amount you paid for the asset you are depreciating. It must be a value or a reference to a cell that contains a value. *Salvage* is the value of the asset at the end of its useful life. Like the cost, this argument must be a value or a reference to a cell that contains one. *Life* is the expected useful life of the asset; that is, the number of years needed to depreciate the asset from its cost to its salvage value. Normally the life of the asset is expressed in years, but it must always be a value or a reference to a value. *Period* is the specific time period for which you are computing the depreciation. Since the double declining balance method of depreciation is an accelerated method that allows you to depreciate more in the early years of an asset's life, it is important to specify the correct period for your calculations. Like the other arguments, *period* must be a value or a reference to one.

Use the @DDB function to build a model that calculates the depreciation expense for each year in an asset's five-year life. Follow these steps:

1. Make these entries:

    A1:   Depreciation Expense Using the Double Declining Balance Method
    A3:   Cost:
    A4:   Salvage Value:
    A5:   Useful Life:
    A6:   Year 1:
    A7:   Year 2:
    A8:   Year 3:
    A9:   Year 4:
    A10:   Year 5:
    A12:   Total Depreciation:
    C3:   11000
    C4:   1000
    C5:   5

C6: [W11] @DDB($C$3,$C$4,$C$5,1)   READY

```
         A         B         C         D         E         F         G
 1  Depreciation Expense Using the Double Declining Balance Method
 2
 3  Cost:                  $11,000.00
 4  Salvage Value:          $1,000.00
 5  Useful Life:                    5
 6  Year 1:                 $4,400.00
 7  Year 2:
 8  Year 3:
 9  Year 4:
10  Year 5:
11
12  Total Depreciation:
```

FIGURE 7-18.   Depreciation for year 1

2. Select /Worksheet Global Format Currency and press ENTER.

3. Move the cell pointer to C3 and select /Range Format Currency, type **2**, and press ENTER. Move the cell pointer to C4 and press ENTER.

4. Move the cell pointer to C5. Then select /Range Format Fixed. Type **0** and press ENTER twice.

5. Select /Worksheet Column Set-Width, press the RIGHT ARROW key twice, and press ENTER. Move the cell pointer to column A, select /Worksheet Column Set-Width, type **11**, and press ENTER.

6. Move the cell pointer to C6, type **@DDB($C$3,$C$4,$C$5,1)**, and press ENTER.

    This formula computes the depreciation expense for the first year, as shown in Figure 7-18. The dollar signs ($) were used so that the formula could be copied, even though it will need to be edited to change the year number.

7. Select /Copy and press ENTER. Move the cell pointer to C7, type **.**, move the cell pointer to C10, and press ENTER.

    The formula has been copied, but each formula must be edited to reference the proper year.

8. Move the cell pointer to C7 and press F2 (EDIT). Press the LEFT ARROW key and then press BACKSPACE to delete the 1. Type **2** and press ENTER.

C12: [W11] @SUM(C6..C10)   READY

```
          A          B          C          D          E          F          G
1  Depreciation Expense Using the Double Declining Balance Method
2
3  Cost:                    $11,000.00
4  Salvage Value:            $1,000.00
5  Useful Life:                      5
6  Year 1:                   $4,400.00
7  Year 2:                   $2,640.00
8  Year 3:                   $1,584.00
9  Tear 4:                     $950.40
10 Year 5:                     $425.60
11
12 Total Depreciation:      $10,000.00
```

FIGURE 7-19.   Copying @DDB

9. Use the same editing technique to change the formulas in A8..A10 to reference the proper year.

10. Move the cell pointer to A12, type **@SUM(C6.C10)**, and press ENTER to produce the results shown in Figure 7-19.

11. Select /File Save, type **DEPREC**, and press ENTER.

12. Select /Worksheet Erase Yes.

@PMT   The *@PMT* function calculates the appropriate payment amount for a loan. The syntax for this function is

@PMT(principal,interest,term of loan)

The *principal* is a numeric value that represents the amount of money borrowed. *Interest* is a numeric value that represents the interest rate. To specify a 9% interest rate, you can use 9% or .09. *Term* is the number of payments for the loan. It is a numeric value and should be expressed in the same time period as the interest.

You can test this function in building a model that determines whether you can afford the monthly payments on your dream home. This model will also use range name references for the function arguments. You learned how to apply these names to cells in Chapter 3, but the process will be reviewed in this example as you apply range names to the principal, interest, and term for the loan before entering the function. Complete these steps:

1. Make the following entries:

A1:	Principal:
A2:	Interest:
A3:	Term:
A5:	Monthly Payments:
C1:	150000
C2:	.09
C3:	20
D3:	years

2. Move the cell pointer to C1, select /Range Name Create, type **PRINCIPAL**, and press ENTER twice.

   This step applies the range name PRINCIPAL to C1.

3. With the cell pointer still in C1, select /Range Format Currency and press ENTER twice.

4. Move the cell pointer to C2, select /Range Name Create, type **INTEREST**, and press ENTER twice.

   This step applies the range name INTEREST to C2.

5. With the cell pointer in C2, select /Range Format Percent and press ENTER twice.

6. Move the cell pointer to C3, select /Range Name Create, type **TERM**, and press ENTER twice.

   This step applies the range name TERM to C3.

7. With the cell pointer in C5, select /Range Format Currency and press ENTER twice.

8. Select /Worksheet Column Set-Width, type **12**, and press ENTER.

9. Type **@PMT(**.

10. Press F3 (NAME), highlight PRINCIPAL, and press ENTER. Type **,**.

11. Press F3 (NAME), highlight INTEREST, and press ENTER. Type **/12** to convert the annual interest rate to a monthly rate. Type **,** (comma).

12. Press F3 (NAME), highlight TERM, and press ENTER. Type *12) to convert the number of years to the number of months. Press ENTER to finalize the entry.

This function shows the use of formulas for function arguments since the interest rate must be divided by 12 to convert the annual percentage to a monthly figure, and the term must be multiplied by 12 to express it as months. 1-2-3 does not object to the use of these formulas since they return the value entries needed for each of the function arguments. The result is shown here:

C5: (C2) [W12] @PMT(PRINCIPAL,INTEREST/12,TERM*12)   READY

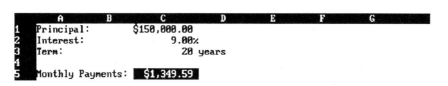

13. Select /File Save, type **PAYMENT**, and press ENTER.

14. Select /Worksheet Erase Yes.

Logical Functions

1-2-3's logical functions allow you to build conditional features into your models. The functions in this category return logical (true or false) values as the result of the condition tests they perform. They are a powerful addition to 1-2-3 because they allow you to alter calculations based on conditions in other locations of the worksheet. This flexibility lets you construct models patterned after "real world" business conditions, where exceptions are prevalent.

These functions let you have more than one calculation for commission payments, purchase discounts, FICA tax, or any other computation requiring multiple calculations that depend on other values in the worksheet. Because these functions frequently use both simple and compound operators and because they are frequently used in combination when making an entry, none of them is covered in this chapter. However, many logical functions will be introduced in Chapter 10 when advanced functions are discussed.

REVIEW EXERCISE

You can apply your new skill with 1-2-3 @functions to building a model that computes total payments for the month, given three different loans. The borrowings will

E5: (C2) [W10] @PMT(B5,C5/12,D5*12)   READY

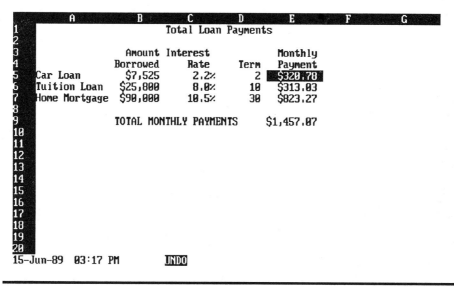

	A	B	C	D	E	F	G
1			Total Loan Payments				
2							
3		Amount	Interest		Monthly		
4		Borrowed	Rate	Term	Payment		
5	Car Loan	$7,525	2.2%	2	$320.78		
6	Tuition Loan	$25,000	8.0%	10	$313.03		
7	Home Mortgage	$90,000	10.5%	30	$823.27		
8							
9		TOTAL MONTHLY PAYMENTS			$1,457.07		

15-Jun-89 03:17 PM   UNDO

FIGURE 7-20. Model for computing payments

comprise a car loan, a tuition loan, and a home mortgage, but three different formulas will be needed since the principal is borrowed for a different amount of time in each case and at different interest rates. Figure 7-20 provides a look at the end result.

1. Enter the labels in C1, B3..E4, B9, and A5..A7.
   Hint: After entry, the /Range Label Right command was used for the labels in B3..E4.

2. Enter the appropriate principal, interest, and term amounts.
   Hint: Interest rates are entered as decimal fractions, as in .022. The /Range Format command is used twice, once to format B5..B7 as Currency with zero decimal places and once to format C5..C7 as Percent with one decimal place.) Also widen columns where needed with /Worksheet Column Set-Width.

3. Enter the formula to compute the car loan payment and format it as Currency with two decimal places.
   Hint: Use @PMT(B5,C5/12,D5*12) and then copy the formula for the other payment computations.

E5: (C2) [W10] @ROUND(@PMT(B5,C5/12,D5*12),2)   `READY`

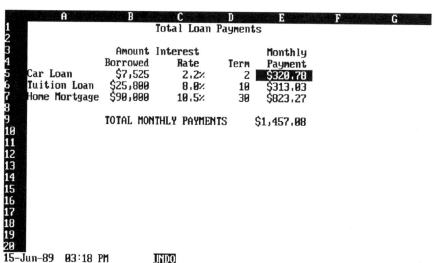

FIGURE 7-21.   Using the @ROUND function to display the correct total

4. Total the payments using the @SUM function and format the total as Currency with two decimal places.

Notice that the total does not seem to match the sum of each of the individual entries; the selected format rounds the display to two decimal places; but the numbers are still stored with all their decimal accuracy. You can solve this problem by using the @ROUND function with each @PMT function.

5. Edit the first payment function and add @ROUND to it to round to two decimal places.

Hint: Press the F2 (EDIT) key, press HOME to move to the front of the entry, type **@ROUND(**, press the END key, type **,2)**, and press ENTER. Copy this formula to E6 and E7.

The resulting model will look like Figure 7-21. The sum will match the total of each of the displayed entries because the extra decimal digits have been eliminated.

REVIEW

- Functions are prerecorded formulas. They are accessed by using the symbol @ followed by a keyword. Most functions also have arguments that define your specific needs to 1-2-3. These arguments are enclosed in parentheses and separated by commas.

- There are eight categories of 1-2-3 functions. Statistical functions perform basic statistical computations. Date and time functions allow you to record dates and times in worksheet cells and work with these special entries in other ways. String functions are designed to provide a way to work with character strings. Math functions perform simple mathematical operations and access to trigonometric calculations. Financial functions compute depreciation and computations involving the time value of money. Special functions are a group of miscellaneous functions that do not fall into any of the other categories. Logical functions allow you to test conditions. Data-management functions allow you to perform computations on entries in a 1-2-3 database.

Functions

Function	Action
@ABS(x)	Computes the absolute value of the number represented by x
@AVG(list)	Computes an average of the value provided
@COUNT(list)	Provides the number of non-blank entries in the list
@DATE(year, month,day)	Records the date number for the date specified
@DAY(date-number)	Extracts a day number from a date number
@DDB(cost,salvage, life, period)	Computes the double declining balance for an asset
@HOUR(time-number)	Extracts the hour number from a time serial number
@INT(x)	Returns the integer portion of the number represented by x
@LEFT(string,n)	Returns a specified number of characters in a string with n determining the number of characters returned
@LOWER(string)	Converts a string to lowercase
@MAX(list)	Returns the maximum value in a list

@MIN(list)	Returns the minimum value in a list
@MINUTE(time-number)	Extracts the minute number from a time serial number
@MONTH(date-number)	Extracts the month number from a date number
@NA	Marks the entry as not available
@PMT(principal, interest,term)	Computes a loan payment
@PROPER(string)	Converts the string to proper case
@REPEAT(string,n)	Duplicates a character string a specified number of times
@RIGHT(string,n)	Extracts a specific number of characters from the right side of a string with n determining the number of characters
@ROUND(x,n)	Rounds the number x to the number of decimal places specified by n
@SECOND(time-number)	Extracts the second number from a time serial number
@SUM(list)	Totals the value entries in the list
@TIME(hour, minute,second)	Records the specified time serial number in a worksheet cell
@UPPER(string)	Converts the entry to uppercase
@YEAR(date-number)	Extracts a year number from a date number

8

CREATING GRAPHS

Creating a Graph
Saving a Graph
Printing a Graph
Review Exercise
Review

The worksheet provides an excellent way to *perform* all your financial projections, but it is not always the best way to *present* the results from these calculations. Important numbers that you want to highlight often get lost in a sea of other figures. How can you make sure that you and others who read your report, which contains hundreds of numbers, will focus on those conditions and trends that you think are important?

One answer is to use 1-2-3's graphics features, which let you present your data in an easy-to-interpret format. Graphs do not present all the specific numbers; instead, they summarize the essence of your data so that you can focus on general patterns and trends. And when you find something in a graph that warrants more detailed analysis, you can still return to the supporting worksheet figures for a closer look.

You do not have to reenter your 1-2-3 data to use the graphics features. You can use the data already entered for your spreadsheet application without making any changes. Nor do you need to learn a new system to create your graphs; 1-2-3's graphics features are accessed through menus that are just like 1-2-3's other menus. You only need to learn a few new commands. Once you have entered your worksheet data, you need make only a few menu selections to present this data in graphic format. (Incidentally, any changes you make to your data will be reflected in your graph.)

To view your graphs on the screen, you need a color monitor or a monochrome (one-color) monitor with a graphics card. But even if you do not have a monitor that will support graphics, you can still make the menu selections that define the graph and save it to disk for printing later on.

Release 2.2 significantly improves the quality of the graphs. This release is designed to take advantage of the new high resolution monitors and provides support for much more detailed graphics. With the improved look of 1-2-3 graphs, you can create professional-looking slides and transparencies for important business meetings.

Release 2.2 and lower releases cannot print a graph directly. Graphs must be saved to disk and printed with the separate *PrintGraph program* or, in Release 2.2, with the Allways add-in that is part of your 1-2-3 package. A separate program is required because 1-2-3's graphics features are so extensive. There are different fonts, different sizes, and color, as well as support for a variety of printers and plotters. If all these options had been placed within 1-2-3's main program , so much memory would have been required that there would have been no room for your own data. The Allways add-in is covered in Chapter 13. This add-in provides additional features that are unavailable in 1-2-3, such as printing a graph and a worksheet on the same page.

This chapter will introduce you to the basic commands for defining a graph. You will learn about some of the special options that produce a more professional product. You will find out how to create and save multiple graphs in a single worksheet file. You will also learn how to obtain a printed copy of a graph using PrintGraph.

CREATING A GRAPH

Creating a basic graph is really quite simple. There are three basic steps. First, decide what type of graph you wish to see. Second, tell 1-2-3 what data to place in this graph. And third, tell 1-2-3 to display the graph for you. Once you have completed these basics, you may want to add further enhancements.

Basic Graphics Terminology

Before you can begin to create your first graph, there are a few basic terms to understand. A sample graph, with the key terms and components marked, is shown in Figure 8-1. A discussion of each of the basic terms follows. More specialized terms are covered along with the implementation of specific features later in the chapter.

DATA SERIES   1-2-3's graphs are designed to show from one to six sets of data values, depending on the type of graph that you select. A set of data values is referred

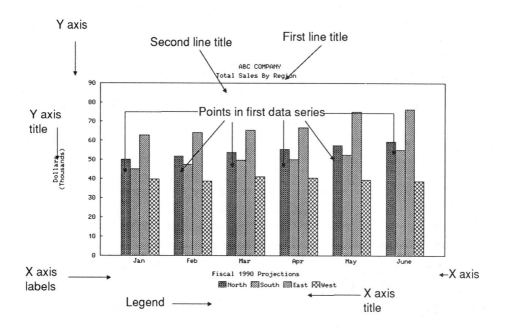

FIGURE 8-1.   A bar graph with titles and legend

to as a *series* and must consist of a range of contiguous cells on the worksheet. A series can represent, for example, sales of a product for a period of six months, the number of employees in the company each year for the last ten years, or the number of rejects on a production line for each of the last 16 weeks.

X AXIS   The individual values in the series are represented as data points along the *X axis,* which is the horizontal axis at the bottom of the graph. Each point along this axis might represent a year, a month, or a quarter. It could also represent a division, a product, or a project. The points along this X axis can be labeled to make it clear what they represent. In addition, a title can be placed along the X axis to describe the general category of data shown along that axis. For example, if each of the points on the X axis represents a month between January and December, an appropriate title for the axis might be Fiscal 90 Projections, which describes the category to which each of these months belongs.

Y AXIS   The *Y axis* is the vertical axis found on most of the graphs that 1-2-3 produces. It is used to measure the relative size of each value within a series. Once you tell 1-2-3 which data to display on the graph, this axis is labeled automatically. 1-2-3 will sometimes represent graph data in thousands or millions and label the Y axis appropriately. You can also make a title for this axis; you might describe the units of measure as dollars, number of employees, or some other appropriate unit of measure for the quantities shown on this axis.

LEGEND   If you choose to show more than one data series on a graph, you can describe each of the series with a *legend* at the bottom of the graph. The legend will show the symbol or pattern used to represent each series in the graph and will describe the data represented by that symbol or pattern.

Entering Some Data
For a Graph

If you have worked through the examples in this book from Chapter 1, you already have a number of worksheets that 1-2-3's graphics features could represent nicely. Even though you have some data for a graph, you will enter a short new worksheet designed to let you work with a small amount of data, yet still experience the maximum number of graphics features. Follow these steps to enter the required data for the examples in this chapter:

1. Make the following entries in the worksheet cells shown:

D1:	' ABC COMPANY
D2:	SALES BY REGION
A5:	North
A6:	South
A7:	East
A8:	West
B4:	Jan
B5:	50000
B6:	45000
B7:	62800
B8:	39550
C4:	Feb
C5:	+B5*1.035

C6:	+B6*1.05
C7:	+B7*1.02
C8:	+B8*.98
D4:	Mar
E4:	Apr
F4:	May
G4:	June

2. Select /Worksheet Global Format Currency, type **0**, and press ENTER.

3. Move the cell pointer to B4, select /Range Label Right, move the cell pointer to G4, and press ENTER.
   This aligns the labels on the right side of the cell as the numbers are aligned.

4. Move the cell pointer to C5, select /Copy, and move the cell pointer to C8. Press ENTER, move the cell pointer to D5, type ., move the cell pointer to G5, and press ENTER again.

5. Move the cell pointer to the following cells and type these numbers:

E6:	50000
F7:	75000
D8:	41000

   Adding these numbers overlays the formulas in those cells and provides more variety in the graph than a growth at a constant rate.

6. Move the cell pointer to C5.

Your entries should look like those in Figure 8-2. Notice that the original formula is not altered by the addition of several numeric constants to the model. You have finished entering the data you will use with the graphics examples. Now it is time to define your requirements for the graph.

Deciding on a Graph Type

1-2-3 offers five different graph types. Your options are line, bar, stacked bar, XY, and pie. A *bar graph* looks like the one shown in Figure 8-1. It uses bars of different heights to represent the data ranges you wish to graph. Bar graphs are especially appropriate when you wish to contrast the numbers in several series.

A *line graph* shows the points in the data range you specify, plotted against the Y axis. The points may be connected with a line, shown as symbols, or both. This type

C5: +B5*1.035   READY

	A	B	C	D	E	F	G	H
1			ABC COMPANY					
2			SALES BY REGION					
3								
4		Jan	Feb	Mar	Apr	May	June	
5	North	$50,000	$51,750	$53,561	$55,436	$57,376	$59,384	
6	South	$45,000	$47,250	$49,613	$50,000	$52,500	$55,125	
7	East	$62,000	$64,056	$65,337	$66,644	$75,000	$76,500	
8	West	$39,550	$38,759	$41,000	$40,180	$39,376	$38,589	
9								

FIGURE 8-2.   Worksheet for using graph features

of graph is an excellent choice for plotting trend data over time, such as sales or expenses. An example of a line graph is shown in Figure 8-3.

A *stacked bar graph* places the values in each of the series you select on top of each other for any one point on the X axis. A stacked bar is a good choice when you wish to see the level of the total as well as each of its components. You might use this

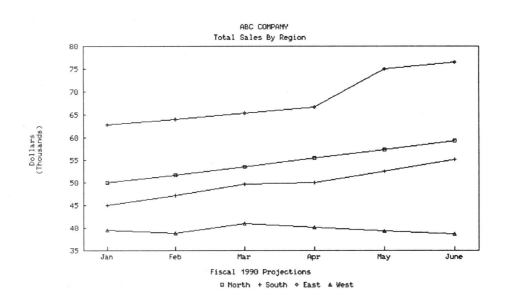

FIGURE 8-3.   A line graph

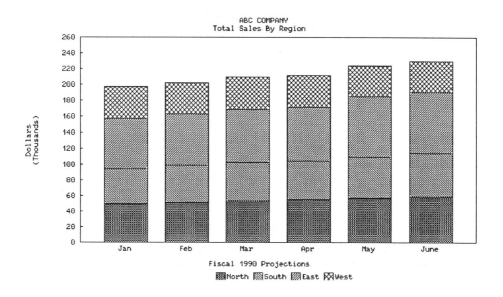

FIGURE 8-4. A stacked bar graph

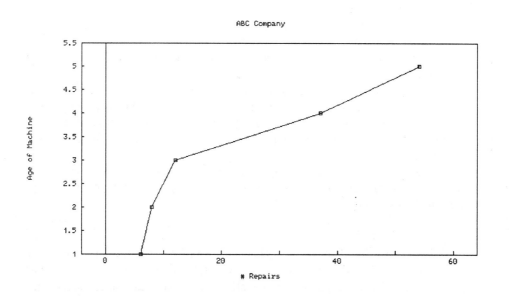

FIGURE 8-5. An XY graph

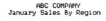
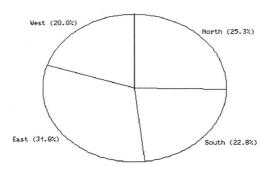

FIGURE 8-6.   A pie chart

type of graph to show the contribution to profit from each of the company's subsidiaries, as shown in Figure 8-4.

An *XY graph* plots the values in one series against the values from a second series. You might use this type of graph to plot age against salary, time against temperature, or machine repairs against the age of the machinery. Figure 8-5 shows an example of an XY graph.

A *pie chart* shows only one range of values. It represents the percent that each value is of the total by the size of the pie wedge assigned to that value. A pie chart is an effective way to show the relative size of different components of a budget or the contribution to profit from different product lines. An example of a pie chart is shown in Figure 8-6.

If you do not choose one of the graph types for your graph, 1-2-3 will use the default type, a line graph. Your first example will be of a bar graph, so use the following steps to make that selection:

1. Select /Graph.

    This will display the main Graph menu as shown in Figure 8-7. Below the menu is the Graph Settings box. From this menu, you can access additional Graph menus that provide additional settings. As you make selections with the

```
C5: +B5*1.035                                                    MENU
Type  X  A  B  C  D  E  F  Reset  View  Save  Options  Name  Group  Quit
Line  Bar  XY  Stacked-Bar  Pie
                         ┌──────── Graph Settings ────────
   Type: Bar                   Titles: First
                                       Second
   X:                                  X axis
   A: B5..G5                            Y axis
   B: B6..G6
   C: B7..G7                                   Y scale:      X scale:
   D: B8..G8                   Scaling        Automatic      Automatic
   E:                         Lower
   F:                         Upper
                              Format        (G)            (G)
   Grid: None    Color: No    Indicator     Yes            Yes

      Legend:         Format:  Data labels:               Skip: 1
   A                  Both
   B                  Both
   C                  Both
   D                  Both
   E                  Both
   F                  Both

22-May-89  04:12 PM
```

FIGURE 8-7.   Main Graph menu and Graph Settings box

Graph menus, 1-2-3 displays the settings in the box. You can use this box to constantly monitor the status of your graph settings. If you want to view the worksheet instead of the settings sheet, press F6 (WINDOW). Pressing F6 (WINDOW) again returns the settings sheet to the screen.

2. Select Type to see the following submenu:

```
C5: +B5*1.035                                                    MENU
Line  Bar  XY  Stacked-Bar  Pie
Line graph
```

3. Select Bar.

Notice that once you have made the type selection, you are returned to the main Graph menu, not to the READY mode. The main Graph menu is another "sticky" menu, like Print. It will stay around so you can make additional selections for defining your graph, disappearing only when you select Quit.

Specifying the Data
To Use in the Graph

There are no defaults for the data to be shown in a graph. If you forget to tell 1-2-3 which data to display on the graph, your graph will be blank. Line, bar, stacked bar, and XY graphs can each show up to six data series or ranges. These graph types can have data assigned to graph ranges A, B, C, D, E, and F in the Graph menu. Pie charts are special; a pie chart can only show one data range. In a pie chart, data is assigned to graph range A.

Follow these steps to assign data to graph ranges A through D in the current graph to see how data is assigned to the various graph ranges:

1. Select A to produce this display:

```
C5: +B5*1.035                                                          POINT
Enter first data range: C5
```

A	B	C	D	E	F	G	H

There is no need to select /Graph because the Graph menu is already on the screen.

2. Move the cell pointer to B5 and type ., move the cell pointer to G5, and press ENTER.

   This step assigns the range B5..G5 to the A range of the graph so that it will now represent the sales for the North region in the months of January through June.

3. Select B and move the cell pointer to B6. Type ., move the cell pointer to G6, and press ENTER.

   This assigns the data for the South region to the B range of the graph.

4. Select C and move the cell pointer to B7. Type ., move the cell pointer to G7, and press ENTER.

   This assigns the data for the East region to the C range of the graph.

5. Select D and move the cell pointer to B8. Type ., move the cell pointer to G8, and press ENTER.

   This assigns the data for the West region to the D range of the graph. Notice that this is the last region for ABC Company so that the E and F ranges are currently unassigned. Also notice that all the ranges assigned have the same unit of measure—dollars. If some ranges were measured in units of products

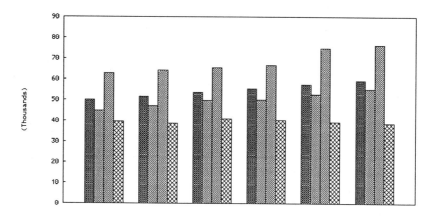

FIGURE 8-8.   Displaying the data in bar graph format

sold and others in dollars, both could not be shown on the same graph. The unit of measure must be the same for all of the data shown on a graph.

Viewing the Graph

Although the graph is not quite finished, you can still view it to see how the various data ranges stack up against each other. Sometimes if one range is either extremely large or extremely small in comparison to the others, it is not practical to graph the data together; the values in the smaller range will seem to blend with the X axis. To view your graph and return again to the menu, follow these steps:

1. Select View.

   If your monitor can display graphics, this command will produce an image that looks like the one in Figure 8-8. All four data ranges are shown on the graph; the A range values are represented by the leftmost bar in each grouping. There are six different points on the X axis, each representing one month in the range. If your monitor can display colors, each range may appear in a different color instead of a different hatch pattern.

2. Press any key to return to the menu display.

1-2-3 offers another method for viewing the current graph. The F10 (GRAPH) key displays the current graph when you are in the READY mode. To try this feature, follow these steps.

1. Select Quit.

    1-2-3 leaves the Graph menu and returns to the READY mode.

2. Press the F10 (GRAPH) key.

1-2-3 displays the graph in Figure 8-8. To return to the READY mode, press any key. You can use this function key when you change the worksheet data a graph uses and you want to see the effect on the graph.

Enhancing the Display

The current graph is not useful. The bars are hatch-marked to distinguish them, but the only way to tell which set of bars represents which set of data is by remembering the sequence in which the different regions were assigned to the graph ranges. Nor can you tell whether the points on the X axis represent years, months, or days and whether the numbers graphed are sales, expenses, or number of employees. Some additional information must be added to the graph in order for it to be useful. In this section you will learn how to add titles to the graph, label the X axis points, and add legends and grid lines.

LABELING THE X AXIS DATA POINTS   Without labels along the X axis it is impossible to tell what each group of values represents. You can solve this problem easily by assigning a range of labels to be displayed along the axis. This range of labels should correspond to the values in the data ranges that have been assigned and should have the same number of entries. Normally you will already have values like this in a column or row of the worksheet. For the current example, the labels that you need for the X axis are in B4..G4.

You can assign these labels to the X axis with the X range option from the Graph menu. Follow these steps to make the assignment:

1. Select /Graph X.

    This will produce a display similar to the one used for the graph data ranges:

```
C5: +B5*1.035                                              POINT
Enter x-axis range: C5
```

```
    A      B      C      D      E      F      G      H
```

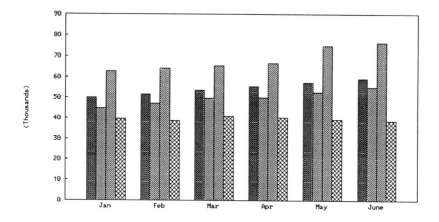

FIGURE 8-9. Adding X axis labels to the bar graph

You must enter the range address you want to use either by typing it or by using the pointing method.

2. Move the cell pointer to B4, type ., and move the cell pointer to G4 before pressing ENTER.

3. Select View to see the graph with the addition of labels along the X axis. Your display should match the one shown in Figure 8-9.

4. Press any key to return to the Graph menu.

Using Release 2.2's Shortcut Approach

If you are using Release 2.2, you can sometimes consolidate range assignments into one easy step. Your data must be in tabular form for this to work with the data used to label the X axis at the top or left side of the detailed entries. Follow these steps to assign all of the data ranges with one command:

1. Select Group. 1-2-3 displays this prompt:

C5: +B5*1.035   **POINT**
Enter group range: C5

(Note that 1-2-3 prompts you with the current location of the cell pointer.)

2. Move to B4, type ., press END, press HOME, and press ENTER to select B4..G8 as the worksheet data range for the data ranges. 1-2-3 displays this prompt:

C5: +B5*1.035   **MENU**
Columnwise Rowwise
Use columns as data ranges

This selection determines whether 1-2-3 divides the worksheet data into graph data ranges according to rows or columns.

3. Select Rowwise.

    1-2-3 automatically assigns the first row in the worksheet range to the X data range, the second row to the A data range, and so forth. By using the /Graph Group command, you can assign all of the graph data ranges at once instead of one at a time.

4. Select View to create the display shown in Figure 8-9.

5. Press any key to return to the Graph menu.

ADDING TITLES   Titles can be added to your graph in four different locations to improve its appearance. You can add a title along either of the axes or at the top of the graph in one or two lines. The menu you will see when you select /Graph Options Titles looks like this:

C5: +B5*1.035   **MENU**
First Second X-Axis Y-Axis
Assign first line of graph title

You will have 39 characters in which to enter any one of these four titles, once you select the option you want. The title can be even longer if you make it by using data that is already stored in a worksheet cell. Follow these steps to enhance your current graph with titles in all four locations:

1. Select Options to produce the following menu:

C5: +B5*1.035   **MENU**
Legend Format Titles Grid Scale Color B&W Data-Labels Quit
Create legends for data ranges

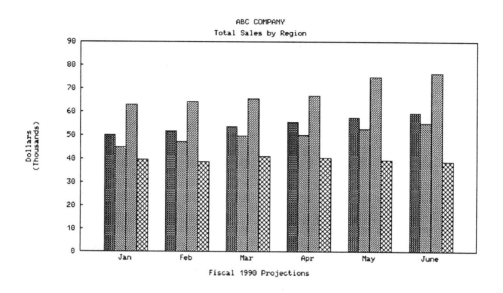

FIGURE 8-10.   Adding titles to the bar graph

2. Select Titles First to add a title at the top of the graph.

3. Type **\D1** and press ENTER.

   This will use the current entry in D1 as the title at the top of the graph. Notice how the Options menu returns to the screen. It too is a "sticky" menu: You must choose Quit in order to leave.

4. Select Titles Second, type **Total Sales by Region**, and press ENTER.

   This time the title was added by typing because there was no entry on the worksheet that exactly matched the desired title.

5. Select Titles X-Axis, type **Fiscal 1990 Projections**, and press ENTER.

6. Select Titles Y-Axis, type **Dollars**, and press ENTER.

7. Select Quit.

   This will exit the Graph Options menu and place you in the main Graph menu.

8. Select View to produce a display with all four titles as in Figure 8-10.

9. Press any key to return to the Graph menu.

ADDING LEGENDS   Legends add clarity to a graph that presents more than one data series by identifying how each data series is represented on the graph. If symbols are used to distinguish the different data series, the legend will consist of the series indicator and the text describing the data shown by that series. If color or hatch patterns are used, a small square of the color or pattern is placed at the bottom of the screen along with the the text description of the series. In Release 2.2, you can add all of the legends at once with a new menu option. Also, 1-2-3 will automatically adjust the legend display to use more than one line if the legend text needs it.

Selecting Legend from the Options menu presents the Legend submenu, as shown here:

```
C5: +B5*1.035                                        MENU
A B C D E F Range
Assign legend for first data range
```

When you select Legend you will be presented with a choice of the same six letters that you used to assign worksheet ranges to the different data series for the graph. Release 2.2 includes a Range option to select a worksheet range for all of the data range legends. To select a legend for a single range, select each of the data series that you assigned and enter a legend for each. You will need to select Legend and the appropriate letter each time until you have assigned a legend entry to each of the data series you used in the graph. Follow these steps to assign the legends for the current graph:

1. Select Options Legend A, type \A5, and press ENTER.

   The label stored in the cell A5 will be used for the legend. Your other option is to type **North** and press ENTER. The advantage of using the label entry in the cell is that if you decide to update it later, the graph title will automatically be updated for you the next time the graph is created.

2. Select Legend B, type \A6, and press ENTER.

3. Select Legend C, type \A7, and press ENTER.

4. Select Legend D, type \A8, and press ENTER.

5. Select Quit.

6. Select View to create the display shown in Figure 8-11.

7. Press any key to return to the Graph menu.

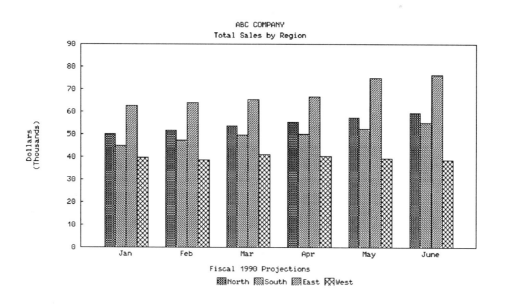

FIGURE 8-11.   Adding a legend to the bar graph

If you are using Release 2.2, you can follow these simpler steps to assign worksheet data as the legend text for the data ranges:

1. Select Options Legend Range. 1-2-3 displays this prompt:

(Note that 1-2-3 prompts you with the current location of the cell pointer as the starting point for the legend range.)

2. Move to A5, type ., press the DOWN ARROW key three times, and press ENTER to select A5..A8 as the worksheet data range for the data range legends.

   1-2-3 automatically assigns the first worksheet cell as the A data range legend, the second worksheet cell as the B data range legend, and so forth.

3. Select Quit.

4. Select View to create the display shown in Figure 8-11.

5. Press any key to return to the Graph menu.

ADDING GRID LINES   *Grid lines* are a series of lines that are parallel to either the X axis or the Y axis and that originate from the markers on the axis. They are designed to help you interpret the exact value of data points by extending either up or to the right from these markers. These lines are called grid lines because choosing to use them in both directions at once will create a grid pattern on your graph.

To get the menu for Grid, select /Graph Options Grid. The grid options can be used with all graph types except the pie chart; grid lines across a pie chart would detract from your ability to interpret the graph. The Grid menu contains these four options:

```
C5: +B5*1.035                                                   MENU
Horizontal Vertical Both Clear
Draw grid lines across the graph
```

With a bar graph, only the first option, Horizontal, is appropriate. This choice will let you interpret the top of each of the bars more accurately. Try it now for the current graph with these entries:

1. Select Options Grid Horizontal.

2. Select Quit to leave the Options menu.

3. Select View to produce the graph shown in Figure 8-12.

4. Press any key to return to the Graph menu.

5. Select Options Grid Clear Quit.

This will remove the horizontal grid lines and return you to the main Graph menu. If you wish to verify that the lines have been removed, you can use the View command.

VIEWING THE GRAPH IN COLOR OR BLACK AND WHITE   If you have a monitor that shows a single color, your only option is to view the graph with the B&W (black and white) option. If you have a color monitor you can select Options Color, and different colors will be used for the various data ranges. Whether you use three colors or a more extensive palette when coloring the graph depends on the graphics support supplied by your system. If you are able to view the system in color, you will want to use the B&W option to switch back to black and white before saving the graph. This option distinguishes the various data series by placing hatch patterns within bars and adding symbols to line graphs. Although the Color option uses color to distinguish

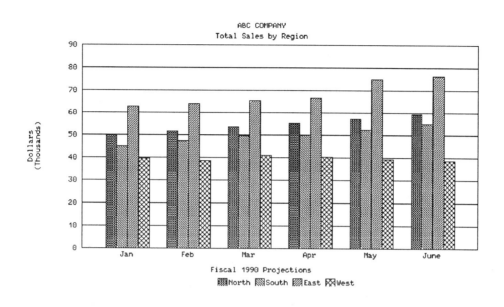

FIGURE 8-12. Adding horizontal grid lines to the bar graph

the various data ranges, these color differences are lost when the graph is printed on a standard black and white printer.

Naming the Current Graph

1-2-3 can only maintain one set of graph definitions at a time unless you assign a name to these definitions. Now that you have completely defined a graph, assign a name to these specifications before you create a second graph. The command to use is /Graph Name Create. Once you have used this command to assign a name, you are free to reset the current graph settings. This lets you start fresh to define a new graph or make a few changes to create a second graph that has many of the same options as the first graph. Follow these steps to assign a name to the current graph settings so you can create additional graphs.

1. Select Name Create.

    You do not need to select /Graph since you are already in the Graph menu.

2. Type **Sls_bar** and press ENTER.

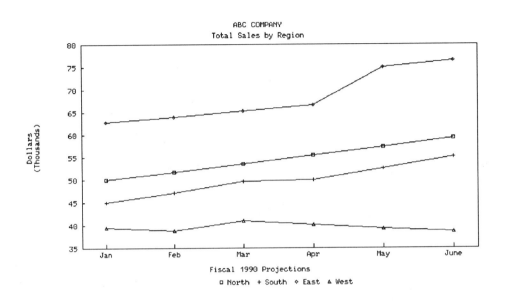

FIGURE 8-13.   Displaying the same data as a line graph

A Look at Some
Other Graph Types

Working with several additional graph types will give you a close-up look at how easy it is to create additional graphs or to change the type for the existing graph. In this section you will use the current data series to create a line graph and a stacked bar graph. Then you will create a pie chart with a subset of this data. Follow these steps to create the three additional graphs:

1. Select Type Line.

2. Select View to display a graph like the one shown in Figure 8-13.
   Notice that different symbols are used for each series shown on the graph. The legend is automatically changed from the hatch patterns to these symbols.

3. Press any key to return to the Graph menu.

4. Select Name Create, type **Sls_line**, and press ENTER.

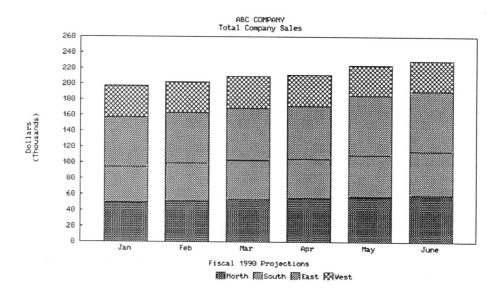

FIGURE 8-14. Displaying the same data as a stacked bar graph

5. Select Type Stacked-Bar.

6. Select Options Titles Second-Line, press ESC to remove the existing title, type **Total Company Sales**, and press ENTER.

   You can use this technique when you want to change any of the current graph specifications.

7. Select Quit and View to display a graph like the one shown in Figure 8-14.

   Notice that the legend is automatically changed back to the hatch patterns.

8. Press any key to return to the Graph menu.

9. Select Name Create, type **Sls_sbar**, and press ENTER.

10. Select Reset to produce this display:

```
C5: +B5*1.035                                              MENU
Graph X A B C D E F Ranges Options Quit
Clear all current graph settings
```

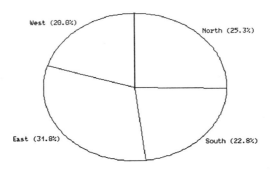

ABC COMPANY
January Sales by Region

West (20.0%)
North (25.3%)
East (31.8%)
South (22.8%)

FIGURE 8-15.   A pie chart

11. Select Graph.
    This will eliminate all the previous graph settings.

12. Select A, type **B5.B8**, and press ENTER.

13. Select X, type **A5.A8**, and press ENTER.

14. Select Type Pie.

15. Select Options Titles First, type **ABC COMPANY**, and press ENTER.

16. Select Titles Second, type **January Sales by Region**, and press ENTER.

17. Select Quit View to view a graph like the one in Figure 8-15.

18. Press any key, select Quit, move your cell pointer to A12, and make these
    entries:

    A12:   1
    A13:   102
    A14:   3
    A15:   4

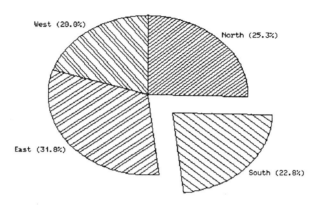

FIGURE 8-16.   A pie chart with shading

With Release 2 or higher, you can use these codes to change the appearance of the graph. First create a range with the same number of value entries as the range shown on the graph. Numbers 0 to 7 are used, each representing a unique hatch pattern. Adding 100 to any one of these entries will explode that piece from the pie (that is, split it off from the pie sections that remain joined).

These values will show as Currency, since that is the Global format. This will not affect their impact on the graph; however, if you find the dollar signs ($) confusing, you can eliminate them with /Range Format General.

19. Select /Graph B, type **A12.A15**, and press ENTER.

20. Select View.

    If you are using Release 2 or higher, notice how the new graph shown in Figure 8-16 differs from the previous one. It is much easier to read and emphasizes the South's contributions.

21. Press any key to return to the Graph menu.

22. Select Name Create, type **Jan_pie**, and press ENTER.

23. Select Quit to return to READY mode.

SAVING A GRAPH

Several aspects of graphs must be saved. You must save the graph definition if you plan to use the graph the next time you work with the current worksheet. Since 1-2-3 cannot print a graph, you must also save the graphic or print image for printing with the PrintGraph or Allways program.

Saving the Worksheet File

After you have created one or more graph definitions, you will want them to be available the next time you work with the current worksheet. To save these graph definitions, save the worksheet file to disk after defining the graphs. Do the following to save the graphs for the Profit file:

Select /File Save, type **Profit**, and press ENTER.

Saving the Graph Image

When you save the worksheet file you do not automatically save the graphic or print image for the current graph. In order to save this image so that you can print it with the PrintGraph or Allways program, you must select /Graph Save. This command saves the file under the name that you specify and adds the filename extension of .PIC to distinguish the file from a worksheet file.

To save multiple graphs for later printing, you must save each one as the current graph, even though the graphs are all defined on the same worksheet. For each graph, choose /Graph Name Use, followed by Save.

Follow these steps to save the graphs created for the Profit worksheet:

1. Select /Graph Save, type **Jan_pie**, and press ENTER.

   Since you exited the Graph menu to save the worksheet, you must now reenter it. The current graphic image was not saved along with the graph definition stored in the worksheet file. Although you are using the same name as you used for the graph specifications on the worksheet, the step you just took creates a unique file. The file that is created with this instruction will be named JAN_PIE.PIC as it is stored on disk.

2. Select Name Use, point to Sls_bar, and press ENTER.

   The bar graph you created will now be the active graph. When you perform another graph save, this is the image that will be saved.

3. Press any key, select Save, type **Sls_bar**, and press ENTER.
   This will save the graphic image of the bar graph you created.

4. Select Name Use, point to Sls_line, and press ENTER.
   The line graph you created will now be the active graph.

5. Press any key, select Save, type **Sls_line**, and press ENTER.

6. Select Name Use, point to Sls_sbar, and press ENTER.
   The stacked bar graph that you created will now be the active graph.

7. Press any key, select Save, type **Sls_sbar**, and press ENTER.

8. Select Quit to exit the Graph menu.

9. Select /Quit Yes.

Depending on how you entered 1-2-3, Quit will return you either to DOS or to the Lotus Access System. If quitting takes you back to DOS you can enter **LOTUS** to place yourself in the Lotus Access System. The following examples assume that you are in the Lotus Access System and are ready to learn how to print the graphs.

PRINTING A GRAPH

As mentioned, you can use the Lotus PrintGraph program to obtain a printed copy of your graphs. Before you can use this program, you must have previously saved the graph in a .PIC file. PrintGraph also must be configured for your system. This should have been completed when 1-2-3 was configured in the installation process. If not, return to Install to add the necessary information to the PrintGraph program. This process is described in Appendix A.

You can also print graphs using the Allways add-in, which is automatically supplied with Release 2.2 and can be purchased for use with Releases 2 and 2.01. This add-in offers additional advanced features that you can also use to print your worksheets. These features are covered in Chapter 13. For now, you can use PrintGraph to print your graphs with its extensive printing features.

The Lotus Access System, which you will use to select the PrintGraph option, is shown here for Release 2.2:

```
1-2-3  PrintGraph  Translate  Install  Exit
Use 1-2-3
```

```
Copyright 1986, 1989 Lotus Development Corp.  All Rights Reserved. V2.2   MENU

Select graphs to print or preview
Image-Select  Settings  Go  Align  Page  Exit

   GRAPHS     IMAGE Settings                      HARDWARE SETTINGS
   TO PRINT   Size                Range colors      Graphs directory:
              Top       .395  X                       A:\
              Left      .750  A                      Fonts directory:
              Width    6.500  B                        A:\
              Height   4.691  C                      Interface:
              Rotate    .000  D                        Parallel 1
                              E                      Printer:
              Font            F
              1  BLOCK1                              Paper size
              2  BLOCK1                                Width      8.500
                                                      Length    11.000

                                                   ACTION SETTINGS
                                                     Pause: No    Eject: No
```

FIGURE 8-17.   The PrintGraph menu in Release 2.2

The PrintGraph menu for Release 1A is very different from the Release 2 menu shown in Figure 8-17. Despite this apparent difference, the features are very similar. It is just that the definition of the various settings is covered by the selection Settings in Release 2 but by two different selections (Options and Configure) in Release 1A. With Release 1A, Options provides access to changing colors, paper size, and action settings. Configure addresses hardware configuration changes such as the directory to use and the output device. This chapter emphasizes the Release 2.2 selections for completing PrintGraph tasks; but even if you are using a lower release, these descriptions should help you make the correct selections.

Selecting Graph Files

Before you can print a graph you must have a copy of it saved as a .PIC file (the type of file that 1-2-3 uses when you select /Graph Save). This file must be in the directory shown on the main PrintGraph menu screen under "Graphs directory." If this description of the directory location for your graph files does not match the location of your .PIC files, you must change the directory.

CHANGING THE GRAPH DIRECTORY   To make this change, enter Settings Hardware to activate this menu:

Specify directory containing graphs
`Graphs-Directory` Fonts-Directory Interface Printer Size-Paper Quit

The graph directory has a default setting of A:\. This means that 1-2-3 will expect to read your graph files from drive A. If you have graph files stored on another drive, you need to change the graphs directory setting. Check the current setting for your graph files now; if a change is required, follow these steps:

1. Select Settings Hardware Graphs-Directory.

2. Type the pathname for your graph files.
   For example, if your graph files are stored on drive C in the directory \123\graphs, you would type this entry:

   C:\123\graphs

3. Press ENTER to finalize the new setting.

4. Select Quit twice to return to the main menu.

TELLING PRINTGRAPH WHICH FILES TO PRINT   The Image-Select option on the main PrintGraph menu allows you to select graphs from the directory listed under "Graphs directory" on the right side of the main PrintGraph screen. Once you select Image-Select, the names of the graph files in this directory will be displayed for you, as shown in Figure 8-18. A highlighted bar will rest on the first filename in the

Select graphs to print

```
GRAPH FILE   DATE      TIME     SIZE
----------------------------------------     Space bar marks or unmarks selection
E            08-03-88  10:20    1362          ENTER selects marked graphs
GRAPH        09-08-88  12:32    4980          ESC exits, ignoring changes
JAN_PIE      02-22-90  20:50    2589          HOME moves to beginning of list
SLS_BAR      02-22-90  20:51    1053          END moves to end of list
SLS_LINE     02-22-90  20:51    1530          ↑ and ↓ move highlight
SLS_SBAR     02-22-90  20:52    1053             List will scroll if highlight
WPCHP17      09-08-88  12:27    4963             moved beyond top or bottom
                                              GRAPH (F10) previews marked graph
```

FIGURE 8-18.   PrintGraph menu for selecting images to print

list. The arrow keys will let you scroll through the list of filenames, moving the highlighted bar through the list until you find a file that you wish to print.

To mark a file for printing, position the highlighted bar on the filename and press the SPACEBAR. If you change your mind, press the SPACEBAR again to undo the selection. After you select the first file you can move the highlighted bar up and down in the list to select as many additional files as you like. 1-2-3 will even remember the order in which you made your selections and print the graphs in that sequence.

If you are uncertain what a graph file contains, you can move the highlighted bar to the filename and press F10. (You may have to change the fonts directory first if it is not in drive A.) 1-2-3 will recreate the chosen graph on your screen for you to review. When you have finished viewing the graph, you can press ESC to return to the selection screen to make additional selections. Once you have marked all the graphs, press ENTER to select the graphs you want for printing. Use these steps to select the graph files created in this exercise:

1. Select Image-Select.

2. Use the highlighted bar and move to JAN_PIE. Press the SPACEBAR to mark the graph with a #.
   Once it is marked, you can make additional selections.

3. Move the highlighted bar to SLS_SBAR and press the SPACEBAR.

4. Move the highlighted bar to SLS_BAR and press the SPACEBAR.

5. Move the highlighted bar to SLS_LINE and press F10 to view the graph.

6. Press ENTER to return to the menu, and then press the SPACEBAR.

Controlling the Settings

The PrintGraph program has a wide variety of settings that allow you to tailor the printing of a graph. Many of these settings are advanced features, best explored only once you have mastered the basics. This section presents the basic settings that you can work with to make PrintGraph respond to your needs. The following menu shows the various aspects of the graphic process that can be changed when you select Settings from the main PrintGraph menu:

Copyright 1986, 1989 Lotus Development Corp. All Rights Reserved. V2.2   **MENU**

Specify graph size, fonts and colors
Image Hardware Action Save Reset Quit

IMAGE SETTINGS   The Image settings allow you to alter features such as size, color, and fonts. Although these features are nice to have available because you can use the default settings, they are not relevant to the basic set of skills you are initially trying to develop.

HARDWARE SETTINGS   You have already explored one hardware setting change: the change to the directory for your graph files. You can also alter the directory where the fonts are stored. The fonts affect the type of printing used for labels throughout the graph. To access these fonts you must be sure that the font files are in the directory shown at the right side of the main PrintGraph menu. If they are not there, you can change this display by using the command /Graphs Settings Hardware Fonts-Directory and typing a new directory name.

CHECKING THE INTERFACE AND PRINTER TYPE   The proper interface and printer type must show on the PrintGraph menu in order for your printer or plotter to produce graphs correctly. Eight different interface options are available, although the first two are used most frequently because they represent standard parallel and serial interfaces. The first option, 1, represents a standard *parallel connection,* which is the most common way of connecting a printer to your system. The second represents a *serial connection,* which is commonly used to connect a plotter to your system. The default value for this setting is 1, which represents a standard parallel interface. If your output device is a plotter, you may need to change this setting to serial. However, consult with your dealer or other knowledgeable source before making these changes.

If you have installed PrintGraph to operate with a variety of printers, the Hardware Printer setting may require frequent change. Each time you want to use a different printer, select PrintGraph Settings Hardware Printer and the output device you want to use for your graphs. If your current setting is blank or needs to be changed, follow these steps:

1. Select Hardware Printer.

2. Select the correct output device from the list of options specified during the Install process. Press ENTER and select Quit.

If no options are displayed it means that you did not install PrintGraph. If the printer type you wish to select is not displayed as an option, return to Install to correct the problem.

SAVING THE CHANGES TO SETTINGS   All the changes you make to the settings are temporary; unless you save them, they will apply only to the current session. When you want to retain the new setting values for subsequent sessions, you

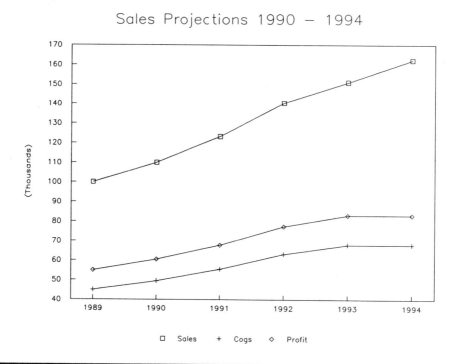

FIGURE 8-19.   A graph printed with the PrintGraph program

must store them in the file PGRAPH.CNF (GRAPH.CNF in Release 1A). To make
the new settings permanent, you must select Save from the Settings menu to store the
settings in the PGRAPH.CNF file. Do the following to save your changes:

Select Save and Quit to return to the main menu.

Unlike other Save operations, here you do not need to enter a filename. 1-2-3 always
uses the same file.

Printing the Graphs

Once you have made all the selections, printing the graph is quite simple. 1-2-3 will
begin printing the graphs you have chosen with Image-Select when you choose Go
from the PrintGraph menu. Pressing the CTRL and BREAK keys simultaneously will

stop the printing if you need to interrupt the process. However, the printer will not stop right away; it will continue to print the lines that have already been transmitted to it. Follow these steps to print the graphs you selected earlier:

1. Check to ensure that your printer is both on and online.

2. Select Go.

3. Once all the graphs have been printed, select Exit. Figure 8-19 shows one of the graphs that was printed.

If you are printing a color graph to a plotter, PrintGraph prompts you to press a key when the pens it lists are loaded before printing a graph. If you have set the Page Eject option to Yes, the printer will advance to the next page after each graph is printed. If you have set the Eject option to No, the printer will use all the space on a page for graphs before advancing the paper. The Pause option allows you to change the paper when a graph is completed. The setting for Pause must be Yes when you want to make this change for a device like a plotter. PrintGraph will continue the printing process until it has completed all the selected graphs, unless you choose to intervene with CTRL-BREAK.

REVIEW EXERCISE

In this chapter, you learned how to use 1-2-3's graph features. The following exercises offer you an opportunity to try these skills using the data from the SALESPRJ file that you created in Chapter 5.

1. Retrieve the SALESPRJ file. If it is unavailable, enter the data in Figure 8-20 in an empty worksheet.

2. Assign the data in B3..G3 to data range X. Assign the data in B4..G4 to data range A. Assign the data in B5..G5 to data range B. Assign the data in B6..G6 to data range C. View the graph. Notice how 1-2-3 creates a line graph because you have not selected a graph type.
   Hint: For Release 2.2, select /Graph Group, select the range B3..G6, and select Rowwise to divide the worksheet range by rows into graph data ranges. For lower releases, select /Graph X and select B3..G3. Then select A and type **B4..G4**. Next select B and type **B5..G5**. Finally select C and type **B6..G6**.

3. Make the current graph a bar graph.
   Hint: Select Type and Bar.

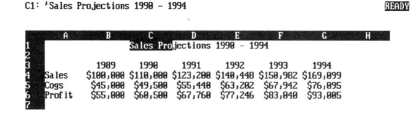

C1: 'Sales Projections 1990 - 1994   READY

FIGURE 8-20.   Worksheet for using graph features

View the graph.

4. Use the labels in A4, A5, and A6 for the legends for the A, B, and C data ranges.
    Hint: For Release 2.2, select Options Legend Range and select the range A4..A6. For lower releases, select Options Legend A and type **\A4**. Then select B and type **\A5**. Next select B and type **\A6**.
    View the graph.

5. Use the contents of C1 as a graph title. Label the X axis "Years" and the Y axis "Dollars." View the graph. It looks like the one in Figure 8-21.
    Hint: To title the graph, select Options Titles First and type **\C1**. To label the X axis, select Titles X-Axis and type **Years**. To label the Y axis, select Titles Y-Axis and type **Dollars**. Then select Quit to return to the main Graph menu.

6. Save the graph settings as SALES_BAR.
    Hint: Select Name Create, type **SALES_BAR**, and press ENTER.

7. Save the graphic image as SALE_BAR.PIC.
    Hint: Select Save, type **SALE_BAR**, and press ENTER.

8. Make the current graph a line graph.
    Hint: Select Type and Line.
    View the graph.

9. Save the graphic image as SALE_LIN.PIC.
    Hint: Select Save, type **SALE_LIN**, and press ENTER.

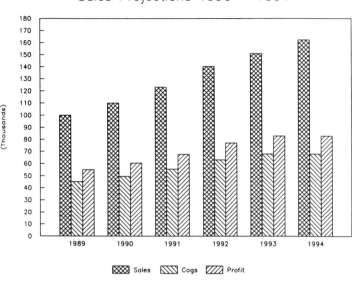

Sales Projections 1990 — 1994

FIGURE 8-21.   Bar graph created from Figure 8-20 data

10. Save the file so the current and named graph settings you have created remain with the worksheet.

    Hint: Select /File Save, press ENTER, and select Replace.

11. Exit 1-2-3 and enter PrintGraph.

    Hint: Select /Quit Yes. Then select PrintGraph from the Lotus Access System.

12. Check if the graphs directory is the same directory that you saved the file to. Change it if necessary.

    Hint: Select Settings Hardware Graphs-Directory, type the directory path you want, and press ENTER. Then select Quit twice to return to the main menu.

13. Check if the fonts directory is the directory that contains 1-2-3 font files. Change it if necessary.

    Hint: Select Settings Hardware Fonts-Directory, type the directory path you want, and press ENTER. Then select Quit twice to return to the main menu.

14. Select SALE_BAR to print. Do not return to the main menu.
    Hint: Select Image, move to the SALE_BAR file, and press the SPACEBAR.

15. Highlight the SALE_LIN file. Press F10. Notice how PrintGraph displays the SALE_LIN graph. Press ESC to return to the graph file list. Press the SPACEBAR to select the file. Press ENTER to return to the main menu.

16. Print the graphs. You may need to put pens in a plotter if you are using one or confirm that the printer or plotter contains a blank sheet of paper. Figure 8-22 shows the SALE_LIN graph printed on a Hewlett Packard LaserJet Series II.
    Hint: Select Go.

17. Exit PrintGraph.
    Hint: Select Exit.

REVIEW

- 1-2-3 can create five different graph types from your worksheet data. It can create bar, line, pie, stacked bar, and XY graphs.

- 1-2-3 can plot up to six series of data in a graph.

- A graph can contain legends to identify the data ranges, grid lines, and titles that enhance its appearance.

- A worksheet has only one current graph at a time. Once you name a graph, you can make a different graph current and still be able to use the named graph at a later time.

- You can save the graph settings by saving the worksheet.

- You can save the graphic image with /Graph Save to save the graph to a file that PrintGraph and Allways can use.

- PrintGraph can print 1-2-3 graphs with a variety of print enhancements. If you prefer you can use the Allways add-in package supplied with Release 2.2 of 1-2-3.

FIGURE 8-22.   Line graph printed with the PrintGraph program

Commands and Keys

Entry	Action
F10 (GRAPH)	Displays the current worksheet
/GA	Graph A assigns worksheet data to the A data range
/GB	Graph B assigns worksheet data to the B data range
/GC	Graph C assigns worksheet data to the C data range
/GD	Graph D assigns worksheet data to the D data range
/GE	Graph E assigns worksheet data to the E data range
/GF	Graph F assigns worksheet data to the F data range

Entry	Action
/GX	Graph X assigns worksheet data to the X data range
/GG	Graph Group assigns worksheet data to all data ranges
/GT	Graph Type selects the current graph type
/GNU	Graph Name Use makes a named graph the current graph
/GNC	Graph Name Create makes the current graph a named graph
/GS	Graph Save saves the graphic image to a .PIC file
/GV	Graph View views the current graph
/GOTF	Graph Options Titles First provides the first line title for the current graph
/GOTS	Graph Options Titles Second provides the second line title for the current graph
/GOTX	Graph Options Titles X-Axis provides the title for X axis in the current graph
/GOTY	Graph Options Titles Y-Axis provides the title for Y axis in the current graph
/GOL	Graph Options Legend assigns legends to the A through F data ranges
/GOGH	Graph Options Grid Horizontal displays horizontal grid lines in the current graph
/GOGV	Graph Options Grid Vertical displays vertical grid lines in the current graph
/GOGB	Graph Options Grid Both displays horizontal and vertical grid lines in the current graph
/GOGC	Graph Options Grid Clear removes grid lines in the current graph
/GOQ	Graph Options Quit returns to the Graph menu
/GOB	Graph Options B&W displays current graph in black and white (monochrome)
/GOC	Graph Options Color displays current graph in color

PrintGraph Commands	Action
I	Image-Select selects the graphic images to print
SHG	Settings Hardware Graphs-Directory selects the directory containing the graph files
SHF	Settings Hardware Fonts-Directory selects the directory containing the font files
SHI	Settings Hardware Interface selects the communications port to the printer
SHP	Settings Hardware Printer selects the printer to use for printing
SS	Settings Save saves the settings made with the Settings menu
G	Go prints the selected graphs
E	Exit leaves PrintGraph

9

DATA-MANAGEMENT BASICS

All the work you have done with 1-2-3 up to this point has been concerned with calculating some type of numeric result. This is the typical application for the 1-2-3 program. However, 1-2-3 also has other features—features that are oriented more toward the management of information than toward calculations. These data-management features are a special group of commands that provide capabilities for the design, entry, and retrieval of information, with or without additional calculations. You can use these commands to keep track of information about your suppliers, clients, or employees.

Since this is a new area of 1-2-3 for you, the first step is to learn some new terms. A *database* is a collection of all the information you have about a set of things. These things can be customers, employees, orders, parts in your inventory, or anything else. If you created a database of employee information, you would place the information about each of your employees in it. All the information about one employee would be in one *record* of the database. A record is composed of all the pieces of information you want to record about each thing in the set, such as one employee. These individual pieces of information in the record are referred to as *fields*. Fields to include in each record in an employee database might contain name, job classification, salary, date of hire, and social security number. Every time you design a new database, you need to decide what fields will be included in each record.

A 1-2-3 database is a range of cells on the worksheet. The database can be in any area of the worksheet you want, but you must put the fields' names in the top row of the range. The records in the database, which contain data for each field, go in the rows beneath the field names.

SETTING UP A DATABASE

To create a new database, first create a list of the fields you plan to use, and then estimate the number of characters required for each field. To make this estimate, total the characters required to store one record in the database. Then estimate the number of records that you will place in the database, and multiply this number by the size of one record to get an estimate of how much memory is required for the database. Next, load 1-2-3 and select /Worksheet Status to see how much memory is available. If the total you need exceeds the amount of memory available, another alternative is required—for example, splitting the database into two sections. Try this process for the employee file you will create.

1. Take a piece of paper and write down this list of field names:

    Last Name
    First Name
    SS#
    Job Code
    Salary
    Location

2. Write the size of the field next to each field name.

    For this example, use 12 characters for the last name, 12 for the first name, 11 for the social security number, 4 for the job code, 8 for the salary, and 3 for the location. This makes a total of 50 characters for one record. (If you want your estimate to be more exact, add 4 for each field since 1-2-3 uses 4 characters to store information about each cell.)

3. Estimate the number of records you plan to eventually enter into the database and multiply this number by the size of one record.

```
A1:                                                              STAT
Press any key to continue...
                        ── Global Settings ──────
     Conventional memory:  111104 of 242576 Bytes (45%)
     Expanded memory:      (None)

     Math coprocessor:     (None)

     Recalculation:
       Method              Automatic
       Order               Natural
       Iterations          1

     Circular reference:   (None)

     Cell display:
       Format              (G)
       Label prefix        '
       Column width        9
       Zero suppression    Off

     Global protection:    Off
```

FIGURE 9-1.   Using the /Worksheet Status command to check available memory

For this example, 100 records is the estimate. Multiplying 100 by 50 results in a product of 5000. This should be well within the limit of any system. However, for those occasions when it is larger, take a look at how to verify this calculation:

4. Select /Worksheet Status and check the amount of available memory.

The amount of memory shown in the worksheet status display in Figure 9-1 is 111,104 bytes—more than enough to accommodate 5000 characters, plus some extra for special options such as formatting. If the amount of available memory exceeds the size requirements of the database, it is safe to proceed. When the size of the database is larger than available memory, you must develop an alternative plan before beginning data entry. One possibility is to disable the Undo feature since it uses half of the available memory.

Choosing a Location

Any area of the worksheet can be used for a database. Normally, when your worksheet serves a dual purpose (for both calculations and a database), place the database below the calculations so it can expand easily. If nothing else is stored on the worksheet, row 1 is as good a starting location as any other.

Entering Field Names

Whatever area you select for your database, record your field names across the top row. Always choose *meaningful names;* they will be used again to invoke the data management features. Meaningful names should be *self-documenting*—that is, they should help clarify what you are doing. Each field name must be contained within a single cell. Field names that span two cells are not acceptable; neither are spaces at the end of a field name. Spaces or special characters in the cell immediately beneath the field name can also cause a problem with some of 1-2-3's data-management features.

To enter the field names in the chosen area, simply type them in their respective cells and adjust the column widths.

1. Enter the field names for the employee database in these cells now:

    A1:   Last Name
    B1:   First Name
    C1:   "SS#
    D1:   Job Code
    E1:   "Salary
    F1:   Location

    Pay special attention to the spelling of field names. When you use the field names in later tasks, they must match exactly if the job is to be completed properly.

2. Move the cell pointer to column A and select /Worksheet Column Set-Width, type **12**, and press ENTER.

3. Repeat step 2 for columns B, C, and E. If you are using Release 2.2, you can select /Worksheet Column Column-Range Set-Width to set the width for columns A through E to 12 and /Worksheet Column Reset-Width for column D.

    These entries should create a display like this:

F1: 'Location   READY

The label entries require a width equal only to the number of characters in the field. The Salary field has been estimated at 8 digits; however, 12 is allowed in the column width for the addition of a dollar sign, a comma, a decimal point, and one extra space to separate the entry from the adjacent fields.

Entering Data

Now that you have entered the field names, you can begin entering the data beneath them. The first record should be entered immediately beneath the field names. Each record will occupy one row; do not skip any row as you begin to enter records.

Make sure that the data you enter in each field is the same type. If a field contains value entries, the entries in all records for this field should contain value entries. If you do not have all the data for a record, you can leave the field blank as long as you do not leave the entire row blank. Except for these few simple guidelines, everything is exactly the same as when entering data in the worksheet environment.

You will need to complete the data entry for the database used throughout the rest of this chapter. The normal procedure for entering records in a database is to enter a complete record at once; however, since it might be easier to complete the entries in one column before moving to the next one, the directions in this chapter are written from that perspective. You can either work from the screen display shown in Figure 9-2 or follow these explicit directions to complete the entries:

1. Place these entries in the Last Name field:

A2:	Larson
A3:	Campbell
A4:	Campbell
A5:	Stephens
A6:	Caldor
A7:	Lightnor
A8:	McCartin
A9:	Justof
A10:	Patterson
A11:	Miller

2. Make these entries in the First Name field:

B2:	Mary
B3:	David
B4:	Keith
B5:	Tom
B6:	Larry
B7:	Peggy

A1: [W12] 'Last Name   READY

	A	B	C	D	E	F
1	Last Name	First Name	SS#	Job Code	Salary	Location
2	Larson	Mary	543-98-9876	23	$12,000	2
3	Campbell	David	213-76-9874	23	$23,000	10
4	Campbell	Keith	569-89-7654	12	$32,000	2
5	Stephens	Tom	219-78-8954	15	$17,800	2
6	Caldor	Larry	459-34-0921	23	$32,500	4
7	Lightnor	Peggy	560-55-4311	14	$23,500	10
8	McCartin	John	817-66-1212	15	$54,600	2
9	Justof	Jack	431-78-9963	17	$41,200	4
10	Patterson	Lyle	212-11-9090	12	$21,500	10
11	Miller	Lisa	214-89-6756	23	$18,700	2
12						

FIGURE 9-2.   The employee database

B8:	John
B9:	Jack
B10:	Lyle
B11:	Lisa

3. Make the following entries in the SS# field:

C2:	'543-98-9876
C3:	'213-76-9874
C4:	'569-89-7654
C5:	'219-78-8954
C6:	'459-34-0921
C7:	'560-55-4311
C8:	'817-66-1212
C9:	'431-78-9963
C10:	'212-11-9090
C11:	'214-89-6756

Notice that a single quotation mark was used at the beginning of each of these entries. The social security numbers must be labels because they include the hyphen character (-). If you forget to start these entries with a label indicator, a negative number will appear in the cell. You will then need to edit the cell entry and insert the label indicator at the beginning.

4. Enter the following job codes:

D2:	23
D3:	23
D4:	12
D5:	15
D6:	23
D7:	14
D8:	15
D9:	17
D10:	12
D11:	23

5. Move the cell pointer to E2, select /Range Format Currency, type 0, press ENTER, move the cell pointer to E11, and press ENTER.

6. Make the following salary entries:

E2:	12000
E3:	23000
E4:	32000
E5:	17800
E6:	32500
E7:	23500
E8:	54600
E9:	41200
E10:	21500
E11:	18700

7. Enter the following location codes:

F2:	2
F3:	10
F4:	2
F5:	2
F6:	4
F7:	10
F8:	2
F9:	4
F10:	10
F11:	2

This completes the entries required to create a database with ten records.

Making Changes

Making changes to entries in the database is no different from making changes in the worksheet data you use. You have two good choices: retype any entry to replace it, or use the F2 (EDIT) technique to make a quick correction. To feel at home with making changes, just as if you were still making worksheet entries, carry out the following steps to change the salary and social security number for Mary Larson:

1. Move the cell pointer to C2, press the F2 (EDIT) key, and move with the LEFT ARROW key until the small cursor is under the 7. Press the DEL key, type **4**, and press ENTER to correct the SS#.

2. Move the cell pointer to E2, press F2 (EDIT), and press the HOME key. Next, press the DEL key, type **2**, and press ENTER to produce the display shown in Figure 9-3.

The other way to update the entries in the database, which you might want to use if the change is extensive, is to retype them.

E2: (C0) [W12] 22000   READY

	A	B	C	D	E	F
	Last Name	First Name	SS#	Job Code	Salary	Location
1						
2	Larson	Mary	543-98-9846	23	$22,000	2
3	Campbell	David	213-76-9874	23	$23,000	10
4	Campbell	Keith	569-89-7654	12	$32,000	2
5	Stephens	Tom	219-78-8954	15	$17,800	2
6	Caldor	Larry	459-34-0921	23	$32,500	4
7	Lightnor	Peggy	560-55-4311	14	$23,500	10
8	McCartin	John	817-66-1212	15	$54,600	2
9	Justof	Jack	431-78-9963	17	$41,200	4
10	Patterson	Lyle	212-11-9090	12	$21,500	10
11	Miller	Lisa	214-89-6756	23	$18,700	2
12						
13						

FIGURE 9-3. Updating the database

SORTING THE DATABASE

1-2-3 provides sort features that can alter the sequence of the records in your database to any sequence you need. If you decide that you would like an employee list in alphabetical order, 1-2-3 can do this for you. If you decide that you want the records in order by job code, salary, or location, 1-2-3 can make this change easily. You will find 1-2-3's sort commands easy to work with, and you will be amazed at how rapidly 1-2-3 can resequence your data.

All the commands that you will need to specify the sort are located on the menu shown in Figure 9-4. You can activate this menu by selecting /Data Sort. The settings sheet, which appears below the menu in this figure, allows you to see at a glance the selections you have already made. You will always want to check the accuracy of the entries shown on this sheet before selecting Go to start the Sort operation.

Defining the Database Location

The first step in resequencing your database is to tell 1-2-3 where the data is located. When you are sorting data, 1-2-3 is not interested in the field names, only in the data values that you expect it to sort. If you accidentally include the field names in this range, 1-2-3 will sort them just as if they were intentionally included as data values.

In defining the area to be sorted, you have the choice of defining some of the records or all of them. Always include all the fields, even if you want to exclude some of the records. This is because excluded fields remain stationary and do not remain with the other portion of the record to which they belong, thus jeopardizing the integrity of

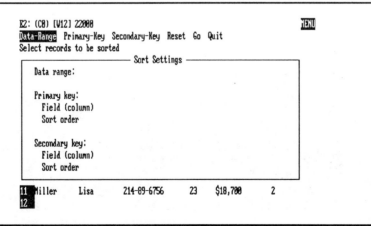

FIGURE 9-4.   The Sort menu and settings sheet

your file. It is therefore a good idea to save the file before sorting in case you accidentally exclude some of the field names. Having Undo enabled is another safeguard, although it will only be effective in reversing the result of a Sort operation if you do so before entering another command. Follow these steps to tell 1-2-3 where the employee records are located:

1. Select /File Save, type **EMPLOYEE**, and press ENTER.

2. Select /Data Sort.

3. Select Data-Range to produce this display:

```
E2: (C0) [W12] 22000                                               POINT
Enter data range: E2
```
A	B	C	D	E	F

4. Press the HOME key. Press the DOWN ARROW key.
   This will position you in A2, right below the first field name. If you had sorted this database previously, you would have had to press ESC first to free the beginning of the range before moving the cell pointer.

5. Type . and press the END key followed by the DOWN ARROW key. Press the END key followed by the RIGHT ARROW key.
   At this point the database range should be highlighted like the one shown in Figure 9-5.

6. Verify that the range you wish to sort is highlighted and press ENTER.

```
F11: 2                                                             POINT
Enter data range: A2..F11
```

	A	B	C	D	E	F
1	Last Name	First Name	SS#	Job Code	Salary	Location
2	Larson	Mary	543-98-9846	23	$22,000	2
3	Campbell	David	213-76-9874	23	$23,000	10
4	Campbell	Keith	569-89-7654	12	$32,000	2
5	Stephens	Tom	219-78-8954	15	$17,800	2
6	Caldor	Larry	459-34-0921	23	$32,500	4
7	Lightnor	Peggy	560-55-4311	14	$23,500	10
8	McCartin	John	817-66-1212	15	$54,600	2
9	Justof	Jack	431-78-9963	17	$41,200	4
10	Patterson	Lyle	212-11-9090	12	$21,500	10
11	Miller	Lisa	214-89-6756	23	$18,700	2
12						

FIGURE 9-5.   Highlighting the range to sort

Defining the Sort Sequence

You can sort your data in sequence by any of the database fields. If you sort by the contents of column D, the database will be in sequence by job code. If you sort by column C, social security number will determine the sequence. Whichever field you choose to sort by, you will also have to decide whether you want the entries to be sequenced from highest to lowest (descending) or lowest to highest (ascending).

1-2-3 refers to the field that determines the sequence of the records after the sort as the *primary key*. It also allows you to establish a *secondary key*. This secondary key, which is optional, is a precaution against duplicates in the primary key. 1-2-3 ignores the secondary key even when you specify one, except where the primary key contains duplicate entries. In that case, the secondary key is used to break the tie.

CHOOSING A PRIMARY KEY   There are three ways to specify the sort sequence. One is to select /Data Sort Primary-Key and point to a cell that contains an entry for the field that will control the order of the records. Another is to type the address of this cell. The third way will work if you have named the first cell in each of the data-entry columns. An easy way to apply these names is to select /Range Name Label Down and specify the range of labels that represent the field names. If you use this approach you can press F3 (NAME) when prompted for a field or a column and select from the list of range names provided. 1-2-3 will display the cell address of the entry on the settings sheet and follow it with the name assigned to the range. The first time the data is sorted, the named cell may be shuffled to a record other than the first record, but this will not affect later use of it because the sort accepts any of the entries with a field. Regardless of the method chosen for specifying the cell, the next prompt you will see asks for the sort order, for which A and D are the only acceptable choices. An A represents ascending sequence and a D represents descending sequence. When 1-2-3 asks for the sort order, a default choice is on the screen. If you want to use it, just press ENTER.

Follow these steps to see the /Data Sort Primary-Key command in action:

1. Select Primary-Key to create this prompt:

```
E2: (C0) [W12] 22000                                          POINT
Primary sort key: E2
```

	A	B	C	D	E	F

2. Move the cell pointer to C2 and press ENTER.
   This selects the social security number as the primary sort key.

3. Type **D** to create the following display:

```
E2: (C0) [W12] 22000                                              EDIT
Primary sort key: C2                    Sort order (A or D): D
```

4. Press ENTER to request descending sequence.

5. Select Go to activate the sort and change the sequence of the records to match Figure 9-6.

   Just defining the sort key does not change the data sequence. You must select Go to tell 1-2-3 that you are ready for the sort to take place.

CHOOSING A SECONDARY KEY   The secondary key is the tie breaker. It resolves duplicate entries and determines which one of the duplicates should be listed first, based on the value of the secondary field. In situations like the last example where social security number was the controlling sequence, a secondary key is not needed. Since the social security number field does not contain legal duplicates, there is no need for a tie breaker. On the other hand, if you want to sort the employee file by last name, a secondary key is appropriate since last names sometimes are duplicated.

The process for specifying the secondary key is the same as the process for specifying the primary key, except that you select /Data Sort Secondary-Key. Try this feature by sorting the employee database in name order, following these steps:

1. Select /Data Sort Reset.

   This cancels the current settings for the data range and for the primary and secondary sort keys.

```
E2: (C0) [W12] 54600                                            READY

         A           B           C        D        E         F
 1  Last Name   First Name       SS# Job Code     Salary  Location
 2  McCartin    John        817-66-1212     15   $54,600        2
 3  Campbell    Keith       569-89-7654     12   $32,000        2
 4  Lightnor    Peggy       560-55-4311     14   $23,500       10
 5  Larson      Mary        543-98-9846     23   $22,000        2
 6  Caldor      Larry       459-34-0921     23   $32,500        4
 7  Justof      Jack        431-78-9963     17   $41,200        4
 8  Stephens    Tom         219-78-8954     15   $17,000        2
 9  Miller      Lisa        214-89-6756     23   $18,700        2
10  Campbell    David       213-76-9874     23   $23,000       10
11  Patterson   Lyle        212-11-9090     12   $21,500       10
12
13
```

FIGURE 9-6.   Records in SS# sequence

E2: (C0) [W12] 32500   READY

	A	B	C	D	E	F
1	Last Name	First Name	SS#	Job Code	Salary	Location
2	Caldor	Larry	459-34-0921	23	$32,500	4
3	Campbell	David	213-76-9874	23	$23,000	10
4	Campbell	Keith	569-89-7654	12	$32,000	2
5	Justof	Jack	431-78-9963	17	$41,200	4
6	Larson	Mary	543-98-9046	23	$22,000	2
7	Lightnor	Peggy	560-55-4311	14	$23,500	10
8	McCartin	John	817-66-1212	15	$54,600	2
9	Miller	Lisa	214-89-6756	23	$18,700	2
10	Patterson	Lyle	212-11-9090	12	$21,500	10
11	Stephens	Tom	219-78-8954	15	$17,800	2
12						
13						

FIGURE 9-7.   Records in sequence by name

2. Select Data-Range, type **A2.F11**, and press ENTER.

3. Select Primary-Key, type **A2**, press ENTER, type **A**, and press ENTER.
   The top cell in the Last Name field was selected as the sort key.

4. Select Secondary-Key, type **B2**, press ENTER, type **A**, and press ENTER.
   The top cell in the First Name field was selected as the secondary key. This key will be used to resolve the tie only when more than one employee has the same last name. In that case, the First Name field will determine which record is placed first.

5. Select Go to resequence the data to the alphabetical name list that is shown in Figure 9-7.

There is no need to quit the Sort menu. Selecting Go to execute the sort will place you back in READY mode after the data has been resequenced. The Quit option is available for occasions when you want to exit the menu without performing the sort.

When you save the worksheet with /File Save, 1-2-3 will save the sort specifications you just entered. The next time you use the worksheet you can execute the sort and change only those options that are different. Be especially careful when updating the data range if you add more fields to the end of the database. If you do not adjust the range, the new fields will remain stationary while the rest of the record is shifted to a new row.

SEARCHING THE DATABASE

As your database grows, it becomes increasingly important to review the information it contains selectively. Once the employee file contains 500 records, it becomes extremely time-consuming to locate all the records that have a job code of 23 by scanning the Job Code column visually.

1-2-3 gives you a way to work with information in your database selectively by means of *exception* or *selective reporting* capabilities. This means you will have a method of selectively presenting information that falls outside of a norm you establish. The selective reporting feature can also provide an easy way to clean up the database or to create reports in response to unexpected requests.

Working with 1-2-3's selective reporting feature requires that you enter your specifications for record selection on the worksheet. These specifications are known as *criteria* and must be entered on the worksheet before invoking 1-2-3's commands.

Once the criteria are entered, you must make various menu selections. All the commands required for working with 1-2-3's selective reporting feature are found in the Data Query menu, which follows:

```
E2: (C0) [W12] 32500                                            MENU
Input Criteria Output Find Extract Unique Delete Reset Quit
Specify range that contains records to search
┌───────────────────────── Query Settings ─────────────────────────┐
│  Input range:                                                     │
│                                                                   │
│  Criteria range:                                                  │
│                                                                   │
│  Output range:                                                    │
│                                                                   │
└───────────────────────────────────────────────────────────────────┘
```

Like the Sort menu, the Data Query menu is "sticky"; in most situations, you will have to make more than one selection from the menu before 1-2-3 will complete your task. As with the Sort menu, you will have a settings sheet on the screen to keep track of the selections you have already made if you are using Release 2.2. You will want to check this sheet carefully after making your entries. A common mistake is to choose the same area of the worksheet for more than one of the selections; this is never correct.

Since the /Data Query feature has a number of steps, the best approach is to look at each step and then try a few examples that combine all of the steps. You will begin by exploring the rules for entering your criteria on the worksheet.

Entering Criteria

You enter criteria on the worksheet to tell 1-2-3 which records you want to work with. 1-2-3 will ignore records that do not match these criteria when you ask the /Data Query feature to perform a task with the database.

The first step in creating criteria is choosing a blank area on the worksheet in which to enter them. The rules for entering criteria differ, depending on whether you are working with label data or value data. Regardless of which type of data you want to enter, the criteria will represent the field name you are attempting to match in the existing records. If you want to match the Job Code field, type **Job Code** in the blank area that you chose. You must enter the field name exactly as it is in the database; that is, with identical spelling. You will then place the criteria specification immediately beneath this field name.

CRITERIA FOR VALUE DATA   You can enter two different types of criteria for matching records when you use a field that contains value entries. One type is *exact entry match criteria,* which places a value that could occur in the field beneath the field name. If you want to search for all records with a 23 in the Job Code field, all you need to do is type **23** beneath the Job Code entry in the criteria area. Make the following entries to set up the exact match criteria:

1. Move the cell pointer to D1, select /Copy, press ENTER, select A13, and press ENTER.

   Copying the field name instead of retyping the field name prevents you from accidentally entering an entry that is different from the field name at the beginning of the database table. When 1-2-3 is looking for an exact match such as in this example, a slight difference between the text in the criteria area and the database table will prevent 1-2-3 from locating the records you want.

2. Move to A14, type **23**, and press ENTER to create the criteria entry shown in Figure 9-8.

These entries do not select any records. They only enable you to use the /Data Query commands to select the records you want. Before moving on to the remaining steps, look at the other types of criteria that are available. In fact, you can set up examples of some of these on the worksheet. You can make multiple-criteria entries in different locations on the worksheet as long as you use them one at a time.

A14: [W12] 23   **READY**

	A	B	C	D	E	F
1	Last Name	First Name	SS#	Job Code	Salary	Location
2	Caldor	Larry	459-34-0921	23	$32,500	4
3	Campbell	David	213-76-9874	23	$23,000	10
4	Campbell	Keith	569-89-7654	12	$32,000	2
5	Justof	Jack	431-78-9963	17	$41,200	4
6	Larson	Mary	543-98-9846	23	$22,000	2
7	Lightnor	Peggy	560-55-4311	14	$23,500	10
8	McCartin	John	817-66-1212	15	$54,600	2
9	Miller	Lisa	214-89-6756	23	$18,700	2
10	Patterson	Lyle	212-11-9090	12	$21,500	10
11	Stephens	Tom	219-78-8954	15	$17,800	2
12						
13	Job Code					
14		23				
15						
16						

FIGURE 9-8.   Entering criteria to select records with a job code of 23

The other type of value criteria is a *comparison formula*. This can be more powerful than exact entry match criteria; it not only performs an exact match but can also identify records whose values are less than, greater than, and not equal to an established value. The variety of logical operators that can be used to express these conditions is shown in Table 9-1.

Although not required because 1-2-3 does not care what field name you use when entering formula criteria, it is worth entering the correct field name on the worksheet at the top of the criteria area to help document the basis of your selection.

=	Equal
>	Greater than
>=	Greater than or equal to
<	Less than
<=	Less than or equal to
<>	Not equal to

TABLE 9-1.   Logical Operators for Building Criteria Formulas

After the field name, the next entry is the formula. The formula is designed to compare the first value in a field against another value. For example, to select records where the salary was greater than $25,000 you could enter the formula +E2>25000. You must use E2 as the cell reference in this formula because you must use the first value in a field. You can use column C for this criteria by following these directions:

1. Move the cell pointer to E1, select /Copy, press ENTER, select C13, and press ENTER.

    Actually, any field name would work equally well. Salary is the recommended entry, however, because it clarifies which field you are using in the comparison.

2. Move to C14, type **+E2>25000**, and press ENTER.

Do not be alarmed that your entry displays a 1 rather than as the formula. The 1 means it is true—E2 is greater than 25,000. If you are intent on seeing it display as you entered it, you can select /Range Format Text on the cell. However, that is not really necessary.

CRITERIA FOR LABEL DATA There are both similarities and differences between the value and label criteria. Exact match entries work the same way as value entries do. You can place a field name in the criteria area and place the label entry you are looking for immediately beneath it. 1-2-3 is not concerned with differences in either capitalization or alignment between the two entries.

Wildcard characters are a new option with label entries. You can make a partial entry and use the asterisk (*) to tell 1-2-3 that you do not care which characters come at the end of the entry as long as the characters that you have specified match. For example, to find all the records where the last name begins with "C," you would enter **Last Name** for the field name in the criteria area and immediately beneath it you would enter **C***. To find all the records where the last name starts with "Camp," you would enter **Camp***. Enter a sample for this type of criteria:

1. Move the cell pointer to A16, type **Last Name**, and move the cell pointer to A17 to finalize.

2. Type **Camp*** and press ENTER.

In Release 2 and higher, there is one additional type of label criteria, which uses string formulas. Since this is an advanced topic, we will address the use of the label criteria you have already entered.

Defining the Database Location

You must tell 1-2-3 where your data is stored before it can search the database for the information you need. In this case, you must include the field names in the range that you provide, since they are an integral part of identifying the information you want to select.

The command by which you specify the location of the database is /Data Query Input. After you select this command, you can point to your data range or type the required cell references as a range address. In both cases the field names must be included. You can select the employee database with these steps:

1. Select /Data Query Input.

2. Press HOME to move the cell pointer to A1, type ., press the END key followed by the DOWN ARROW key, and then press the END key followed by the RIGHT ARROW key.

   The database area should be highlighted as shown in Figure 9-9. Notice that the field names are included in this area.

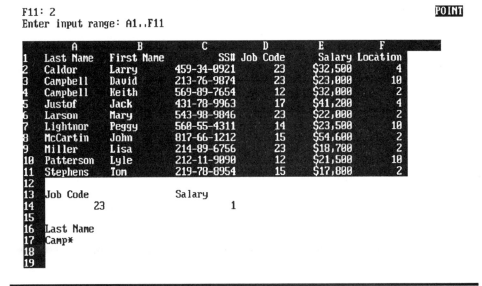

FIGURE 9-9.   Selecting the area for /Data Query Input

3. Press ENTER to finalize.

The menu will remain on the screen for additional selections, such as the criteria location and the type of selection you want performed.

Telling 1-2-3 Where You Have Stored the Criteria

1-2-3 uses criteria to determine which records from the database will be used to fill your request. You have already entered several sets of criteria on the worksheet. Now you need to choose one set that 1-2-3 can use to check each record in the database. 1-2-3 will ignore records that do not meet these criteria.

To define the location of your criteria on the worksheet, select /Data Query Criteria. Earlier than Release 2.2, the command was /Data Query Criterion. Remember that the criteria must already be stored on the worksheet from the READY mode before you can use this command effectively. First use the criteria that searches all the records to find those that contain a job code of 23. Follow these steps:

1. Select Criteria.

2. Move the cell pointer to A13, type ., press the DOWN ARROW key once, and press ENTER.

Now all you need to do is tell 1-2-3 to highlight records that match the criteria.

Finding Matching Records

1-2-3's /Data Query Find command highlights records that match the criteria you have defined. If there are multiple entries that match, the records are highlighted one at a time. 1-2-3 begins at the top of the database, highlighting the first record that matches, and lets you use the arrow keys to move to other records that match the criteria. If the number of fields exceeds the width of the screen, you can also use the arrow keys to view other fields within a highlighted record. You cannot move to records that do not match the criteria; the highlighted bar automatically skips over them.

You completed the preliminary steps for Find when you entered your criteria on the worksheet and then defined its location as well as the location of the data. Now, whenever you select Find, the criteria that was defined and referenced with Criteria will be used. The data referenced with the range input will be searched for matching records. Because the preliminaries have been completed, only one step is needed to highlight the first record.

A2: [W12] 'Caldor   FIND

	A	B	C	D	E	F
1	Last Name	First Name	SS#	Job Code	Salary	Location
2	Caldor	Larry	459-34-0921	23	$32,500	4
3	Campbell	David	213-76-9874	23	$23,000	10
4	Campbell	Keith	569-89-7654	12	$32,000	2
5	Justof	Jack	431-78-9963	17	$41,200	4
6	Larson	Mary	543-98-9846	23	$22,000	2
7	Lightnor	Peggy	560-55-4311	14	$23,500	10
8	McCartin	John	817-66-1212	15	$54,600	2
9	Miller	Lisa	214-89-6756	23	$18,700	2
10	Patterson	Lyle	212-11-9090	12	$21,500	10
11	Stephens	Tom	219-78-8954	15	$17,800	2
12						
13	Job Code		Salary			
14	23		1			
15						
16	Last Name					
17	Camp*					
18						
19						

FIGURE 9-10.   Finding the first matching record

1. Select Find to produce the display shown in Figure 9-10.

   Notice that the first record containing a job code of 23 was classified as matching the criteria, and that it is currently highlighted.

2. Press the DOWN ARROW key to move to the next record with a job code of 23, as shown in Figure 9-11.

3. Press the UP ARROW key to move back to the previous record.

4. Press ESC to return to the Data Query menu.

Extracting Matching Records

The Find operation is useful when you need to answer a question quickly or take a quick look at someone's record. You can specify the criteria to have these records selectively highlighted for you. The problem with Find is that the data does not stay on the screen. Often when you move to the second record, the first record disappears from view (the database is probably larger than your small example). The *Extract* operation can solve this; it permits you to selectively copy fields from the database to

A3: [W12] 'Campbell   FIND

	A	B	C	D	E	F
1	Last Name	First Name	SS#	Job Code	Salary	Location
2	Caldor	Larry	459-34-0921	23	$32,500	4
3	Campbell	David	213-76-9874	23	$23,000	10
4	Campbell	Keith	569-89-7654	12	$32,000	2
5	Justof	Jack	431-78-9963	17	$41,200	4
6	Larson	Mary	543-98-9846	23	$22,000	2
7	Lightnor	Peggy	560-55-4311	14	$23,500	10
8	McCartin	John	817-66-1212	15	$54,600	2
9	Miller	Lisa	214-89-6756	23	$18,700	2
10	Patterson	Lyle	212-11-9090	12	$21,500	10
11	Stephens	Tom	219-78-8954	15	$17,800	2
12						
13	Job Code		Salary			
14	23		1			
15						
16	Last Name					
17	Camp*					
18						
19						

FIGURE 9-11.   Finding the second matching record

a new area on the worksheet. As you extract this information, you can also use the fields in any sequence in the output area you are building.

To use Extract, you must complete a preliminary step from READY mode. This step involves constructing an output area in a blank area of the worksheet. You create the output area by placing the field names you wish recorded in this area at its top. Any sequence is acceptable as long as the names are an exact match with the ones in the top row of the database in terms of spelling, capitalization, and alignment.

SETTING UP AN OUTPUT AREA   You must choose a location for the output of the Extract command and prepare it to receive data. One approach is to leave some blank rows at the bottom of the database and place the output area beneath this area. This way you will not find yourself moving the output area as the database expands. Another approach is to place the output area to the right of the database so you do not need to worry about the amount of expansion that will be required. Once you have selected the location, enter the names of the fields you want copied from matching records. Remember, you will not need to include every field, and the fields you choose do not need to be placed in the same sequence as those in the database. You may want to copy the field names to the output area from above the database. This strategy eliminates all possibilities of a difference in spelling, capitalization, or alignment. Complete this task now for the employee file by following these steps.

1. Select Quit to return to READY mode.

    You cannot build the output area from the Data Query menu. You must exit it and return after you have completed the needed cell entries.

2. Move the cell pointer to A41, type **First Name**, and move the cell pointer to B41 to finalize the entry.

3. Type **Last Name** and move the cell pointer to C41.

4. Type **"Salary** and move the cell pointer to D41 to finalize.

5. Type **Job Code** and press ENTER.

This is all that is required to set up the output area like the following:

D41: 'Job Code   READY

You are ready to take a look at the remaining menu commands required to complete the Extract operation. The first command you need is /Data Query Output so that you can tell 1-2-3 where the output area is located. You can define the row containing the field names you just entered as the output area. This would be row 41 in the current example. Be aware that 1-2-3 will use all the rows from this point to the end of the worksheet to write matching records. You can also select the row containing the field names and an appropriate number of rows beneath it. If you choose the latter approach, the output area you choose must be large enough to contain all the selected records or you will get an Error Message rather than the results you are looking for.

PERFORMING THE EXTRACT   Once you have completed the preliminaries you have done the difficult work. Now all that is required is selecting Extract from the menu. Try this now with your data:

1. Select /Data Query Output. Move the cell pointer to A41, type ., press END, press the RIGHT ARROW key, and press ENTER.

2. Select Extract.

3. Select Quit to return to READY mode.

Move the cell pointer so you can view the entries that have been copied to the extract area. They should look like the ones in Figure 9-12.

```
A41: [W12] 'First Name                                            READY

        A           B          C        D       E        F
11  First Name  Last Name     Salary Job Code
12  Larry       Caldor        $32,500      23
13  David       Campbell      $23,000      23
14  Mary        Larson        $22,000      23
15  Lisa        Miller        $18,700      23
16
17
```

FIGURE 9-12.   Extracting matching records

Trying a Few More Examples

You entered more than one set of criteria as you looked at some of the ways that criteria could be entered in worksheet cells. You can try an extract with the remaining two sets of criteria, using just a few easy steps. First use the criteria that selects records where the salary entry is greater than $25,000, and then use the criteria that selects records where the last name begins with "Camp." Follow these steps:

1. Select /Data Query Criteria, type **C13.C14**, and press ENTER.

   This is where you stored the criteria to select records by the Salary field. You can use the same input area and the same output area as in your previous request without making another entry.

2. Select Extract to produce the list shown in Figure 9-13.

3. Select Criteria, type **A16.A17**, and press ENTER.

```
A41: [W12] 'First Name                                            READY

        A           B          C        D       E        F
11  First Name  Last Name     Salary Job Code
12  Larry       Caldor        $32,500      23
13  Keith       Campbell      $32,000      12
14  Jack        Justof        $41,200      17
15  John        McCartin      $54,600      15
16
17
```

FIGURE 9-13.   Extracting records with salary greater than $25,000

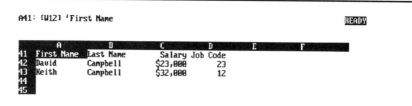

FIGURE 9-14.   Extracting records where the last name begins with Camp

This will use the criteria you entered earlier, which selects last names that begin with Camp*. If you choose to point to this criteria rather than typing the range address, press ESC first.

4. Select Extract to produce the data shown in Figure 9-14.

5. Select Quit to return to READY mode.

SPECIAL FEATURES

Now that you have completed the basics of data management, you may want to take a look at some of 1-2-3's data-management features. These include a short-cut approach to executing a Query operation, referencing the database with a range name, and the powerful database statistical functions.

Using a Short-Cut Approach

There is a short-cut approach to reexecuting a /Data Query command. However, it requires that certain conditions be met. The first condition is that the database be the exact same size and in the exact same location as when the last query was executed. The second condition is that your criteria must be the same size and shape as when the last query was executed. They can have new values or check new fields, as long as the location of these criteria is the same. The third condition is that if you are performing Extract operations, the output area must be the same size and shape as in the last query. The fourth and last condition is that you must be performing the same /Data Query operation. If you performed an Extract last time, you must perform an Extract this time. If all of these conditions are met you can reexecute the last Query operation by pressing F7 (QUERY).

A17: [W12] 'L*   READY

	A	B	C	D	E	F
1	Last Name	First Name	SS#	Job Code	Salary	Location
2	Caldor	Larry	459-34-0921	23	$32,500	4
3	Campbell	David	213-76-9874	23	$23,000	10
4	Campbell	Keith	569-89-7654	12	$32,000	2
5	Justof	Jack	431-78-9963	17	$41,200	4
6	Larson	Mary	543-90-9846	23	$22,000	2
7	Lightnor	Peggy	560-55-4311	14	$23,500	10
8	McCartin	John	817-66-1212	15	$54,600	2
9	Miller	Lisa	214-89-6756	23	$18,700	2
10	Patterson	Lyle	212-11-9090	12	$21,500	10
11	Stephens	Tom	219-78-8954	15	$17,800	2
12						
13	Job Code		Salary			
14	23		1			
15						
16	Last Name					
17	L*					
18						
19						

FIGURE 9-15.   Changing the criteria to select records where the last name begins with L

Try this by carrying out the following directions to update the criteria:

1. Move the cell pointer to A17, type **L***, and press ENTER as shown in Figure 9-15.

2. Press F7 (QUERY), and then press PGDN twice to produce the display shown in Figure 9-16.

This is a handy feature if you need to perform multiple Query operations. You only need to use the menu the first time. Then you can type new values in the criteria area if you wish, and press F7 (QUERY) to have 1-2-3 use the new criteria.

Naming the Database

Using a name rather than a range address to refer to the database can provide flexibility. 1-2-3 permits you to assign a name to a range of cells. If you expand this range of cells by inserting blank rows or columns in the middle, the range referenced by the name will be expanded automatically. If a built-in function or formula references the name rather than an address, the built-in function is automatically adjusted for any change in the range.

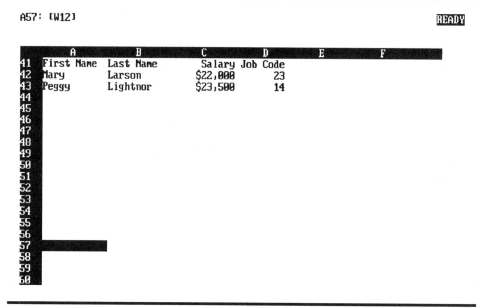

FIGURE 9-16.   Extracting records where the last name begins with L

You can assign names with the /Range Name Create command, which was first introduced in Chapter 3. Try it now with the employee database by following these steps:

1. Select /Range Name Create, type **EMPLOYEE**, and press ENTER.

2. Press ESC and then HOME. Type **.** and then press END followed by DOWN ARROW, END followed by RIGHT ARROW, and ENTER.

You will now be able to reference the range A1..F11 by the name EMPLOYEE. If you insert blank rows or columns in the middle of your database and make entries, the reference to EMPLOYEE will make these available immediately.

USING THE DATABASE STATISTICAL FUNCTIONS

The database statistical functions are a special category of built-in functions that are designed to work exclusively in the data-management environment. Like other built-in functions, they are prerecorded formulas that can perform calculations for you with a minimum of work on your part. Unlike other built-in functions, they operate on a database and require that you establish criteria for which records are to be included in the calculations they perform.

All the database statistical functions have the same format for their arguments. They are patterned after the following:

@DFUNCTION (database,offset in database,criteria location)

The first argument in all these functions is the location of the database. The range that you use to identify this location should include the field names as well as the data. The second argument, the offset, is the column number of the field that you want used in the calculations. This column number is always one less that what you would expect with the ordinary way of counting. 1-2-3 refers to the first column in the database as column 0 and increments this by one for each column to the right. Since you have no control over 1-2-3's procedures, you will have to adjust your way of thinking when using these functions. The last argument is the location of the criteria. These criteria are defined in the same way as the ones you used with Extract and Find in the Data Query menu. You must record them on the worksheet before you include their location in the function. Putting a few of these to work will clarify exactly how you work with them.

Using @DAVG

The @DAVG function allows you to compute the average for a field in a selected group of database records. You can use this function to determine the average salary for employees with a job code of 23. You can use the criteria you entered for the /Data Query feature. Just follow these steps:

1. Move the cell pointer to A21. Type **Average Salary for Job Code 23:** and move the cell pointer to D21 to finalize your entry.

2. Type **@DAVG(EMPLOYEE,4,A13.A14)** and press ENTER.

Notice that the database reference uses the range name, EMPLOYEE, which includes the field names, all records, and all fields. The offset is 4 because you are referring to the fifth column and 1-2-3 starts with column 0 rather than column 1. The criteria location uses the entries in A13 and A14 to select the records whose salary entries will be included in the average. The results follow:

D21: @DAVG(EMPLOYEE,4,A13..A14)   READY

Using @DSUM

The @DSUM function follows the same pattern as the @DAVG function. If you want to total one of the fields in the database for all records with a job code of 23, you can use it without entering criteria again. Follow these steps:

1. Move the cell pointer to A22. Type **Total Salaries for Job Code 23:** and move the cell pointer to D22 to finalize your entry.

2. Type **@DSUM(EMPLOYEE,4,A13.A14)** and press ENTER.

The results of this calculation follow:

D22: @DSUM(EMPLOYEE,4,A13..A14)   READY

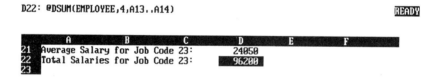

Using @DCOUNT

The @DCOUNT function is used to selectively count the number of non-blank entries in records that match your criteria. It follows the same pattern as the other database functions and operates on the entries in the column specified by the offset.

You can use this function to count the number of employees with a job code of 23. Follow these steps to enter the function:

1. Move the cell pointer to A23. Type **Number of Employees in Job Code 23:** and move the cell pointer to D23 to finalize your entry.

2. Type **@DCOUNT(EMPLOYEE,3,A13.A14)** and press ENTER.

The results of this calculation follow:

```
D23: @DCOUNT(EMPLOYEE,3,A13..A14)                              READY
```

```
         A           B          C          D        E        F
21 Average Salary for Job Code 23:       24050
22 Total Salaries for Job Code 23:       96200
23 Number of Employees in Job Code 23:       4
24
```

The Count operation is performed on the Job Code field. This will effectively give you a count of the records coded as job code 23. If the Job Code field were blank, the records could not be selected as matching the criteria for job code 23; therefore the @DCOUNT function does not count records that do not match.

Using @DMIN

The @DMIN function searches for the minimum value in the column specified. Only records that match your criteria are eligible for this minimum comparison. This provides a convenient way to determine the lowest salary paid to an individual in location 2 or the lowest salary paid to someone with job code 23. This time you will change the criteria and then enter the formula to determine the lowest salary in location 2. Follow these steps:

1. Move the cell pointer to E13 and type **Location**.

2. Move the cell pointer to E14 and type **2**.

3. Move the cell pointer to A24 and type **Minimum Salary for Location 2:**. Then move the cell pointer to D24 to finalize your entry.

4. Type **@DMIN(EMPLOYEE,4,E13.E14)** and press ENTER to produce these results:

```
D24: @DMIN(EMPLOYEE,4,E13..E14)                              READY
```

```
         A           B          C          D        E        F
21 Average Salary for Job Code 23:       24050
22 Total Salaries for Job Code 23:       96200
23 Number of Employees in Job Code 23:       4
24 Minimum Salary for Location 2:       17800
25
```

```
A1: 'Item                                                      READY

        A         B       C        D        E          F        G
 1  Item      Part_No  Cost     Vendor   Date_Purchased
 2  Chair     AX-9087  $121.50  ABC        05-Mar-89
 3  Table     RT-8976  $350.89  Royston    20-Jan-89
 4  Credenza  PY-8921  $289.50  ABC        15-Dec-88
 5  Stand     RW-2167  $127.00  Crawford   13-Jan-89
 6  Desk      WL-0976  $890.99  Royston    14-Feb-89
 7
```

FIGURE 9-17.   A database to record purchases

REVIEW EXERCISE

You can try out your new skills with 1-2-3's data-management features by creating the database in Figure 9-17. Use the data shown in this figure to guide your entries. Be certain that you use the date functions covered in Chapter 7 for the entry of the dates. The first date entry can be completed by typing **@DATE(89,03,05)** and pressing ENTER.

After completing your entries, follow these steps to format the entries and try out the sort, query, and database statistical functions.

1. Format C2..C6 as Currency with two places. Format E2..E6 as Date 1. Widen the column width for column E to 10.

    Hint: Use the /Range Format and /Worksheet Column commands.

2. Establish criteria for vendor ABC in A18..A19, and use the Find command to highlight records where the vendor is ABC.

    Hint: Enter the criteria on the worksheet first by placing **Vendor** in A18 and **ABC** in A19. Next select /Data Query, specify the input as A1..E6, specify the criteria as A18..A19, and then choose Find from the menu. Press ESC and then choose Quit to exit from the Query menu.

3. Sort the database by part number within vendor; that is, Vendor will be the primary key and Part_no will be the secondary key.

    Hint: Use /Data Sort Data-Range to define A2..E6 as the range. Select Primary-Key and type **D2**. Type an **A** and press ENTER for ascending order. Select Secondary-Key and type **B2**. Type an **A** and press ENTER for ascending order. Select Go to sort the data.

E12: (C2) [W14] @DAVG(A1..E6,2,B18..B19)   READY

	A	B	C	D	E	F	G
1	Item	Part_No	Cost	Vendor	Date_Purchased		
2	Chair	AX-9087	$121.50	ABC	05-Mar-89		
3	Credenza	PY-8921	$289.50	ABC	15-Dec-88		
4	Stand	RW-2167	$127.00	Crawford	13-Jan-89		
5	Table	RT-8976	$350.89	Royston	20-Jan-89		
6	Desk	WL-0976	$890.99	Royston	14-Feb-89		
7							
8							
9							
10							
11	Average cost of ABC purchase				$205.50		
12	Average cost of Royston purchase				$620.94		
13							
14							
15							
16							
17							
18	Vendor	Vendor					
19	ABC	Royston					
20							

08-Jul-89   04:42 PM   UNDO

FIGURE 9-18.   A sorted database with @DAVG functions

4. Use the database statistical functions to compute the average cost of purchases from ABC and Royston. You can use the locations shown in Figure 9-18 for the additional criteria that you type in B18..B19 or choose another location. Labels were added in A11..A12 to describe the computations placed in E11..E12; you can use any location you choose. The cells containing the formulas were formatted as Currency with two decimal places.

REVIEW

- You can create a database with 1-2-3 by using a tabular area on the worksheet. Your first step should be comparing your storage needs with the available memory in your computer.

- Field names are placed one per cell across the top row of the table. Rows beneath the field names are used for the data in the database records.

- You can resequence the records in a 1-2-3 database with the /Data Sort command. The records are specified as the data range for the sort. Primary and secondary keys can be selected to control the sequence of the records. Once your specifications are defined, the Go option will sort the records.

- 1-2-3's /Data Query command allows you to select records of interest in the database. You can highlight matching records with the Find option or copy them out to a new area on the worksheet if you set up an output area and then use Extract. Only records that match your criteria or specifications are highlighted or copied.

- The database statistical functions are @ functions that work with the records in a 1-2-3 database and the criteria you have established to select records of interest. You can obtain a total, average, minimum, or maximum, and you can perform other statistical computations on a selected group of your records with these functions.

Commands and Keys

Entry	Action
F7 (QUERY)	Repeats the most recent Query operation
/DQC	/Data Query Criteria defines for 1-2-3 the specification you have entered on the worksheet
/DQE	/Data Query Extract writes copies of records meeting the specifications in the criteria area to the output area
/DQF	/Data Query Find highlights records matching the criteria
/DQI	/Data Query Input defines for 1-2-3 the database records for the Query operation
/DQO	/Data Query Output defines the output area for a /Data Query Extract operation
/DSD	/Data Sort Data-Range defines the records to be sorted
/DSG	/Data Sort Go performs the Sort operation
/DSP	/Data Sort Primary-Key defines the primary sort sequence for 1-2-3
/DSS	/Data Sort Secondary-Key defines the secondary sort sequence for 1-2-3
@DAVG	Computes an average of a specified field in the records matching your specifications
@DCOUNT	Computes a count of the non-blank entries in a specified field for the records matching your specifications

| @DMIN | Determines the minimum value in a specified field in the records matching your specifications |
| @DSUM | Computes the sum of a specified field in the records matching your specifications |

10

USING ADVANCED FUNCTIONS

Adding Logic to Your Calculations
Turning Label Entries into Serial Date and Time Values
Manipulating Labels
Review Exercise
Review

You have already learned how to use some of the basic built-in functions that 1-2-3 has to offer. These provide an excellent way of handling everyday tasks such as totaling a column of numbers or rounding the result of a calculation to two decimal places.

In addition to these built-in functions, 1-2-3 also has a number of more sophisticated and specialized functions that can significantly help you to handle complex business needs. This chapter will show you how to use a number of these functions. In Chapter 7, the functions were organized by category. Here, although a particular category of functions is addressed, the focus is on the integration of the functions with an application example. In many instances, several functions are combined to resolve a specific application problem. This is especially important for the more complex functions; new users need to understand how to apply these functions to the business problems they face.

ADDING LOGIC TO YOUR CALCULATIONS

According to 1-2-3's rules, you can place only a single entry into a worksheet cell. Therefore, only one formula can be stored in each worksheet cell. This can be limiting, especially considering the many exceptions and special rules that apply to the calculations performed every day in a business setting. For example, when you give a customer a purchase discount, you may not want to multiply the purchase amount by a fixed percentage. The amount of the discount might depend on the size of the sale, whether the sale is cash or credit, and the amount purchased by the customer on an annual basis. Regular 1-2-3 formulas can calculate a discount based on a fixed percentage, but they cannot cope with all these conditions. Fortunately, 1-2-3 has a number of built-in functions that can step in to fill this need. These functions let you add logic processing to your calculations and let you make your calculations on the basis of any conditions you wish to apply.

Creating a Salary Projection Model

The first example you will explore creates a salary model. With this model, you can estimate the various components of salary expense. After projecting a salary increase with a percentage growth factor, you can also estimate other salary expenses, such as your FICA contribution as an employer and the cost of the benefits you are supplying for different personnel classifications. You can easily adapt the model to meet other conditions and situations—either by adding new expense categories (patterning calculations after the examples provided) or by altering the formulas for the existing calculations. Since this model is dependent on the @IF function, it is a good idea to review how the @IF function works before starting the model.

USING @IF   The *@IF* function lets you test a condition to determine the appropriate value for a cell. @IF is one of the most powerful built-in functions because it frees you from the limitation of deciding on one formula for a cell. Now you can set up two different values for a cell and determine which one to use, based on other conditions in the worksheet. You can create two or more discount levels, payroll deductions, commission structures, or other calculations involving more than one alternative.

The @IF function uses three arguments, in this sequence:

@IF(condition to test,value if true,value if false)

The first argument, *condition to test,* can be any logical expression that can be evaluated as true or false. Examples are A1>9, C2=G10, and A2+B6>C3*H12. The expression returns a value of true only if the condition specified is met. For example, in the first expression, true will be returned only if A1 is greater than 9. If this expression evaluates as true, the cell will take on the value specified in the second argument of the function.

The second argument for the @IF function, *value if true,* is the value the cell will use if the condition is true and can take several forms. It can be an actual numeric value, a formula that needs to be calculated, or another @IF statement to be checked if multiple levels of conditions must be met before an action is determined. In Release 2 and higher, this argument can be a string value as long as it is enclosed in double quotation marks.

The third argument, *value if false,* is the value the cell containing the @IF statement will assume if the condition in the function is false. All the conditions mentioned for *value if true* also apply here.

Release 2 and higher also allow strings to be used with the logical @IF condition. For example, you could have an entry such as @IF(A10="Chicago",F2,G2). If A10 contains Chicago, the cell containing this entry will take on the value of F2. If A10 contains anything else, the cell containing the function will be equal to G2.

MAKING THE ENTRIES IN THE SALARY MODEL   To minimize your entries, enter data for only a few employees. Then a simple Copy operation and additional data entry allow you to expand this model to include as many employees as you want. The model you will be building is shown in Figure 10-1. Follow these explicit instructions for your entries:

1. Select /Worksheet Erase Yes to clear the worksheet.

2. Select /Worksheet Column Set-Width, type **13**, and press ENTER.
   This will widen column A to accept the name entries.

G4: @IF(D4>=7,@IF(E4>50000,20000+(E4-50000)*0.02,E4*0.2),E4*0.14)   `READY`

	A	B	C	D	E	F	G
1			Salary Expense Projections				
2		1990	Job	1991			
3	Name	Salary	Increase Class	Salary	FICA	Benefits	
4	Jones, Ray	$25,000	7.00%	3	$26,750	$2,009	$3,745
5	Larkin, Mary	$29,000	5.00%	9	$30,450	$2,287	$6,090
6	Harris, John	$45,000	6.50%	7	$47,925	$3,599	$9,585
7	Parson, Mary	$55,900	5.50%	9	$58,975	$3,605	$20,179
8							

FIGURE 10-1.   Completed salary model

3. Make these entries on the worksheet:

A3:	Name
A4:	Jones, Ray
A5:	Larkin, Mary
A6:	Harris, John
A7:	Parson, Mary
B2:	'1990
B3:	Salary
B4:	25000
B5:	29000
B6:	45000
B7:	55900
C1:	Salary Expense Projections
C3:	Increase
C4:	.07
C5:	.05
C6:	.065
C7:	.055
D2:	Job
D3:	Class
D4:	3
D5:	9
D6:	7
D7:	9
E2:	'1991
E3:	Salary
F3:	FICA
G3:	Benefits

4. Move the cell pointer to C4, select /Range Format Percent, and press ENTER, Move the cell pointer to C7 and press ENTER again.

5. Move the cell pointer to D4, select /Range Format Fixed, type **0**, and press ENTER. Move the cell pointer to D7 and press ENTER again.

6. Select /Worksheet Global Format Currency, type **0**, and press ENTER to produce the display in Figure 10-2.

All the remaining entries in this model must be calculated. Standard formulas will not work; various factors affect the computed results, and a regular formula cannot deal with these exceptions. After analyzing each of the

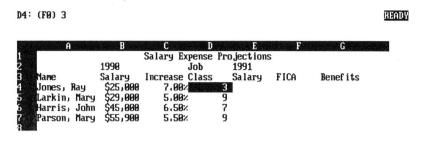

D4: (F0) 3   READY

	A	B	C	D	E	F	G
1			Salary	Expense	Projections		
2		1990		Job	1991		
3	Name	Salary	Increase	Class	Salary	FICA	Benefits
4	Jones, Ray	$25,000	7.00%	3			
5	Larkin, Mary	$29,000	5.00%	9			
6	Harris, John	$45,000	6.50%	7			
7	Parson, Mary	$55,900	5.50%	9			
8							

FIGURE 10-2.   Salary model before adding formulas

required conditions, enter an @IF statement that captures the essence of how you would perform these calculations manually under all circumstances.

FICA is not computed by the same method for all wage levels. It is calculated at 7.51% unless the individual earns more than the established cap amount for FICA. If earnings exceed the cap amount, you will only pay an employer's FICA contribution on the cap amount. You can record this with the @IF function if the condition to be tested is recorded in the function and the two different methods for performing the FICA computation are recorded as the values for true and false conditions.

Follow these directions for making your entries:

7. Move the cell pointer to E4, type **+B4∗(1+C4)**, and press ENTER.

   This formula calculates the projected salary for 1991, based on the increase percentage.

8. Select /Copy, press ENTER, move the cell pointer to E5, type **.** (period), move to E7, and press ENTER.

9. Move the cell pointer to F4 and type **@IF(E4<48000,E4∗.0751,48000∗.0751)**. Then press ENTER.

   The essence of this function is to check whether the salary is less than $48,000 and, if it is, to multiply the salary by 7.51%. If it is not less than $48,000, the rate will be applied to $48,000, the amount chosen for this example as the arbitrary limit for FICA payments. You now have the rules for two different ways to perform the FICA calculation, depending on the amount of the salary.

F4: @IF(E4<48000,E4*0.0751,48000*0.0751)   READY

	A	B	C	D	E	F	G
1			Salary Expense Projections				
2		1990		Job	1991		
3	Name	Salary	Increase	Class	Salary	FICA	
4	Jones, Ray	$25,000	7.00%	3	$26,750	$2,009	
5	Larkin, Mary	$29,000	5.00%	9	$30,450	$2,287	
6	Harris, John	$45,000	6.50%	7	$47,925	$3,599	
7	Parson, Mary	$55,900	5.50%	9	$58,975	$3,605	
8							

FIGURE 10-3.   Salary model with @IF formulas for FICA calculation

10. Select /Copy, press ENTER, move the cell pointer to F5, and type . (period). Then move the cell pointer to F7 and press ENTER.

The results will look like the worksheet in Figure 10-3. Naturally, if you had more records on your worksheet, you could copy this formula farther down the worksheet than cell F7 before finalizing the copy.

In this case, the @IF function provided just the solution you needed. The next problem for the salary expense model involves calculating the cost of benefits. You can also perform this calculation with @IF, but because of its complexity you will require multiple levels of @IF statements.

The hypothetical model you are creating requires an answer to two different conditions concerning benefits. According to the company's specifications for the calculations, the first question concerns the job class of the employee. Executives have a job class greater than or equal to 7 and their benefits are calculated under different rules than are the benefits for nonmanagement employees. Even once the job class is decided, however, there is still the salary factor, which can affect the estimated benefit amount.

In the current example, benefits for executive employees are calculated as 20% of the executive's salary unless the executive makes more than $50,000, which classifies the person as senior executive management. In this case, the computation is $20,000 plus 2% of the amount over $50,000. For nonexecutive employees, the calculation is a little different; it is always computed as 14% of the projected salary. All this may sound a little complex at first; but if you stop and think about it for a minute, you realize that you have no difficulty making these computations by hand. The trick is to record all these conditions in a worksheet cell. Following these directions will do this for you:

11. Next you should move the cell pointer to cell G4 and then you should type **@IF(D4>=7,@IF(E4>50000,20000+(E4– 50000)*.02,E4*.2),E4*.14)**.

This formula examines all the necessary conditions. The condition in the first @IF checks to see if the job class is greater than or equal to 7. If this condition is true, the second @IF becomes the value of this cell and must be evaluated. The second @IF condition checks the salary to see if it is greater than $50,000 and, depending on the result of this condition test, computes the benefit expense to be either $20,000 plus 2% of the amount over $50,000 or 20% of the salary.

There is yet another condition, one that occurs when the job class is less than 7. In this case the benefit expense is 14% of the salary.

These multiple levels of conditions are frequently referred to as *nested @IF* statements. They are a little complicated but worth the investment of time for the flexibility they offer.

12. Select /Copy, press ENTER, and move the cell pointer to G5. Type ., move the cell pointer to G7, and press ENTER.

Your salary model is now complete and should match the model shown earlier in Figure 10-1. If you have other salary expenses you can alter the model to include them and then save it.

13. Select /File Save, type **SALARY**, and press ENTER before clearing memory.

Or, if you do not wish to save this model, you can clear it by selecting /Worksheet Erase Yes.

Calculating the Net Purchase Price

The next model you will build also needs the flexibility that occurs when logic is incorporated in worksheet cells. Since calculating a net purchase price involves calculating varying purchase discounts and applying shipping costs, numerous conditions need to be considered. In this case, the @IF function would be a cumbersome solution; many levels of nesting would be required to solve the problem. There are several additional functions in 1-2-3 that offer a wide range of options. The two that you will examine now are the @VLOOKUP function, which builds a table of codes and associated values on the worksheet for reference, and the @INDEX function (available in Release 2 and higher), which also builds a table of values but uses a different approach for finding the correct entry. First you will examine each of the functions. Then you will enter the basics of the model. Finally you will apply the

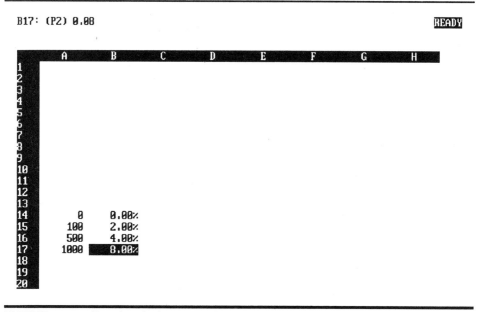

FIGURE 10-4.   Entering the lookup table codes and values

information you have obtained on the inner workings of the two functions to complete the model.

USING @VLOOKUP   The *@VLOOKUP* function allows you to search a table that you have entered on the worksheet for an appropriate value to use in your worksheet. When you create the table that @VLOOKUP will be referencing, you must store the codes that will be looked up in a column on the worksheet. The values that you wish to correspond to each of these codes will be stored in the columns to the right of the codes. Figure 10-4 shows a table of codes in column A, and the associated return values for each code in column B. You must understand the way that @VLOOKUP works before you even enter the codes and associated values in the table.

The @VLOOKUP function uses three arguments, in this sequence:

@VLOOKUP(code to be looked up,table location,offset)

The first argument is *code to be looked up*—the entry in your worksheet, which will be compared against the column of table values. When numeric values are used,

1-2-3 looks for the largest value in the table that is not larger than the code you have supplied. The codes should be in ascending order. If the first code in the column is larger than the code you supply, you will get an ERR condition. When string values are used (permissible only with Release 2 and higher), the search is always for an exact match. This means that 1-2-3 will use a case-sensitive search; CLEVELAND will not match Cleveland.

Since a table must be at least two partial columns on the worksheet, the second argument, *table location,* will always be a range reference to at least two partial columns on the worksheet. This reference must include the table codes as well as the return values.

The third argument, *offset,* tells 1-2-3 how many columns to the right of the code column to use when obtaining the return values. This argument allows you to create tables that are more than two columns wide.

USING @INDEX   The *@INDEX* function also requires you to enter a table on the worksheet, but you do not enter values for matching. Every entry in the table is designed to be a return value. Which of these return values to use is determined by the row and column number you specify.

The @INDEX function uses three arguments, in this sequence:

@INDEX(table location,column number,row number)

Table location is the address of all the codes in the table. For example, the table location of the entries shown in the lower middle of Figure 10-5 is D15..F19. The *column number* is the number of the offset column, which contains the value you wish to use. The leftmost column in the table has a column offset of 0, with the column offset number increasing by 1 for each column as you move to the right. The *row number* is the number of the row you wish to use. The same numbering scheme is used: The upper row is row 0 and each row farther down in the table is incremented by 1.

@INDEX is ideal for applications in which your data values can be used to access the correct value in the table. Computing shipping costs is a good example, if the cost is determined by weight and distance and values can be assigned for each. Shortly, you can put the @INDEX function to work computing shipping costs.

CREATING THE PURCHASE MODEL   To compute a net purchase price, you need to know the following basic components: the item purchased, the purchase price and quantity, the purchase discount amount, the shipping weight, and the customer's shipping zone. All items weigh between one and five pounds and all customers are assigned a shipping zone from 1 to 3, depending on their distance from a regional warehouse.

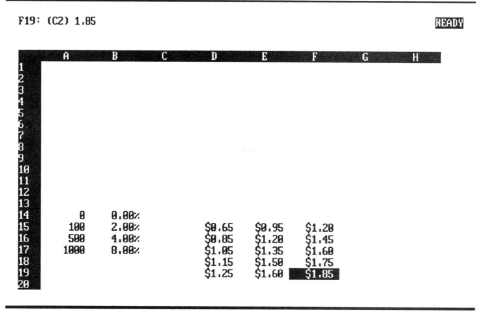

F19: (C2) 1.85   READY

FIGURE 10-5.   Entering the index table values

Purchase discounts are computed on the extension of the item's cost—that is, you multiply the number of units by the unit price. Shipping costs are added after calculating purchase discounts. The discount rate applied increases with the size of the purchase. For a purchase of $100, a 2% discount is given; for $500, a discount of 4% is given; and for $1000 or more, an 8% discount is given. You can construct the @VLOOKUP table with these entries:

1. Move the cell pointer to A14, type **0**, and press ENTER.

    Normally, you would use a location farther away from the data to allow for expansion. For now, however, you will find it easier to view the entries while building your formulas.

2. Enter these table codes and their associated values:

    A15:   100
    A16:   500
    A17:   1000
    B14:   0
    B15:   .02
    B16:   .04
    B17:   .08

This completes the table entries for the @VLOOKUP table. You still need to enter the values for shipping costs, but this time you will use an index table. For purchase discounts, the index table is not an option because of the wide gap between entries. You would need an index table with 1000 entries, even though only three discounts need to be stored. All these extra entries would be necessary because of the @INDEX function's method of finding a return value based on the row and column location. Continue with the entries for the shipping table:

3. Move the cell pointer to D15, type **.65**, and press ENTER.

    This is the value that will be used for the shipping cost of a one-pound item shipped to zone 1.

4. Complete the entries as follows:

D16:	.85
D17:	1.05
D18:	1.15
D19:	1.25
E15:	.95
E16:	1.20
E17:	1.35
E18:	1.50
E19:	1.60
F15:	1.20
F16:	1.45
F17:	1.60
F18:	1.75
F19:	1.85

    Once you have entered the tables, enter the data in the main section of your model.

5. Move the cell pointer to A1 and begin making these entries:

A1:	Item
A2:	Number
A4:	X5401
A5:	YT45
A6:	CF514
A7:	RT908
A8:	R4312
B1:	Units
B2:	Purchd

B4:	3
B5:	7
B6:	12
B7:	5
B8:	10
C1:	Unit
C2:	Cost
C4:	25.50
C5:	38
C6:	47.50
C7:	150
C8:	12.50
D2:	Weight
D4:	1
D5:	3
D6:	4
D7:	1
D8:	2
E2:	Zone
E4:	2
E5:	0
E6:	1
E7:	2
E8:	1
F2:	Discount
G1:	Shipping
G2:	Cost
H1:	Net
H2:	Price

6. Move the cell pointer to C4, select /Range Format Currency, press ENTER, move the cell pointer to C8, and press ENTER again.

7. Move the cell pointer to F4, select /Range Format Currency, press ENTER, move the cell pointer to H8, and press ENTER.

8. Move the cell pointer to D15, select /Range Format Currency, press ENTER, move the cell pointer to F19, and press ENTER.

9. Move the cell pointer to B14, select /Range Format Percent, press ENTER, move the cell pointer to B17, and press ENTER.

B14: (P2) 0   READY

	A	B	C	D	E	F	G	H
1	Item	Units	Unit				Shipping	Net
2	Number	Purchd	Cost	Weight	Zone	Discount	Cost	Price
3								
4	X5401	3	$25.50	1	2			
5	YT45	7	$30.00	3	0			
6	CF514	12	$47.50	4	1			
7	RT900	5	$150.00	1	2			
8	R4312	10	$12.50	2	1			
9								
10								
11								
12								
13								
14	0	0.00%						
15	100	2.00%		$0.65	$0.95	$1.20		
16	500	4.00%		$0.85	$1.20	$1.45		
17	1000	8.00%		$1.05	$1.35	$1.60		
18				$1.15	$1.50	$1.75		
19				$1.25	$1.60	$1.85		
20								

FIGURE 10-6.   Purchase model without formulas

This completes the data entry. The model is ready for the formulas and should now appear as shown in Figure 10-6. Naturally, other fields, such as customer name and shipping address, still need to be added. However, these are not important for your purposes at this time.

The formula for the purchase discount will use the @VLOOKUP function. The first argument will be the purchase amount, which must be computed by multiplying the units times the unit cost. This value will be looked up in the table stored in A14..B17. 1-2-3 does not attempt to find a match. Instead, it searches for the largest value in column A that is not greater than the purchase amount. It then returns the value in column B from the same row. The table location will be specified as the second argument. The third argument tells 1-2-3 which column in the table to use for the return value. In the current example, this number is 1, indicating that 1-2-3 should use the values in column B, since those values are one column to the right of the table codes.

10. Move the cell pointer to F4 and type **@VLOOKUP(**.

11. Move the cell pointer to B4, type *, move the cell pointer to C4, and type , (comma).

12. Move the cell pointer to A14 and press F4 (ABS).

This will place dollar signs ($) in front of the row and column portion of the address, making it an absolute reference to the beginning of the table. You need an absolute reference because you want the table reference to remain the same regardless of where you copy the formula.

13. Type . and move the cell pointer to B17.

14. Type ,1)*(B4*C4) and press ENTER.

This formula will look up a discount percentage appropriate for the purchase amount and multiply by the amount of the purchase. In this case the discount is zero, since the purchase amount is $76.50.

15. Select /Copy, press ENTER, and move the cell pointer to F5. Type . (period), move the cell pointer to F8, and press ENTER.

The purchase discount has been computed for all the entries on the model that appears in Figure 10-7.

16. Move the cell pointer to G4 and type @INDEX(.

F4: (C2) @VLOOKUP(B4*C4,$A$14..$B$17,1)*(B4*C4)   READY

	A	B	C	D	E	F	G	H
1	Item	Units	Unit				Shipping	Net
2	Number	Purchd	Cost	Weight	Zone	Discount	Cost	Price
3								
4	X5401	3	$25.50	1	2	$0.00		
5	YT45	7	$38.00	3	0	$5.32		
6	CF514	12	$47.50	4	1	$22.00		
7	RT908	5	$150.00	1	2	$30.00		
8	R4312	10	$12.50	2	1	$2.50		
9								
10								
11								
12								
13								
14	0	0.00%						
15	100	2.00%		$0.65	$0.95	$1.20		
16	500	4.00%		$0.85	$1.20	$1.45		
17	1000	8.00%		$1.05	$1.35	$1.60		
18				$1.15	$1.50	$1.75		
19				$1.25	$1.60	$1.85		
20								

FIGURE 10-7.   Computing purchase discounts

17. Move the cell pointer to D15 and press F4 (ABS).

    This will make the table reference absolute, which will allow the formula to be copied.

18. Type . and move the cell pointer to F19.

19. Type , (comma) and move the cell pointer to E4. Type , again and move the cell pointer to D4.

    In this step you have specified E4, the zone, as the column to use for the return value and D4, the weight, as the row.

20. Type)*, move the cell pointer to B4, and press ENTER.

    This completes the formula, which will find the cost of shipping one item from the index table and then multiply it by the number of items.

    Note to Release 1A users: Since Release 1A does not have the @INDEX function, you can modify the application by adding a column of codes in column C to the left of the shipping costs. You can use this code and the offset option in @VLOOKUP to control the value returned from this table. Assuming you made this alteration to the worksheet entries, you could use a formula like this:

    @VLOOKUP(D4,$C$15.$F$19,E4+1)*B4

    Notice that 1 is added to the zone to option values of 1, 2, and 3, which will access the table offset columns.

21. Select /Copy, press ENTER, move the cell pointer to G5, type . (period), move the cell pointer to G8, and press ENTER.

22. Move the cell pointer to H4, type +B4*C4 −F4+G4, and press ENTER.

    This formula calculates the net purchase price by extending units times unit cost, subtracting the discount, and adding the shipping cost. Once it is copied to the other rows, your model is complete.

23. Select /Copy, press ENTER, move the cell pointer to H5, type . (period), move the cell pointer to H8, and press ENTER.

    Figure 10-8 shows the resulting calculations in column H.

24. Select /Worksheet Erase Yes to clear memory, or select /File Save to create a copy of the model on disk before clearing memory.

H4: (C2) +B4*C4-F4+G4   `READY`

	A	B	C	D	E	F	G	H
1	Item	Units	Unit				Shipping	Net
2	Number	Purchd	Cost	Weight	Zone	Discount	Cost	Price
3								
4	X5401	3	$25.50	1	2	$0.00	$4.35	$80.85
5	YT45	7	$38.00	3	0	$5.32	$8.05	$260.73
6	CF514	12	$47.50	4	1	$22.00	$19.20	$566.40
7	RT900	5	$150.00	1	2	$30.00	$7.25	$727.25
8	R4312	10	$12.50	2	1	$2.50	$13.50	$136.00
9								
10								
11								
12								
13								
14	0	0.00%						
15	100	2.00%		$0.65	$0.95	$1.20		
16	500	4.00%		$0.85	$1.20	$1.45		
17	1000	8.00%		$1.05	$1.35	$1.60		
18				$1.15	$1.50	$1.75		
19				$1.25	$1.60	$1.85		
20								

FIGURE 10-8.   Completed purchase model

Checking Entries for Errors

Data-entry errors can cause serious problems in worksheet accuracy. There are no
facilities for validity checks; you make entries directly into each worksheet cell.
However, there is a group of logical functions that can be used in combination with
the @IF function to alert you to potential error conditions in certain fields. These
functions can check a cell to see if it contains a number or a string value. They can
also check for NA, which indicates that an entry is not available, or ERR, which
indicates an error condition in a formula. The @ISNUMBER and @ISSTRING
functions are only available in Release 2 and higher.

These are the functions and the checks they perform:

@ISERR(value)	Checks for a value of ERR in a cell
@ISNA(value)	Checks for a value of NA in a cell
@ISNUMBER(value)	Checks for a numeric value in a cell
@ISSTRING(value)	Checks for a string value in a cell

In all four functions, the argument *value* is normally a cell address that references a cell you want checked. In the first function, 1 representing true is returned if the cell has a value of ERR. In the second, 1 is returned if the cell has a value of NA. The @ISNUMBER function returns 1 if the cell contains a number. @ISSTRING returns 1 if the cell contains a string.

Although these functions can be used alone, they are most frequently combined with the @IF statement, as in

@IF(@ISNUMBER(A6),"A6 is numeric","A6 is not numeric")

This @IF statement checks to see if @ISNUMBER(A6) returns a 1 for true or 0 for false. If the result of this test is true, "A6 is numeric" will be placed in the cell containing the function. If the condition tests false because A6 does not contain a numeric value, the phrase "A6 is not numeric" will be placed in the cell that contains this function.

You will build two short models to look at the effect of two of these functions. You will see from these examples that it is easy to enter an error-checking formula once and copy it down the column. You can scan data for errors but it is much easier to scan a special column where messages are used to flag error conditions.

CHECKING FOR MISSING DATA   The first example you will enter works with the @NA function. This function serves as a place marker for missing data. The model records the order number, order date, quantity, and price, and computes a total. If the price is missing, @NA is inserted in its place. When the order total is computed by multiplying quantity by price, if the value for a price is NA, the total for that item is NA. To prevent this, insert a message that is more noticeable. Complete these steps to create the model:

1. Move the cell pointer to A1 and select /Worksheet Column Set-Width, type **13**, and press ENTER.

2. Make these entries on the worksheet:
A2:	Order Number
A3:	12760
A4:	12781
A5:	12976
B2:	Date
B3:	'01-Oct-89

B4:	'01-Oct-89
B5:	'02-Oct-89
C2:	Quantity
C3:	3
C4:	4
C5:	12
D2:	Price
D3:	3.5
D4:	@NA
D5:	12.25
E2:	Total

Notice that the dates in column B were entered as labels. This is not the usual format entered for dates, since the @DATE function will create a date number that can be used in calculations. However, label entries were used because there is no need to use them in calculations. Later in this chapter, you will look at the features of another built-in function that can convert these labels to date numbers.

3. Move the cell pointer to D3, select /Range Format Currency, and press ENTER. Move the cell pointer to E5 and press ENTER.

Now that you have completed the preliminary entries, it is time to enter a formula in E3 that will test the price for the first entry for a value of NA. If a true condition is returned, the cell should take on the value NA; if a false condition is returned, the cell will have the value that is computed by multiplying price by quantity. Follow these steps to have the error-checking formula placed in column E.

4. Move the cell pointer to E3, enter **@IF(@ISNA(D3),"Missing Unit Price",C3*D3)**, and press ENTER.

5. Select /Copy and press ENTER. Move the cell pointer to E4, type . (period), move the cell pointer to E5, and press ENTER.

The worksheet looks like the one in Figure 10-9. Notice that the message "Missing Unit Price" flags the record that has no price entry. This is not necessary when you have only three records; but when you have hundreds, this message can save you a lot of time.

6. Select /Worksheet Erase Yes to clear memory.

Remember to first select /File Save if you want to retain a copy of this example.

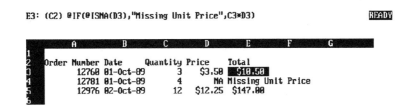

E3: (C2) @IF(@ISNA(D3),"Missing Unit Price",C3*D3)   READY

	A	B	C	D	E	F	G
1	Order Number	Date	Quantity	Price	Total		
2							
3	12760	01-Oct-89	3	$3.50	$10.50		
4	12781	01-Oct-89	4	NA	Missing Unit Price		
5	12976	02-Oct-89	12	$12.25	$147.00		

FIGURE 10-9.   Order data with @ISNA used to locate missing information

CHECKING FOR NON-NUMERIC DATA   You may have an application where you want to require your computer operators to enter numeric values in certain key fields. Although there is no direct way to lock out unacceptable input, you can display an Error Message if non-numeric data is entered. If you have Release 2 or higher, you can use a combination of @ISNUMBER and @IF to handle this task for you. First, make a few entries in an address file. Then add a formula that checks the first ZIP code field to see if it contains a number, since the application is designed to accept a five-digit ZIP code for persons living in the United States. If the field does not contain a numeric entry, a message will display.

Follow these directions to make the entries in the file:

1. Move the cell pointer to A1, select /Worksheet Column Set-Width, type **15**, and press ENTER.

2. Move the cell pointer to B1, select /Worksheet Column Set-Width, type **20**, and press ENTER.

3. Make these entries in the worksheet cells shown:

A3:	Name
A4:	John Smith
A5:	Jill Brown
A6:	Harry Olson
A7:	Mary Greene
B3:	Address
B4:	'1215 East 11th St.
B5:	'41 S. Main St.
B6:	'1111 G St. NW
B7:	'42 Stone Ct.

C1:	Client Listing
C3:	City
C4:	Towson
C5:	Akron
C6:	Austin
C7:	Berea
D3:	State
D4:	New York
D5:	Ohio
D6:	Ohio
D7:	Michigan
E3:	Zip Code
E4:	98765
E5:	45321
E6:	r567w1
E7:	44040
F3:	Zip Code Errors

Notice that a single quotation mark was used at the front of the address entries to ensure that the entries were treated as labels. The only task remaining is to enter the error-checking formula:

4. Move the cell pointer to F4, type **@IF(@ISNUMBER(E4)," ","ERROR - Zip Code must be numeric")**, and press ENTER.

   Although you may actually want to enter ZIP codes as labels, this example assumes you do not want to. The formula provides an example of the type of error checking you can have 1-2-3 perform. The formula bases the result of the @IF test on whether or not the referenced cell contains a number. If it does, a blank (enclosed with the set of quotation marks) is placed in the cell. If the entry is not numeric, an Error Message is placed at that location. Naturally you can choose any Error Message you like and may prefer an entry like "Invalid Zip Code."

5. Select /Copy, press ENTER, move the cell pointer to F5, type . (period), move the cell pointer to F7, and press ENTER again.

   The worksheet looks like the one in Figure 10-10.

6. Select /Worksheet Erase Yes to clear memory.

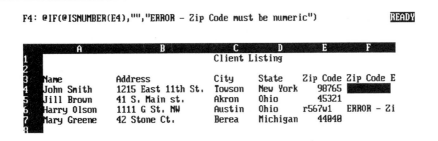

F4: @IF(@ISNUMBER(E4),"","ERROR - Zip Code must be numeric")   READY

	A	B	C	D	E	F
1			Client Listing			
2						
3	Name	Address	City	State	Zip Code	Zip Code E
4	John Smith	1215 East 11th St.	Towson	New York	98765	
5	Jill Brown	41 S. Main st.	Akron	Ohio	45321	
6	Harry Olson	1111 G St. NW	Austin	Ohio	r567w1	ERROR - Zi
7	Mary Greene	42 Stone Ct.	Berea	Michigan	44040	
8						

FIGURE 10-10.   Using @ISNUMBER to locate incorrect ZIP codes

TURNING LABEL ENTRIES INTO SERIAL DATE AND TIME VALUES

Both date and time entries can require extra effort, especially when you have an entire column of date entries to make. The @DATE and @TIME functions that you used in Chapter 7 each require three arguments. In addition, the year-month-day sequence of the date arguments differs from the sequence in which most users would ordinarily enter dates. There are functions that allow you to convert either the date or time, entered as a label in one of the date or time display formats, to a valid date or time number. @TIMEVALUE is the function that changes a label entry in a valid time format to a time number. @DATEVALUE is the function that converts a label in a valid date format to a valid date number. Both these functions are available only in Release 2 and higher.

Using Dates from Label Entries To Compute Rental Fees

Figure 10-11 presents a few records that were entered with the dates stored as labels in columns C and D. The fact that all the calculations are displayed as zeros in column E suggests a problem with the calculation of the amount due. This problem is caused

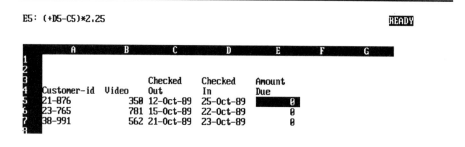

FIGURE 10-11.   Dates stored as labels

by the manner in which the dates were entered. Because the formula for amount due subtracts the date in D5 from the date in C5, 1-2-3 is expecting values in these cells. A date number would meet this requirement, but label entries do not. These dates were entered as labels, which means that they cannot be used in arithmetic calculations. You can correct this problem with a few modifications to the formula, but first enter the basic data that the model will use. Follow these steps to completion:

1. Move the cell pointer to column A, select /Worksheet Column Set-Width, type **13**, and press ENTER. Use this same procedure to widen columns C and D to 11.

2. Make these entries:

A4:	Customer-id
A5:	'21-876
A6:	'23-765
A7:	'38-991
B4:	Video
B5:	350
B6:	781
B7:	562
C3:	Checked
C4:	Out
C5:	'12-Oct-89
C6:	'15-Oct-89
C7:	'21-Oct-89
D3:	Checked

E5: (C2) (@DATEVALUE(D5)-@DATEVALUE(C5))*2.25   READY

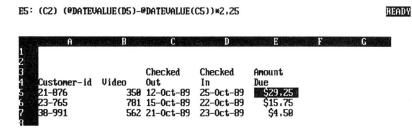

	A	B	C	D	E	F	G
1							
2							
3			Checked	Checked	Amount		
4	Customer-id	Video	Out	In	Due		
5	21-876		350 12-Oct-89	25-Oct-89	$29.25		
6	23-765		781 15-Oct-89	22-Oct-89	$15.75		
7	30-991		562 21-Oct-89	23-Oct-89	$4.50		
8							

FIGURE 10-12.   Using @DATEVALUE for date labels in formulas

D4:	In
D5:	'25-Oct-89
D6:	'22-Oct-89
D7:	'23-Oct-89
E3:	Amount
E4:	Due

The formula for the amount due in Figure 10-11 was entered as (D5–C5)*2.25. The erroneous results showed you that a different formula is required when dealing with label entries.

3. Next you move the cell pointer to E5. Then type (@DATEVALUE(D5)–@DATEVALUE(C5))*2.25 and press ENTER.

4. Select /Range Format Currency and press ENTER twice.
    This format will be copied when you copy the formula to other cells in the range.

5. Select /Copy and press ENTER. Move the cell pointer to E6, type . (period), move the cell pointer to E7, and press ENTER.
    Now that the label entries have been converted to date numbers, they can be used in formulas without causing an error, as the worksheet in Figure 10-12 shows.

6. Select /Worksheet Erase Yes to clear memory or save the worksheet with the /File Save command.

Turning Time Labels into Hours for Billing Clients

The @TIMEVALUE function converts a label entry in a valid time format to numeric time representation, which is suitable for use in any calculation. The format of the function to handle this conversion is @TIMEVALUE(time string). This conversion is one way to avoid the need for the three arguments that @TIME requires. It can also correct mistakes in data entry in which times were accidentally entered as labels. To try this function with a short example, follow these steps:

1. Move the cell pointer to column C, select /Worksheet Column Set-Width, type **13**, and press ENTER.

2. Move the cell pointer to E5, select /Range Format Date Time, type **4**, move the cell pointer to E7, and press ENTER.

3. Make these worksheet entries:

A3:	Job
A4:	Number
A5:	1
A6:	2
A7:	3
B3:	Time
B4:	In
B5:	'8:05 AM
B6:	'8:10 AM
B7:	'8:30 AM
C4:	Repair
C5:	Tires
C6:	Brakes
C7:	Steering
D3:	Time
D4:	Out
D5:	'9:17 AM
D6:	'10:34 AM
D7:	'1:18 PM
E3:	Elapsed
E4:	Time

   It is possible to enter these times without the AM or PM designation for the entries before 1:00 PM. It is also possible to enter these designations in lowercase, as in 9:05 am or 10:16 pm.

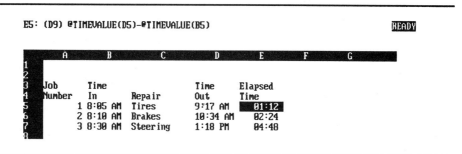

E5: (D9) @TIMEVALUE(D5)-@TIMEVALUE(B5)   READY

A	B	C	D	E	F	G
Job	Time		Time	Elapsed		
Number	In	Repair	Out	Time		
1	8:05 AM	Tires	9:17 AM	01:12		
2	8:10 AM	Brakes	10:34 AM	02:24		
3	8:30 AM	Steering	1:18 PM	04:48		

FIGURE 10-13.   Using @TIMEVALUE for time labels in formulas

4. Next you move the cell pointer to E5. Then type **@TIMEVALUE(D5)– @TIMEVALUE(B5)** and press ENTER.

5. Select /Copy, press ENTER, move the cell pointer to E6, type **.** (period), move the cell pointer to E7, and press ENTER.

   The results look like the worksheet in Figure 10-13.

6. Select /Worksheet Erase Yes to clear memory.

MANIPULATING LABELS

Release 2 and higher have an entire category of built-in functions that only operate on label or string entries. Release 1A, however, has none of these functions, so if you are working with Release 1A, skip this section.

The string functions provide a variety of character-manipulation formulas that give you flexibility in arranging your text entries. They are extremely useful for correcting data-entry errors and for restructuring worksheet data for a new application.

The unique feature of the string functions is that many of them work with individual characters in the string. When 1-2-3 works with individual characters, its numbering system is different from yours. 1-2-3 considers the first character in the string to be in the 0 position of the string. Since 1-2-3 will not adjust its numbering scheme, in order to work with 1-2-3's numbering method you will have to adjust your method of counting.

Replacing Incorrect Characters

You can replace characters with a text string without retyping the entire string. You can use this feature to change slash characters to hyphens, or to change a part number into a warehouse location. The function is extremely flexible; you can replace multiple characters with one character, or you can replace one character with multiple characters.

The function you will use to make these replacements is @REPLACE. It uses four arguments, in this sequence:

@REPLACE(original string,start location,number of characters,new string)

The first argument is the *original string* or, more likely, a reference to the cell containing the original string.

The second argument, *start location,* is the position number in the original string at which you want to begin the replacement. Remember that when 1-2-3 calculates the position number, it begins with position 0 for the first character in the string.

The third argument, *number of characters,* tells 1-2-3 how many characters to remove from the string. This argument offers considerable flexibility. You can specify 0 characters to have the new string inserted in the original string. When the number of characters is greater than the length of the new string, the string that is returned by this function will be shorter than the original. When the number of characters is the same as the number of characters in the original string, the entire string will be replaced.

The last argument, *new string,* is a series of characters enclosed in quotation marks, or a reference to a cell that contains a string. When there are no characters between the quotation marks, the new string is empty (" ") and @REPLACE will simply delete the characters from the original string.

You will work with an example that will alter a series of part numbers on the worksheet. The existing part numbers have three sections, each separated by slashes (/). @REPLACE will change the first slash to - (hyphen) and will delete the middle section of the entry. Follow these steps to take a look at @REPLACE in action:

1. Make the following entries:

A1:	Part Number
A2:	AB/567/8907
A3:	VB/907/6754
A4:	JK/675/8752
A5:	LK/999/5544
C1:	Altered Part Number

Your worksheet should now look like this:

C1: 'Altered Part Number   READY

```
      A          B          C          D          E          F          G          H
1  Part Number            Altered Part Number
2  AB/567/8907
3  UB/907/6754
4  JK/675/8752
5  LK/999/5544
6
```

2. Move the cell pointer to C2, type **@REPLACE(A2,2,5,"-")**, and press ENTER.

    The character in position 2 is a slash because position 2 refers to the third character in the string. The next argument tells the function to remove the slash (/) and the next four characters from the string. This removes both slashes and the three characters between them. These five characters are replaced with a single - (hyphen).

3. Select /Copy, press ENTER, move the cell pointer to C3, type . (period), move the cell pointer to C5, and press ENTER.

    The results are as follows:

C2: @REPLACE(A2,2,5,"-")   READY

```
      A          B          C          D          E          F          G          H
1  Part Number            Altered Part Number
2  AB/567/8907            AB-8907
3  UB/907/6754            UB-6754
4  JK/675/8752            JK-8752
5  LK/999/5544            LK-5544
6
```

4. Select /Worksheet Erase Yes to clear memory.

Using Part of a Name Entry

Some of the string functions allow you to dissect a string entry and restructure the original entry into a string that looks quite different. These features can be useful; they can alter names entered as John Smith to Smith, John, or just Smith if you are only interested in the last name. Unless you have worked with the string functions for a while, however, you may have to experiment a bit to come up with the correct solution. The difficulty in creating the correct formula arises, in part, because meaningful activities with these functions frequently require the use of a number of functions in one formula.

    You will create a string formula that extracts the last name from an entry that looks like John Smith. This will require three built-in functions: @MID, @FIND, and

@LENGTH. First you need to take a look at these functions and the arguments you will use with them.

USING @FIND   Use the *@FIND* function whenever you wish to locate the position of a string within a string. You can use it to locate the position of a blank space between first and last name, for example. When you combine the position of the blank space with the result of other functions, you can change a name that is sequenced as first name/last name to a name that is sequenced as last name/comma/first name.

The *@FIND* function uses three arguments, in this sequence:

@FIND(search string,string to be searched,starting location)

The *search string* is a character sequence or a reference to a cell that contains a character sequence to be found in the second argument, *string to be searched*. As with the other string functions, when the characters are entered directly into the function, they must be enclosed in quotation marks. The length of *search string* must be at least one character less than the length of *string to be searched*. The function is case-sensitive in its search, so you will want to differentiate carefully between upper- and lowercase.

One option is to store the string directly in the function. The string can also be stored in a cell, and the cell address where it is stored can be used as a function argument. The maximum length of this string is 240 characters.

The last argument, *starting location,* is the position in *string to be searched* at which you want to begin your search. 1-2-3 counts the leftmost character in the string as 0, causing you to make a mental adjustment as you specify the place to begin.

If you were to enter **"@FIND("-","213-28-7865",4)**, the result 6 would be returned. (Remember that 1-2-3 begins counting with position 0.) Even though 1-2-3 begins at position 4 when it determines what location the search string matches, it determines the position number based on its position from the far left of the string. After looking at the other two functions, you will use @FIND to build the formula that extracts the last name.

USING @MID   You can use the *@MID* function whenever you want to extract a portion of a string. Unlike @RIGHT and @LEFT, which only extract from the beginning or the end of a string, @MID can be used to extract a portion from the center of a string. This function offers the ultimate in flexibility; you can start anywhere in the string and extract as few or as many characters as you want.

The function uses three arguments, in this sequence:

@MID(string,start number,number of characters)

The first argument, *string*, is any group of characters, a reference to a group of characters, or a string formula.

Start number is the first character position you wish to extract from the string. If you choose to extract the first letter in the string, this is referred to as position 0.

The last argument, *number of characters*, is a number representing how many characters to extract from the string. The range of acceptable values has an upper limit of 240 and a lower limit of 0. The entry @MID("abcdefghi",3,3) would return def.

USING @LENGTH   The *@LENGTH* function returns the number of characters in a string. It is a count of those characters. It is not the same as the position number of the last character, which will always be one less than the string length. @LENGTH is written as @LENGTH(*string*). For example, @LENGTH("Profit") equals 6, while the position number of the "t" is 5. Since this is the last function needed for your formula, you are ready to put all three together to access the last name.

COMBINING THE THREE FUNCTIONS   Extracting the last name from entries that look like the name John Smith can be quite a challenge. The @RIGHT function cannot handle the task because last names have varying numbers of characters. You can use the three functions just discussed in combination to handle the task. Follow these steps to test the process:

1. Make these worksheet entries:

    A1:   John Smith
    A2:   Jim Pearson
    A3:   Rob Smithfield
    A4:   Ken Horn

2. Select /Worksheet Column Set-Width, type **15**, and press ENTER.

3. Move the cell pointer to A10, press the SPACEBAR once, and press ENTER.
    This step will not appear to have an effect on the cell, but it alters it to contain one blank space. This is quite important: It is the character you will be searching for within the name to identify the end of the first name.

4. Next you should move the cell pointer to cell B1 and then you should type **@MID(A1,@FIND($A$10,A1,0)+1,@LENGTH(A1))**.

5. Select /Copy, press ENTER, move the cell pointer to B2, type . (period), move the cell pointer to B4, and press ENTER.

Each of the entries in column B shows the last name of the individual listed in column A, like this:

`B1: @MID(A1,@FIND($A$10,A1,0),@LENGTH(A1))`

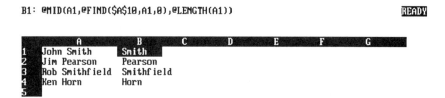

```
          A             B            C        D        E        F        G
1  John Smith      Smith
2  Jim Pearson     Pearson
3  Rob Smithfield  Smithfield
4  Ken Horn        Horn
5
```

The formula will work for all first- and last-name entries, regardless of the length of each component. If the entries in column A contained middle names, a different formula would be required.

Combining Numbers and Strings

String and number entries cannot be combined into one cell because string and numeric data have different attributes. String data cannot be used to perform calculations; numeric data is not affected by changes in label alignment. Although you cannot negate any of the basic attributes of strings or values, you can change one type of entry to the other type with built-in functions.

There is one built-in function that turns strings into numeric values and another function that converts numeric values into strings. You can use them when you want to perform arithmetic operations on a string that looks like a number. The *@VALUE* function uses a string as its argument and returns the number with which you will be able to perform the desired operation. The *@STRING* function converts a number into a character string. These functions are also useful when you want to concatenate (combine) a numeric branch number or a date with some text data to produce a heading for a report. After conversion with the @STRING function, this is possible.

The @STRING function uses two arguments, with one representing the number to be converted and the other representing the number of decimal places that the string will display. It looks like this:

@STRING(number,number of decimal places)

The first argument, *number,* can be an actual numeric value or a reference to a value. The second argument, *number of decimal places,* is the number of decimal places that you want the converted string to display. If the original number has more decimal places than the number you specify, a string will be created by a rounded representation of the original number. If the number of decimal places in the original number is shorter, zeros will be used for padding.

You will make entries that allow you to test the workings of the @STRING function as it converts numeric data, so that it can be concatenated with character data to produce the report heading. These are the steps required to complete the test example:

1. Select /Worksheet Erase Yes to remove the previous entries.

2. Make these entries:

A3:	Dept:
A4:	Headcount:
B3:	400
B4:	50

3. Move the cell pointer to column A, select /Worksheet Column Set-Width, type **10**, and press ENTER.

4. Move the cell pointer to B1, type +**"January Budget Report for Department "&@STRING(B3,0)**, and press ENTER to produce these results:

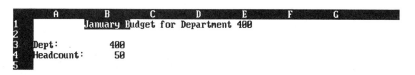

```
B1: +"January Budget for Department "&@STRING(B3,0)                    READY
```

```
           A           B           C          D          E          F          G
 1                  January Budget for Department 400
 2
 3    Dept:            400
 4    Headcount:        50
 5
```

This formula starts with a + to make 1-2-3 use the entry as a value. This may seem contradictory, but all formulas are value entries even if they are string formulas. The string that is included in the formula is enclosed within quotation marks, which are required for all text not stored in a cell. The ampersand (&) joins (or concatenates) the two components of a string, and the @STRING function creates a string from the value in B3. The arguments for this function tell 1-2-3 to show zero decimal places when the conversion is made.

As you work with additional string entries, keep in mind that the conversion can take the opposite approach and turn strings into numeric entries with @VALUE.

REVIEW EXERCISE

This chapter has introduced you to several powerful functions that can enhance your models. Trying another example that uses these powerful functions will help give you the confidence to use them in your own models. The following example creates a property comparison model.

1. Erase the current worksheet so you can start with an empty worksheet.
   Hint: Select /Worksheet Erase Yes.

2. Set the width of column A to 14, column B to 8, column C to 6, column D to 23, and column E to 21.
   Hint: For each column, select /Worksheet Column Set-Width, type the column width, and press ENTER.

3. Set the format of the range B4..C7 to the currency Format with 0 decimal places.
   Hint: Select /Range Format Currency, type 0, press ENTER, select range of B4..C7, and press ENTER.

4. Make these entries on the worksheet:
A2:	Address
A4:	'513 Curtis
A5:	5234
A6:	'11335 West
A7:	'110 Main
B2:	Cost
B4:	65000
B5:	74000
B6:	78000
B7:	"$70,000
C2:	Taxes
D1:	Error Checking
D2:	Address
E2:	Cost

5. Use the @REPEAT and @LENGTH functions to place below the column headings in row 2 a hyphenated line that is the same length as the column headings.
   Hint: Enter **@REPEAT("-",@LENGTH(A2))** in A3. Then select /Copy, press ENTER, select the range B3..E3, and press ENTER.

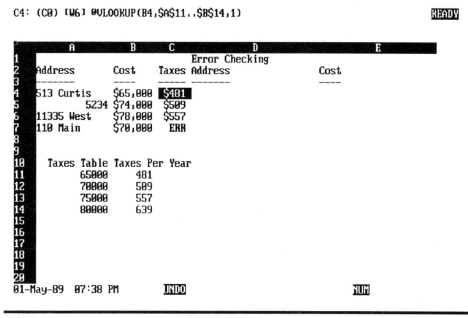

C4: (C0) [W6] @VLOOKUP(B4,$A$11..$B$14,1)   READY

```
         A            B        C            D                E
 1                             Error Checking
 2   Address        Cost     Taxes Address            Cost
 3   -------        ----     ----- -------            ----
 4   513 Curtis    $65,000   $481
 5        5234     $74,000   $509
 6   11335 West    $78,000   $557
 7   110 Main      $70,000    ERR
 8
 9
10   Taxes Table Taxes Per Year
11       65000      481
12       70000      509
13       75000      557
14       80000      639
15
16
17
18
19
20
```
01-May-89   07:38 PM   UNDO   NUM

FIGURE 10-14.   Property listing with @LOOKUP used for property taxes

6. Add the following data starting in column A, which lists the property taxes for different property values:

```
10   Taxes Table Taxes Per Year
11       65000      481
12       70000      509
13       75000      557
14       80000      639
```

7. Use the @VLOOKUP function and the property tax table you created to compute the property tax in column C for each property. The worksheet is shown in Figure 10-14.

   Hint: Enter **@VLOOKUP(B4,$A$11..$B$14,1)** in C4. Then copy the formula by selecting /Copy, pressing ENTER, selecting the range C5..C7, and pressing ENTER again.

   Notice that 1-2-3 returns ERR for the last property. While you can visually check the address and cost entries with a small worksheet like this, you will want to use formulas instead. Formulas allow you to automatically check your worksheets when there are too many entries to visually check each one.

8. Enter the formula **@IF(@ISSTRING(A4)," ","Address must be a label")** in column D for the rows containing addresses, to ensure that all addresses are entered correctly.

    Hint: After entering the first formula in D4, select /Copy, press ENTER, select the range D5..D7, and press ENTER.

    Notice that the @IF formula returns an Error Message in D5 because you entered a number in A5.

9. Move to A5 and enter **'5234 North**.

10. Enter the formula **@IF(@ISNUMBER(B4)," ","Cost must be a label")** in column E for the rows containing entries to check that all costs are entered correctly.

    Hint: Enter this formula in E4 then select /Copy, press ENTER, select the range E5..E7, and press ENTER.

    Notice that the @IF formula returns an Error Message in E7 because you entered a label in B7.

11. Move to B7 and enter **70000**. The final worksheet looks like the one in Figure 10-15.

12. Save this model as PROPERTY or erase the worksheet if you do not wish to save this model.

    Hint: Select /File Save, type **PROPERTY**, and press ENTER, then select /Worksheet Erase Yes.

REVIEW

- The @IF function lets you create a formula that can provide more than one result. The result returned by the formula depends on a condition. The condition is an expression that evaluates as true or false. With Release 2 and higher, you can include strings in the condition or choose to return a string rather than a value.

- You can place one @IF statement inside another @IF statement by using the second @IF as the entry that is used when the condition evaluates as either true or false. This process of using one @IF inside another @IF is referred to as nesting @IF statements.

- @VLOOKUP allows you to search a vertical table for an entry stored in the worksheet. @VLOOKUP searches the first column of the table for the entry

```
B7: (C0) [W8] 70000                                              READY
```

```
         A           B       C           D                  E
 1                               Error Checking
 2  Address         Cost    Taxes Address                 Cost
 3  -------         ----    ----- -------                 ----
 4  513 Curtis      $65,000 $481
 5  5234 North      $74,000 $509
 6  11335 West      $78,000 $557
 7  110 Main        $70,000 $509
 8
 9
10     Taxes Table Taxes Per Year
11           65000       481
12           70000       509
13           75000       557
14           80000       639
15
16
17
18
19
20
01-May-89  07:38 PM            UNDO                      NUM
```

FIGURE 10-15.   Property listing with @ISSTRING and @ISNUMBER to detect errors

stored in the worksheet. Once it locates a matching entry it returns a value from the same row of the table.

- @INDEX also returns a value from a table. @INDEX does not search for a matching entry. You must supply the row and column offset from the beginning of the table. The @INDEX function returns the entry in the cell with the specified offset in the table.

- 1-2-3 provides several functions that are used to check for errors. By using these functions you can check entries in other worksheet cells and plan appropriate actions. These functions can also be used with @IF to return different results depending on whether these special functions return true or false. The @ISERR function tests to determine if a cell equals ERR. @ISNA tests to determine if a cell equals NA. The @ISNUMBER function tests to determine if a cell contains a number, and @ISSTRING tests to determine if a cell contains a string.

- Other 1-2-3 functions convert one type of data to another. @DATEVALUE converts a string containing a date to a date number. @TIMEVALUE converts a string containing a time to a time number. @VALUE converts a string containing a number to a value. @STRING converts a value to a string.

- The string functions in Release 2 and higher manipulate and return strings. @REPLACE replaces part of one string with another. @FIND finds the position within a string that contains another string. @MID returns a portion of a string. @LENGTH returns the length of a string.

Functions

Entry	Action
@IF	Returns one value if the condition tested is true and another value if false
@VLOOKUP	Compares a worksheet entry against table entries and returns a value from the same row in the table
@INDEX	Returns a value from the specified row and column of a table
@ISNA	Returns 1 if a value equals NA, otherwise returns 0
@ISERR	Returns 1 if a value equals ERR, otherwise returns 0
@ISNUMBER	Returns 1 if a value is a number, otherwise returns 0
@ISSTRING	Returns 1 if a value is a string, otherwise returns 0
@MID	Returns characters from a string starting at any position in the string
@FIND	Returns the position at which a character string starts in another character string
@REPLACE	Replaces characters in one string with another character string
@LENGTH	Returns the length of a string
@STRING	Returns a string obtained by converting a number entry to a string entry
@VALUE	Returns a value obtained by converting a string containing numeric digits to a value entry

11

ADVANCED FILE-MANAGEMENT TECHNIQUES

Saving a Section of the Worksheet
Combining Information from Other Files
into the Current Worksheet
Using Links to Incorporate Data from Other Worksheets
Importing Text Data
Review Exercise
Review

By now you are probably an expert at the basic file-management features for saving and retrieving your worksheet files. These commands are the workhorses of the file commands because they play a central role in every worksheet session. A number of other file-management commands are used less commonly but provide some powerful options that you will want to incorporate into your set of skills.

In this chapter you will learn to use the extract feature to save a small portion of the worksheet in a worksheet file. This feature will let you transfer account names or end-of-period totals to another worksheet without having to reenter any of the data. You will also learn to use the 1-2-3 combine features, which let you combine an entire file or a range of data with the file currently in memory. With Release 2.2 you can also combine information from several files into one worksheet with the file link features. This new method is easier and less error prone because you can even update the links for shared network files at any time with the /File Admin Link-Refresh command. These new techniques allow you to bring data into memory from disk without wiping out the current entries in the worksheet, as /File Retrieve does. Finally, you will explore a feature that enables you to import text data from a word processing program or other source into your 1-2-3 worksheet. This feature brings the lines of your word processing document into the current worksheet as a column of long label entries. Or, if you prefer, you can use one of the Data menu selections to split these long labels into individual cell entries. Together, these new commands provide ways to increase productivity by letting you reuse existing data rather than having to reenter it. The commands also let you consolidate the numbers in individual worksheets to compute a total automatically.

SAVING A SECTION OF THE WORKSHEET

In this section, you will examine the commands that let you save a range on a worksheet to a file without having to save the entire worksheet. You will have complete control over the amount of data that is saved to this file, and you can use it to start a new worksheet application. You can also add the data in this file to an existing application, using the 1-2-3 commands covered later in this chapter.

Why Would You Want to Save Part of a Worksheet?

You may be wondering what purpose can be served by saving a portion of a current worksheet to a file. One of the advantages is that this approach lets you continue very large applications when you are running out of memory. Suppose that you have a model in which you are recording detailed expenses by department for 1990. You have been monitoring the amount of available memory month by month and have come to the realization that you will not be able to fit an entire year's worth of information in memory at once. One approach open to you is to record expenses for the first quarter or six months in one worksheet and use other worksheets for the remaining periods. However, this strategy alone will not provide all the information you need. You will have all the detailed expenses, but you will not have a total of all the expenses for the year, which is likely to be just as important as the detail.

1-2-3's /File Xtract command will let you total each expense category on the worksheet that contains the expenses for the first quarter, and save those totals separately in a worksheet file. The worksheet containing the totals can be used as the basis for the second quarter worksheet. This same process can be used at the end of the second and third quarters so that the worksheet with the fourth quarter figures will be able to present a total for the entire year.

This same capability can be used in the data-management environment, as a database begins to grow too large for the worksheet. You can sort the worksheet and save one or more categories of data with the /File Xtract command. This data can be used as the basis for a second database, containing only those categories of data that you have saved with /File Xtract.

You could use the /File Xtract command on the employee database discussed in Chapter 9 to split the database by an alphabetical break if it became too large. Perhaps you could divide records by placing records with last names beginning with the letters "A" through "M" in one database, and placing the others in a separate database. Other potential divisions would be by location codes or job codes.

The ability to extract information from a worksheet can also be useful when you wish to save data-entry time. You can use a worksheet containing a list of all your account names to save these names into a file by themselves. Anyone starting a new application that required these names could retrieve the extract file to begin their application.

Different Options for Saving

There is more than one way to create the extract file. You can save just the values in the range selected, or if you prefer you can save the formulas. This chapter will help you examine both prospects so that you can become familiar with some of the potential sources of problems when saving formulas.

Whether you plan to save formulas or values, the command that you will use is /File Xtract. The spelling is a little different than you might expect because of 1-2-3's commitment to having only a single command that begins with a given letter in a menu. The "E" is already used for the Erase command, which accounts for the novel spelling of Xtract.

The menu that /File Xtract presents looks like this:

You can try each of these options in the next two sections.

SAVING VALUES   When you choose to save as Values, 1-2-3 will save the current values of the cells you select in a worksheet file. This file will have a filename extension of .WKS or .WK1, depending on which release of 1-2-3 you are using.

The extracted data is placed in the new file beginning in cell A1. The portion of the new file that contains data will be determined by the size and shape of the data being saved. It will retain its original size and shape, although each cell's address will be determined by its offset from the beginning of the range. The same offset will be used in the new file, but the origin is always A1.

When you select the Values option, calculated results and labels will be retained in the new file. All formulas are replaced by the result of the formula calculations. This is a convenient way to carry the result of calculations forward to a new worksheet without having to bring the data forward, as would be required when saving formulas.

When you select /File Xtract Values, 1-2-3 asks for the name of the file to store the data in, using a prompt message like this:

You have the same options as with the /File Save command. You can type the name of a new file and 1-2-3 will store your data in that file. You can type the name of an existing file, specify the range to be saved, and 1-2-3 will prompt you with this message:

```
A1:                                                              MENU
Cancel  Replace  Backup
Cancel command -- Leave existing file on disk intact
        A        B        C        D        E        F        G        H
```

Building a small model is a good way to test the operation of the /File Xtract command. The model will present the detailed sales data for each month in the first quarter and sum this data to provide an end-of-quarter figure. Although there is not enough data to cause a condition with insufficient memory, the concept and potential actions required are exactly the same as you would need with much larger models. Follow these steps to create this practice example:

1. Select /Worksheet Erase Yes to ensure that the worksheet is blank.

2. Select /Worksheet Column Set-Width, type **18**, and press ENTER.

3. Complete these entries:

A3:	Sales - Product 1
A4:	Sales - Product 2
A5:	Sales - Product 3
B2:	"Jan
B3:	1200
B4:	4400
B5:	5400
C2:	"Feb
C3:	1500
C4:	5600
C5:	7800
D2:	"Mar
D3:	1100
D4:	7800
D5:	9900
E2:	"Qtr1
E3:	@SUM(B3.D3)
E4:	@SUM(B4.D4)
E5:	@SUM(B5.D5)

4. Move the cell pointer to E3.

 After moving to E3, your worksheet may resemble Figure 11-1.

5. Select /File Xtract Values.

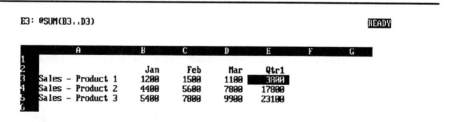

FIGURE 11-1.   Data for the first quarter

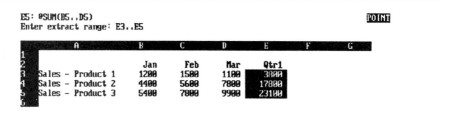

FIGURE 11-2.   Selecting an extract range

6. Type **QTR1VALU** and press ENTER.

   QTR1VALU will be the name of the file used for this extract.

7. Expand the range by moving the cell pointer to E5 so that it looks like the highlighted range in Figure 11-2.

8. Press ENTER to finalize.

   The current value of these three cells will be written to the filename specified.

9. Select /File Save, type **1ST_QTR**, and press ENTER to save the original file.

10. Select /File Retrieve, type **QTR1VALU**, and press ENTER.

This will place the three values in cells A1, A2, and A3. Your screen will look like this:

You will have an opportunity to work with this extract file again later. You will learn how to place its contents anywhere you like in the worksheet by combining it with an existing worksheet.

SAVING FORMULAS   Saving formulas is just as easy as saving values, but before you use this option you must consider how you will use the file and what it will contain. If you save the formulas without the data they need, will there be data on the new worksheet for them to operate on? Do they contain relative references that will be adjusted when they are placed in the new worksheet? Will the adjustments that are made be logical? In many cases, the answer to these questions is no, indicating that another approach would be preferred, but there are situations in which it is convenient to be able to save the formulas.

You will want to save the quarter totals as values to look at the differences. Follow these steps to complete the exercise:

1. Select /File Retrieve, type **1ST_QTR**, and press ENTER to recall the original worksheet.

2. Move the cell pointer to E3, if not already there.

3. Select /File Xtract Formulas.

4. Type **QTR1FORM** and press ENTER.
   QTR1FORM will be the name of the file used for this extract.

5. Expand the range by moving the cell pointer to E5 and press ENTER to finalize.
   The formulas or values in these three cells will be written to the filename specified.

6. Select /File Retrieve, type **QTR1FORM**, and press ENTER to produce this display:

A1: @SUM(IT1..IV1)   READY

Notice that the formulas were adjusted for the new worksheet. This situation has a high potential for error because the formulas might not be adjusted as you would expect. In this particular case, the Values option meets your needs better. Later, you will see the package work with formulas when you use the /File Combine Add command and only the current value of the formula.

COMBINING INFORMATION FROM OTHER FILES INTO THE CURRENT WORKSHEET

The /File Retrieve command has a /Worksheet Erase command built right into it. Every time you select /File Retrieve, the file in memory will be replaced by the contents of the file you are bringing in from the disk. In many cases this is exactly what you need. But in others, you might prefer to retain the current contents of memory and bring information into memory from disk to add to the current data. The /File Combine command provides this capability and performs the Release 2.2 file link features covered later in the chapter. You will want to review the /File Combine command capabilities and then contrast them with the file linking ability covered later.

In this section you will examine each of the File Combine menu options separately in order to understand the functions they serve. These components will then be joined in examples to help you understand their sequence and their relationship to the File Combine menus.

Applications for the Combine Operation

There are many applications for the /File Combine command. This feature has three options, with a menu like this:

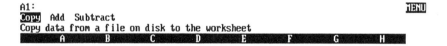

The first option copies data from disk to an area of the worksheet and replaces the contents of that area with what is on the disk. This option would be useful for adding a list of account names that are stored in a file created with the /File Xtract command.

The second option adds the data on the disk to the data already in memory. Each value in the file will be added to a corresponding value in the current worksheet. The corresponding value is determined by the cell pointer location at the time the command is invoked. This option would let you automate the consolidation of sales or expenses for all the units within a company to produce a total company report.

The third option is subtraction. This option could be used to remove the results for a subsidiary from the total company reports.

A1: [W25] 'Cash   READY

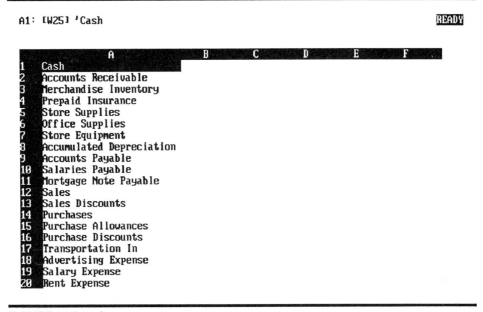

	A	B	C	D	E	F
1	Cash
2	Accounts Receivable
3	Merchandise Inventory
4	Prepaid Insurance
5	Store Supplies
6	Office Supplies
7	Store Equipment
8	Accumulated Depreciation
9	Accounts Payable
10	Salaries Payable
11	Mortgage Note Payable
12	Sales
13	Sales Discounts
14	Purchases
15	Purchase Allowances
16	Purchase Discounts
17	Transportation In
18	Advertising Expense
19	Salary Expense
20	Rent Expense

FIGURE 11-3.   Account names

Deciding How Much
Data to Combine

You have two options when combining a file with the current worksheet: to combine everything in the file, or on whether to combine the contents of a range name. The option you choose depends if the file contains data you do not want to combine.

USING AN ENTIRE FILE   When you combine an entire file, everything in the file will be placed within the current worksheet. Which combining method to use depends on which selections you make. Figure 11-3 shows a list of account names that are stored in a file named ACCOUNTS. The current worksheet shown in Figure 11-4 can use this list of names. The result of combining ACCOUNTS with the current worksheet is shown in Figure 11-5. The accounts were put just where they were needed by the placement of the cell pointer in A5 before the Combine operation was invoked with the menu.

A5:   READY

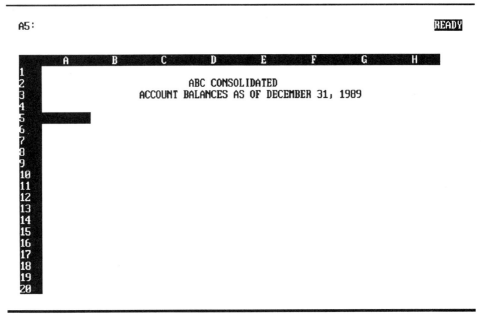

FIGURE 11-4.   Worksheet requiring account names

A5: 'Cash   READY

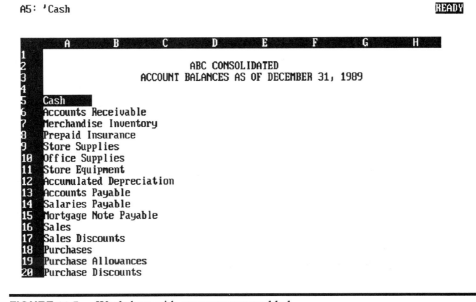

FIGURE 11-5.   Worksheet with account names added

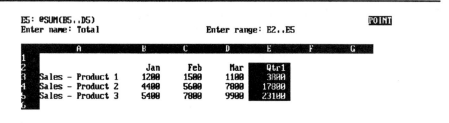

FIGURE 11-6.   Naming a range to use later with /File Combine

USING A RANGE   You were introduced to range names in the second chapter. Ranges of cells can be assigned range names for a variety of reasons. For example, names can be added to improve the readability of formulas. They can also be used to let you combine less than an entire file with the current worksheet.

If you want to transfer numbers to another worksheet, you can create an extract file for each group of numbers you wish to transfer. But a far easier approach is to use the /Range Name command in the sending file, save that file, and use the /File Combine command with the Named/Specified-Range option to obtain the data you need in a receiving file. While you can combine ranges by providing a range address instead of a range name, range names are easier to remember than range addresses which prevents mistakes.

To try this with the 1ST_QTR file you created earlier, follow these steps:

1. Select /File Retrieve, type **1ST_QTR**, and press ENTER.

2. Move the cell pointer to E2 and select /Range Name Create.

    You are including the label Qtr1 in this range in order to see how the label is handled.

3. Type **Total** and press ENTER.

4. Move the cell pointer to E5 to produce the display in Figure 11-6.

5. Press ENTER.

    Both the label and formulas are now named Total. Later, if you use this named range with /File Combine, the combination method you select will determine whether the current value of the formula or the formula itself is used. The command you select will also determine whether the label at the top of the formulas is used. This will be more clear after you have examined the options for combining in more detail.

6. Select /File Save, press ENTER, and select **Replace**.

This is required to save the assigned range names on the disk.

Methods for Combining

There are three different methods for combining data in a file with the current contents of memory. Each method has a completely different effect on the current worksheet, so be certain that you understand each one clearly before using these features on your own applications. It is also recommended that you save the current worksheet before you begin. That way, if you use the wrong method, you can retrieve the worksheet from disk and try again.

You will need to build a new worksheet model to use with the Combine options. Follow these directions:

1. Move the cell pointer to B2, select /Range Erase, move the cell pointer to E5, and press ENTER.

   This is a short-cut approach to creating the new model, since you need the same entries and width for column A.

2. Make these worksheet entries:

B2:	"Qtr1
C1:	Sales Summary by Quarter
C2:	"Qtr2
D2:	"Qtr3
E2:	"Qtr4
F2:	"Total
F3:	@SUM(B3.E3)

3. Select /Copy, press ENTER, move the cell pointer to F4, type ., move to F5, and press ENTER.

The model shell is now ready to receive data from the various quarters and looks like the worksheet in Figure 11-7.

The Combine options provide the perfect solution because they do not destroy the current model as you bring the quarter totals in from other files. The data that you will be bringing in must be on disk, either as a range in a complete model or as an extract file that contains only the data you need.

COPYING TO THE CURRENT WORKSHEET   The /File Combine Copy command is used when you have data stored on disk, and you want to replace a section of the current worksheet. To bring this data into the current worksheet, position the cell

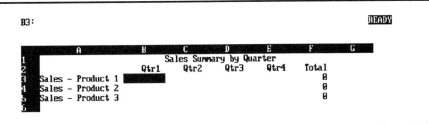

FIGURE 11-7.   Worksheet before /File Combine command

pointer carefully; this is what will control the placement of the data. Use the values you stored in QTR1VALU for this example. Follow these directions:

1. Move the cell pointer to B3.

2. Select /File Combine Copy.

3. Select Entire-File.

4. Type **QTR1VALU** and press ENTER to produce the results shown in Figure 11-8.

Notice that each of the values in this small file is placed on the model and the entries are included in the total.

Try the same exercise with the formulas you stored in QTR1FORM, using these steps:

1. Move the cell pointer to B3, select /Range Erase, move the cell pointer to B5, and press ENTER.

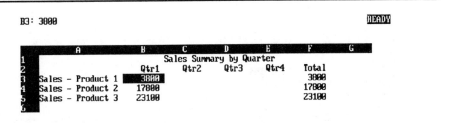

FIGURE 11-8.   Copying data to the worksheet with /File Combine Copy

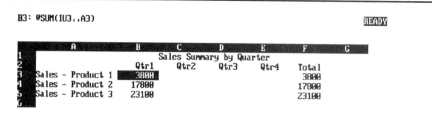

FIGURE 11-9.   Combining formulas without the cells they reference

2. Select /File Combine Copy.

3. Select Entire-File.

4. Type **QTR1FORM** and press ENTER to produce the results shown in Figure 11-9.

Notice that everything appears the same at first glance. But a look at the formula in the control panel shows that everything is not the same; this formula includes entries from most of the columns. In this instance, the formulas have the potential to cause nothing but trouble, as the CIRC status indicator at the bottom of the screen tells you. It says that the worksheet contains a formula reference to itself.

Another problem to be on the lookout for is incorrect cell pointer placement or a lack of knowledge of the exact contents of an extract file or a range. If you were to position the cell pointer in the wrong place and use the /File Combine command, you could wind up with results like the one shown in Figure 11-10. Notice how everything has shifted by one row, making the model useless.

FIGURE 11-10.   Misjudging cell pointer's position for /File Combine

ADDING TO THE CURRENT WORKSHEET   When you use the /File Combine
Add command, values will be added to the existing values. Which values are added
is determined by cell pointer position and placement of the file values within the file.
If the worksheet cells are blank, the only difference between Copy and Add is that
Add ignores labels. Follow these steps to try the new command:

1. Move the cell pointer to B3, select /Range Erase, move the cell pointer to B5,
   and press ENTER.

2. Move the cell pointer to B2.
   You will be using the named range Total in the 1ST_QTR file this time.
   Since the label Qtr1 is included in the range, you need to move the cell pointer
   to B2 so that the first value in the file will be matched with B3.

3. Select /File Combine Add Named/Specified-Range.

4. Type **Total** and press ENTER.

5. Type **1ST_QTR** and press ENTER to produce the results shown in Figure 11-11.
   Try this again to see if it really adds.

6. Select /File Combine Add Named/Specified-Range.

7. Type **Total** and press ENTER.

8. Type **1ST_QTR** and press ENTER. Move the cell pointer to B3 to see the value
   7600 in B3, as in Figure 11-12.

You can see that each of the numbers in the current worksheet doubled, as the numbers
on the file were added to the current worksheet again.

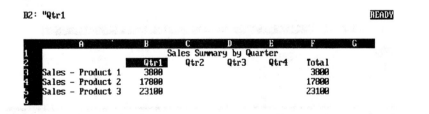

FIGURE 11-11.   Copying data to the worksheet with /File Combine Add

B3: 7600   READY

```
          A          B        C        D        E        F          G
 1                        Sales Summary by Quarter
 2                      Qtr1     Qtr2     Qtr3     Qtr4     Total
 3  Sales - Product 1   7600                                7600
 4  Sales - Product 2  35600                               35600
 5  Sales - Product 3  46200                               46200
 6
```

FIGURE 11-12. Adding a range to the worksheet twice

SUBTRACTING FROM THE CURRENT WORKSHEET   The /File Combine Subtract command is the exact opposite of the Add option. It subtracts the values stored on disk from the current worksheet cells. This command depends on the cell pointer location and the offset within the file that controls which numbers will be subtracted from which entries. You can try this by subtracting the last entry you added to the worksheet, following these steps:

1. Select /File Combine Subtract Entire-File.

   Since you will use the QTR1VALU file, leave the cell pointer in B3, since there is no need to have the cell pointer in B2. This file does not have a label before the numeric values the way the named range did.

2. Type **QTR1VALU** and press ENTER to produce the results shown in Figure 11-13.

   Each of the entries returned to the original values as the Subtract operation was completed.

3. Select /File Save, type **QTRTOTAL**, and press ENTER to save this new file.

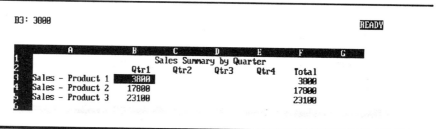

B3: 3000   READY

```
          A          B        C        D        E        F          G
 1                        Sales Summary by Quarter
 2                      Qtr1     Qtr2     Qtr3     Qtr4     Total
 3  Sales - Product 1   3000                                3000
 4  Sales - Product 2  17000                               17000
 5  Sales - Product 3  23100                               23100
 6
```

FIGURE 11-13.   Subtracting data from the worksheet with /File Combine Subtract

USING LINKS TO INCORPORATE DATA FROM OTHER WORKSHEETS

The /File Combine commands provide a set of tools for using data from other worksheets in the current one. Data from other files that is combined with the current worksheet is not automatically updated when there are changes in the original files from which you obtained the data. When you use the /File Combine command to reference data in other worksheet files, you must repeat the /File Combine commands every time you use the worksheet to ensure that the data is still current.

If you are using Release 2.2, however, you have another way of updating the worksheet data. This update is accomplished by establishing links to data in other worksheet files. 1-2-3 will update the links that you establish every time you retrieve the file containing the links. If you are working on a network, and other users may be updating the values of the data your worksheet is linked to, Release 2.2 even provides a command to refresh the links. All you need to do is select /File Admin Link-Refresh.

As an example of the file link feature, the summary worksheet that you create to combine expenses can contain formulas that reference the totals in the supporting worksheets. The summary worksheet is referred to as the *target file* because it will contain data stored in the other files. The files that contain the data are referred to as the *source files* because they are the source of the data you need. If the data in a source file changes, 1-2-3 changes the cells that reference the data in the source file each time you retrieve the target file that contains the links or select the /File Admin Link-Refresh command.

Release 2.2 supports a one-to-one link between worksheet cells. A one-to-one link is established when one cell in the target file obtains the value of a single cell in a source file. When a cell in the target file references the value of a cell in a source file, the cell cannot include other functions or formula operators; it must be a simple cell reference.

Using the File Links

To include a value from another file, you must specify the worksheet file from which you want to obtain the value as well as the worksheet cell address or range name. If the file is not on the current drive or in the current directory, you will need to specify this information along with the filename. If the filename has an extension other than .WK1, as in .WKS for a link to a Release 1A worksheet, you must specify the filename extension. The filename must also be enclosed in a set of double angle brackets, as in +<<BUDGET.WK1>>A2, which links the current cell in the target file worksheet to cell A2 in the BUDGET worksheet.

Follow these easy steps to establish a link from the current cell to a cell in a source file worksheet:

1. Type + to tell 1-2-3 that you are starting a formula.

2. Type << to enter the left side of a set of angle brackets. Use the less-than symbol (<) to create these brackets.

3. Enter the filename.

   Although 1-2-3 does not require you to include the directory name or the file extension unless you are using a directory other than the current directory or an extension other than .WK1, you may want to develop the habit of entering it anyway. Then you will not need to worry about which directory is current when you establish the link. 1-2-3 assumes that the file has a .WK1 extension unless you provide another extension.

4. Enter the right side of the set of angle brackets by typing >>. Use two greater-than symbols to create these brackets.

5. Enter a reference to the cell that contains the value you want to link to, such as B10.

   This reference can be entered as a cell address or a range name. If the range name is assigned to more than one cell, 1-2-3 uses the cell in the upper left corner of the range.

6. Press ENTER to finalize the entry.

1-2-3 finds the value in the source file worksheet and displays the current value in the cell containing the link in the target file worksheet.

A cell that references an external worksheet cell cannot include other formula features of 1-2-3. Thus, +<<BUDGET.WK1>>A2*<<BUDGET.WK1>>B3 would not be an acceptable entry. Nor can the external worksheet cell reference be an argument for a function in the cell, so @PMT(<<FINANCE.WK1>>A3,B3,C7) would not be acceptable. If you try using a file link with other formula features, 1-2-3 places the worksheet in EDIT mode and prompts you to fix the error.

If you are using a worksheet with file links in a network environment, you may want to confirm that file links are using the most up-to-date values of the cells in the other worksheets. This is necessary because other users may be updating entries in the source file while you are working in the target file. Before printing or making decisions based on the information in the target file, you may want to refresh the links to data in the source file. To do so, select /File Admin Link-Refresh. This command checks all external file links. If any have changed, 1-2-3 updates the value in the current worksheet.

USING FILE LINKS FOR A CONSOLIDATED WORKSHEET   Consolidating quarterly sales data provides a practical application for the use of external file links. Follow these steps to create a consolidated worksheet using file links:

1. Select /File Retrieve, type **1ST_QTR**, and press ENTER.

    This contains the first quarter of data that you want to consolidate. Notice that the data that you will include in the consolidation is stored in E3, E4, and E5. You can use this worksheet as the basis for the second quarter's data.

2. Complete these entries:

B2:	"Apr
B3:	1400
B4:	6000
B5:	8900
C2:	"May
C3:	1100
C4:	5600
C5:	7600
D2:	"Jun
D3:	1300
D4:	6400
D5:	8000
E2:	"Qtr2 *type in, or edit cell and replace 1 with 2.

    These entries produce the result shown in Figure 11-14.

E2: "Qtr2   READY

	A	B	C	D	E	F	G
1							
2		Apr	May	Jun	Qtr2		
3	Sales – Product 1	1400	1100	1300	3800		
4	Sales – Product 2	6000	5600	6400	18000		
5	Sales – Product 3	8900	7600	8000	24500		
6							

FIGURE 11-14.   Worksheet containing second quarter data

3. Select /File Save, type **2ND_QTR**, and press ENTER to save this new file. Notice that the data that you will include in the consolidation is stored in E3, E4, and E5.

4. Select /File Retrieve, type **QTRTOTAL**, and press ENTER.

5. Select /Range Erase, select B3..B5, and press ENTER.
   Since you can use external file references instead of the /File Combine commands, you will want to remove the old data first.

6. Enter **+<<1ST_QTR>>E3** and press ENTER. The formula looks like this:

```
B3: +<<1ST_QTR.WK1>>E3                                          READY
```

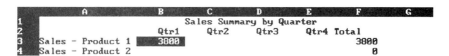

```
           A           B        C        D        E       F      G
1                           Sales Summary by Quarter
2                         Qtr1     Qtr2     Qtr3    Qtr4 Total
3    Sales - Product 1   3800                              3800
4    Sales - Product 2                                        0
```

1-2-3 adds .WK1 to the filename for you. The value 3800 is the one that the 1ST_QTR.WK1 file has stored in E3. If the values in 1ST_QTR.WK1 later change, 1-2-3 will use the updated value when you retrieve this file. Since this external file link is a formula, you can use the Copy command to copy it for the other products.

7. Select /Copy, press ENTER, move to B4, type . (period), move to B5, and press ENTER to copy the formula from B3 to B4..B5.
   Notice how 1-2-3 automatically adjusts the cell reference in the formula as you copy it. You cannot copy the formula to the next column because the second quarter column uses a different worksheet file, making it easier to type the external reference in the correct way than to edit it.

8. Move to C3, enter **+<<2ND_QTR>>E3**, and press ENTER.
   1-2-3 adds .WK1 to the filename for you. The value 3800 is the one that the 2ND_QTR.WK1 file has stored in E3. If the value in E3 in 2ND_QTR.WK1 later changes, 1-2-3 will use the updated value when you retrieve the file. Since this external file link is a formula, you can use the Copy command to copy it for the other products.

9. Select /Copy, press ENTER, move to C4, type . (period), move to C5, and press ENTER to copy the formula from C3 to C4..C5. The worksheet now looks like the one in Figure 11-15.

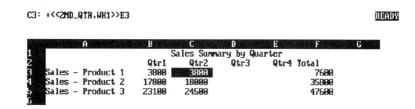

FIGURE 11-15.   External file links to obtain data from another worksheet

The real advantage of using file links instead of the /File Combine commands becomes apparent when the data changes. To see the effect of changing the data, follow these steps:

1. Select /File Save, press ENTER, and select Replace to save the QTRTOTAL file.

2. Select /File Retrieve, type **2ND_QTR**, and press ENTER.

3. Move to D3, enter **1700**, and press ENTER.

   The new value automatically updates the Product 1 total in E3. If you used the /File Combine commands to consolidate data, the consolidated data would not contain the updated number. If you create a file link between the consolidated worksheet and the supporting worksheet, 1-2-3 will update the values for you.

4. Select /File Save, press ENTER, and select Replace to save the 2ND_QTR file.

5. Select /File Retrieve, type **QTRTOTAL**, and press ENTER. The worksheet looks like the one in Figure 11-16.

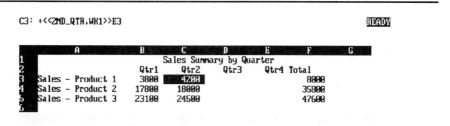

FIGURE 11-16.   File links refreshed to show updated data

In the new worksheet, 1-2-3 updated the file links when you retrieved the file.

LISTING THE EXTERNAL FILE LINKS   As you develop models with external file links, it can become difficult to remember all the source files to which a worksheet is linked. To quickly remind you which files the current worksheet uses, 1-2-3 has the /File List Linked command. When you select this command for the QTRTOTAL file, 1-2-3 displays this result:

```
C3: +<<2ND_QTR.WK1>>E3                                              FILES
Enter extension of files to list: C:\123NEW\1ST_QTR.WK1
         1ST_QTR.WK1    04/29/89        12:41        1811
1ST_QTR.WK1    2ND_QTR.WK1
```

This screen lists the files to which QTRTOTAL is linked. From this display, you can press ENTER to return to the worksheet.

You can also use the /File Admin Table Linked command to create a table of the links to the current file in an empty area of the worksheet. The first step is determining an empty area of the worksheet that is at least four columns wide and contains enough rows to list all the current links plus a couple of extra rows. Once you have determined the area you are going to use, you can invoke the command and highlight the cells for the table. 1-2-3 will write the current file path and filename in the first column and include additional information such as date, time, and file size.

IMPORTING TEXT DATA

1-2-3 provides a feature that allows you to transfer data from a word processor or any other program that can create ASCII text files. This data will be brought into 1-2-3 as a long label. Each line in the word processing document will be one label, with the end result of the transfer being a column of long labels. Although the entries may appear to reside in separate fields due to the data alignment in the original word processor, this is not the case. There is no automatic way to use a portion from the center of the long label without the Release 2 and higher /Data Parse command, which you will examine later.

Why Put Text Data
In the Worksheet?

The worksheet seems to be the place for calculations and other methods of rigorous analysis. Why would anyone want to put word processing data on the worksheet? One possible reason is a significant savings in data-entry time. If you have account names, employee numbers, inventory items, or other lists of text data in a word processing document and find that the same information is required in the spreadsheet environment, why retype it when you can have the package duplicate it for you? You will be assured of data consistency between the two applications.

Bringing the Data
Into the Worksheet

Bringing data into the worksheet involves several steps. Before you can enter 1-2-3 commands, you must complete preliminary tasks. The data you wish to access must be saved in a word processing file before you attempt the Import operation.

You should use a word processing program to try this exercise. You will also want to check your word processor's documentation to ensure that you use the correct option for creating an ASCII text file without all the edit characters. Some word processors create the document and require you to strip off special characters to create an ASCII file; others have an option for creating it directly.

Do not be concerned if you do not have a word processor to try this exercise with. You can still practice this command by entering the data shown in Figure 11-17 into the worksheet and printing this worksheet to a file using the /Print File command. Specify the range just as if you were printing it to your printer. In fact, the only differences are that you must specify a filename for saving the data and you should choose Options Other Unformatted from the Print menu before printing to the disk. This process will create a text file for you, and it will automatically have the filename extension of .PRN that you need to import the data.

```
C:TRANS123.PRN L5      C33         Insert
┌────────────── N O N D O C U M E N T   E D I T   M E N U ──────────────┐
│   CURSOR      SCROLL        DELETE     OTHER           MENUS           │
│ ^E up       ^W up        ^G char    ^J help         ^O onscreen format │
│ ^X down     ^Z down      ^T word    ^I tab          ^K block & save    │
│ ^S left     ^R screen up ^Y line    ^U turn insert off ^P print controls │
│ ^D right    ^C screen    Del char   ^N split the line  ^Q quick functions │
│ ^A word left   down      ^U undo    ^L find/replace  Esc shorthand     │
│ ^F word right            ^B top bit    again                          │
└──────────────────────────────────────────────────────────────────────┘
Smith, John    500     2500    12                                  <
Brown, Jill    330     1200    18                                  <
Stick, Jim     600     9000    12                                  <
Parks, Mel     120     5600    18                                  <
Appel, Jon     900     1350    12                                  <
                                                                   <
                                                                   <
                                                                   <
                                                                   <
                                                                   <
                                                                   <
                                                                   <
                                                                   <
                                                                   <
                                                                   <
```

FIGURE 11-17.   Text data entered with WordStar

Figure 11-17 shows data that was entered with WordStar. You can duplicate these entries with your word processor, and then import that data into 1-2-3. Follow these steps:

1. Select /Quit Yes to exit 1-2-3. Load your word processor, enter the data shown in Figure 11-17, and save the file as a text file with a filename extension of .PRN and the name TRANS123 (making it TRANS123.PRN).

   If your word processor assigns its own file extensions, you will have to rename the file in step 3. If you print a 1-2-3 file to disk rather than to the printer, 1-2-3 creates an ASCII text file on the disk with a filename extension of .PRN. It is unlikely that your word processor follows the same naming convention; it is very likely that you will have to rename the text file to change the extension name.

2. Exit your word processor.

3. Use the DOS RENAME command if you do not have a filename extension of .PRN.

Using the /File Import command is the next step. This command can bring up to 2048 lines of text data into the worksheet in Release 1A. In Release 2 and higher, the limit on the size of the imported file is 8192 lines. Each line can have a maximum of 240 characters.

You have two basic options for importing text data into your worksheet. After selecting /File Import, you can choose either Text or Numbers. Your choice will affect the manner in which the data is placed on the worksheet. Use the Text option when you want to import the entire file, including all the label entries. Use the Numbers option when you want to strip away everything but the numbers.

If you import the data in Figure 11-17 with the Text option, each line of the word processing document will become one long, left- aligned label. You will have an entire column of left-aligned labels. If you have Release 2 and higher, you can use the /Data Parse command to split these long, left-aligned labels into entries for individual cells.

If you select the Numbers option, only characters enclosed in double quotes and numbers will be imported. Characters not in quotation marks as well as blanks will be eliminated in the import process. Each number in a line of the text file will generate a numeric cell entry, and each quote-enclosed label will create a left-justified label cell. Entries from the same line of a text file will produce entries in the same row of the worksheet, proceeding from the left to the right of the row with each new entry.

You will want to try both File Import options with the data you entered a few minutes ago. Continue with these steps:

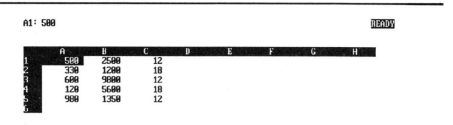

FIGURE 11-18.   WordStar data imported as numbers

1. Reload 1-2-3 or select /Worksheet Erase Yes to ensure that memory is clear.

2. Select /File Import Numbers to produce this result:

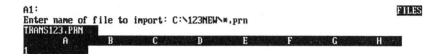

3. As 1-2-3 searches the disk for all the files with the filename extension .PRN, select a text file from the list presented to produce the display shown in Figure 11-18.

    Notice how each column of numbers from the text file is a separate column in 1-2-3.

4. Clear memory by selecting /Worksheet Erase Yes.

5. Select /File Import Text and select TRAN123.PRN to produce the results shown in Figure 11-19.

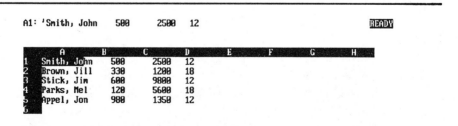

FIGURE 11-19.   WordStar data imported as text

Notice the difference between this example and the earlier one. All these entries are stored in column A as long labels. There is no automatic way to work with the second number in the first row because it is not easily accessible. It is buried in the middle of a long label entry. (Note that if you used tabs to separate the columns in your word processing document, Release 2 and higher will expand these tabs correctly, while Release 1A will not.)

Separating the Text Data
Into Fields with /Data Parse

It is great to display data from your word processor in the worksheet environment, but the data imported with the Text option is not especially useful in its current format. Importing the data as numbers does not solve the problem, since only numeric entries and quote-enclosed labels are brought over to the spreadsheet application.

You cannot use the data imported as Text in calculations and cannot reference any of the individual pieces of information separately. The Release 2 and higher /Data Parse command offers a solution to this problem. "Parse" is a fancy word that has been used by programmers for a long time. In 1-2-3, it means splitting the long label entries into smaller pieces. You can use it to split the long labels created by /File Import into separate cell values. Using /Data Parse to accomplish this task is a multi-step process. You must create a pattern that will be used for the Parse operation, define the labels to be parsed, define the area in which the newly generated cell values should be stored, and tell 1-2-3 to begin the Parse operation. The menu that provides these options is accessed by selecting /Data Parse and is shown here:

```
A1: 'Smith, John   500     2500   12                              MENU
Format-Line  Input-Column  Output-Range  Reset  Go  Quit
Create or edit a format line at the current cell
                          ────── Parse Settings ──────
    Input column:
    Output range:
```

CREATING A FORMAT LINE   The format line is an edit pattern that will be used against each long label to determine how it should be split into its component parts and what each component should look like. Each cell in the column of long labels will have this format line applied to it unless another format line is encountered within the column. At that point, the new format line will be used until the end of the labels or until another format line is encountered.

1-2-3 makes its best guess at the format that should be used for each component, using the symbols shown in Table 11-1 to present each of the options. It makes its

Character	Meaning
D	Marks the first character of a date block
L	Marks the first character of a label block
S	Indicates that the character below should be skipped during the Parse operation; this character is never generated by 1-2-3, but you can enter it when you are editing a format line
T	Marks the first character of a time block
V	Marks the first character of a value block
>	Indicates that the block started by the letter that precedes it is continued; the entry that began with a letter will be placed in one worksheet cell until a skip or another letter is encountered
*	Represents a blank space immediately below the character; this position can become part of the block that precedes it if additional space is required

TABLE 11-1.   Format line characters for data parse

determination from the entries in the line at which you place your cell pointer, and it inserts a new line and positions the format line immediately above this. When it encounters a space in the label it assumes that a field has ended.

If you want, you can create many format lines for one column of labels; however, each of them must be generated separately. Despite the fact that you can create multiple format lines, some consistency in the organization is required. You would not want to create a format line for each line that is parsed.

Try creating a format line by moving the cell pointer to the column of long labels you imported. Follow these steps:

1. Move the cell pointer to A1.

    This is the top entry in the column of long labels generated with /File **Import**.

2. Select /Data Parse.

3. Select Format-Line.

    This produces the following menu of Format-Line options:

```
A1: 'Smith, John    500      2500   12                                    MENU
Create  Edit
Create a format line at the current cell
                              ── Parse Settings ──────────
 ┌─────────────────────────────────────────────────────────────┐
 │  Input column:                                                │
 │                                                               │
 │  Output range:                                                │
 └─────────────────────────────────────────────────────────────┘
```

4. Select Create.

1-2-3 will insert a blank line above the cell pointer's location and generate a format line at that location. The line generated for your data should look like this:

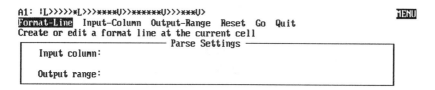

If you were to continue with /Data Parse and use this format line, five fields would be generated. A separate field would be generated for both the first and last names. If you want both the first and last names in the same cell, you will need to modify the format line. The CALC indicator will be turned on at the bottom of the screen, but there is no cause for concern.

MODIFYING THE FORMAT LINE   You can modify the format line that was generated by selecting Format-Line again, since the Data Parse menu remains on the screen for further selections. This time you will choose Edit to make your changes. Try this technique to alter the two name fields to make them one field. Follow these instructions to make the change:

1. Select Format-Line.

2. Select Edit to edit the format line. Press the DOWN ARROW key so the initial Data Parse settings box will disappear temporarily to show the format line and the worksheet data. The worksheet looks like the one in Figure 11-20.

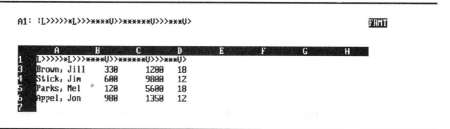

FIGURE 11-20.   Editing the format line

```
A1: !L>>>>>*L>>****U>>*****U>>***U>                                    FRMT

      A       B       C       D      E       F       G      H
1 L>>>>>>>>>>****U>>*****U>>***U>
3 Brown, Jill    330     1200    18
4 Stick, Jim     600     9800    12
5 Parks, Mel     120     5600    18
6 Appel, Jon     980     1350    12
7
```

FIGURE 11-21.   Edited format line

The OVR indicator is turned on to indicate that you are in overstrike mode. Any character you type will replace a character in the existing format line. You can use the arrow keys to change which rows appear, although the format line always appears in the first line.

3. Move the cell pointer to the * that precedes the second "L," and type >> to change the display to look like the worksheet in Figure 11-21.
   This will cause the two name fields to be combined into one field.

4. Press ENTER to finalize.

PRODUCING THE FINAL PRODUCT   There are still a few more steps. You have to tell 1-2-3 where the input is located and where you would like to store the output of the Parse operation. Your last step is to select Go from the menu so that 1-2-3 will apply the information entered in the preliminary steps to your column of long labels, producing individual entries.

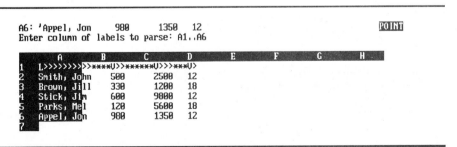

```
A6: 'Appel, Jon    980     1350    12                                  POINT
Enter column of labels to parse: A1..A6

      A       B       C       D      E       F       G      H
1 L>>>>>>>>>>****U>>*****U>>***U>
2 Smith, John    500     2500    12
3 Brown, Jill    330     1200    18
4 Stick, Jim     600     9800    12
5 Parks, Mel     120     5600    18
6 Appel, Jon     980     1350    12
7
```

FIGURE 11-22.   Selecting the data to parse

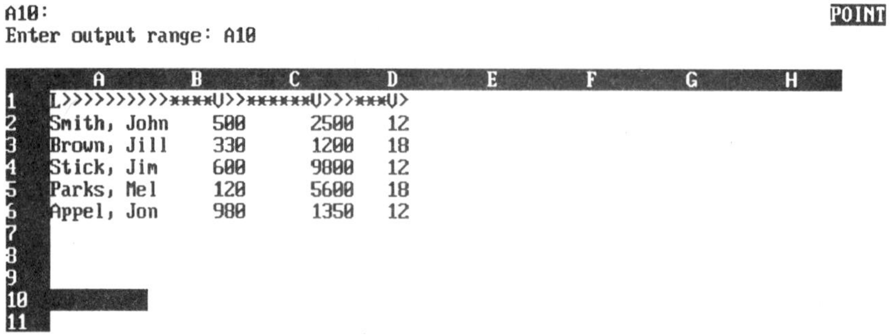

```
A10:                                                              POINT
Enter output range: A10

        A         B         C         D     E     F     G     H
1  L>>>>>>>>>>****U>>******U>>>***U>
2  Smith, John    500      2500      12
3  Brown, Jill    330      1200      18
4  Stick, Jim     600      9000      12
5  Parks, Mel     120      5600      18
6  Appel, Jon     900      1350      12
7
8
9
10
11
```

FIGURE 11-23.   Selecting where 1-2-3 places the parsed data

Follow these steps to define the input and output areas and create the finished product:

1. Select Input-Column. Then highlight A1..A6 with the cell pointer as in the worksheet in Figure 11-22. You must include the format line in the input column.

2. Press ENTER.

3. Select Output-Range and move the cell pointer to A10, as in Figure 11-23.
   You can position the cell pointer in the upper left corner of the range rather than calculating the exact space requirements and making a mistake.

4. Press ENTER and select Go to produce the results in Figure 11-24.

5. Select /Worksheet Column Set-Width, type **11**, and press ENTER to expand the column width, as shown in Figure 11-25.

This conversion required a number of steps and would not be a worthwhile investment of time for so little data. With volumes of data, however, this command can help you be more productive and save hours of time.

```
A10: 'Smith, John                                                   READY

         A         B         C         D       E       F       G       H
1   L>>>>>>>>>>***U>>******U>>***U>
2   Smith, John    500      2500      12
3   Brown, Jill    330      1200      18
4   Stick, Jim     600      9000      12
5   Parks, Mel     120      5600      18
6   Appel, Jon     980      1350      12
7
8
9
10  Smith, Jo      500      2500         12
11  Brown, Ji      330      1200         18
12  Stick, Ji      600      9000         12
13  Parks, Me      120      5600         18
14  Appel, Jo      980      1350         12
15
```

FIGURE 11-24.   Imported data that has been parsed

```
A10: [W11] 'Smith, John                                             READY

         A         B         C         D       E       F       G
1   L>>>>>>>>>>***U>>******U>>***U>
2   Smith, John    500      2500      12
3   Brown, Jill    330      1200      18
4   Stick, Jim     600      9000      12
5   Parks, Mel     120      5600      18
6   Appel, Jon     980      1350      12
7
8
9
10  Smith, John    500      2500         12
11  Brown, Jill    330      1200         18
12  Stick, Jim     600      9000         12
13  Parks, Mel     120      5600         18
14  Appel, Jon     980      1350         12
15
```

FIGURE 11-25.   Widening column A for readability

D2: "Price   READY

	A	B	C	D
1		1989		1990
2	Item	Price	% Chg	Price
3	Transparencies	$37.00	$0.05	
4	Felt-tip pens	$7.00	$0.07	
5	Walnut credenza	$109.50	$0.12	
6				

FIGURE 11-26.   Worksheet entries for price projection model

REVIEW EXERCISE

This chapter has taught you several new skills that you will use for your worksheet. To further enhance your skills with these advanced file-management techniques, try these exercises to create price and sales projection worksheets:

1. Erase the current worksheet.
   Hint: Select /Worksheet Erase Yes.

2. Set the column width for all columns to 15.
   Hint: Select /Worksheet Global Column-Width, type **15**, and press ENTER.

3. Set the format for all cells to Currency with two decimal digits.
   Hint: Select /Worksheet Global Format Currency, and press ENTER.

4. Make the entries shown in Figure 11-26. Enter the years as right-aligned labels.

5. Enter the formula +B3*(1+C3) in D3. Copy this formula to D4..D5.
   Hint: Enter formula shown above. Then select /Copy, press ENTER, select D4..D5, and press ENTER again.

6. Set the format for the percentage change to show the numbers as percentages with two digits after the decimal point. The results appear in Figure 11-27.
   Hint: Move to Column C. Select /Range Format Percent, press ENTER, specify range of C3..C5, and press ENTER again.

7. Name the cells containing the item names as ITEM_NAMES.
   Hint: Move to A3. Select /Range Name Create, type **ITEM_NAMES**, press ENTER, highlight A3..A5, and press ENTER again.

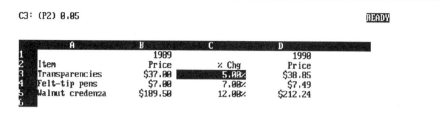

C3: (P2) 0.05   READY

	A	B	C	D
1		1989		1990
2	Item	Price	% Chg	Price
3	Transparencies	$37.00	5.00%	$38.85
4	Felt-tip pens	$7.00	7.00%	$7.49
5	Walnut credenza	$189.50	12.00%	$212.24
6				

FIGURE 11-27.   Completed price projection model

8. Name the cells containing the 1990 prices as 1990_PRICE.

     Hint: Move to Column D. Select /Range Name Create, type **1990_PRICE**, press ENTER, highlight D3..D5, and press ENTER again.

9. Save the values of the cells containing the 1990 prices as PRICE_90. Since you have named the range containing the 1990 prices, you can provide the range name instead of the range address.

     Hint: Select /File Xtract Values, type **90_PRICE**, press ENTER, then type **1990_PRICE**, and press ENTER again.

10. Save this file as PRICES.

     Hint: Select /File Save, type **PRICES**, and press ENTER.

11. Erase the PRICES worksheet from 1-2-3's memory.

     Hint: Select /Worksheet Erase Yes.

     At this point you are ready to create a new worksheet that uses the information in the PRICE_90 worksheet. To make the new worksheet easier to create, you can use the data from the PRICES worksheet in your new worksheet.

12. Set the column width for all columns to 15.

     Hint: Select /Worksheet Global Column-Width, type **15**, and press ENTER.

13. Move to A4.

14. Copy the ITEM_NAMES range from the PRICES worksheet into this worksheet.

     Hint: Select /File Combine Copy Named/Specified Range. Then type **ITEM_NAMES**, press ENTER, type **PRICES**, and press ENTER again.

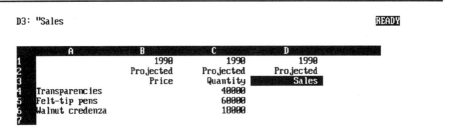

FIGURE 11-28.   Worksheet entries for sales projection model

15. Make the entries shown in Figure 11-28.

16. Set the format of B4..B6 and D4..D6 to Currency with two decimal digits.
    Hint: Select /Range Format Currency, press ENTER, select B4..B6, and press
    ENTER again. Then perform the same steps for the D4..D6 range.

17. Enter the formula +B4*C4 in D4. Copy this formula to D5..D6. The worksheet
    looks like the one in Figure 11-29.
    Hint: Enter **+B4*C4** in D4. Then select /Copy, press ENTER, select C5..C6,
    and press ENTER again.
    At this point, only the price data is missing. You can try several methods of
    entering the price data into the worksheet.

18. Move to B4.

19. Copy the price values in the PRICE_90 file.
    Hint: Select /File Combine Copy Entire-File, type **PRICE_90**, and press
    ENTER.

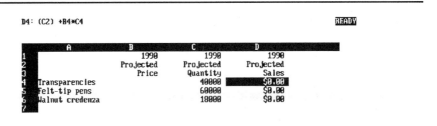

FIGURE 11-29.   Sales projection model with prices missing

Notice that the worksheet contains the values for the 1990 prices because the values were extracted to the PRICE_90 file.

20. Erase the 1990 prices.

    Hint: Select /Range Erase, select B4..B6, and press ENTER.

21. Add the price values in the PRICES file.

    Hint: Select /File Combine Add Named/Specified Range. Then type **1990_PRICE**, press ENTER, type **PRICES**, and press ENTER.

    Notice that the worksheet contains the values for the 1990 prices, instead of the formulas that the PRICES worksheet has, because the values are added to the PRICE_90 file. If you have Release 2.2, try the next three steps to create an external file link to incorporate the 1990 prices from the PRICES worksheet file into this worksheet.

22. Erase the 1990 prices.

    Hint: Select /Range Erase, select B4..B6, and press ENTER.

23. Enter **+<<PRICES>>1990_PRICE** in B4 and copy this formula to B5..B6. The results are shown in Figure 11-30.

    1-2-3 uses the first cell in the 1990_PRICE range for B4 and adjusts the row the file link uses as the formula is copied to B5 and B6.

24. Save this worksheet as SALES_90.

    Hint: Select /File Save, type **SALES_90**, and press ENTER.

    This chapter also introduced the /Data Parse command to break long labels into smaller cells. You can use this worksheet to try these features by printing it to a file and importing it. If you are using Release 1A, you can print the file and import it, but you cannot parse the data.

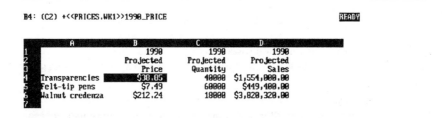

FIGURE 11-30.   Sales projection model with prices added

```
A1: 'Transparencies         38.85        40000  $1,554,000.00                    READY

      A        B         C      D       E        F         G          H
1  Transparencies        38.85         40000  $1,554,000.00
2  Felt-tip pens          7.49         60000    $449,400.00
3  Walnut credenza      212.24         18000  $3,820,320.00
4
```

FIGURE 11-31.   1-2-3 print file imported into a new worksheet

25. Print the range A4..D6 of this worksheet to a file called PARSE with no margins and no headers, footers, or page breaks.

    Hint: Move to A4. Select /Print File, type **PARSE**, and press ENTER. Select Range, type a period, press END, press HOME, and press ENTER. In Release 2.2, select Options Margin None to remove the margins. In other releases, select Options Margin Top, type **0**, and press ENTER; select Margins Bottom, type **0**, and press ENTER; select Margins Left, type **0**, and press ENTER; select Margins Right, type **240**, and press ENTER. Then select Other Unformatted Quit Go Quit to print the file.

26. Erase the SALES_90 worksheet from 1-2-3's memory.

    Hint: Select /Worksheet Erase Yes.

27. Import the PARSE.PRN file into the new 1-2-3 worksheet as long labels. The worksheet looks like the one in Figure 11-31.

    Hint: Select /File Import Text, type **PARSE**, and press ENTER.

28. Create a format string that looks like this:

```
      A        B         C      D       E        F         G          H
1  L>>>>>>>>>>>>*********U>>>>*********U>>>>**U>>>>>>>>>>>>
3  Felt-tip pens          7.49         60000    $449,400.00
4  Walnut credenza      212.24         18000  $3,820,320.00
```

    Hint: Select /Data Parse Format-Line Create.

29. Select the imported rows to parse.

    Hint: Select Input-Column, select A1..A4, and press ENTER.

30. Select A10 as the destination for the parsed data.

    Hint: Enter Output-Range, select A10, and press ENTER.

```
A1:  :L>>>>>>>>>>>>>∗∗∗∗∗∗∗∗∗U>>>>∗∗∗∗∗∗∗∗∗∗U>>>∗∗U>>>>>>>>>>>>>        READY
```

```
         A        B        C        D        E       F        G        H
1   L>>>>>>>>>>>>>∗∗∗∗∗∗∗∗∗U>>>>∗∗∗∗∗∗∗∗∗∗U>>>∗∗U>>>>>>>>>>>>>
2   Transparencies           38.85           40000  $1,554,000.00
3   Felt-tip pens             7.49           60000    $449,400.00
4   Walnut credenza         212.24           18000  $3,820,320.00
5
6
7
8
9
10  Transpare    38.85    40000  1554000
11  Felt-tip      7.49    60000   449400
12  Walnut cr   212.24    18000  3820320
13
14
15
16
17
18
19
20
```

FIGURE 11-32.   Parsed data

31. Parse the data using the settings you have entered. The results appear in Figure 11-32.

   Hint: Select Go.

REVIEW

- You can extract a portion of a worksheet to another worksheet file with the /File Xtract command. This command copies either values (formulas are converted to their value in the new worksheet) or formulas (formulas remain intact). The Formulas option should only be used if the cells the formulas reference are part of the range extracted to the new file. Once a file is extracted, you can retrieve it and use it just as you would with other worksheet files.

- You can combine the values of a range or entire worksheet file into the current worksheet file with the /File Combine command. You must be careful where the cell pointer is when you perform this command because the cells copied into the current worksheet have the same relative distance to the cell pointer's position as they have in their original file to the upper left corner of the range or worksheet. The Combine option lets you copy (incoming data replaces current worksheet data), add (incoming numbers are added to the current worksheet data), or subtract (incoming numbers are subtracted from the current worksheet data).

- A Release 2.2 worksheet can contain external file links, which return the value of a cell in another worksheet. Cells containing an external file link have a +, the filename in double angle brackets (<<>>), and the cell address or range name of the cell in the target file worksheet. The links are updated when you retrieve a file or when you select the /File Admin Link-Refresh command.

- 1-2-3 can import, or bring in, data from another computer program if the other computer program can produce an ASCII text file without the edit characters. The imported data can be separated into long labels, with each line in the imported data converting into a long label entry within a cell, or into a series of individual cell entries for each line if the data is separated by commas or spaces and the text data is enclosed in quotes.

- The /Data Parse command available in Release 2 and higher can break labels into smaller cell entries. It also converts the label data into numbers, dates, and times if the appropriate format-line characters are used. The format line determines how 1-2-3 divides the text into cells.

Commands

Entry	Action
/FXV	/File Xtract Values copies the values in a worksheet range to a new worksheet file
/FXF	/File Xtract Formulas copies the formulas in a worksheet range to a new worksheet file
/FCC	/File Combine Copy copies a range or worksheet from another file to the current worksheet
/FCA	/File Combine Add adds range or worksheet data from another file to the current worksheet
/FCS	/File Combine Subtract subtracts range or worksheet data from another file to the current worksheet
/FIT	/File Import Text brings data into 1-2-3 and stores the data as long labels
/FIN	/File Import Numbers brings data into 1-2-3 and stores numbers and characters enclosed in quotes in individual cells

/DPFC	/Data Parse Format-Line Create creates a format line to parse label data
/DPFE	/Data Parse Format-Line Edit edits a format line to parse label data
/DPI	/Data Parse Input-Column selects the format line and input labels to parse
/DPO	/Data Parse Output-Range selects the area to which 1-2-3 copies the parsed data
/DPG	/Data Parse Go parses the data using the other /Data Parse command selections
/FAL	/File Admin Link-Refresh refreshes external file links

12

CREATING 1-2-3 MACROS

What Are Keyboard Alternative Macros?
Macro Building Blocks
Creating a Few More Macros
Special Macro Topics
Review Exercise
Review

Many 1-2-3 users are intimidated by macros. They have heard about the failures that others have experienced when attempting to use them. But this failure is not inevitable; in fact, if you use the step-by-step approach presented in this chapter, you will have no need for concern. There is no reason why you cannot be just as successful with macros as you are with 1-2-3's /Range Format and /File Save commands.

In their simplest form, macros are nothing more than a way to automate the selections you have been making from 1-2-3's menus. These macros are referred to as *keyboard alternative macros*. In their most complex form, macros provide an entire programming language with the special 1-2-3 command language instructions. Attempting to use the most sophisticated form of macros without mastering the keyboard variety is a little like practicing diving before you have learned to swim. If you jump in at the deep end of the pool without knowing how to swim to the edge, you will be well over your head and doomed to failure. Clearly, using the command language macros before mastering the keyboard alternative variety is asking for problems; why, then, do so many new users use this approach? Fortunately, the material in this chapter introduces the material in a logical sequence to help you avoid this problem.

This chapter will introduce you to a step-by-step approach to the creation of keyboard alternative macros that can ensure your success. You will learn how to enter menu selections and special keyboard entries in worksheet cells for later execution. You will learn 1-2-3's rules for naming macros and how you can execute the macro instructions you have stored. You will also learn how to use Release 2.2's Learn feature to significantly reduce the effort involved in the creation of keyboard alternative macros. You will create several ready-to-use macros, which will be your foundation for creating macros that fit your particular needs. Since macros are based on a series of building blocks, you will need to learn something about each of the building blocks before creating a macro. In this chapter you will be introduced to the building blocks and then combine them in your first macro example, before making your entries.

WHAT ARE KEYBOARD ALTERNATIVE MACROS?

Keyboard alternative macros are nothing more than a column of label entries that have a special name assigned to them. The contents of the label entries are the sequence of 1-2-3 keystrokes that you want 1-2-3 to execute for you. Once the keystrokes are entered in the column of worksheet cells, you will use the /Range Name Create command to assign a name to the top cell in the macro. You can use \ and a single letter for the macro name or use a longer entry up to the 15 character limit for range names. If you choose \ and the single letter, you can execute the macro by holding down the ALT key and the letter used in the macro name or by pressing ALT-F3 (RUN) and selecting the name from the list of macro names. If you use the longer entry option for the name, your only alternative is to press ALT-F3 (RUN) and select the macro name. When you save the worksheet on which you entered the macro, you save the macro for later use with the worksheet on which it was entered. If you were to use the macro on another worksheet, you would have to reenter it, use the /File Combine command covered in Chapter 11, or use the more sophisticated Macro Library option covered in more advanced books on 1-2-3.

Keyboard alternative macros provide a wealth of time-saving features. You can use them to automate printing, formatting, or any other 1-2-3 task that can be handled with menu selections. After you have learned the basics, you will want to examine the tasks you execute repeatedly. The more frequently a task is performed, the greater the potential payback of automating it with macro instructions. Some users find that data-management tasks such as sorting and extracting are the most important to automate; other users give printing or formatting the highest priority because they use these commands most frequently. Although the macros in the remainder of the chapter have widespread application, only you can decide which tasks offer you the greatest payback when automated.

MACRO BUILDING BLOCKS

The secret to creating macros that run correctly the first time you try them is having a structured approach that you use consistently for each new macro you create. At first glance the steps recommended here might seem unnecessarily time-consuming; however, you will find that they guarantee immediate success and thereby save debugging time.

The first step to successful macros is to lay out a road map of where you want to go with the macro. Whether you type the macro entries or use the Learn feature's recorder to place them on the worksheet, you need to test the instructions that you hope will get you there. If you are not using the recorder, you may want to test the instructions before entering them on the worksheet. After the instructions are stored on the worksheet you will need to name them. Documenting the workings of the macro is an often overlooked step, but it can guarantee continued trouble-free execution. Complete this step for every macro. Only then will you be ready to try your new macro.

You can examine each of these steps more closely in the sections that follow.

Knowing Where You Are
Going Before Beginning

If you are typing the macro entries, the only way to guarantee first-try success for every macro is to try the 1-2-3 instructions that you want to store in a macro and to monitor their effect on the worksheet. This happens automatically when you use the Learn feature because 1-2-3 is executing and recording the instructions as you enter them.

If you are typing the macro entries, write each command on a piece of paper as you enter it. If the results meet your needs, you can enter the keystrokes you have written on your sheet of paper as a series of label entries on the worksheet. If the commands do not perform the required tasks, you can alter them and try again. Once you discover the correct combination of menu requests, you have a guarantee (if you enter them carefully) that they will function. You have already tried these commands and ensured their correct operation before recording them. The other objective of this planning phase for the macro is to ensure that you have not forgotten any of the requirements. Planning is required if you use the recorder approach as well, because you must understand the path of the specific commands that you will need.

Recording Menu Selections

You will want to select an out-of-the-way location on the worksheet for recording your macro commands. With Release 2, 2.01, or 2.2, put them at the far right side of the worksheet. With Release 1A, you need to moderate how far to the right you store the macro commands; Release 1A uses memory less efficiently when information is scattered on the worksheet.

To prevent 1-2-3 from executing the menu commands you want to record, begin the macro sequence with an apostrophe so that it is treated as label. Indicate each request for the menu with a slash, and record each menu selection as the first letter of the selection. To record the keystrokes necessary to obtain a worksheet status display, type '/ws or '/WS in the cell. Case is never important when you are entering menu selections.

In addition to entering the menu selections, you sometimes have to indicate that the ENTER key would be pressed if you were entering the command sequence from the keyboard. In a macro, this key is represented by the tilde mark (~). When you are entering data other than menu selections, such as a filename or a range name, enter the names in full. For example, to record the keystrokes necessary to retrieve a file named Sales, you would enter '/frSales~ in the macro cell.

Menu selections should always be recorded with the first letter of the selection. Typing the full name of the command is not a substitute for the first letter and will cause errors in the macro. While it is possible to select commands by pointing to the menu selections through the successive use of the RIGHT ARROW key, followed by the use of the ENTER key, this should be avoided in macros. In subsequent releases of the product, Lotus might alter the sequence of the menu selections, causing the cursor-movement method to fail. However, you can be assured that the first letters of the selections are not likely to change. This guarantees that your macros will be compatible with future releases of the 1-2-3 product.

Recording Special Keys

There are a number of special keyboard keys, such as the function and arrow keys, that you will want to include in your macros. These keys and the macro keywords that stand for them are shown in Table 12-1. Notice that all the special keywords are enclosed in curly brackets or braces ({ }). You will find it easy to remember most of these words; they are the same words you probably connect with the special keys—for example, EDIT represents F2. The only thing you will need to remember is to use the braces like this: {EDIT}. Without the braces, 1-2-3 will not recognize the entry as a special key.

There are several special keys that cannot be represented in a macro. The NUM LOCK key has no representation and must be turned on by the operator if a macro requires

Cursor-Movement Keys	Keywords
UP ARROW	{UP} or {U}
DOWN ARROW	{DOWN} or {D}
RIGHT ARROW	{RIGHT} or {R}
LEFT ARROW	{LEFT} or {L}
HOME	{HOME}
END	{END}
PGUP	{PGUP}
PGDN	{PGDN}
CTRL-RIGHT ARROW	{BIGRIGHT}
CTRL-LEFT ARROW	{BIGLEFT}

Editing Keys	Keywords
DEL	{DEL}
INS	{INS}
ESC	{ESC}
BACKSPACE	{BACKSPACE} or {BS}

Function Keys	Keywords
F1 (HELP	{HELP} Release 2.2 only
F2 (EDIT)	{EDIT}
F3 (NAME)	{NAME}
F4 (ABS)	{ABS}
F5 (GOTO)	{GOTO}
F6 (WINDOW)	{WINDOW}
F7 (QUERY)	{QUERY}
F8 (TABLE)	{TABLE}
F9 (CALC)	{CALC}
F10 (GRAPH)	{GRAPH}
ALT-F7 (APP1)	{APP1} Release 2.2 only
ALT-F8 (APP2)	{APP2} Release 2.2 only
ALT-F9 (APP3)	{APP3} Release 2.2 only
ALT-F10 (APP4 or ADD-IN)	{APP4} Release 2.2 only

TABLE 12-1.   Special Keys in Macro Commmands

it. The use of the SCROLL LOCK key follows the same procedure, since it too cannot be represented. CAPS LOCK also has no representation, although this is less important than the other two keys; you will be able to control capitalization if you are requested to input directly during a macro. If macro instructions include cell entries for other parts of the worksheet, you will get to choose whether to make these entries upper- or lowercase when building the macro. The case you choose will be maintained when the macro is executed.

CURSOR-MOVEMENT KEYS   When you are creating a macro, movement of the cell pointer to the right will be represented by {r}, {RIGHT}, or {right}. The Learn feature uses the abbreviated form shown first. The Learn feature records every press of a key even if the same key is pressed multiple times, as in {u}{u}{u} to represent pressing the UP ARROW key three times. When you type the entries you can enter {UP 3}, or {U 3} as a shortcut.

Case is never important for the special macro words, although uppercase will be used throughout this chapter. Movement to the left is {LEFT}, movement down is {DOWN}, and movement up is {UP}.

In Release 1A, moving the cursor up three cells is represented by {UP}{UP}{UP}. If you have a long distance to move, you will want to explore GOTO, listed with the function keys, to avoid all the entries required by Release 1A. In Release 2 there is a short-cut approach that lets you enter this same instruction as {UP 3}.

When you are working from the keyboard, the effect of the HOME key depends on whether you are in READY mode or EDIT mode. This is also true in the macro environment. If you record {HOME} in a macro, its effect will depend on what you are having the macro do for you. If you have placed 1-2-3 in EDIT mode, the instruction will take you to the left side of the entry in the current cell; otherwise, it will place you in A1.

The END and arrow key combinations are supported in macros. You can enter {END}{RIGHT} to have the cell pointer moved to the last occupied cell entry on the right side of the worksheet. To specify paging up and down, you can use {PGUP} and {PGDN}.

FUNCTION KEYS   With the exception of the function keys to run macros, all function keys can be represented by special macro keywords. To use F2 (EDIT), you would enter {EDIT}. The F5 (GOTO) key is another key that is used frequently. To record the fact that you want the cell pointer moved to D10, you would make this entry in a macro:

{GOTO}D10~

Notice that the cell address you want the cell pointer moved to is placed outside the braces and is followed by a tilde (~). Remember that the tilde represents the ENTER key and is required to finalize the request, just as you would press ENTER to finalize if you were executing the command directly.

Other keys required frequently are F6 (WINDOW) and F9 (CALC). As you might expect, {WINDOW} is the macro representation for F6 and {CALC} is the macro representation for F9. The remaining function keys are shown in Table 12-1.

THE EDIT KEYS   In addition to F2 (EDIT), which places you in the EDIT mode, there are several keys that are used frequently when you are correcting cell entries.

The ESC key can remove an entry from a cell and can delete a menu default, such as a previous setup string. This option allows you to cancel the default and make a new entry. ESC is used in a macro just as it is outside a macro except that braces are required. The entry would therefore be {ESC}.

To delete a character to the left of the cursor while in EDIT mode, or to delete the last character entered, use either {BS} or {BACKSPACE} in your macro. To delete the character above the cursor from EDIT mode, use {DEL} or {DELETE}. For example, you could create a macro that requests a change in the label prefix to center justification. The sequence of entries in a macro would be

{EDIT}{HOME}{DEL}^~

This is exactly the same sequence of keys that you would press if you were typing the request to be executed directly, rather than storing the keystrokes in a macro.

In Release 2, repeat factors can also be used with these keys. {DELETE 4} is equivalent to pressing the DELETE key four times. {BACKSPACE 7} will delete seven characters to the left of the cursor on the edit line.

Creating the Macro

As you may recall, we promised you not the fastest path to macro entry but the fastest path to a macro that would run correctly the first time you tried it. Your first step in creating a macro will be to make a plan and to try your plan before recording your first keystroke. This step is the critical one if you want to ensure success.

PLANNING THE MACRO   If you are thinking of creating a macro, you must have a task that you want to automate. For your first example, you will automate a request for formatting, based on the assumption that you need to format data as Currency frequently and would like to create a macro that will save you a few keystrokes. Your first step is to ask yourself which 1-2-3 commands you normally use to handle this task. The answer should be the /Range Format Currency command sequence. Also ask yourself if you want the macro to specify the number of decimal places and the range for formatting or whether you want the operator to complete the instruction from the keyboard. For your example, the number of decimal places will be supplied but the range will be controlled by the operator at execution.

Once your decisions are made, you will want to test the series of instructions you plan to use before typing them. If you are using 1-2-3's Learn feature, covered later in this chapter, you can use your trial run to capture the keystrokes. Either way, you will need some test data on the worksheet before beginning. Follow these directions for creating test data to see if the formatting commands and subsequent macro function correctly.

1. Make the following worksheet entries:

   A1:   2
   A2:   5
   A3:   4
   A4:   9
   A5:   7
   C6:   8
   C7:   9
   C8:   3

   There is nothing special about these entries. They are just a few numbers that will be stored in the default format of General and that will provide practice entries for formatting. Copy them across the worksheet to create additional entries.

2. Move the cell pointer to A1, select /Copy, and press the END key followed by the DOWN ARROW key. Press ENTER, move the cell pointer to B1, type . (period), move the cell pointer to F1, and press ENTER.

3. Move the cell pointer to C6, select /Copy, move the cell pointer to C8, and press ENTER. Move the cell pointer to E6, type ., move the cell pointer to F6, and press ENTER to create this display:

C6: 8   READY

	A	B	C	D	E	F	G	H
1	2	2	2	2	2	2		
2	5	5	5	5	5	5		
3	4	4	4	4	4	4		
4	9	9	9	9	9	9		
5	7	7	7	7	7	7		
6			8		8	8		
7			9		9	9		
8			3		3	3		
9								

   This provides a little variety in the length of the column of numbers you will be formatting with your macro once it is created. Now you are ready for a trial run of the instructions you plan to enter.

4. Move the cell pointer to A1.

   This is the first cell you will format. The movement of the cell pointer could be incorporated in the macro, but it would eliminate some of the macro's flexibility and is probably not desirable.

5. Enter / and write a slash on the piece of paper on which you are recording the keystrokes from the trial.

6. Select Range and write "R" on the piece of paper.

7. Select Format and write "F" on the piece of paper.

8. Select Currency and write "C" on the piece of paper.

9. Type **0** and write "0" on the piece of paper.

10. Press ENTER and write a tilde (~) on the piece of paper.

    Notice how every keystroke that you enter, whether it is from the menu or just a keyboard entry, should be written on the piece of paper. Most beginners would skip steps 5 through 10. This is the very cause of failure in their macros. Once you become a 1-2-3 expert and have all the menu selections committed to memory, there is no problem with skipping the writing. But until you reach that point, the importance of these steps cannot be overemphasized.

11. Press ENTER again to record the range selection. However, do not write this down; you are leaving the range selection up to the user when the macro is executed.

12. Select /File Save, type **NUMBERS**, and press ENTER.

This will save a copy of the numeric entries in the NUMBERS file. You can retrieve it at a later time to practice with this or other macros.

MAKING THE MACRO ENTRIES   The macro entries you need to make are written on your sheet of paper. All you need to do now is record these entries on the worksheet. You can record them all in one cell or you can split them into more than one cell—as long as the cells are contiguous in a column on the worksheet. With such a short macro it will not make much difference, but as your macros become longer, you may want to split them well before you reach the 240-character limit for a cell entry. Keeping the length of an individual cell entry to a minimum will allow you to document each step in the macro.

Normally you would place your macro to the right side of the worksheet. Since this is your first macro, however, you will want to keep it in view as it executes, so place it in the lower portion of column B. Follow these steps to record the macro keystrokes you have written on your sheet of paper:

1. Move the cell pointer to B15.

2. Type **'/r** and then move the cell pointer to B16.

   The apostrophe is used to prevent immediate execution of your entries. The slash represents the request for the menu and the "R" is used to invoke the Range commands (the "R" can be either lower- or uppercase).

3. Press the DOWN ARROW key, type **fc0~**, and press ENTER.

These entries tell 1-2-3 that you want to use the Format option and have selected Currency with 0 decimal places as the format you want to use.

   This is all that is required for entering any macro. The only mandatory step that remains is naming the macro.

Naming the Macro

Now that you have recorded all the keystrokes, you are ready to name the macro. Before doing this you will want to position the cell pointer on the top cell in the macro, as this is the only cell that you will name. You will use the /Range Name Create command that you were introduced to in earlier chapters to apply the name to this cell. You must assign a name of not more than 15 characters, or a special name consisting of a backslash and a single letter, to the cell. The backslash identifies your entry as a macro name, which will allow you to execute the macro with the ALT key and the letter used in the macro name. This naming convention lets you create 26 unique, quickly executable macros on one worksheet, since 1-2-3 does not distinguish between upper- and lowercase letters in a macro name.

   If you follow the recommendation of positioning the cell pointer before you begin, the process is quite simple. You will only need to press ENTER after typing the name to have the name applied to the macro. Saving a macro after you name it will save both the macro entries and the name, so they will be available when you use the worksheet.

   Follow these steps to name the formatting macro you just entered.

1. Move the cell pointer to B15.

2. Select /Range Name Create.

3. Type \c and press ENTER twice.

This will apply the name to the current cell.

Theoretically, you can now execute the macro; however, it is best to document it first. If you do not take the time to document your work now, you will never do it; later, it will be difficult to remember what name you chose for the macro and what each step accomplishes unless you document it.

Documenting the Macro

You will want to develop a few easy documentation rules for yourself so that your documentation is always stored in the same place. A good strategy to use for documentation is to place the macro name in the cell immediately to the left of the top cell in the macro. If the macro is named \a, you would enter '\a in this cell. The apostrophe is required to prevent the backslash from being interpreted as a repeating label indicator and filling your cell with the letter "a."

A good area to use for documenting the macro is the column of cells to the right of the macro instructions. Depending on the length of the macro instructions, this documentation may extend one or more cells to the right of the macro column. Entering a brief description of every command can make the purpose of the macro much clearer when you go back to examine it at a later time.

Follow these steps to document the formatting macro:

1. Move the cell pointer to A15, type '\c, and press ENTER.

2. Move the cell pointer to C15, type **request Range command**, and press ENTER.

3. Move the cell pointer to C16, type **select Currency format with 0 decimal places,** and press ENTER.

The macro is now ready to execute with the instructions in the next section.

Executing the Macro

Once you have entered and named a macro, you can use it whenever you wish. Whenever you have a macro that requires the cell pointer to be positioned in a certain cell, you will need to put the cell pointer there before you execute the macro. The cell pointer does not need to be on the macro itself in order to execute it. After you have positioned your cell pointer, you can execute the macro by holding down the ALT key and, while the key is pressed, pressing the letter key you used in your macro name. The macro will begin executing immediately. Follow these instructions to try your new formatting macro:

1. Move the cell pointer to B1.

2. Press the ALT key and, while holding the key down, type **c**, and then release the ALT key.

   This causes the macro to execute. This particular macro requests formatting and ends in time for you to complete the range that should be formatted.

3. Move the cell pointer to B5 and press ENTER.

   The entries in B1..B5 should now be formatted as Currency with 0 decimal places. You will want to try this again to see how flexible the macro is.

4. Move the cell pointer to C1 and press the ALT key and type **c**. Move the cell pointer to C8 and press ENTER to create this display:

C1: (C0) 2   READY

	A	B	C	D	E	F	G	H
1	$2	$2	$2	2	2	2		
2	5	$5	$5	5	5	5		
3	4	$4	$4	4	4	4		
4	9	$9	$9	9	9	9		
5	7	$7	$7	7	7	7		
6			$8		8	8		
7			$9		9	9		
8			$3		3	3		
9								
10								
11								
12								
13								
14								
15	\c	/r	request Range command					
16		fc0~	select Currency format with 0 decimal places					
17								

This time the entries in C1..C8 are formatted. This same macro can format one cell or a large range of cells. Try the macro several more times with the remaining numeric entries on the worksheet.

5. Select /File Save, press ESC, type **FORMAT**, and press ENTER to save this example.

6. Select /Worksheet Erase Yes to clear the worksheet from memory.

Using 1-2-3's Learn Feature

If you have Release 2.2 of 1-2-3, you can use the Learn feature of the package to record keyboard alternative macros rather than typing them. This approach offers a couple of major advantages. First, you can try out your plan for a macro and have 1-2-3 record your entries. If you make a few mistakes, you do not need to start over because you can edit the entries that 1-2-3 places on the worksheet with the same techniques you have used for changing any entry. Second, when you have 1-2-3 record the keystrokes you do not need to remember the keywords that 1-2-3 uses for the function keys and other special keys. All you need to do is press the proper key and 1-2-3 will record it in the macro cells correctly.

Release 2.01 also has a Learn feature as part of the optional Value Pack. The Lotus HAL package also has a capability that allows you to record 1-2-3 keystrokes. Each of these works a little differently than Release 2.2 and is not compatible with Release 2.2. You will need to consult the documentation for these other products if you want to use their features rather than the Learn feature of 2.2.

To use 1-2-3's Learn feature you must follow several steps. First you must tell 1-2-3 where to record the keystrokes. Then you must start the recording and remember to stop it when you are finished. You can try out this procedure with a macro that will correctly format three date entries. First, place the date entries on the worksheet using the @DATE function covered in Chapter 7:

1. Type **@DATE(89,7,15)** in A1 and then press the DOWN ARROW key.

2. Type **@DATE(90,4,15)** in A2 and then press the DOWN ARROW key.

3. Type **@DATE(89,5,30)** in A3 and then press the DOWN ARROW key.

Now you are ready to explore the Learn feature.

SPECIFYING A LEARN RANGE   Just as you selected an out-of-the way location for macros when you typed them, you will normally want to choose the same type of location when 1-2-3 is recording them. To specify this range, select /Worksheet Learn. 1-2-3 prompts you for a learn range. Highlight the range you wish to use. You can move the cell pointer to the beginning of the range, type a period, and move to the end of the range to highlight all the cells in the range.

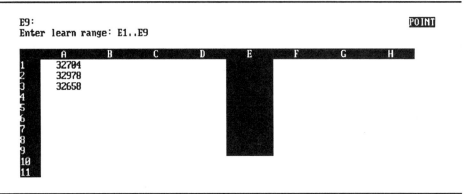

FIGURE 12-1.   Specifying a learn range

When you press ENTER, 1-2-3 remembers this location as an area in which it can record your keystrokes when you ask it to start recording for you.

For the date macro you want to record, follow these steps to specify a range:

1. Select /Worksheet Learn Range.

    The other two menu selections under Learn are used to erase a learn range that you no longer need or to cancel the definition of a learn range.

2. Move the cell pointer to E1, type . (period), and move the cell pointer to E9.

    Your screen should look like the one in Figure 12-1. In this example, a location that would allow you to see the entire example at one time was selected rather than an out-of-the-way location.

3. Press ENTER to finalize your selection.

TURNING ON THE LEARN FEATURE   Just as a telephone answering machine does not begin recording your messages until you attach the unit to your phone and turn it on, 1-2-3 does not begin recording keystrokes when you tell it where to store them. You must start the Learn feature and its recorder by pressing ALT-F5 (LEARN). Since this action tells 1-2-3 to immediately begin recording keystrokes, you should position your cell pointer where you want to begin working with worksheet data in the macro before doing this.

For the current worksheet follow these steps:

1. Move the cell pointer to A1 by pressing the HOME key.

2. Press ALT-F5 (LEARN).

    1-2-3 will place a LEARN indicator in the bottom line of your screen to indicate that it has started to record your keystrokes. This indicator will remain until you press ALT-F5 (LEARN) again.

3. Select /Range Format Date 1 to select Date format 1.

4. Press the DOWN ARROW key twice to highlight the range of the three dates, and press ENTER.

    You will not see 1-2-3 record anything in the learn range yet as it is always a step behind in writing the information to the worksheet.

5. Select /Worksheet Column Set-Width, type **10**, and press ENTER.

    Notice that when you start entering this new command, 1-2-3 writes the previous command to the worksheet.

6. Press ALT-F5 (LEARN) to stop recording.

    The LEARN indicator is removed from the bottom of the screen, but a CALC indicator appears. This indicator is there because 1-2-3 has not as yet placed the last instruction recorded in the learn range.

7. Press F9 (CALC) and the last instruction will be added. Your screen will look like the one in Figure 12-2.

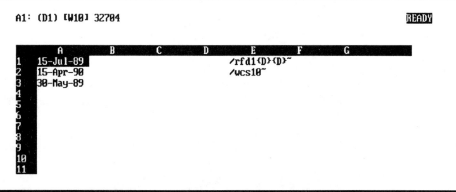

A1: (D1) [W10] 32704   READY

	A	B	C	D	E	F	G
1	15-Jul-89				/rfd1{D}{D}~		
2	15-Apr-90				/wcs10~		
3	30-May-89						
4							
5							
6							
7							
8							
9							
10							
11							

FIGURE 12-2.   Keystrokes recorded in the learn range

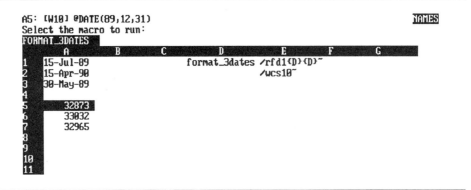

FIGURE 12-3. Running the macro

8. Move the cell pointer to D1, type **format_3dates**, and press ENTER.

9. Select /Worksheet Column Set-Width and type **14** to widen the column.

10. Select /Range Name Labels Right to use this entry to name the top cell in the macro. Press ENTER.

    The /Range Name Labels Right command allows you to specify a columnar range of labels and applies those labels as names for the cells to the immediate right of each cell in the range.

11. Type three more date numbers as shown here:

    A5:   @DATE(89,12,31)
    A6:   @DATE(90,6,8)
    A7:   @DATE(90,4,2)

12. Move the cell pointer to A5 and try the macro by pressing ALT-F3 (RUN). Highlight the name of the macro as shown in Figure 12-3 and then press ENTER.

    1-2-3 will format the cells as dates, as shown in Figure 12-4.

CREATING A FEW MORE MACROS

Now you have created your first two macros, but you haven't begun to experience the variety that macros can offer. You can follow the instructions in this section to create

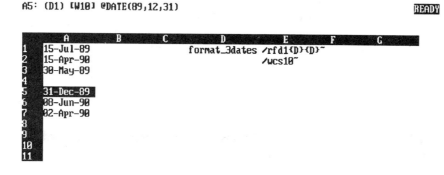

A5: (D1) [W10] @DATE(89,12,31)   READY

	A	B	C	D	E	F	G
1	15-Jul-89			format_3dates	/rfd1{D}{D}~		
2	15-Apr-90				/wcs10~		
3	30-May-89						
4							
5	31-Dec-89						
6	08-Jun-90						
7	02-Apr-90						
8							
9							
10							
11							

FIGURE 12-4.   Result from the macro

two more macros. This practice should help you improve your skill level with macro instructions.

Creating a Print Macro

Print macros are useful because print must be created from most worksheets periodically. In addition, by adding instructions in a print macro you can add any special form feeding, range printing, headers, footers, borders, or extra copies. Make these entries to provide a few lines of data to print:

1. Select /Worksheet Erase Yes, select /Worksheet Column Set-Width, type **15**, and press ENTER.

2. Place these entries on the worksheet:

    A1:   Name
    A2:   John Smith
    A3:   Bill Brown
    A4:   Karen Hall
    A5:   Janice Gold
    B1:   Salary
    B2:   25600
    B3:   45300
    B4:   18900
    B5:   42500
    C1:   Location

C2:	Dallas
C3:	Chicago
C4:	Dallas
C5:	Chicago

Your worksheet should look like this:

C5: 'Chicago   READY

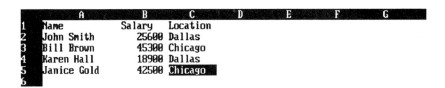

Now you are ready to create a print macro. It will print two copies of the data you just entered on the worksheet.

3. Make these entries to create the macro:

F2:	' \p
G2:	'/pp
H2:	Invoke print printer command
G3:	rA1.C5~
H3:	Specify range
G4:	g
H4:	Begin printing
G5:	pa
H5:	Page and align
G6:	g
H6:	Print a second copy
G7:	pa
H7:	Page and align
G8:	q
H8:	Quit the print menu

4. Move the cell pointer to G2, select /Range Name Create, type **\p**, and press ENTER twice. If you prefer, you can also move the cell pointer to F2 and use the /Range Name Labels Right command to name the top cell in the macro code.

Make sure your printer is on and online before following the directions in the next instruction.

5. Press ALT and type **p** to execute the macro and print the worksheet.

Creating a Macro
to Insert Rows

You can create a macro to insert one or more blank rows in a worksheet, and use it with the print data you entered for the last example. A macro like this will be useful if you work frequently in the data-management environment and want to have some blank rows between the field names. Since blank rows can cause problems for the Query commands, you can have one macro to add them when you need them and another macro to remove them again. In this section, you will create a general-purpose macro: It will insert blank rows anywhere. If you wish, you can add a {GOTO} instruction to position the cell pointer right below the field names, so that the blanks are automatically inserted at the correct location for a database. To create a macro to insert blank rows, follow these instructions:

1. Place the following entries in the cells listed, using an apostrophe in front of the entry for S2 and T2:

S2:	\i
T2:	/wi
U2:	Request worksheet insert
T3:	r
U3:	Specify rows
T4:	{DOWN}~
U4:	Move down to insert 2 rows

2. Move the cell pointer to S2, select /Range Name Labels Right, and then press ENTER to name the top cell in the macro.

3. Move the cell pointer to A2.

4. Press ALT and type **i** to execute the macro.

   The macro will insert blank rows in the worksheet, and it will look like this:

A2: [W15]   READY

	A	B	C	D	E	F	G
1	Name	Salary	Location				
2							
3							
4	John Smith	25600	Dallas			\p	/pp
5	Bill Brown	45300	Chicago				rA1.C5~
6	Karen Hall	18900	Dallas				g
7	Janice Gold	42500	Chicago				pa
8							g
9							pa
10							q
11							

Inserting blank rows in the macro itself is one possibility when you add rows. You must be especially careful because 1-2-3 adds the rows across all the columns, and this addition may cause computational problems elsewhere in the worksheet.

5. Select /Worksheet Erase Yes.

SPECIAL MACRO TOPICS

There are many macro options—so many, in fact, that complete books are written on the subject. This chapter cannot cover all possible options, but it can show you a few of particular interest that go beyond the simpler keyboard alternatives to add command language ability, minus all the complexity. In this section you will take a look at a few of the special options, as well as at several command language instructions.

Creating Automatic Macros

1-2-3 has a unique feature that lets you create an automatic macro. Every time a worksheet containing an automatic macro is retrieved, 1-2-3 immediately executes the macro without requiring you to press any keys, as long as /Worksheet Global Default Autoexec has not been set to No.

There are numerous applications for a macro that executes as soon as you retrieve the worksheet file containing it, once you begin to use the advanced command language features. For now, there are still a few applications for an automatically executing keyboard macro. For example, you might want to create a worksheet in which the input area is immediately erased. This means that even if the file is saved with previous data, the slate will be wiped clean with each new retrieval and you will be ready for data input.

The only difference between an automatic macro and one that you must execute is the name that you assign to it. An automatic macro must be named \0 (zero).

You can put the automatic macro to use with a model that calculates the monthly payments on a loan. The model is designed to function regardless of the principal, interest, or time. So that you can easily tell what data elements have been entered for each use of the model, the old data fields will be erased and new entries will be made. Follow these directions to set up the basic model before setting up the automatic macro:

1. Move the cell pointer to column E, select /Worksheet Column Set-Width, type **1**, and press ENTER.

2. Move the cell pointer to column G, select /Worksheet Column Set-Width, type **1**, and press ENTER.

3. Move the cell pointer to B3, type **Enter desired borrowings:**, and move the cell pointer to E2.

4. Type **************.

5. Select /Copy, press ENTER, move the cell pointer to E4, and press ENTER. Move the cell pointer to E3 and type *****.

6. Move the cell pointer to B6, type **Enter interest rate:**, and move the cell pointer to B10.

7. Type **Enter term in years:** and move the cell pointer to B13.

8. Type **** Your Payments Will Be **** and move the cell pointer to F13.

9. Type **@PMT(F3,F6/12,F10*12)** and press ENTER.
   Everything is now entered for this model, except for a few more asterisks to form boxes on the data-entry form and except for the data itself.

10. Move the cell pointer to E2, select /Copy, press the DOWN ARROW key twice to move to E4, and press ENTER. Move the cell pointer to E5 and press ENTER.

11. Keeping the cell pointer in E2, select /Copy, press the DOWN ARROW key twice to move to E4, and press ENTER. Move the cell pointer to E9 and press ENTER.

12. Add the remaining three asterisks to complete the boxes by placing an asterisk in G3, G6, and G10.

13. Move the cell pointer to F13, select /Range Format Currency, and press ENTER twice.
    You have already completed quite a bit of work, but you have yet to enter the automatic macro. Follow these instructions to create the macro:

14. Move the cell pointer to B21, type **'/reF3~**, and move the cell pointer to B22.

15. Type **'/reF6~** and move the cell pointer to B23.

16. Type **'/reF10~** and move the cell pointer to B24.

17. Type {**GOTO**}**F3~** and move the cell pointer to B21.

The tilde mark (~) is a very important part of the last three steps. It is easy to forget, but make the effort to remember; problems will occur if you leave it off.

18. Select /Range Name Create, type **\0**, and press ENTER twice.

19. Move the cell pointer to A21, type **^\0**, and press ENTER.

20. Make the following documentation entries:

    C21:   Erases previous borrowing entry
    C22:   Erases previous interest rate
    C23:   Erases previous term
    C24:   Positions the cell pointer for the first entry

21. Make these entries to perform the first payment calculation:

    F3:   65000
    F6:   .1025
    F10:   30

Your display should now match Figure 12-5.

22. Select /File Save, type **PAYMNT**, and press ENTER.

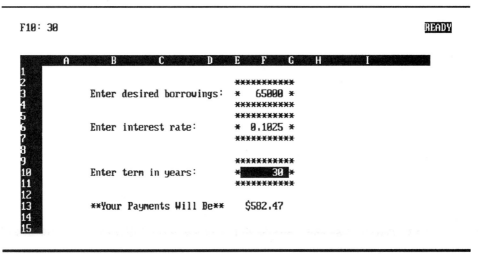

FIGURE 12-5.   Calculating a payment amount

23. Select /File Retrieve, point to PAYMNT in the list of filenames, and press ENTER.

    If the macro does not begin executing immediately, select /Worksheet Global Default Autoexec Yes Update, save the worksheet, and retrieve it again.

24. Complete entries in F3, F6, and F10 to calculate a new payment with different numbers.

Adding Sophistication with a Few Command Language Instructions

You have already explored the workings of the keyboard alternative macros. The command language instructions make up a complete programming language for 1-2-3 instructions. However, you can look at just a few that can add power to your macros. The macro instructions in this sections are the Release 2 versions of the instructions. Some of the features covered in this section are also available in Release 1A, but the commands are different. Release 1A commands, which are quite different from the Release 2 versions, will not be covered. If you plan to use the command language instructions extensively, you will want to acquire an upgraded version of 1-2-3 anyway in order to have access to a full set of commands.

Each of the special command language commands uses braces around the keyword entry for the command, as in {QUIT}, the command that ends a macro. Some of the command language commands also use arguments similar to the built-in functions' use of arguments. These arguments refine the use of the command to a specific situation. They look something like this:

{BRANCH End}

This command will cause the macro to begin executing the instructions stored at the range named End. Notice that the command language argument is also enclosed within the braces.

BRANCHING WITHIN A MACRO   The *{BRANCH}* command allows you to change the flow of execution within a macro to another location on the worksheet. This location can be specified as a cell address or a range name. The format of the command is {BRANCH *location*}. This command is seldom used alone; normally, it is combined with a condition test that will cause the macro to branch only if a certain condition is true.

This command does not alter the location of the cell pointer. It is not related to the command {GOTO}, which is designed to position the cell pointer rather than to alter the flow of execution of a macro.

ADDING A COUNTER   A *counter* will permit you to count the number of times that you have executed a group of instructions. This is the typical use for a counter; to use it in that way, however, you must combine it with other instructions in this section. For now, you will find out how counters are established; then, later in this section, you will see how it is combined with other instructions to create a macro that executes certain instructions repetitively. As you learn more about the macro, you will find that 1-2-3 has a {FOR} instruction that automatically initializes a counter and increments it for you. You may want to use this option later; when beginning to work with macros, however, you will find it more beneficial to establish your own counter so you can understand exactly what is happening.

A counter can be a cell address or a range name that you have assigned to a cell address. Once you decide on a location to use for a counter, you should reserve the location's use for this counter.

The *{LET}* command is used to set the value for a counter. When used in a macro with repetitive processing, {LET} must be used in two different ways: first, to initialize the value of the variable at the start of the macro, and second, to increment the variable each time you process the repetitive instructions within the macro. To use A1 as a counter and initialize it to zero, you could use this instruction at the beginning of the macro:

{LET A1,0}

To increment this counter within a macro after completing an iteration of the processing, you could use this instruction:

{LET A1,A1+1}

This instruction is written to work regardless of the current value of A1, as long as it contains a value entry.

The two instructions affecting the value of the counter might be incorporated in a macro that performs repetitive processing something like this:

```
\m        {Let A1,0}

          Top ...

          {LET A1,A1+1}

          End {QUIT}
```

You would enter the instructions to be executed repetitively in the section between Top and End. Top represents the beginning of the repetitive section. End marks the first instructions following the section that would be executed repetitively. Naturally, other instructions must be added to control the flow of execution.

ADDING A CONDITION CHECK   Just as the @IF function is one of the most powerful built-in function tools, the *{IF}* macro instruction is one of the most powerful command language instructions. It serves a similar purpose because it also allows you to deal with logical conditions. Its power is far more extensive because it lets you perform any other macro instruction, depending on the result of the condition test. It is not limited to controlling the value of a single cell the way that @IF is. In fact, the {IF} command is normally combined with {BRANCH} to completely change the execution flow within a macro.

Any condition can be tested. In macros where you have established a counter to control processing, the condition that is normally checked is the value of the counter. If the condition tested is true, the command on the same line as the {IF} will be executed. You might find a line like this within a macro:

{IF A1>10}{BRANCH End}

This line checks the value of A1. If A1 is greater than 10, the macro will branch to the range named End and execute the macro instructions it finds at that location.

ACCEPTING INPUT FROM THE KEYBOARD   There are several commands that let you accept data from the keyboard while a macro is executing. The simplest of these is *{?}*. When a macro encounters this special entry, it suspends execution and waits for input from the keyboard. When the operator presses ENTER, the macro continues where it left off.

You can use this feature to create a macro that removes the repetition involved in entering a series of built-in functions. You can supply the variable portion of the function and have the macro automate the entry of the portion that does not vary.

A macro like this enters the date for you; all you need to supply is the year, month, and day:

X	Y	Z
1 \d	@DATE(	Start date function
2	{?}	Wait for year to be input
3	,	Add comma after year
4	{?}	Wait for month to be input
5	,	Add comma after month
6	{?}	Wait for day to be input
7	)~	End function and finalize with ENTER
8	/rfd1~	Format entry as a date

Make sure that you place an apostrophe in front of the entries in X1, Y1, Y3, Y5, Y7, and Y8 to ensure that the contents of these cells are interpreted as labels.

If you like, you can enter this macro and give it a name. The following section provides a version of this same macro that is a bit more sophisticated. It incorporates several advanced macro features into the macro and creates a macro that will enter ten dates. You will use a slightly different strategy with this macro and document each instruction immediately after entering it. This will help you understand what each step is doing.

BUILDING A DATE-ENTRY MACRO   This section combines the advanced features just discussed in a working macro example. It uses the concept of a counter, branching, and keyboard input all in one macro, since it is common to include multiple advanced instructions in a macro. Follow these directions to enter the macro:

1. Select /Worksheet Erase Yes, move the cell pointer to J1, select /Worksheet Column Set-Width, type **23**, and press ENTER. Type **{LET A1,0}** and move the cell pointer to K1.

2. Type **Initialize A1 to 0 as a counter** and move the cell pointer to J2.

3. Type **{IF A1=10}{BRANCH End}** and move the cell pointer to K2.

4. Type **Check for max value in the counter** and move the cell pointer to J3.

5. Type **{LET A1,A1+1}** and move the cell pointer to K3.

6. Type **Increment counter** and move the cell pointer to J4.

7. Type **'@DATE(** and then move the cell pointer to K4.

   The apostrophe is required to prevent 1-2-3 from interpreting @ as a value entry in the cell.

8. Type **Enter first part of function** and move the cell pointer to J5.

9. Complete the remaining entries like this:

J5:	{?}
K5:	Pause for the entry of the year
J6:	,
K6:	Enter the comma separator
J7:	{?}
K7:	Pause for the entry of the month
J8:	,
K8:	Enter comma separator
J9:	{?}
K9:	Pause for the entry of the day
J10:	)~
K10:	Generate close and finalize
J11:	{DOWN}
K11:	Move the cell pointer down one cell
J12:	{BRANCH Top}
K12:	Begin Loop again
J13:	{UP}{END}{UP}
K13:	Move to the top of the date column
J14:	'/rfd1
K14:	Invoke date entry
J15:	{END}{DOWN}~
K15:	Expand format range
J16:	'/wcs12~
K16:	Widen column
J17:	{QUIT}
K17:	End macro after 10 entries and format

The {QUIT} command is the only one that has not been discussed. It is used to end the execution of a macro just as a blank cell will do. Using {QUIT} rather than a blank cell makes it clearer that you intend the macro to end at that point.

```
I1: '\z                                                                 READY

        I               J                    K      L       M       N
1    \z          {LET A1,0}           Initialize A1 TO 0 as a counter
2    Top         {IF A1=10}{BRANCH End} Check for max value in the counter
3                {LET A1,A1+1}        Increment counter
4                @DATE(               Enter first part of function
5                {?}                  Pause for the entry of the year
6                ,                    Enter comma separator
7                {?}                  Pause for the entry of the month
8                ,                    Enter comma separator
9                {?}                  Pause for the entry of the day
10               )~                   Generate close and finalize
11               {DOWN}               Move the cell pointer down one cell
12               {BRANCH Top}         Begin Loop again
13   End         {UP}{END}{UP}        Move to the top of the date column
14               /rfd1                Invoke date entry
15               {END}{DOWN}~         Expand format range
16               /wcs12~              Widen column
17               {QUIT}               End Macro after 10 entries and format
18
```

FIGURE 12-6. A macro to enter dates

10. Enter these labels in the cells specified:

    I1:   '\z
    I2:   Top
    I13:   End

    Move the cell pointer to I1. The macro should now match Figure 12-6.

11. Select /Range Name Labels Right, expand the range to I13, and press ENTER.

    The /Range Name Labels Right command saves you from having to use the /Range Name Create command three times. It assigns the labels in the range you specify to the entries in the cells immediately to the right of the cell containing the label.

12. Move the cell pointer to D1 and press and release ALT-Z to execute the macro.

You can enter anything you want for the year, month, and day for each date as long as the entries are valid and you press ENTER after each entry. Figure 12-7 shows one set of date entries that were completed with the macro.

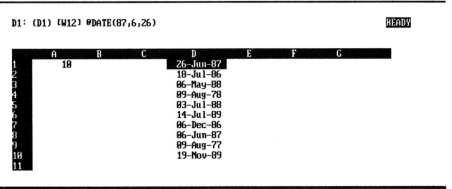

FIGURE 12-7.   Dates entered with the macro

Debugging Macros

The debugging process involves testing and correcting macros to ensure that you are obtaining the desired results. One of the most common mistakes users make in creating keyboard macros is forgetting to enter the tilde mark to represent each time the ENTER key is pressed. When you add command language commands to a macro, you do not have the ability to test it completely before entering it.

1-2-3 has a STEP mode that executes a macro one keystroke at a time. This allows you to follow its progress and spot the area of difficulty if problems are encountered. In Release 2.2, pressing the ALT and F2 keys simultaneously will turn on the STEP mode. In Release 2, pressing the SHIFT and F2 keys simultaneously will turn on the STEP mode. In Release 1A, pressing the SHIFT key plus the F1 key activates the STEP mode. Since this is a toggle process, holding the keys down too long will toggle the STEP mode into the off position again. When this mode is operational, you will see the word STEP at the bottom of your screen, as shown in Figure 12-8.

When the STEP mode is on, any macro you invoke will be executed one step at a time. You will press the SPACEBAR each time you are ready for the next keystroke. In Release 2.2, 1-2-3 displays its location in the macro. It shows the current cell address within the macro and its contents, and even uses a small highlight to mark the current keystroke. This information is displayed on the bottom line of the screen. The menu selections invoked will display in the control panel to provide information on the operation of the macro. You will not be able to input direct commands while the macro is executing. SST will appear at the bottom of the screen while the macro is executing. In Release 2.2, SST only appears when the macro is waiting for input.

```
I1: '\z                                                              READY
        I            J              K      L       M       N
1   \z          {LET A1,0}       Initialize A1 TO 0 as a counter
2   Top         {IF A1=10}{BRANCH End} Check for max value in the counter
3               {LET A1,A1+1}    Increment counter
4               @DATE(           Enter first part of function
5               {?}              Pause for the entry of the year
6               ,                Enter comma separator
7               {?}              Pause for the entry of the month
8               ,                Enter comma separator
9               {?}              Pause for the entry of the day
10              )~               Generate close and finalize
11              {DOWN}           Move the cell pointer down one cell
12              {BRANCH Top}     Begin Loop again
13  End         {UP}{END}{UP}    Move to the top of the date column
14              /rfd1            Invoke date entry
15              {END}{DOWN}~     Expand format range
16              /wcs12~          Widen column
17              {QUIT}           End Macro after 10 entries and format
18
19
20
01-May-89  07:21 PM        UNDO           STEP
```

FIGURE 12-8. Placing the macro in STEP mode

To stop a malfunctioning macro, press the CTRL and BREAK keys simultaneously. This cancels the macro operation immediately and presents an error indicator at the upper right corner of the screen. Pressing ESC will return you to READY mode so you can make the necessary corrections to your macro.

Follow these instructions to try a macro in STEP mode:

1. Select /File Retrieve, type **FORMAT,** and press ENTER.

2. If you are using Release 2.2, press the ALT and F2 keys. If you are using Release 2, press the SHIFT and F2 keys. If you are using Release 1A, press the SHIFT and F1 keys.

3. Move the cell pointer to F1, press ALT, and type **c.**

4. Press the SPACEBAR to execute a keystroke.

5. Continue pressing the SPACEBAR until you are asked to supply the range to format.

6. Press the END key followed by the DOWN ARROW key, and then press ENTER.

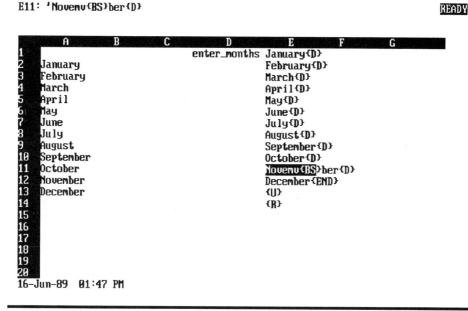

FIGURE 12-9.   Macro entries

7. Execute step 2 again to toggle the STEP mode into the off position.

8. Select /Worksheet Erase Yes.

REVIEW EXERCISE

Although practice will improve your skill level with all 1-2-3 tasks, it is especially important with macros because a number of steps are required to achieve successful results. For practice, you will create a macro that enters the month names in a column beginning at the cell pointer. You can use this same approach to enter account names or part numbers if you need to use them in a number of places within one model. You can follow these steps, which even include a deliberate mistake and its correction, if you are using Release 2.2. If you are using a different release, you will need to make minor modifications to allow for the direct entry of the data without the Learn feature:

1. Use E1..E20 as your learn range.
    Hint: Select /Worksheet Learn Range, highlight E1 through E20, and press ENTER.

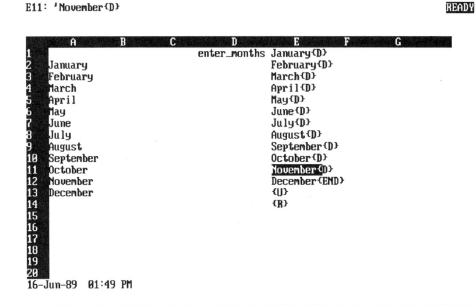

E11: 'November{D}   READY

FIGURE 12-10.   Corrected macro entries

2. Start recording the keystrokes as you begin a trial run in A2. Make a deliberate mistake in typing November by entering **Novemv**. Then press the BACKSPACE key and type **ber**. Move to B2 after typing December.

   Hint: Move the cell pointer to A2 and press ALT-F5 (LEARN) before starting to type the month names.

3. Use enter-months for the macro name.

   Hint: Remember to turn off the Learn feature by pressing ALT-F5 (LEARN). Press F9 (CALC) to record the last instruction and record the macro name in cell D1. You can use either /Range Name Create or /Range Name Label Right to name the top cell in the macro. Your entries will look like those in Figure 12-9 if you move the cell pointer to E11, where 1-2-3 has recorded the mistake and its correction.

4. Correct the entry in this cell.

   Hint: Press F2 (EDIT) to make the correction. The final entries will look like those in Figure 12-10.

REVIEW

- 1-2-3's keyboard alternative macros allow you to perform repetitive tasks with ease. You can type the keystrokes in a cell or use 1-2-3's Learn feature to record them. Once they are named you can execute all the keystrokes with one request.

- To record function keys and special keys, you must use 1-2-3's keywords enclosed in braces ({ }). To record menu selections, use the first character in each command name. To record entries, type them as you would without a macro.

- Macros are entered in a group of contiguous cells in a column of the worksheet. If you are typing the entries, each one must be a label entry.

- You can use two different methods for naming macros. In both cases, only the top cell in the macro is named. Your selection will determine how you can execute the macro. If you use \ and a single letter, you can press ALT and type the letter to execute the macro. If you use a regular range name, you will need to use F3 (RUN) to execute the macro.

Commands and Keys

Entry	Action
ALT-*letter*	Executes a macro
ALT-F2	Enables STEP mode
ALT-F3	Executes a macro
ALT-F5	Enables Learn feature
/RNLR	/Range Name Labels Right applies names to cell immediately to the right
/WL	/Worksheet Learn specifies a learn range for 1-2-3

13

USING ALLWAYS

Working with Add-ins
Using the Features of Allways
Review Exercise
Review

The output devices connected to most computers are able to support features that just a few years ago were only available to publishers with access to sophisticated typesetting equipment. These features have come to be called desktop publishing.

The Print menus in 1-2-3 and its PrintGraph program create professional-looking output but do not fully use the desktop publishing features of your printer. A separate add-in program is provided with Release 2.2 to add these features to 1-2-3. Add-ins are not automatically part of 1-2-3's feature set until they are attached. After attaching an add-in, you can invoke it at any time and its features will be accessible from menus in much the same way that regular 1-2-3 menu commands are. The add-in that adds desktop publishing features to 1-2-3 is called Allways. Although it is a separate program, a copy of it is included with every copy of 1-2-3 Release 2.2. To install Allways you will need a hard disk and a minimum of 128K of memory above the requirements of 1-2-3. Allways can also be used with earlier versions of 1-2-3 since it was originally designed and sold as a separate add-in.

Although Allways is an add-in, you will soon learn to rely on its abilities so much that you will begin to think of its features as an integral part of 1-2-3. With Allways you can use as many as eight different fonts per printout to change the size and appearance of the characters. A set of soft fonts is provided with Allways. This means that you have definitions of each of the characters stored on disk and can use these fonts with dot-matrix or laser printers. You can also continue to use the "native" fonts that your printer has built into it or that you have added by installing a cartridge. You can boldface or underline individual cell entries or ranges. You can use shading, lines, and boxes to highlight important information in a report. You can adjust the width of one or more columns or change the height of rows. You can also print graphs and worksheet text on the same page with flexible sizing options, if your printer is capable. Menus similar to the 1-2-3 menus and immediate changes in the appearance of the screen with a graphics monitor known as WYSIWYG (what you see is what you get) make the features of this add-in simple to master. After a little practice with the exercises in this chapter, you will consider yourself a spreadsheet publishing expert.

In this chapter you will learn how to use some of the basic features of Allways. First, you will want to take a look at some of the basic procedures for using add-ins. As you work through the Allways features you will be expanding your knowledge of spreadsheet publishing concepts as well as the specific features of Allways. You will also learn the techniques needed to attach or invoke other 1-2-3 Release 2.2 add-in programs.

WORKING WITH ADD-INS

1-2-3 add-in programs are separate programs that have been designed to attach to 1-2-3 through its Add-in Manager. These add-ins can be attached to 1-2-3 to allow them to function without removing 1-2-3 or the current worksheet from memory. Because these add-ins have additional memory requirements, you may not be able to leave Undo enabled unless you have expanded memory on your system.

Attaching an Add-in

When an add-in program is attached to 1-2-3, you define how you want to invoke the features of the add-in. You can invoke it through menu selections or through a short-cut feature known as a *hot key*. When the hot-key option is chosen, you select one of the allowable function keys at the time you attach the add-in. To execute a hot-key add-in, you press the ALT key in combination with the function key selected at the time of attachment.

If you are using Release 2.2, you will want to disable the Undo feature before attaching Allways if you only have conventional memory in your machine. Select /Worksheet Global Default Other Undo Disable Quit. Then use the following steps to attach Allways after following the installation instructions for Allways that appears in Appendix A:

1. Select /Add-in. 1-2-3 displays this Add-in Manager menu:

```
A1:                                                                    MENU
Attach  Detach  Invoke  Clear  Quit
Load an add-in program into memory
```

2. Select Attach.

   This invokes the Add-in Manager and displays a menu listing the names of all the add-in files in 1-2-3's directory.

3. Highlight the name of the add-in you wish to attach as shown here:

```
A1:                                                                    FILES
Enter add-in to attach: C:\123R22\*.ADN
ALLWAYS.ADN        MACROMGR.ADN      ALLWAYS\
```

4. Press ENTER.

5. Type **7** to assign the add-in to the ALT-F7 key combination.

6. Select Quit to return to READY mode.

If you had wanted to use the features of Allways immediately, you would have selected Invoke.

   1-2-3 assigns the hot key ALT-F10 to the add-in menu when it is not assigned to an add-in. When you press this hot key, 1-2-3 displays the Add-in Manager menu just as if you had selected /Add-in. Once you assign an add-in to a function key, the number does not appear the next time you select /Add-In Attach.

Invoking an Add-in

Once an add-in is attached it can be invoked by selecting Invoke from the Add-in Manager menu or by its hot key if one was assigned when the add-in was attached. If you attempt to invoke an add-in before attaching it, its name will not appear in the list of add-in options after you select Invoke from the Add-in Manager menu. If no add-ins are attached, an error message will indicate that at the bottom of the screen.

   To invoke an add-in with a hot key assigned, press ALT and the function key assigned. To invoke an add-in without a hot key assigned, follow these steps:

1. Type / (slash) and select Add-in from the main menu.

   Alternatively you can press ALT-F10 if this key combination is not used as a hot key for an add-in.

2. Select Invoke.

3. Highlight the name of the attached add-in you wish to invoke (for this example, ALLWAYS.ADN) and press ENTER.

   When Allways is invoked. Allways displays its opening screen then how Allways will print your spreadsheet. You can return to 1-2-3 by pressing ESC.

4. Press ESC to return to 1-2-3.

Eliminating the Attachment
For an Add-in

Once an add-in is attached, it will remain attached even if you deactivate it by returning to 1-2-3. This means that you can invoke it again and again, whenever you want. It also means that some of your computer's memory is allocated to the add-in. If you know you are not going to use the add-in again, the best approach is to eliminate its attachment to 1-2-3. This can be accomplished in two ways.

If you only want to eliminate the attachment for one add-in, select Detach from the menu for the Add-in Manager. To eliminate all the attachments for add-in with one command, select Clear from the Add-in Manager menu. Any remaining add-ins are detached when you quit 1-2-3.

If you are using Release 2.2, you can remove the attachment for Allways and reattach it by following these steps:

1. Select /Add-in.

2. Select Detach, highlight Allways, and press ENTER. Then, select Quit.

3. Press ALT-F7 and notice that this combination no longer invokes Allways.

4. Select /Add-in.

5. Select Attach.

6. Highlight Allways in the list of selections and press ENTER.

7. Type **7** to attach Allways to the ALT-F7 key combination.

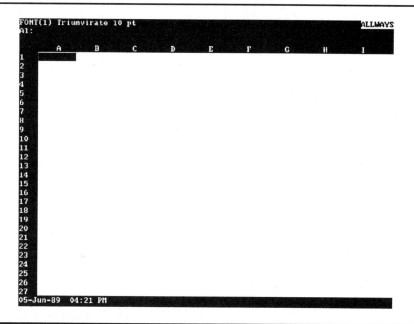

FIGURE 13-1.   Allways screen with a blank worksheet

8. Select Quit to return to READY mode in 1-2-3 or select Invoke, highlight Allways, and press ENTER to work with Allways. Figure 13-1 shows the Allways display when you invoke it with no worksheet active.

USING THE FEATURES
OF ALLWAYS

Allways provides support for printing information stored on a worksheet and 1-2-3 graph images. The worksheets and graphs are created by using menu selections covered in earlier chapters. Rather than printing the worksheet with the Print commands covered in Chapter 6, you can invoke Allways and enhance the worksheet entries before printing them.

Unlike PrintGraph, Allways does not require that you exit 1-2-3 to start another program when you want a printout of a graph. In addition, Allways can print a graph on the same page as text entries from a worksheet program and allows you to change fonts, the range of worksheet cells occupied by the graph, and colors.

Because Allways provides desktop publishing features, it has many options that deal with page layout. In 1-2-3 itself, page layout options are limited and affect every entry on the sheet instead of individual cell entries. Many features of Allways, like the /Range Format commands in 1-2-3, are oriented toward changing the appearance of a range of worksheet cells. There are many more options with Allways, however. Before looking at the menu commands necessary for a full implementation of these features, you will want to enhance your understanding of the general concepts that apply to using desktop publishing features.

The Concept of Changing
A Worksheet with Allways

In Chapter 6, you learned that 1-2-3's Print menus offered a few features to control the layout of the page. By defining margins and specifying different print ranges you learned that you had some control over page appearance. The use of printer setup strings allowed you to pass a message to your printer at the beginning of the Print operation or for various rows within the document. Although these features added flexibility to page appearance, there were many restrictions, such as the inability to use a particular print feature for an entry within a row if the worksheet had multiple entries within the row. Allways will make 1-2-3 users' presentations more sophisticated without changing the 1-2-3 worksheet data in any way.

After attaching Allways, you can invoke it with ALT-F10, by selecting Invoke, highlighting, it and pressing ENTER, or with a hot key such as ALT-F7 if you assigned one. The worksheet currently in memory will then be presented on the Allways display. Although it is the same information found on the worksheet, it looks a little different in Allways because the display simulates the appearance of the information on a printed page.

Once you invoke Allways, the worksheet becomes frozen. Although you can change the worksheet's appearance, you cannot update values in the worksheet. If you need to change a worksheet value, you must return to 1-2-3. Even though you cannot change any of the entries stored in worksheet cells when Allways is active, you can make significant changes to the appearance of the information. Like 1-2-3, Allways has a menu that displays at the top of the screen after you press the slash key. Menu selections are made by entering the first letter of the desired selection or by highlighting the desired selection and pressing ENTER to complete the selection. Allways has other similarities to 1-2-3 that will contribute to a feeling of instant familiarity with the product. You will notice a mode indicator in the upper right corner that tells you what Allways is doing at any given moment. Allways also uses function keys to perform some tasks. As in 1-2-3, you can invoke the Help feature by pressing F1. The F3 key displays a list of range names or filenames for your selection. The F5 key is a GOTO key. Other function key assignments for Allways are as follows.

F4	Zooms out to reduce the size of entries on the screen
SHIFT-F4	Zooms in to increase the size of entries on the screen
F6	Toggles between graphics display mode and text display mode
F10	Toggles the display of graphs on and off

Unlike 1-2-3, Allways provides a set of *accelerator keys* that you can use to request features without the need for many selections. These accelerator keys change the format of the current cell or the range selected before pressing the accelerator key. Table 13-1 lists the accelerator keys. You would press a key combination at the location where you want to begin the special feature and again after you want to stop using it.

ALT-B	Boldface On/Off
ALT-G	Grid lines On/Off
ALT-L	Lines Outline/All/None
ALT-S	Shading Light/Dark/Solid/None
ALT-U	Underline Single/Double/None
ALT-1	Font 1 (Triumvirate 10 point)
ALT-2	Font 2 (Triumvirate Italic 10 point)
ALT-3	Font 3 (Triumvirate 14 point)
ALT-4	Font 4 (Triumvirate 20 point)
ALT-5	Font 5 (Times 10 point)
ALT-6	Font 6 (Times Italic 10 point)
ALT-7	Font 7 (Times 14 point)
ALT-8	Font 8 (Times 20 point)

TABLE 13-1.   Allways Accelerator Keys

You can use the options in the Allways menu to change the appearance of your worksheet. Just as you do in 1-2-3, invoke the menu in Allways by typing / to produce a menu like this:

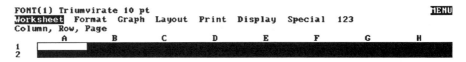

Commands in the Format menu selection will allow you to change fonts and use boldface, underlining, and other features. Allways will display the text on the screen as it will print, using a WYSIWYG interface. Also, format changes will appear in the top line of the control panel as you move the cell pointer around on the worksheet. The entries are not coded like 1-2-3's but are spelled out.

Another difference between the menu selections in Allways and 1-2-3 is that you will not find a File selection to save and retrieve files. The selections you make with Allways will be saved if you return to 1-2-3 and save your 1-2-3 file. Allways will store your formatting settings to a file with the same name as the worksheet it formats and an .ALL extension. Since there is no way you can end Allways without returning to 1-2-3, this should help you remember to save your changes. When you retrieve your 1-2-3 file at another time, all of your Allways changes will be available if you attach Allways.

Changing Fonts

The selection of fonts for your entries will alter the typeface and the size of the characters. The term *typeface* refers to the style of print characters. These characters may be somewhat plain without any embellishments at the ends of the simple straight lines used to construct each of the letters in the character set. Fonts without embellishments are referred to as *sans serif fonts*. Fonts with embellishments at the ends of the lines that form the letters are known as *serif fonts*. Figure 13-2 shows the default fonts that are shipped as part of the Allways package. These are the fonts that you see

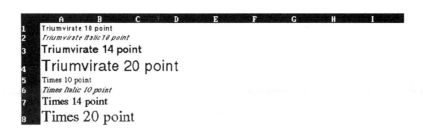

FIGURE 13-2. Sample of fonts available in Allways

initially when you select a font for your worksheet. You can use any of the 54 fonts that come with Allways, however, in addition to any of the fonts that your printer or a cartridge provides.

The fonts shipped with the Allways package are soft fonts, which means that they are defined by the software and do not require the insertion of font cartridges in your printer. You may be able to buy other fonts on cartridges or disks from your printer manufacturer or other outside companies. Once your printer has access to a particular font, the characters of the font are created by a grid pattern of wires inside your printer. This grid can create any graphic pattern by using or not using any of the wires. Although Allways will support the use of font cartridges for your printer, there are 54 fonts included with the package. The eight default fonts use a serif font called Times and a sans serif font called Triumvirate.

The size of the characters is another important component of a font. Size is measured in points for laser printers. Allways uses this same measurement scheme. Each point is 1/72 of an inch. Normally 10- or 12-point fonts are used for regular spreadsheet entries. Headings may use 12- or 24-point fonts and fine print may be displayed with a 5- or 7-point font.

USING DIFFERENT FONTS   You can use as many as eight fonts on any output created with Allways. The fonts available at any one point are part of a selectable font set. For different worksheets you might have a different set of fonts. The first font in any set is always the font used as the default, which means that it will be used for all entries unless you select a different font with the Format Font command or an accelerator key. When you format part of the worksheet to use a different font, the column may need to be resized to fit all of the characters. When worksheet entries are printed with the default font, you do not have to change the column width because Allways defines the column widths according to the size of the default font.

To look at the application of different fonts for a worksheet, you will want to complete the entries shown in Figure 13-3. Follow these step-by-step directions:

1. Select /Worksheet Golbal Format , (comma), type 0, and press ENTER.

2. Move the cell pointer to C2, type **ABC COMPANY**, and press the DOWN ARROW key.

3. Type **Unit Sales By Region** and move the cell pointer to A6.

4. Complete the following entries:
   A6:   Tires
   A7:   Radios
   A8:   Tuners
   A9:   Sky-views
   B5:   "North

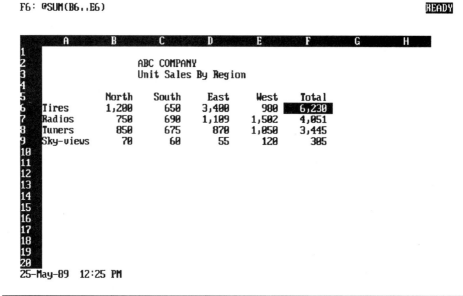

F6: @SUM(B6..E6)   READY

FIGURE 13-3.   Worksheet for demonstrating Allways features

B6:	1200
B7:	750
B8:	850
B9:	70
C5:	"South
C6:	650
C7:	690
C8:	675
C9:	60
D5:	"East
D6:	3400
D7:	1109
D8:	870
D9:	55
E5:	"West
E6:	980
E7:	1502
E8:	1050
E9:	120
F5:	"Total
F6:	@SUM(B6..E6)

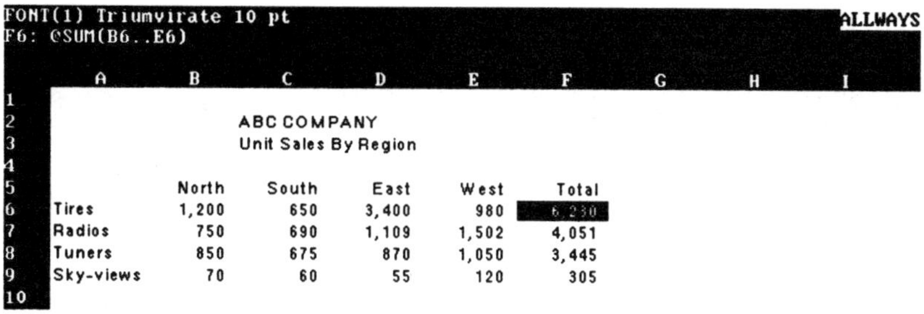

```
FONT(1) Triumvirate 10 pt                                           ALLWAYS
F6: @SUM(B6..E6)

         A        B        C        D        E        F        G        H        I
1
2                          ABC COMPANY
3                          Unit Sales By Region
4
5                 North    South     East     West    Total
6    Tires        1,200      650    3,400      980    6,230
7    Radios         750      690    1,109    1,502    4,051
8    Tuners         850      675      870    1,050    3,445
9    Sky-views       70       60       55      120      305
10
```

FIGURE 13-4.   Allways screen showing worksheet from Figure 13-3

5. With your cell pointer on F6, select /Copy, press ENTER, move the cell pointer to F7, and type . (period). Move the cell pointer to F9 and press ENTER to complete the Copy operation.

   With the model entries completed you are ready to invoke Allways and make the font changes using these additional steps:

6. Press ALT-F7 to invoke Allways, assuming you attached it according to the directions provided earlier in the chapter.

   Your screen shows the model as it will print with Allways and will match Figure 13-4.

7. Move the cell pointer to C2 by pressing the F5 (GOTO) key, typing C2, and pressing ENTER.

8. Select /Format Font to activate the menu and tell Allways that you want to use a different font for a range.

   Allways will display eight font selections that are part of its font set. As you become familiar with the default fonts, you will make use of the accelerator keys to quickly set the font of a worksheet range. Allways uses ALT-1 through ALT-8 for each of the fonts. Since this is the first font selection you are making, you will want to use the selection box Allways provides.

9. Select Triumvirate 14 from the font list by using the UP and DOWN ARROW keys to move to Triumvirate 14 and pressing ENTER.

   If you try typing a letter to select a font, Allways interprets the letter as trying to select another menu option from the Format Font menu. To choose

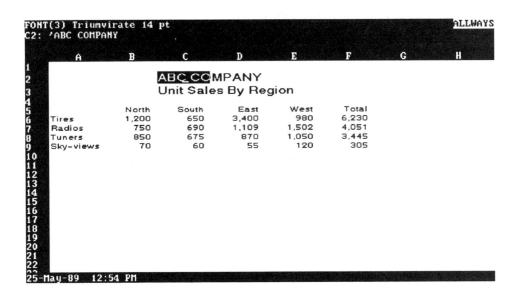

FIGURE 13-5.   Changing the font size to emphasize text

an option from a box like the one on the screen, you must point to it with the arrow keys. Allways will prompt you for the range you want to format with this font.

10. Move the highlight to C3 to expand the range and then press ENTER. Your screen will show the range in the new format as in Figure 13-5. Notice that the entire entry for C2 and C3 is displayed in the new font, including the portion of the entries that borrows space from the cell in column D. The control panel also shows your font selection.

Allways has other alternatives for selecting ranges to format and keys to press to select the format. You can also select a range by moving to the first cell that you want to format and typing a period before moving the cell pointer to the opposite side of the range. Then you can use the accelerator keys to format the range. To try this with the worksheet you have created, follow these steps:

1. Move the cell pointer to A6 and type . (period). The control panel changes to show that you are selecting a range instead of a single cell.

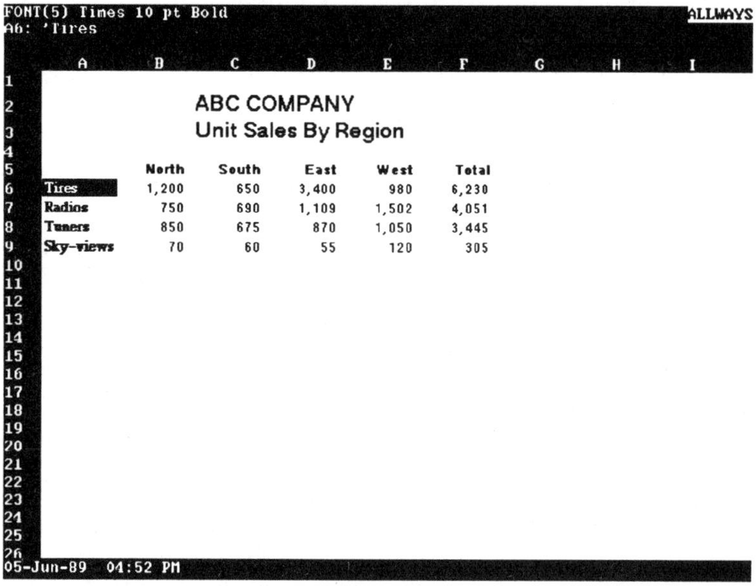

FIGURE 13-6.   Worksheet after changing fonts

2. Press the DOWN ARROW to highlight A6..A9. Allways highlights the range that you have selected.

3. Press ALT-5 to select Times 10 point.

4. Press ALT-B for the accelerator key to make this same range boldface.

5. Press ESC to remove this range selection.

6. Move the cell pointer to A5 and select /Format Bold Set. Next, move the cell pointer to F5 and press ENTER. The Times 10-point font is still displayed except that it is in boldface. Your screen will look like the one in Figure 13-6.

CHANGING THE FONT SET   When you first install Allways, your font set is created from eight of the soft fonts provided with Allways. This means that you have access to four Triumvirate fonts and four Times fonts in the default font set. You also have the ability to replace any of these default fonts with fonts directly supported by your printer or another soft font. If you have a printer that supports font cartridges, you can tell Allways which of these fonts you are using and they will also be available for your selection.

To replace an existing font, follow these steps:

1. Select /Format Font.

2. Highlight the font you want to remove from the font set.

3. Select Replace.

4. Highlight the font in the list that you wish to use as the replacement, and press ENTER.

5. Highlight the font size in the list that you wish to use as the replacement, and press ENTER.

6. Select Quit.

To configure Allways to use other cartridges, follow these steps:

1. Select /Print Configuration Cartridge.

2. Highlight the desired cartridge in the list and press ENTER.

3. Select Quit to leave the Configuration menu.

The cartride fonts will now be included in the list of fonts to select from when you replace a font.

Other Formatting
Options in Allways

In addition to changing fonts and using boldface anywhere in a row of the worksheet, you can alter the appearance of cell entries in other ways. For a range as small as one cell or as large as all your spreadsheet entries, you can use single or double underlining, color selections, shading, and an outline around each cell.

ADDING LINES   You can add lines at any side of a cell or a range of cells. If you use the outline feature, you can completely outline all the walls of each cell in a range.

If you are discussing eliminating the Sky-views product line, you may want to outline the entries in that row. Move the cell pointer to B9 and then follow these steps.

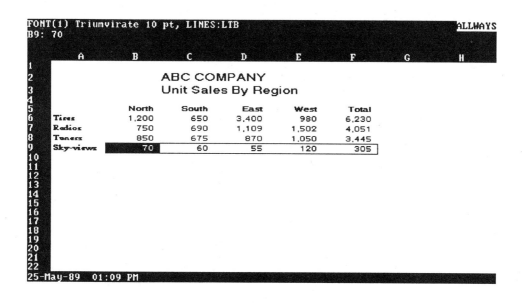

FIGURE 13-7.   Outline added to worksheet range

1. Select /Format Lines Outline.

2. Move the cell pointer to F9 and press ENTER.

   A box is drawn around the outer edges of all the cells in the range. The selection All would draw a box around each cell in the range.

Your screen will look like the one in Figure 13-7 with a selection of Outline and like the one in Figure 13-8 with a selection of All.

REMOVING A FORMAT OPTION   You can remove any format that you add to a worksheet range. The /Format Reset command strips away any format changes made and displays the entries in Font 1 format.

To eliminate the outline around the Sky-views entries, follow these steps:

1. Select /Format Reset with the cell pointer still in B9.

2. Expand the range by moving the cell pointer to F9 and pressing ENTER.

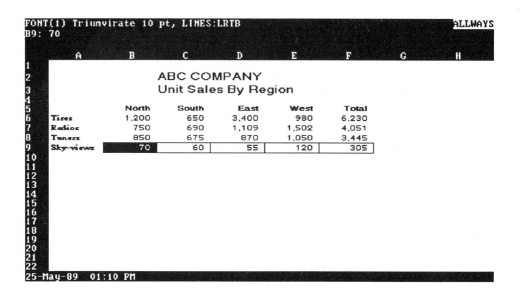

FIGURE 13-8.   Outline added to cells in a range

ADDING SHADING   You can add three levels of shading to one or more cells in the worksheet. Allways supports light, dark, and solid black shading levels. The /Format Shade command will add shading to a preselected range or prompt you to select a range to format. The ALT-S accelerator key will lightly shade the current cell or selected range. If you press ALT-S again, Allways uses medium shading instead. If you press ALT-S a third time, Allways uses dark shading. Pressing it once more removes the existing shading.

To use light shading on numbers in the Total column, follow these steps:

1. Move the cell pointer to F6.

2. Select /Format Shade Light.

3. Move the cell pointer to F9 and press ENTER.

Your screen now looks like the one in Figure 13-9.

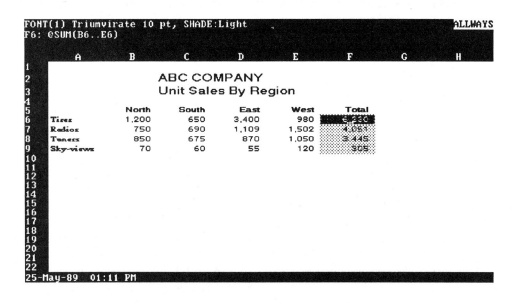

FIGURE 13-9.   Range formatted for light shading

ADDING UNDERLINING   You can underline text with either single or double underlining. Single underlining differs from a line at the bottom of the box in that it is only added for the length of the cell entries, not the entire cell width. Double underlining underlines the entire cell's width. To underline the titles at the top of the screen, follow these steps:

1. Move the cell pointer to C2.

2. Select /Format Underline Single.

3. Move the cell pointer to C3 and press ENTER.

Your screen will display underlining beneath the entire entry in C2 and C3. If you decide to remove the underlining but want to leave other format changes such as the font intact, use the /Format Underline Clear command.

The ALT-U accelerator key quickly underlines text. Pressing ALT-U once adds single underlining to the current cell or selected range. Pressing ALT-U again changes single underlining to double underlining. Pressing ALT-U a third time removes the underlining. Try it using these steps:

1. Type . (period) and press the DOWN ARROW to select the range C2..C3.

2. Press ALT-U to change the single underlining to double underlining. Notice that instead of underlining the entry, Allways creates double underlining that is the width of column C.

3. Press ALT-U again to remove the double underlining.

Changing Column Widths
And Row Heights

You can change the width of a column in the Allways display and printout without affecting the column width in your 1-2-3 spreadsheet. Row heights are normally adjusted for the font size selected but can also be changed to a custom height. To change the column width, use the /Worksheet Column Set-Width command to specify a specific size. The row height is changed with the /Worksheet Row Set-Height command.

The column width can be adjusted more precisely in Allways than in 1-2-3. The columns are measured in terms of the number of characters of the default font, which is initially a 10-point font that will display in the column. You can change to fractional sizes like 11.42 if you wish to accommodate the exact width needed for a different font.

To change the column width for column A, follow these steps:

1. Move the cell pointer to column A.

2. Select /Worksheet Column Set-Width.

3. Press the RIGHT ARROW key five times and press ENTER.
   To reset the column width to 1-2-3's width, select /Worksheet Column Reset. Try this command now:

4. Select /Worksheet Column Reset.

Allways resets the column width to the default column width.

Row heights are uniform initially, but as you select different fonts, Allways automatically adjusts the height to properly display the data. You can establish a specific height for a row by selecting /Worksheet Row Set-Height and pressing the DOWN or UP ARROW key to reserve sufficient space. Try this now by moving to row 5 and entering the command. To reset the row height so that Allways adjusts it automatically, select /Worksheet Row Auto.

Label Alignment

Allways does not have an option for changing the label alignment. You must return to 1-2-3 and change the label prefix to alter the label alignment.

It is important to note that Allways does treat label alignment a little differently and may display labels differently than 1-2-3 does. In 1-2-3, labels that are centered or right-aligned but exceed the width of the cell will be left-aligned. This is not true in Allways because Allways will allow these entries to spill over to adjacent cells, displaying part of a centered label to the right of its cell and part to the left.

If you return to 1-2-3 and change the label prefix at the front of C2 and C3 to a caret and then invoke Allways again, you will see a difference. Follow these steps:

1. Select /Quit.

2. Move the cell pointer to C2.

3. Press the F2 (EDIT) key, press HOME, and press the DEL key. Type ^ and press ENTER.

4. Move the cell pointer to C3 and repeat the procedure described in step 3.

5. Press ALT-F7 to invoke Allways, and notice how the labels are centered on column C even though they were left-aligned in 1-2-3. Figure 13-10 shows the Allways screen.

6. Select /Quit to return to 1-2-3. Change the label indicators back to ' and then invoke Allways again.

Changing the Page Layout

You can change several options that control what a printed page of your output will look like. With the /Layout PageSize command you can select one of the standard sizes that Allways supports or enter your custom requirements. You can also change the margins or add a header or a footer. Follow these steps for a look at the options:

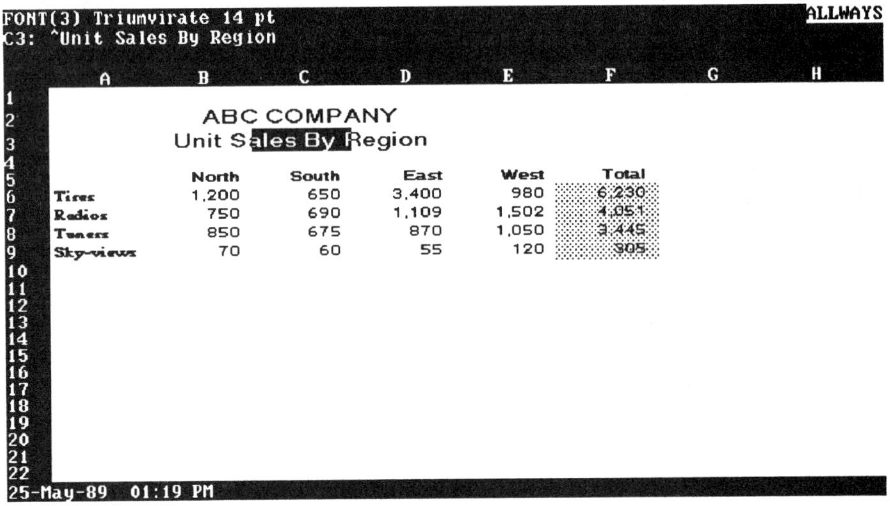

```
FONT(3) Triumvirate 14 pt                                    ALLWAYS
C3: ^Unit Sales By Region

        A         B         C         D        E         F      G      H
 1
 2                      ABC COMPANY
 3                   Unit Sales By Region
 4
 5                  North     South      East     West      Total
 6      Tires       1,200       650     3,400      980      6,230
 7      Radios        750       690     1,109    1,502      4,051
 8      Tuners        850       675       870    1,050      3,445
 9      Sky-views      70        60        55      120        305
10
11
12
13
14
15
16
17
18
19
20
21
22
25-May-89   01:19 PM
```

FIGURE 13-10.   Labels centered with Allways

1. Select /Layout PageSize and look at the list of options.

2. Press ESC to leave the current choice unchanged, although it would be possible to select another size for a special need.

3. Select Margins from the Layout menu. You could select and enter a new number for any margin.

4. Select Top, type **2**, and press ENTER.

5. Select Quit to exit the Margin menu.

Printing the Allways Document

Once you have made all the changes you need, you can print the document. You must print it from Allways to see the enhancements you have made in the printout. All of the Allways options for printing can be accessed by selecting /Print. You can define any size range you wish and can print this range with all its enhancements to the printer or to a file. You can also choose to print more than one copy of the selected range.

To specify the print range, select /Print Range Set, highlight the desired range, and press ENTER. You can use the /Print Range Clear command to eliminate a print range. Try this now with the current worksheet:

1. Select /Print Range Set.

2. Press the HOME key to move to A1.

3. Type . and then the END key followed by the HOME key to move to the last non-blank cell on the worksheet.

4. Press ENTER.

5. Select Go from the menu to print a copy.

CHANGING THE PRINT SETTINGS   Allways has print settings that allow you to further customize your output. You can use these options to print multiple copies of your output or to print a selected range of pages.

To print two copies of output, follow these steps:

1. Select /Print Settings Copies.

2. Type **2** and press ENTER.

3. Select Quit to exit the Settings menu.

To print a selected range of pages, follow these steps:

1. Select /Print Settings Begin.

2. Type the number of the first page you wish to print and then press ENTER.

3. Select End, type the number of the last page you want to print, and press ENTER.

4. Select Quit.

Adding Graphs to the Display

Allways supports the display of graphs created in 1-2-3 by placing these graphs in a range of the worksheet. Allways automatically sizes the graph for the size of the selected range. You will be able to print the graphs on the same page as worksheet text because Allways uses the same Print commands to print a worksheet whether it consists of worksheet entries, graphs, or a combination of both.

To display a graph on the worksheet you will need to have a copy of the desired 1-2-3 graph saved as a .PIC file on disk. These graph files are created with 1-2-3's /Graph Save command once a graph is displayed in 1-2-3. Once you have stored the graph files on disk in 1-2-3, displaying them in Allways is as simple as selecting /Graph Add and choosing the name of the .PIC file.

To add a couple of graphs to the current display, follow these steps.

1. Select /Quit to return to 1-2-3. The 1-2-3 worksheet will display again.

2. Select /Graph to invoke 1-2-3's Graph menu. Select Type Bar.
    You will create two graphs—a bar graph and a pie chart. If you have never created a 1-2-3 graph before, you will want to be sure to look at the details in Chapter 8.

3. Select Group, highlight A6..E9, press ENTER, and select Columnwise so that 1-2-3 divides the range into data series according to columns.
    If you are using Release 1A, 2, or 2.01, you must select each range individually. For the X range, select X to specify the X range, highlight A6..A9, and press ENTER. For the A range, select A to specify the A range, highlight B6..B9, and press ENTER. For the B range, select B to specify the B range, highlight C6..C9, and press ENTER. For the C range, select C to specify the C range, highlight D6..D9, and press ENTER. For the D range, select D to specify the D range, highlight E6..E9, and press ENTER.

4. Select Save, type **BAR1**, and press ENTER.
    You could have added legends and titles to the graph with the techniques used in Chapter 8, but instead you will have a quick graph to use with Allways without any further entries.

5. Select Reset Graph to clear the bar graph specifications.

6. Select Quit to leave the Graph menu. Enter the numbers **1** through **4** in G1..G4 to use later for establishing hatch-mark patterns.
    This step must be completed while you are in READY mode.

7. Select /Graph Type Pie.

8. Select A, highlight B6..B9, and press ENTER.

9. Select X, highlight A6..A9, and press ENTER.

10. Select B to establish hatch-mark patterns, highlight G1..G4, and press ENTER.

11. Save the graph by selecting Save, typing **PIE1**, and pressing ENTER.

12. Select Quit to return to READY mode.
    You now have two 1-2-3 .PIC files on your disk that you can print with PrintGraph or Allways.

13. Select /Range Erase, highlight G1..G4 and press ENTER since the hatch pattern codes are not needed anymore.

You can add the graphs to the Allways display with these steps:

1. Press ALT-F7 to invoke Allways again.

2. Move the cell pointer to A11.

3. Select /Graph Add.

4. Highlight BAR1 and press ENTER.

5. Move the cell pointer to D26 and press ENTER.
   The bar graph now appears on your Allways screen as in Figure 13-11.

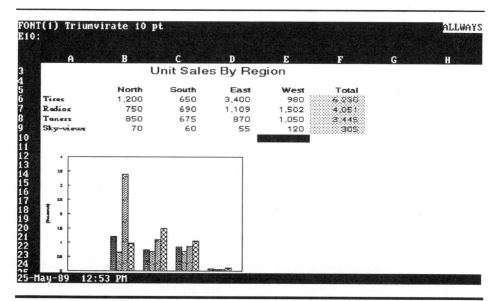

FIGURE 13-11.   Adding a bar graph

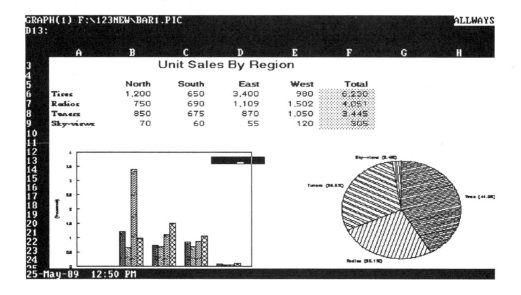

FIGURE 13-12.   Two graphs added

6. Move the cell pointer to E10.

7. Select /Graph Add.

8. Highlight PIE1 and press ENTER.

9. Move the cell pointer to I27 and press ENTER.

The two graphs display on the Allways sheet and can be printed. Figure 13-12 shows the Allways sheet with two graphs added. If the /Display Graphs command is set to No, only the X pattern shown in Figure 13-13 will appear on your screen.

Printing Graphs with Allways

Printing a graph with Allways is no different from printing a worksheet that contains text. You will use the same menu selections to specify the range of the worksheet that

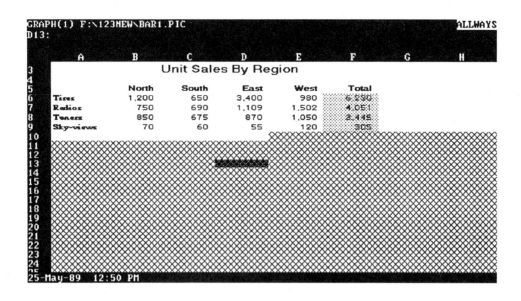

FIGURE 13-13.   Allways display with /Display Graphs set to No

contains graphs. You can also make other menu selections to change settings if desired. When you are ready to print the graph, select Go from the Print menu.

REVIEW EXERCISE

You can try out some of the Allways features by first entering the budget analysis data shown in Figure 13-14. The worksheet uses a default format of comma with 0 decimal places. Column A's width is 18. The column headings are right-aligned. The formula in D4,+B4-C4 is copied to D5..D8.

1. After making the entries, attach and invoke Allways, and then display the heading in B1 in a Times 14-point font.
   Hint: Use /Format Font.

2. Use the Times 10-point font for the entries in A4..A8 and B3..D3. Also use bold on these entries.
   Hint: Use /Format Font and /Format Bold Set.

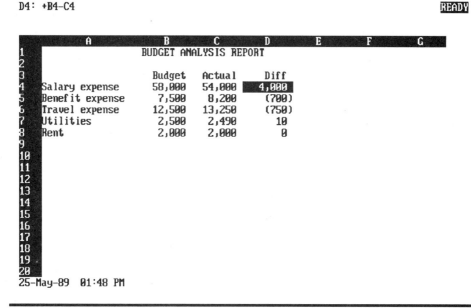

FIGURE 13-14.   Budget analysis worksheet

3. Use light shading to show the over-budget difference computations in D5 and D6.

   Hint: Use /Format Shade Light and select D5..D6 as range and press ENTER. Your Allways screen will look like the one in Figure 13-15.

4. Print two copies of the worksheet from Allways.

   Hint: Use /Print Settings, /Print Set, and /Print Range Go.

5. Return to 1-2-3 and create a bar graph that shows the Budget figures as the A range and the Actual numbers as the B range. Save the graph, and then return to Allways and add it to the display.

   Hint: Use /Quit to leave Allways. Create the graph by selecting /Graph Type Bar Group, choosing the range A4..C8, selecting Columnwise Save, typing filename, pressing ENTER, and selecting Quit. To add the graph to the worksheet in Allways, invoke Allways, move to where you want to add the graph (such as A10) and select /Graph Add. Highlight the name of the graph image file and press ENTER.

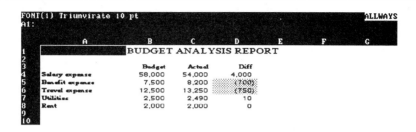

FIGURE 13-15.   Budget analysis after formatting by Allways

REVIEW

- Allways allows you to significantly enhance the appearance of printed output.

- As a first step you must attach Allways by pressing ALT-F10 and selecting Attach from the menu for the Add-in Manager. You can assign Allways to one of the hot keys (ALT-F7 through ALT-F10).

- To invoke Allways once it is attached, press the hot key assigned or press ALT-F10 and select Invoke from the menu.

- You can activate the Allways menu by typing / (slash). Typing a **Q** with the menu active returns you to 1-2-3. You can also leave Allways by pressing ESC when the Allways mode indicator is on the screen.

- You can change the appearance of the worksheet with the many Allways format options. Graphs can be displayed in any range of the worksheet if you have a 1-2-3 graphic image file stored on disk.

- Column widths and row heights can also be changed with Allways. When you return to 1-2-3, changes made with Allways will not be apparent on your 1-2-3 screen. Saving a 1-2-3 file will save your Allways modifications, making them available again the next time you load the spreadsheet and invoke Allways.

Commands and Keys

Entry	Action
/AA	/Add-In Attach loads an add-in to memory
/AC	/Add-In Clear unloads all add-ins from memory
/AD	/Add-In Detach unloads an add-in from memory

| /AI | /Add-In Invoke starts a loaded add-in |
| /AQ | /Add-In Quit leaves the Add-In Manager menu |

Allways Commands

Entry	Action
/Quit	/Quit returns you to 1-2-3
/DG	/Display Graphs toggles the display of graphs on and off
/DZ	/Display Zoom enlarges or contracts the worksheet display
/FFB	/Format Font Bold applies boldface to the selected range
/FFD	/Format Font Default restores or updates the default font set
/FFL	/Format Font Library allows you to access the Allways fonts library file
/FFR	/Format Font Replace replaces a font in the Allways font set
/FFU	/Format Font Use allows you to select a font for a specific range
/FL	/Format Lines adds lines or an outline around cells
/FR	/Format Reset eliminates formatting
/FS	/Format Shade adds light, dark, or black shading
/FU	/Format Underline adds or clears single or double underlining
/GA	/Graph Add adds a graph to a range on the worksheet
/GR	/Graph Remove removes a graph from the worksheet
/LP	/Layout PageSize sets the dimensions of a printed page
/LM	/Layout Margins allows you to change any of the page margins
/PG	/Print Go starts printing
/PR	/Print Range clears or sets the print range
/PS	/Print Settings allows you to specify the number of copies and a range of pages to print
/SC	/Special Copy copies formats from one range to another
/WCR	/Worksheet Column Reset reestablishes the same column width used by 1-2-3
/WCS	/Worksheet Column Set-Width alters the column width
F1	Activates help
F3	Displays range or filenames for your selection
F4	Zooms out to reduce the size of entries on the screen
F5	Moves to a worksheet cell
F6	Toggles between graphics display and text display mode
F10	Toggles the display of graphs on and off
SHIFT-F4	Zooms in to increase the size of entries on the screen

INSTALLING 1-2-3
AND ALLWAYS

This appendix is designed to serve as an introduction to installing Lotus 1-2-3 on your system. It will cover 1-2-3 installation on various types of equipment. Whether you use a hard disk or a floppy disk, you will find detailed instructions to ensure that the installation process proceeds smoothly. In addition, this appendix includes directions for installing Allways, which requires a hard disk.

If your copy of 1-2-3 has already been installed by your computer dealer or someone else in your organization, you do not need to read this appendix. If your copy of 1-2-3 is still covered in shrink wrap, you will need to install the package. The same is true for Allways. In that case you will find this appendix to be a valuable reference for the steps that you must take. It will also provide some information on various equipment options to help you make intelligent selections during the installation process.

Before beginning with specifics, this appendix will introduce the hardware options and the various system components. You cannot install 1-2-3 or Allways if you do not have at least some general knowledge about the system you will be using. In order for the Install program to configure your copy of 1-2-3 and Awsetup to set up your copy of Allways to run with your specific hardware components, you must be able to tell the program what those components are.

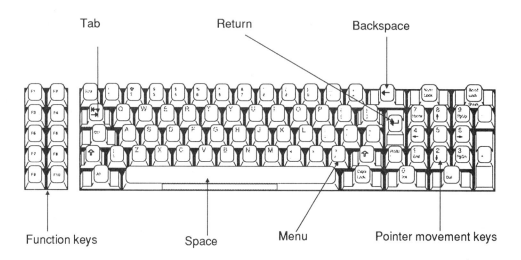

FIGURE A-1.   Regular keyboard

YOUR EQUIPMENT

1-2-3 and Allways are designed to run on a personal computer or on one of the newer 80286- or 80386-based machines such as an AT or a PS/2 from IBM, or a compatible computer. Because the compatible market is constantly changing, you will need to check with your dealer for the most up-to-date list of certified compatibles. In case of doubt, have the dealer demonstrate 1-2-3 and Allways on the machine you are considering.

Throughout this appendix, the assumption is made that you have an IBM PC, XT, AT, or PS/2. The regular keyboard that the PC and XT use is shown in Figure A-1. The enhanced keyboard that the AT and PS/2 use is shown in Figure A-2. If you have a certified compatible, look at the keyboard of your machine to locate the keys shown in the two figures on your own system.

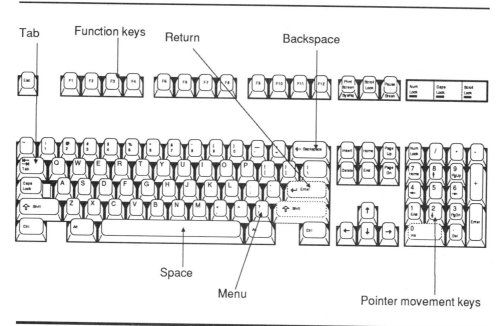

FIGURE A-2.   Enhanced keyboard

Minimum Configuration

The minimum system configuration required for 1-2-3 is listed in Table A-1. An optimal configuration for your application may require more equipment. Notice the differences in memory and disk drive support among the different versions. The minimum memory in Release 2.2 is 384K, which is greater than the 256K required for Releases 2 and 2.01, the 192K for Release 1A, and the 128K for Release 1. Also, Release 2 and higher can be used with one double-sided disk, whereas Release 1A requires either two disks or a hard disk and one double-sided disk. All of the releases can use a hard disk, although you must continue to use the System disk with Release 1A or 1. Using a hard disk to store the 1-2-3 program files prevents you from frequently having to change disks and improves the speed with which 1-2-3 performs the tasks you direct. Release 2 and higher can use expanded memory if you add a card that follows the Lotus/Intel/Microsoft (LIM) Expanded Memory Specification 2.2.

Release 1A	Release 2	Release 2.2
IBM PC, XT, AT, PS/2 or compatible	IBM PC, XT, AT, PS/2 or compatible	IBM PC, XT, AT, PS/2 or compatible
Keyboard	Keyboard	Keyboard
192K RAM	256K RAM	384K RAM
2 double-sided/double-density (DSDD) disk or 1 hard disk and 1 DSDD disk	1 DSDD disk or 1 hard disk	1 DSDD disk or 1 hard disk with 1,700,000 bytes free
Monochrome or color monitor	Monochrome or color monitor	Monochrome or color monitor

TABLE A-1.   Minimum Configuration

Allways has its own minimum configuration. Allways only runs on a computer with a hard disk. It needs an additional 128K of RAM and 1MB (1 megabyte or one million bytes) on the hard disk.

ADDING MEMORY   The models you create are limited by the amount of memory on your system. Operating 1-2-3 at the lowest memory level possible, you can use all of the package features but you are restricted in the size of your data files, the size of your spreadsheet applications, and the number of files you have in memory. If you plan to build large models, you will want to consider expanding the memory of your machine. Network and TSR software can still be used with 1-2-3 and Allways, but those other programs further limit the size of your worksheets. If you are using Allways or other add-ins with 1-2-3, you may want to disable Undo so that your worksheets do not run out of memory.

With Release 2, you also have the option of expanding memory beyond the standard 640K. To do this, select a card that conforms to the Lotus/Intel/Microsoft Expanded Memory Specification 2.2, such as the Above Board card. With these cards, 1-2-3 can use up to 4 MB of memory (approximately 4,000,000 characters) above the 640K memory limit. This expanded memory will allow you to build large data files and spreadsheets with the 1-2-3 program. You will need to run the expanded-memory management software that comes with your card before 1-2-3 can access this additional memory.

Release 2 and higher also support the addition of a math coprocessor. The 8087, the 80387, and the 80287 coprocessor chips are supported and are automatically recognized once they are installed. Spreadsheet models with a significant number of calculations are calculated much faster with one of these chips added to the motherboard of your machine.

KEYBOARD   You will begin using the keyboard in this appendix as you work with the Install program. Any directions given will refer to key names on the regular or enhanced keyboard. The enhanced keyboard offers a second set of movement keys as well as the numeric keypad so that you can use the numeric keypad for numbers while you use the second set of movement keys for moving in 1-2-3. Pressing the key labeled NUM LOCK toggles the numeric keypad between movement keys and number keys. Other keyboard types usually have the same keys, but you must look for where these keys are located.

MONITOR   Monitors can be described using two features. The first feature varies depending on whether the monitor can display multiple colors. Monitors come in two basic varieties, color and monochrome. Monochrome implies one color. This may be white, green, or amber on black. Normally a monochrome monitor will display only text, although you can add cards such as an Enhanced Graphics Adapter or a Hercules card. Even with the graphics adapter, a monochrome monitor will display one-color graphs. A color monitor can display graphs in color as well as use color for highlighting some of the 1-2-3 screens; for example, it can use red for the error indicator and blue to highlight menu choices.

The second feature of a monitor is the resolution, or how many dots of light your monitor can display across the screen—the more dots your monitor uses to fill the screen, the sharper the images it displays. The different types of monitor resolution are described with letters like CGA, EGA, and VGA. When you install 1-2-3 you will have to select the type of display you want based on the monitor's resolution and manufacturer.

PRINTERS   If you have both a dot-matrix and a letter-quality printer, you may want to use the letter-quality device for text and use the dot-matrix device to print graphics. If you have both a dot-matrix printer and a laser printer, you can use the dot-matrix for draft copies and the laser for the final output. On a network you may have a variety of output devices from which to select, including a plotter for graphics and a laser printer for professional-looking text and graphics output.

To connect any of these printers to your system, you will also need a cable and an available port. It is possible to connect printers to both parallel and serial ports as long as they are compatible, but there are some special settings if you use a serial connection. First, you must set the printer's baud rate to control the speed of data transfer. At any baud rate except 110 you should also set 1 stop bit, 8 data bits, and no parity. With a speed of 110 there should be 2 stop bits. Once the program is loaded, use the /Worksheet Global Default Printer Interface command and select the baud rate that matches your printer's rate. This is done by typing /**WGDPI**, pointing to the baud rate you need, and pressing ENTER. This change is saved with the /Worksheet Global Default Update command (/WGDU). If you are purchasing your system at the same time as you acquire 1-2-3, your dealer will usually assist you with this installation.

A plotter provides another option for producing graphs. With most devices you can use either paper or transparencies in your plotter with the appropriate pens to create the display medium of your choice. Since 1-2-3 supports only a limited number of plotters, you will want to ensure that the one you purchase is on the acceptable list; otherwise, it may not function with 1-2-3.

ADDING DISK DRIVES   1-2-3 offers several possibilities for storing the 1-2-3 programs and your data. With Release 2 and higher, you can store the 1-2-3 programs on your hard disk and use a hard disk or a floppy disk to store your data. Hard disks offer the advantage of storing large amounts of information. A hard disk that holds 100MB of information is equivalent to 278 floppy disks. Your computer may have one or two disk drives. When two disks are next to each other, the one to the left or above the other is usually referred to as drive A. The one to the right or below the other is usually referred to as drive B. If your computer only has one drive, it is drive A. Before you can store data on a floppy disk, the disk must be prepared. Use the FORMAT command described in your operating system manual or review the section "Using /System to Prepare a Disk" in Chapter 4 before storing data on floppy disks.

Another possibility is running 1-2-3 using floppy disks. You can use one or two drives with 1-2-3. If you only use one disk, you will find that the required disk swapping is quite cumbersome. Data cannot be stored on the System disk containing the program and Help files, and so you will find yourself changing disks frequently.

If you have two drives, one drive can be used for the program and the other can be used for data. This will work whether both drives are floppy disk drives or one is a hard disk drive and one is a floppy disk drive. The best configuration for using 1-2-3 is to have a hard disk drive along with a floppy disk drive so that you can load all the 1-2-3 programs on the hard disk and have the flexibility of storing data files on either the hard disk or a floppy disk. You will then be able to switch from 1-2-3 to Translate or PrintGraph without having to search for the proper disk, since all three programs will be on your hard disk. Also, with a hard disk you will be able to store files that exceed a floppy disk's capacity.

The Operating System

The operating system is the control program that resides in the memory of your computer regardless of the software you are working with. It controls the interface between the various devices and establishes the format for data storage on disk. The different releases of 1-2-3 are compatible with different versions of the DOS operating system. Since DOS is absolutely essential to using your computer and its software, make sure you have a version of DOS that is compatible with your release of 1-2-3.

Release 1A of 1-2-3 was designed to run under DOS 1.1 or higher. With Release 2 and higher, the version number for DOS depends on the type of system you have. For the IBM PC, PC XT, Portable, P, and 3270-PC, use DOS 2.0 or higher. For the IBM PC AT, use DOS 3.0 or higher. Using the IBM PCjr with the Utility program requires DOS 2.1. With the Compaq machines, use 2.02 or higher; and with the AT&T, use 2.11 or higher. All this may seem a bit confusing, but your dealer can advise you based on your configuration.

Noting Your Equipment

You are now ready to proceed with the steps needed to install your 1-2-3 disks. First, however, make a note of your hardware configuration. Table A-1 provides a convenient form for doing this. You will want this information available when you use 1-2-3's Install program and Allways' Awsetup program.

INSTALLING 1-2-3

The purpose of installation is to register your disks with your name and your company name and to tailor your 1-2-3 disks to run with your specific hardware configuration. If 1-2-3 only ran with one type of hardware, this step would not be necessary. Since it is necessary, however, you should remember that it offers you an advantage: You can continue to use the package even if you change your hardware configuration to include a plotter, a new printer, or a different monitor.

Preliminary Steps

When you purchase 1-2-3, the package you receive contains an envelope with several disks, the number of which depends on the disk size and the release of 1-2-3. 1-2-3 comes either on 3 1/2-inch disks or 5 1/4-inch disks. They provide the same information, and you should choose the size your disk drive is designed to accept. The disks have names on them that describe the function of the files on the disk. (With 3 1/2-inch disks, the data from several disks is combined on one disk.) The instructions that follow describe the disks for Release 2.2 and, in parentheses, for other releases.

The *Install disk* (called the Utility disk in previous releases) contains the installation program, Install, which copies the necessary files to your computer. The *Install Library disk* (combined with the Install disk for 3 1/2-inch disks) contains the driver files 1-2-3 uses to interface with the equipment you have. The *System disk* contains the program files 1-2-3 runs to execute 1-2-3. Releases 2 and 2.01 include a second backup System disk in case your original one is destroyed. Release 2.2 is not copy protected, so you can make your own backups. The *PrintGraph disk* contain the files for the PrintGraph program, which prints 1-2-3 files. The *Translate disk* contains 1-2-3's Translate program, which translates a data file from one format to another so you can use 1-2-3 data with other programs and use data from other programs in 1-2-3. The *Help disk* contains the file 123.HLP that 1-2-3 uses to provide HELP screens when you press F1 (HELP). The *Sample Files disk* (called the View of 1-2-3 in Releases 2 and 2.01 and the Tutorial disk in Release 1A) contains the sample files 1-2-3 provides to let you try its features without affecting your own data. If you will be using 1-2-3 from a floppy disk drive, the Install program copies the necessary drivers to the System disk. If you plan to use 1-2-3 from a hard disk drive, the Install program tells 1-2-3 which driver files to use.

You will want to complete several preliminary steps with this set of disks before running Install. First, register your 1-2-3 disks. Then locate your DOS disk, all of the 1-2-3 disks, and the same number of blank formatted disks (unless you have a hard disk). Since the steps required for installation with a hard disk are different from those required with floppy disks, the procedures will be covered separately once you have registered the floppy disks.

Registering Your Floppy Disks

Release 2.2 does not copy protect the disks as earlier versions of 1-2-3 do. Instead, you must register the disks before you can run 1-2-3. When you register your disks, you will enter a name and a company name. This information is stored on a disk that cannot change. If you try running 1-2-3 without registering it first, 1-2-3 will display a reminder to tell you that you must use the Init program first. To use the Init program to register the disks, follow these steps:

1. Insert the System disk in drive A.

2. Type **INIT** and press ENTER.

3. Press ENTER twice after reading the message on each screen.

4. Type your name and press ENTER. The Init program displays it again and asks for a confirmation.

5. Type **Y** and press ENTER to accept the name.

6. Enter your company name and press ENTER. Again, the Init program redisplays your entry and prompts you for confirmation.

7. Type **Y** and press ENTER to accept the company name. Init reads other information from the System disk. Then Init shows all of the information that it will register on the disk.

8. Press ENTER to accept this information and write it to the disk. The Init program displays a message indicating that you are ready to install 1-2-3.

9. Press ENTER to end the Init program. When the DOS A> prompt returns, you are ready to use the Install program.

Installing with Floppy Disks

Use the instructions in this section if you have a system with one or two disk drives but no hard drive. The basic steps of installation, in this case, are making backup copies of the Lotus disks, copying critical DOS files to the disks, and running the Lotus installation program. Because you will not be using a hard drive, you will not be able to use Allways. The installation instructions given here are for Release 2.2. If you have an uninstalled copy of an earlier release, read the instructions at the front of your Lotus manual, as there are a few differences in the installation process between releases.

MAKING BACKUP DISKS   Before you use the 1-2-3 disks to create worksheets, you want to protect your investment from accident. If you are using 1-2-3 from floppy disks, you should back up the disks. If an accident should ever happen to your backup disks, you can use the originals. It is worthwhile to back up all the disks, even if you think you will not use some of them. After completing the backup, store the original disks in a safe place and use the backups.

The procedure for backing up the disks is as follows:

1. Format as many disks as you have 1-2-3 disks by placing your DOS disk in drive A and a blank disk in drive B and typing **FORMAT B: /S**. The /S will put part of DOS on the disk. When the Format operation is complete, DOS will prompt you to create another disk. Respond by typing **Y** and pressing ENTER until all blank disks are formatted. If you only have one disk drive, you must wait until DOS prompts you to insert the disk to be formatted and then place it in drive A.

2. Label each of the disks so that they have the same titles as the original disks.

3. With DOS loaded in your system, place one of the 1-2-3 disks in drive A and a formatted blank disk in drive B.

4. Type **COPY A:*.* B:** /V and press the ENTER key. Lotus recommends the use of the Copy command rather than Diskcopy because the /V parameter for Copy causes DOS to verify each file after it is copied to ensure that it matches the original exactly.

    With a one-drive system, DOS will prompt you to take the disks in and out several times, since DOS can copy only a limited amount of data at one time.

5. Once the first disk has been copied, remove both the original and the copy from the drives and apply the label to the newly copied disk. Then proceed to copy the other disks.

If you use the copies and store the originals, you can remedy a failure in one of the copies by making another copy from the original disk.

COPYING COMMAND.COM TO YOUR DISKS   Although it is not possible to place all of the DOS files on your Lotus disks because of space limitations, you may want to place the DOS COMMAND.COM file on the disks. This will prevent an Error Message from appearing every time you exit 1-2-3 or one of the other programs. If you choose to omit this step, you will see the Error Message "Insert disk with COMMAND.COM in drive A and strike any key when ready" every time you exit 1-2-3 or an auxiliary program.

You will probably want to add COMMAND.COM to the System disk, PrintGraph, and the Translate disk. Placing COMMAND.COM on the disks will not make the disks bootable, however, so you will have to load DOS into your system before beginning to work with any of these programs. The following directions for copying COMMAND.COM are for a two-drive system, but you can easily adapt them to a one-drive system by using the instructions in the preceding section.

1. Insert your DOS disk in drive A and boot your system if the DOS A> prompt is not on your screen.

2. Place your System disk in drive B without a write-protect tab.

3. Type **COPY A:COMMAND.COM B:** /V and press ENTER.

    This will copy COMMAND.COM to drive B and verify the copy to ensure that it is correct.

4. Remove the System disk. Repeat the procedure for the Translate disk and the PrintGraph disk.

Hardware

Computer manufacturer   _____

Computer model   _____

Graphics card   _____

Monitor   _____

RAM   _____

Printer manufacturer/model   _____

Printer interface
(serial or parallel)   _____

Plotter model   _____

Plotter interface
(serial or parallel)   _____

Disk drives—number and type
(Hard vs. Floppy)   _____

Software

DOS version number   _____

Lotus 1-2-3 version   _____

FIGURE A-3.   Configuration worksheet

You are now ready to install 1-2-3 for your equipment. Make sure that you have your completed equipment configuration worksheet (Figure A-3) handy.

RUNNING INSTALL WITH A FLOPPY DISK SYSTEM   It is possible to use your 1-2-3 package without running the Install program, but without it you will not be able to use a printer or display a graph. Since you probably will want to do at least one of these things eventually, you might as well complete the installation now. You will want to start the Install program directly from DOS, so make sure the DOS disk is in drive A. Then boot your system. Once you see the A> DOS prompt, follow these steps:

1. Place the Install disk in drive A. Type **Install** and press ENTER.

2. Press ENTER after reading the opening screen.

3. Replace the Install disk with the Install Library disk if you are using 5 1/4-inch disks when Install prompts you to change the disks. Press ENTER.

4. Replace the current disk with the System disk when Install prompts you to change the disks. Press ENTER.

5. Since this is a first-time installation, select that option from the menu screen presented (see Figure A-4). Install will then take you on a guided tour through the entire installation process.

6. Install wants to ensure that you can use the numeric keypad to select options in the Install program. Press the key labeled NUM LOCK if NUM appears in the bottom of the screen. Press ENTER to continue.

7. Install will ask you if your monitor can display graphs, if you have a text printer, and if you want to print graphs. After you select Yes or No, you will be asked to select the monitor and the text and graphics printers in your configuration. Figures A-5 and A-6 show two of the selection screens that will be presented to you during installation. Refer to the equipment configuration you listed on your worksheet to supply the correct selections. When you select a printer, the Install program displays manufacturers. After you select a manufacturer, Install displays additional selection boxes from which you select the printer model.

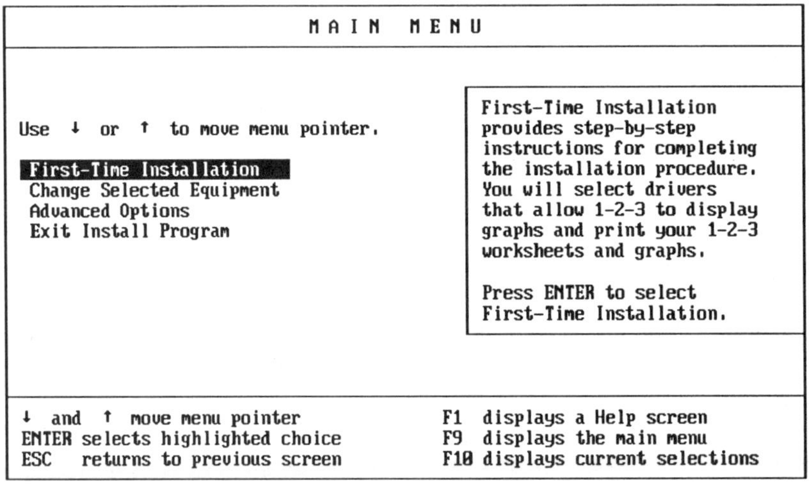

```
                        M A I N   M E N U

 ┌─────────────────────────────┐ ┌─────────────────────────────┐
                                   First-Time Installation
 Use  ↓  or  ↑  to move menu       provides step-by-step
 pointer.                          instructions for completing
                                   the installation procedure.
 ┌─────────────────────────────┐  You will select drivers
 │ First-Time Installation     │  that allow 1-2-3 to display
 └─────────────────────────────┘  graphs and print your 1-2-3
 Change Selected Equipment         worksheets and graphs.
 Advanced Options
 Exit Install Program              Press ENTER to select
                                   First-Time Installation.



 ↓ and ↑ move menu pointer         F1  displays a Help screen
 ENTER selects highlighted choice  F9  displays the main menu
 ESC   returns to previous screen  F10 displays current selections
```

FIGURE A-4.   Install's main menu

```
                     S I N G L E   M O N I T O R

 IBM/Compaq Video Graphics (VGA 80 x 25)
 IBM/Compaq Video Graphics (VGA 80 x 43)
 IBM/Compaq Video Graphics (VGA 80 x 50)     Select this if you want to use
 IBM/Compaq Enhanced Graphics (EGA 80 x 25)  a color or single-color
 IBM/Compaq Enhanced Graphics (EGA 80 x 43)  (monochrome) monitor
 IBM Multi-Color (MCGA) Color                with an IBM or Compaq Video
 IBM Multi-Color (MCGA) Monochrome           Graphics Adapter (VGA) to
 IBM color card, color monitor              display text and graphs,
 IBM color card, single-color monitor       and you want a standard
 Hercules Graphics card (80 x 25)           80 x 25 screen display.
 Hercules Graphics card (90 x 38)
 Hercules RamFont - Combined (90 x 25)
 Hercules RamFont - Combined (90 x 38)
 Toshiba T3100/T5100 (80 x 25)
 Toshiba T3100/T5100 (80 x 50)
 Use ↓ to see more selections below.

 ↓  and  ↑  move menu pointer         F1  displays a Help screen
 ENTER selects highlighted choice     F9  displays the main menu
 ESC   returns to previous screen     F10 displays current selections
```

FIGURE A-5.   Selection of monitor display options

```
                     T E X T   P R I N T E R (S)

   Anadex
   C. Itoh
   Canon                              Select the brand name of your
   Diablo                             text printer from the list on
   Epson                              the left by highlighting it
   GE/Genicom                         and pressing ENTER. If you
   HP                                 have more than one text
   IBM                                printer, you can return to
   IDS                                this list and select another.
   Inforunner
   Infoscribe                         To cancel a selected printer,
   MPI                                highlight the brand name and
   NEC                                press DEL.
   Okidata
   Printek
 Use ↓ to see more selections below.

 ↓  and  ↑  move menu pointer         F1  displays a Help screen
 ENTER selects highlighted choice     F9  displays the main menu
 ESC   returns to previous screen     F10 displays current selections
```

FIGURE A-6.   Selection of printer manufacturers

8. If you are creating only one set of installation parameters, you will want to save your selections as 123.SET. When Install asks if you want to name the driver set, select No, and Install will automatically use the 123.SET filename to store your selections. If you plan to create two or more sets, you can start over with the First-Time Installation option for each driver. It is important that you use a different name for each driver. Once Install knows the settings file name, it is ready to copy the .SET file to the other disks.

9. Replace the System disk with the Install Library disk (Install disk for 3 1/2-inch disks) when Install prompts you to change the disks. Press ENTER.

10. Replace the current disk with the System disk when Install prompts you to change the disks. Press ENTER.

11. Replace the System disk with the PrintGraph disk if you are using 5 1/4-inch disks when Install prompts you to change the disks. Press ENTER.

12. Replace the current disk with the Translate disk when Install prompts you to change the disks. Press ENTER. This completes the installation process and you are ready to exit the Install program.

13. Press the DOWN ARROW three times and press ENTER to select End Install Program.

14. Press the DOWN ARROW and ENTER to select Yes, which confirms that you want to exit the Install program. The Install program is removed from memory and the DOS A> prompt reappears.

While you are using the Install program, you may want to press F10 to view your current selections (you will see something like Figure A-7), or you may want to alter some of the advanced options such as sort sequences that will control the order that 1-2-3 uses for resequencing information in its data-management environment. The only way to access the advanced options is to select Modify Current Driver Set from the Advanced Options menu. This will be covered in the "Modifying the Current Driver" section later in this chapter. You have the option of placing numbers first or last in the sort sequence with one of the advanced installation options.

Installing 1-2-3 on a Hard Disk

Installing with a hard disk is actually a little easier than installation with a floppy disk system. You will not have to make separate backup copies of the Lotus disks because

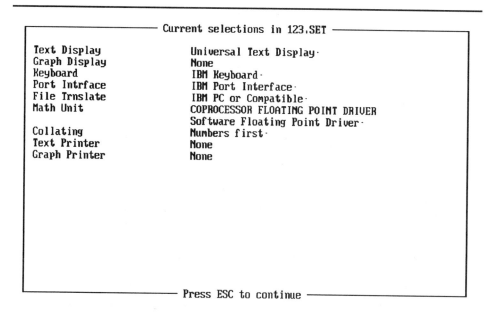

```
┌──────────────── Current selections in 123.SET ────────────────┐
│                                                                │
│   Text Display          Universal Text Display·                │
│   Graph Display         None                                   │
│   Keyboard              IBM Keyboard·                           │
│   Port Intrface         IBM Port Interface·                     │
│   File Trnslate         IBM PC or Compatible·                   │
│   Math Unit             COPROCESSOR FLOATING POINT DRIVER       │
│                         Software Floating Point Driver·         │
│   Collating             Numbers first·                         │
│   Text Printer          None                                   │
│   Graph Printer         None                                   │
│                                                                │
│                                                                │
│                                                                │
│                                                                │
│                                                                │
│                                                                │
│                                                                │
│                 ──────── Press ESC to continue ────────        │
└────────────────────────────────────────────────────────────────┘
```

FIGURE A-7.   Install listing current selections

you will be copying them to your hard disk and can therefore use your original disks as backups. This eliminates the formatting step to prepare the disks and expedites the installation program because you will not have to change disks. Everything that Install needs will already be on your hard drive.

You will have one additional step—establishing a subdirectory for your 1-2-3 files—with this approach. Subdirectories provide a method for establishing different categories of information on your disk. They can save a significant amount of time because 1-2-3 will only have to search through a section of the entries on the disk rather than through a directory with an entry for every file.

The instructions for this section assume that DOS is on your hard drive and that you are using Release 2.2 of 1-2-3. Unlike previous releases, Release 2.2 does not require you to execute a special program to have 1-2-3 work on your hard disk without a System disk in drive A. The installation for Release 2 and 2.01 is similar, but you must use the Copyon and Copyoff programs to run 1-2-3 without a System disk in drive A.

ESTABLISHING A SUBDIRECTORY   The preliminary steps for a hard disk installation will proceed quickly. You need only set up your 1-2-3 subdirectory and copy the files to the hard disk.

1. Start DOS in your system without a disk in drive A. This will force your system to boot from the copy of DOS stored on your hard disk, drive C.

2. Enter the date if you do not have a clock card. The format you should use is 12-15-89 for a date of December 15, 1989. Press ENTER after supplying the date.

3. Enter the time in the form HH:MM. If the time is 1:30 P.M., for example, type **13:30** and press ENTER. If there is a clock card in your system, you do not have to enter the time.

Now establish the subdirectory that will contain all your 1-2-3 files. These instructions use a subdirectory name of 123, but the choice of a name is yours.

1. At C>, the DOS prompt, type **MD \123** to make a subdirectory called 123. This directory will be immediately below the root directory for your disk. If you have an existing \123 subdirectory, you will want to use a different name so that the Release 2.2 files will not overwrite your other program files.

2. Make 123 the current directory by typing **CD \123**.

You now have a directory to which you can copy all your 1-2-3 files. This is a real convenience because it will save you from having to swap disks as you transfer from 1-2-3 to PrintGraph to Translate.

1. Place your 1-2-3 System disk in drive A and close the door.

2. Type **COPY A:*.* C:**. This will copy all of the files to the hard disk. Remove the System disk from drive A.

3. Repeat this with every disk. When you have completed the process, every file from every disk will reside in the 123 directory. If you need space on your hard disk for other applications, you can omit copying the sample worksheets.

RUNNING INSTALL WITH A HARD DISK SYSTEM   If the DOS C> prompt is on your screen, type **Install** and press ENTER. The rest is easy, since all of the installation files you will need are now on your hard disk. With the information from Figure A-3 handy, follow these steps to provide the information Install needs:

1. Press ENTER after reading the opening screen.

2. Since this is a first-time installation, select that option from the menu screen presented (see Figure A-4). Install will then take you on a guided tour through the entire installation process.

3. Install wants to ensure that you can use the numeric keypad to select options in the Install program. Press the key labeled NUM LOCK if NUM appears in the bottom of the screen. Press ENTER to continue.

4. Install will ask you if your monitor can display graphs, if you have a text printer, and if you want to print graphs. After you select Yes or No, you will be asked to select the monitor and the text and graphics printers in your configuration. Figures A-5 and A-6 show several of the selection screens that will be presented to you during installation. Refer to the equipment configuration you listed on your worksheet to supply the correct selections. When you select a printer, the Install program displays manufacturers. After you select a manufacturer, Install displays additional selection boxes from which you select the printer model.

5. If you are creating only one set of installation parameters, you will want to save your selections as 123.SET. When Install asks if you want to name the driver set, select No, and Install will automatically use the 123.SET filename to store your selections. If you plan to create two or more sets, you can start over with the First-Time Installation option for each driver. It is important that you use a different name for each driver. Once Install knows the settings file name, it creates the .SET file.

6. Press the DOWN ARROW three times and press ENTER to select End Install Program.

7. Press the DOWN ARROW and ENTER to select Yes, which confirms that you want to exit the Install program. The Install program is removed from memory and the DOS C> prompt reappears.

While you are using the Install program, you may want to press F10 to view your current selections (you will see something like Figure A-7), or you may want to alter some of the advanced options such as sort sequences that will control the order that 1-2-3 uses for resequencing information in its data-management environment. The only way to access the advanced options is to select Modify Current Driver Set from the Advanced Options menu. This will be covered in the "Modifying the Current Driver" section later in this chapter. You have the option of placing numbers first or last in the sort sequence with one of the advanced installation options.

With Install completed, you are now ready to use 1-2-3. You can display graphs and interface with your printer or plotter. Switching between 1-2-3 programs will be easy; all the Lotus files are stored on your disk.

USING INSTALL AFTER INSTALLING 1-2-3

Once you have installed 1-2-3, you may continue to use the Install program. You will use the Install program if you want to create more than one driver set. You may need to change the hardware configuration to include another printer or screen display. You may also want to change the sort order 1-2-3 uses for the /Data Sort command.

Creating More Than One Driver Set

If you use your Lotus software on more than one computer or if you frequently alter the configuration of your system, you will want more than one driver set. This will allow you to switch from one driver set to another without having to change the installation parameters each time.

If you use more than one driver set, pick a meaningful driver name for each, such as 2MONITOR, PLOTTER, or HOME. You can use up to eight characters for the first part of the name. You must avoid the following symbols: , . ; : / ? * ^ + = < > [ ] \ '. Install adds a .SET extension to the filename, as in COLOR.SET.

Use the First-Time Installation option to create each driver set. Save each driver set under a different name. You may want to store each multiple driver set on a separate disk or in a different directory, if you want to use different drivers with the files in different drives or directories. In this case, you will not want to save the driver set to the Translate and PrintGraph disks.

To use a driver set other than 123.SET, copy it to the 1-2-3 System disk before starting the program from a disk. Another option is to specify the pathname of the driver set when you start 1-2-3, as in 123 C:\BUDGET\HOME.SET. The pathname is the drive designation followed by the directory and filename. On a floppy disk without subdirectories, simply give the drive designation and the filename, separated by a backslash (\).

Modifying the Current Driver

Install has two options for modifying the existing 1-2-3 driver sets. They are Change Selected Equipment and Advanced Options. The Change Selected Equipment option changes a driver set file. The Advanced Options option selects drivers and other settings that the driver set file selects and other settings that 1-2-3 uses.

To change the drivers that the current driver set file selects, select Change Selected Equipment. Then select whether to change the screen display, text printer, or graph printer. When Install displays the list of available screen or printer drivers, select the appropriate one and press ENTER. For printers you will need to make additional selections.

If you want to modify the drivers selected by a driver set file other than the current driver set file, you must make that driver set file current. First select Advanced Options. Then select Make Another Driver Set Current and enter the driver name that you want to modify. If you do not select a driver set file, Install uses 123.SET. Then select Modify Current Driver Set. This displays a screen like the one in Figure A-8. As the figure indicates, 1-2-3 uses separate drivers for the text screen and the graph

```
To change a driver, highlight the driver type and press ENTER.  Only drivers
that you can change appear.  If you don't know how to combine Text and
Graph Display drivers, use the Change Selected Equipment, main menu option.

Return to menu          Leave driver list
Text Display            Universal Text Display·
Graph Display           None
Port Intrface           IBM Port Interface·
Math Unit               COPROCESSOR FLOATING POINT DRIVER
                        Software Floating Point Driver·
Collating               Numbers first·
Text Printer            None
Graph Printer           None
```

FIGURE A-8.   Install menu for modifying current driver set

screen. If you only selected one monitor, Install selected the graph screen driver and text screen driver based on the selection you made for the screen display. This screen also includes other options that you did not select when you created the driver set, but you can change these now.

CHANGING THE DISPLAY   The display driver may need to be changed if you want to change the initial display driver or you want to use different drivers for graphs and text. Several of the monitors can use more than one display driver. For example, if you are using a monitor with a VGA display, you may want to see how your graphs will look to someone with an EGA monitor. To change a display driver, select Text Display or Graph Display. The Install program lists the possible selections with a triangle next to the display driver that is currently selected. When you select a different driver, Install replaces the current selection with the new selection.

If you want to select the display drivers as you did when you created the driver set, select Return to menu and then select Change Selected Equipment and Screen Display. This assigns the text display and graph display drivers at the same time.

CHANGING THE PRINTER   The printer driver may need to be changed if you change the printer or you want to add another one. 1-2-3 allows up to four text printer drivers and unlimited graph print drivers. To add or change a printer driver from the screen in Figure A-8, select Text Printer or Graph Printer. The Install program lists the possible printer manufacturers with a triangle next to the printer manufacturer that you have selected. To add another printer driver, select the printer driver you want to add. Then make the additional menu selections appropriate for the printer. This selects the printer driver that you added as the secondary printer driver. To remove a printer driver, select Text Printer or Graph Printer and press DEL after highlighting the manufacturer and the model.

To select a printer driver for 1-2-3, use the /Worksheet Global Default Printer Name command. Then type the number that represents the selected driver. To select a printer driver for PrintGraph, use the /Settings Hardware Printer command and select the printer driver from the list that PrintGraph displays. Notice that some printer selections made in Install have two or more selections in PrintGraph because some printers have multiple density or color selections for printing. If you want many graph printer drivers selected with the driver set and you are using 1-2-3 on floppy disks, you should only change the driver set on the PrintGraph disk so you do not run out of room on the other disks.

CHANGING THE SORT ORDER   The Collating option allows you to change the collating sequence for the existing driver set. Install provides three options: ASCII, Numbers first, and Numbers last. If you are not familiar with sorting sequences, look

```
┌──────────────────────── Help Screen ─────────────────────────┐
│                                                               │
│ The collating sequence determines the order in which 1-2-3 sorts entries │
│ that include both numbers and letters.  Here are the results of a sort in │
│ ascending order, depending on which collating sequence you choose:        │
│                                                               │
│                                                               │
│ Numbers first            Numbers last           ASCII         │
│ ─────────────            ─────────────           ─────────────  │
│ 22 Rye Road              One emerald city        22 Rye Road   │
│ 23 Chestnut Avenue       One Emerson Place       23 Chestnut Avenue │
│ 39 Columbus Street       Parkway Towers          39 Columbus Street │
│ One emerald city         Three Center Plaza      One Emerson Place  │
│ One Emerson Place        22 Rye Road             One emerald city   │
│ Parkway Towers           23 Chestnut Avenue      Parkway Towers     │
│ Three Center Plaza       39 Columbus Street      Three Center Plaza │
│                                                               │
│ Note that ASCII is identical to Numbers first, except that uppercase letters │
│ come before lowercase.  Earlier releases of 1-2-3 use the ASCII collating    │
│ sequence.                                                     │
│                                                               │
└──────────────────── Press ESC to leave Help ─────────────────┘
```

FIGURE A-9.   HELP screen illustrating different sort options

at the Install HELP screen shown in Figure A-9 for a sample of the three options. The sort order for each option is as follows:

- ASCII: Blank cells, followed by labels and values in ASCII order. Capitalization will affect the sort order with this choice. This selection also makes @ functions case-sensitive and can have serious implications for formulas containing string functions that are used in computations or for the criteria area with /Data Query commands.

- Numbers last: Blank cells, label entries with letters in alphabetical order, label entries beginning with numbers in numeric sequence, labels beginning with special characters, and then values.

- Numbers first: Blank cells, labels beginning with numbers in numeric sequence, labels beginning with letters in alphabetical order, labels beginning with special characters, and then values.

To change the collating sequence, select Collating from the menu and then select the sort order you want from the submenu.

Saving the Driver Files

Once you have changed your driver file's display, printer, and sort configurations, you need to save them so that the driver file will contain your new selections. To save the driver file, select Return to menu and then select Save Changes. When 1-2-3 displays the filename, edit it if you want the new settings saved with a different filename. When the filename is correct, press ENTER to save the updated changes. When the new driver set file is saved, you are instructed to press F9 to return to the last menu or press ENTER to leave Install. After pressing ENTER, you must select Yes to confirm that you want to leave Install.

Changing Other
Configuration Parameters

Most of the hardware configuration options are specified in the installation process. However, two additional options that could require frequent change are changed directly from 1-2-3. One is the disk drive assignment for data files, and the other is the printer settings. The disk drive assignment can be changed from the default drive of C:\123R3 to another drive. The command to do this within 1-2-3 is /Worksheet Global Default Directory. Printer settings can be changed with /Worksheet Global Default Printer. The changes made with this command can be saved with /Worksheet Global Default Update.

INSTALLING ALLWAYS

After you have installed 1-2-3 on a hard disk, you are ready to install Allways. Unlike the 1-2-3 installation program, the Allways installation program selects the printers you will use and copies the files for you. To install Allways, follow these steps:

1. Insert the Allways Setup disk in drive A. You can also use drive B.

2. Type **A:** and press ENTER to make drive A the current drive.

3. Type **AWSETUP** and press ENTER to start the Allways setup program.

4. Press ENTER after reading the opening screen.

5. Press ENTER to select First-Time Installation.

6. Enter the drive and directory containing the 1-2-3 files if they are not in C:\123. When the drive and directory are correct, press ENTER. Awsetup cannot install Allways without modifying 1-2-3 files. The drive and directory also tell Awsetup where on the hard disk to copy the Allways files.

7. Awsetup will prompt you to find out whether it has selected the correct display driver. If the selection is correct, press ENTER. If it is incorrect, select No and select the correct display driver from the list. If your screen cannot display graphs, you can still use Allways but your screen will not display the worksheet as Allways will print it. When Allways uses the correct display driver and can display graphics, it creates a what-you-see-is-what-you-get (WYSIWYG) display.

8. Awsetup will prompt you to select the correct printer from the list. Highlight your printer and press ENTER. Since Allways stores the printer information on disks 2 through 5, it will prompt you to enter one of those disks in the current drive. After you replace the Setup disk with the disk the Awsetup program requests, press ENTER. Awsetup will copy this information to the Allways subdirectory under the 1-2-3 directory. Once it has copied the files, Awsetup prompts if you want to choose another printer.

9. Select Yes if you will use Allways with another printer and repeat step 7, or select No. Once the printers are selected, Awsetup copies the fonts from the disks.

10. For each of the disks, starting with the Setup disk, insert the disk when Awsetup prompts you and press ENTER. Once the fonts are copied, the installation program is complete.

11. Select Exit to DOS and then select Yes to confirm that you want to leave Awsetup. When the DOS prompt returns, you are ready to use Allways.

GLOSSARY

@ Function   A prerecorded formula that is already stored internally in 1-2-3. You can access these functions by following a set of rules stating that built-in functions are accessed with @ followed by a keyword and, in most cases, a set of parentheses around specific arguments that provide the values the functions will use. Functions have different areas of applications including statistical, mathematical, and financial. For example, @SUM(A1..B10) will total all the values in the cells within the range A1..B10. You can use functions as part of another formula or function, as in @PMT(@SUM(A4..A10),C5,D10).

Absolute   A type of reference used in a worksheet formula. An absolute cell reference always refers to the original cell regardless of where the formula is copied. An absolute reference is distinguished from other types of references by the dollar sign ($) in front of both the row and the column portion of the address. Examples are $A$2, $D$50, $Z$3.

Alignment   The placement of a label entry within a cell. 1-2-3 allows left, right, or center alignment of label entries within a cell. Special label indicators are used to control the alignment. The caret (^) is used for center alignment, an apostrophe (') for left alignment, and the double quotation mark (") for right alignment.

Allways   An add-in package that 1-2-3 provides with Release 2.2. This add-in program prints worksheets and graphs, offering printer enhancements such as bold-face, underlining, and character sizing. This package can also be purchased for Releases 2 and 2.01.

Arguments   Individual values, quote-enclosed labels, range references, or range names that define how you wish to use a built-in function or a command language instruction. The number and type of arguments supplied will depend on the function or command language instruction selected. When cell references are included in your arguments, you have the option of typing the reference or pointing to the cell or range you wish to select.

Arithmetic Operators   Symbols used in 1-2-3 formulas to define the type of mathematical operation to be performed. When more than one arithmetic operator is included in a formula, they are evaluated from left to right, using a priority order for the operators. The valid arithmetic operators and their order of precedence is

^	Exponentiation
+, −	Positive, negative number
*, /	Multiplication, division
+, −	Addition, subtraction

Parentheses can be used to override the order of precedence.

ASCII   A format for file storage in which text and special characters are assigned code numbers. This standard coding system facilitates the exchange of information between programs, since a standard code represents each character. 1-2-3 is able to bring ASCII data into the worksheet with the /File Import command. The characters in the acronym ASCII represent American Standard Code for Information Interchange.

Axis   The horizontal (X axis) or vertical (Y axis) line that provides the framework for the construction of most types of graphs. The X axis is used to represent the categories in the data series that are being plotted. The Y axis functions as a scale for a quantitative measurement of the data shown on the graph.

Backup   A copy of a file (with a slightly different name so the operating system can distinguish it from the original file) used to store data in case you lose the newest version. The Release 2.2 File commands provide the option of saving to a backup when you try saving a file to an existing filename. The backup copy of the file has a .BAK extension.

Built-in Function   *See @ Function.*

Cell   A single location on the worksheet. You have the option of storing a number, label, or formula in a worksheet cell. Other characteristics, such as label alignment and formatting, can also be specified for one or more worksheet cells.

Cell Pointer   The highlighted bar that marks the current cell on the worksheet. The cell pointer can be moved with the arrow keys and with other special keys such as HOME, END, PGUP, PGDN, and the F5 (GOTO) key.

Cell Reference   A reference to a worksheet cell in a formula. There are three types of cell references that you can use: a relative reference (A1), an absolute reference ($A$3), and a mixed reference (A$4 or $A4).

Circular Reference   A reference that depends on itself to calculate a result. For example, if a formula were stored in A1 as +A3/A1*2, this would be a circular reference. This particular example is a direct use of a reference to the cell itself. In many cases, the dependence on itself is indirect. 1-2-3 will place a CIRC indicator at the bottom of the screen when a worksheet contains a circular reference. In Release 2 and higher, you can use the /Worksheet Status command to identify the first cell causing the circular reference.

Column   The vertical division of the worksheet, consisting of one cell from each row of the worksheet in a vertical column. A column of cells on the worksheet can be widened or narrowed as well as hidden with Release 2 and higher.

Column Width   The number of characters that can be stored in a column. You can change this number globally or for an individual column. The default column width is 9 characters. In Release 2 and higher, you can widen a column to 240 characters; in Release 1A, you can widen it to 72. The narrowest width permissible for all releases is 1 character.

Command Language   The advanced macro commands that make up the 1-2-3 macro command language. These commands provide a full programming language to 1-2-3 users that can extend the usefulness of the macro features beyond a duplication of 1-2-3 menu commands. The command language instructions all appear within braces ({ }) and many use one or more arguments to refine their tasks. For example, {LET A1,0} is a command language instruction.

Configuration File   The file that contains the default parameters for 1-2-3. Some of the options can be set with the /Worksheet Global Default command. Choosing the

Update option from this same menu can update this file so that your changes are present in subsequent 1-2-3 sessions.

Control Panel   The area at the top of the 1-2-3 screen, consisting of three lines. The top line displays the current cell address, cell contents, and cell characteristics. The top line also displays a mode indicator in the right corner, which informs you that 1-2-3 is ready to process a new task or shows the current task. The second line serves a dual purpose. In EDIT mode, it functions as the edit line for altering your data. In MENU mode, the current menu is displayed in this line. The third line provides a description of the current menu selection in MENU mode.

Criteria   Specifications for searching the database. These criteria are entered on the worksheet and the Data commands are invoked to copy, highlight, or delete records that match the criteria you have entered.

Current Directory   The current location for 1-2-3's data files. The /File Directory command allows you to change the current disk drive and subdirectory. The File commands use the current directory unless another one is provided. The PrintGraph program also has menu options for changing the default directory for both graph and font files.

Database   A collection of individual pieces of data about a group of objects. In 1-2-3, a database is an organized structure for storing items of information (fields) about objects on the worksheet. Taken together, all the data about one object in the set is considered to be a record, which is stored across a row of the worksheet. Fields are stored vertically in columns of the worksheet, with a record having one value in each field. There are numerous 1-2-3 commands to select records from the database, as well as commands to sort it in a new sequence.

Data Series   A set of related data that is included in a graph that 1-2-3 takes from a worksheet. An example of data series is sales for each month of several products, where each product is a different series. 1-2-3 can include up to six data series in a graph.

Debugging   The process of removing errors from a computer program. Since macros can be used to write a program within 1-2-3, it is appropriate to refer to the process of testing and eliminating errors from a macro as debugging.

Desktop Publishing   Computer programs that help you to design output to enhance the basic appearance and print the enhanced output. Allways offers this feature for your worksheets and graphs.

Edit   The process of making corrections to an entry without having to completely reenter the data.

Edit Line   The second line of the control panel. This is the line where 1-2-3 displays your data as you enter it. This line also displays data that is being edited.

End   In READY mode, this indicates that you want to move your cursor to the last entry in a specific direction. After pressing END, you will always press an arrow key to indicate the direction you want to move. In EDIT mode, END takes you to the last character in a cell.

Erase   To remove from the worksheet or disk file. There are /Worksheet Erase and /Range Erase commands in 1-2-3's menus. The /Range Erase command removes the entries from the cells you specify. The /Worksheet Erase command removes the current worksheet files from memory completely. It requires a confirmation before proceeding with this option. The /File Erase command makes the space a file is using available for the storage of new files and alters the entry in the file directory.

Error Message   A message that appears at the lower left corner of the screen when an error condition is encountered. This message will appear when the printer is not ready or when the disk is full. Press F1 (HELP) to see a more complete description.

Expanded Memory   Memory greater than 640K. This memory is added on an expansion card to the motherboard of a standard PC.

Extended Memory   Memory in computers that use 80286 and 80386 processors, such as the newer model PS/2 machines and ATs. Since DOS cannot access this memory, it is unavailable to all releases except 3.0.

External File Links   A formula in a Release 2.2 worksheet that references data in another cell in another 1-2-3 worksheet. Release 2.2 formulas that use a value from another file have the formula +<<FILENAME.WK1>>CELL_ADDRESS. 1-2-3 updates these links with the /File Admin Link-Refresh command.

Extract   The process of pulling selected information from a database. Before you can use the /Data Extract command to accomplish this, you must set up an output and a criteria area on the worksheet.

Field Names   The names that are used for the types of data stored in a database. In an employee database, some of the field names you might have are Last Name, Job Code, and Salary. In 1-2-3 they are always stored at the top of a column, with the values for each record placed beneath them.

File   An organized collection of data on the disk. 1-2-3 uses filename extensions to distinguish between the various types of files it stores on disk. Print files have a filename extension of .PRN, worksheet files have an extension of .WKS (Release 1A) or .WK1 (Releases 2, 2.01, and 2.2), and graph files have an extension of .PIC.

Filename   The name that is used to access data stored on a disk. This name must follow standard DOS rules and consist of from 1 to 8 characters in the name portion of the entry. It may also include an optional 1- to 3-character filename extension. If this extension is used, a period will separate it from the filename. 1-2-3 will provide most file extensions for you.

Fonts   A set of characters in a specific typeface. 1-2-3's graphic features support various fonts for use in printing graphs, titles, legends, and labels. With the Allways add-in, you can use fonts for your worksheet data.

Format   The type of display used to present values. The format displayed may portray less internal accuracy than the package can support. Some of the permissible formats are currency, percent, scientific notation, and date.

Formula   An entry in a worksheet cell that performs a calculation. A formula in 1-2-3 can be up to 240 characters long.

Function Keys   Special keys at the left or top of the keyboard that give you quick access to some of 1-2-3's features. 1-2-3 may use these keys differently from the way that other packages use the same keys; each software vendor may use them in any way it chooses.

Graph   A representation of numeric worksheet data in a graphic format, which permits easy interpretation of results. 1-2-3 supports five graph formats: pie charts, line graphs, XY graphs, bar charts, and stacked bar charts.

Grid Lines   Horizontal and vertical lines that can be added to a graph to aid interpretation of the data points. These lines extend from the points on one or both axes.

Header   A line that can be printed at the top of every page. This line can include a report name, the preparer's name, the date, the page number, or any other information you would like printed at the top of each page of a report.

Home   The A1 location on the worksheet screen. In EDIT mode, the home position is the first character in the entry being edited.

Import   The process of bringing text into the worksheet. Text can be imported with the /File Import command as numbers or text. The Text option brings in the complete line in the text file as a long label. The Numbers option only brings in the numeric values and character data enclosed in quotes from a line of text but stores each one as a separate cell entry across a row of the worksheet.

Label   A series of up to 240 characters to be treated as text. Label entries cannot be used in arithmetic formulas. In Release 2 and higher, you can use labels in special string formulas and functions.

Label Indicator   The special character at the beginning of a cell entry that identifies the entry as a label. If you enter a non-numeric character in a cell, 1-2-3 will generate this indicator for you. If you want to enter a numeric character as a label, you must first enter the label indicator unless you want 1-2-3 to treat the entry as a value. The default label indicator is an apostrophe, indicating that the entry should be left-aligned within the cell. A double quotation mark can be used for right alignment, a caret symbol can be used for center alignment, a backslash can be used to repeat a label for the length of the cell, and a vertical bar can be used to include printer codes and page breaks in a worksheet.

Legend   A description, added to the bottom of a graph, that distinguishes one set of data on the graph from other data series that may also be shown. If a hatch pattern is used to shade bars, the legend identifies which data set each pattern represents. If symbols are used to mark the various points on a line graph, the legend identifies the symbol that represents each series.

Logical Operator   Used when you want 1-2-3 to evaluate an expression to determine whether it is true or false. The simple logical operators are as follows.

=	Equal to
>	Greater than
>=	Greater than or equal to
<	Less than
<=	Less than or equal to
< >	Not equal

In addition, three compound logical operators are used to join logical expressions: #AND, #OR#, and #NOT#. An example is @IF(A1>7 #AND# B3=6,0,12).

Macro   A form of shorthand that allows you to record 1-2-3 formulas in worksheet cells easily and to execute these same entries as commands at a later time. Macros also extend beyond this and allow you to create complete applications with your own menus and other features, using the extensions that the command language instructions provide.

Macro Keyword   An instruction from 1-2-3's macro command language that appears in braces and is used with arguments to make your specific needs known to 1-2-3. A macro keyword might look something like this in a macro:

{LET A1,1}

Macro Library   A collection of macros stored in a separate file so that you can use one macro in several worksheets.

Macro Recorder   When you use the Learn feature, 1-2-3 stores the macro representation of all of your keystrokes on the worksheet. You can use the cells containing the macro symbols for keystrokes as the basis for a macro.

Margin   The amount of white space around a printed document. 1-2-3 has default settings for a top, bottom, right, and left margins but allows you to change any of them.

Math Coprocessor   A special chip that can be added to your computer to enhance the processing speed.

Menu   A selection of features presented in a horizontal line at the top of the screen. You can activate each menu option by pointing to it and pressing ENTER or by typing the single letter beginning the selection.

Minimum Recalculation   How Release 2.2 recalculates the values in your work-sheet so that the value of the cell will only be recalculated when it contains a formula that references a cell that has changed. This feature shortens the time between when you enter a value and when 1-2-3 updates the cells in the worksheet to reflect the new value.

Mode Indicator   The indicator in the upper right corner of the 1-2-3 display screen, which lets you know what 1-2-3 is doing at any point. 1-2-3 will be waiting to process your next request only when this indicator reads READY.

Operator Precedence   The order in which the operators are processed. A list from the highest to the lowest priority follows. In formulas containing multiple operators with the same priority level, these operators are evaluated from left to right.

( )	Parentheses for grouping
^	Exponentiation
+−	Positive and negative indicators
/*	Division and multiplication
+−	Addition and subtraction
< > <= >= <>	Logical operators
#NOT#	Complex Not indicator
#AND#	Complex And indicator
#OR#	Complex Or indicator
&	String operator

Parse   To divide long pieces of data into smaller pieces of data. You can use the /Data Parse command to break long labels into smaller ones.

Pointing   A method for building worksheet formulas. With the pointing method, you type the special characters and arithmetic operators but you point to the cell addresses of interest.

PrintGraph   A program that prints your 1-2-3 graphs. This program is included in your 1-2-3 package and allows 1-2-3 to interface with a variety of printers and plotters. It provides a variety of options, including different characters sets (fonts), colors, sizes, and rotation. If you have the Allways add-in, you also have the option of printing graphs with Allways, which allows you to use Allways features and to print graphs and worksheets on the same page.

Protected Mode   A mode of memory addressing used on 80286 and 80386 machines that have more than 640K of memory. Although Release 2.2 and lower do not use the additional memory, you may use this memory to run other programs.

RAM   Random Access Memory. The location where your computer stores temporary information such as programs as they execute and the data the program uses; it can also be used as a temporary disk on which to store information until the computer is rebooted.

Range   A group of cells on the worksheet. There are many commands in 1-2-3's menus that will operate on ranges, including /Range Erase, /Range Format, and /Range Name.

Range Name   A name that you assign to a group of cells on the worksheet. This name can be from 1 to 15 characters in length. It can be used anywhere you would have used a range address to refer to the same cells. If you assign names to all ranges used in formula calculations, your formulas will be self-documenting.

Range Reference   A reference to one or more cells on the worksheet. To specify a range reference, use two cells at opposite corners of the range. For example, A1..A10, A2..B4, B4..A2, and A1..A1 are all valid ranges. Like a cell reference, a range reference can be relative, absolute, or mixed.

Recalculation   The process of reevaluating all the formulas on the worksheet. The default for 1-2-3 is to use automatic recalculation, which means that every time you make a change to a cell entry, every formula on the worksheet will be reevaluated. If you disable the automatic recalculation, you will need to press F9 (CALC) when you want to recalculate the worksheet. Release 2.2 uses minimal recalculation so your worksheets are updated quickly.

Relative   A type of cell reference used in formulas. A relative reference is entered as a reference to a specific cell in the original formula, but when this formula is copied the reference is updated based on the new location. It will still represent a cell with the same relative direction and distance as the original cell reference, but the reference will not be to the exact same cell as the original. A relative reference to a cell might look like A1, M2, or B5. It is the default reference type that is placed into a formula built with the pointing method, unless you take special action to override this default.

Rounding The process of affecting the internal precision of a number in memory. You can use 1-2-3's @ROUND function to reduce this internal precision. A number stored as 123.567 will be stored as 123.57 after being rounded to two decimal places. If this same number is rounded to a whole number, it will be 124. You can control which numbers are rounded and the place at which you would like rounding to occur. This is different from formatting, which changes the number's appearance but does not change how 1-2-3 stores the value and uses it in calculations.

Row A horizontal line of consecutive cells on the worksheet. With Release 1A, there are 2048 rows on the worksheet; with Release 2, there are 8192 rows.

Settings Sheet A screen display that appears in several Release 2.2 screens that display settings for options in the current menu. For example, the settings sheet for the Print menus displays the settings made with any command accessed through the Print menus.

Setup String A series of characters transmitted to the printer to activate certain printer features. Each printer has its own set of characters for its features. On a Hewlett Packard LaserJet Series II printer, the print font is returned to Courier from the Letter Gothic font with a setup string of \027(s10H.

String A series of characters. Release 2 and higher of 1-2-3 have several features that work with strings. You can use the concatenation character (&) to join two strings. Release 2 and higher also have a number of built-in functions that focus on string manipulation.

Titles The text characters that are used to provide description on a graph. They can be placed at the top of the graph or along the X axis or Y axis. In the worksheet environment, titles can also refer to the data that you want to freeze on the top or left side of the screen as you scroll the cell pointer down or to the right.

Undo Removes the effect of the last change that you made since 1-2-3 was in the READY mode. This feature is enabled and disabled with the /Worksheet Global Default Other Undo command. Enabling Undo reduces the memory available for your worksheet files.

Value A number or formula entry on the worksheet.

Window   A portion of the screen used to show another part of the same worksheet.

Worksheet   The entire electronic sheet of paper that 1-2-3 creates in the memory of your computer system. This worksheet is composed of many cells organized into rows and columns.

X Axis   The horizontal axis on a graph. This is the axis on which the categories of a data series are shown.

Xtract   A File menu selection that creates a worksheet file containing a subset of the current worksheet. Only the range you specify will be saved to the worksheet file with this operation. You will have the option of saving formulas or values to this file. If you choose, you can create this file as a snapshot of the current worksheet with only labels and values stored in the new file. Xtract should be distinguished from Extract, which is used in the data-management environment to copy information from the database to another area of your worksheet. Release 2.2 offers external file links as another option to refer to data in another worksheet file.

Y Axis   The vertical axis on a bar, line, or XY graph that measures quantitative units such as dollars, units sold, or number of employees.

1-2-3'S BUILT-IN FUNCTIONS

Function	Type	Available Only in Release 2 and Higher
@@(cell)	Special	*
@ABS(number)	Math	
@ACOS(number)	Math	
@ASIN(number)	Math	
@ATAN(number)	Math	
@ATAN2(x,y)	Math	
@AVG(list)	Statistical	
@CELL(attribute string,range)	Special	*
@CELLPOINTER(attribute string)	Special	*
@CHAR(code)	String	*
@CHOOSE(number,list)	Special	
@CLEAN(string)	String	*
@CODE(string)	String	*
@COLS(range)	Special	*
@COS(number)	Math	
@COUNT(list)	Statistical	
@CTERM(interest,future value, present value)	Financial	*
@DATE(year,month,day)	Date & Time	
@DATEVALUE(date string)	Date & Time	*

501

Function	Type	Available Only in Release 2 and Higher
@DAVG(input range,offset column, criteria range)	Database	
@DAY(date number)	Date & Time	
@DCOUNT(input range,offset column, criteria range)	Database	
@DDB(cost,salvage,life,period)	Financial	*
@DMAX(input range,offset column, criteria range)	Database	
@DMIN(input range,offset column, criteria range)	Database	
@DSTD(input range,offset column, criteria range)	Database	
@DSUM(input range,offset column, criteria range)	Database	
@DVAR(input range,offset column, criteria range	Database	
@ERR	Special	
@EXACT(string1,string2)	String	*
@EXP(number)	Math	
@FALSE	Logical	
@FIND(search string,entire string, starting location)	String	*
@FV(payment,interest,term)	Financial	
@HLOOKUP(code to be looked up, table location, offset)	Special	
@HOUR(time number)	Date & Time	
@IF(condition to be tested,value if true, value if false)	Logical	
@INDEX(table location,column number, row number)	Special	
@INT(number)	Math	
@IRR(guess,range)	Financial	
@ISERR(value)	Logical	
@ISNA(value)	Logical	
@ISNUMBER(value)	Logical	
@ISSTRING(number)	Logical	*
@LEFT(string,number of characters to be extracted)	String	*
@LENGTH(string)	String	*

Function	Type	Available Only in Release 2 and Higher
@LN(number)	Math	
@LOG(number)	Math	
@LOWER(string)	String	*
@MAX(list)	Statistical	
@MID(string,start number,number of characters	String	*
@MIN(list)	Statistical	
@MINUTE(time number)	Date & Time	*
@MOD(number,divisor)	Math	
@MONTH(date number)	Date & Time	
@N(range)	String	*
@NA	Special	
@NOW	Date & Time	*
@NPV(discount rate,range)	Financial	
@PI	Math	
@PMT(principal,interest,term of loan)	Financial	
@PROPER(string)	String	*
@PV(payment,periodic interest rate, number of periods)	Financial	
@RAND	Math	
@RATE(future value,present value, number of periods)	Financial	*
@REPEAT(string,number of times)	String	*
@REPLACE(original string,start location,# characters,new string)	String	*
@RIGHT(string,number of characters to be extracted)	String	*
@ROUND(number to be rounded, place of rounding)	Math	
@ROWS(range)	Special	*
@S(range)	String	*
@SECOND(time number)	Date & Time	*
@SIN(number)	Math	
@SLN(cost,salvage value,life of the asset)	Financial	*
@SQRT(number)	Math	
@STD(list)	Statistical	
@STRING(number,number of decimal places	String	*
@SUM(list)	Statistical	

Function	Type	Available Only in Release 2 and Higher
@SYD(cost,salvage value,life,period)	Financial	*
@TAN(number)	Math	
@TERM(payment,interest,future value)	Financial	*
@TIME(hour, minute,second)	Date & Time	*
@TIMEVALUE(time string)	Date & Time	*
@TRIM(string)	String	*
@TRUE	Logical	
@UPPER(string)	String	*
@VALUE(string)	String	*
@VAR(list)	Statistical	
@VLOOKUP(code to be looked up, table location, offset)	Special	
@YEAR(date number)	Date & Time	

TRADEMARKS

COMPAQ®	COMPAQ Corporation
HAL™	Lotus Development Corporation
IBM®	International Business Machines Corporation
IBM® PC AT	International Business Machines Corporation
IBM® PC XT	International Business Machines Corporation
Intel®	Intel Corporation
Lotus®	Lotus Development Corporation
Microsoft®	Microsoft Corporation
MS-DOS®	Microsoft Corporation
1-2-3®	Lotus Development Corporation
OS/2™	International Business Machines Corporation
Zenith™	Zenith Data Systems

Index

Essential 1-2-3 Release 2.2 Commands

Worksheet Commands

Alters format of all worksheet cells

Alters width of all worksheet columns

Sets recalculation to automatic

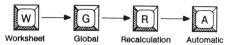

Sets recalculation to manual

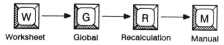

Determines whether \O macros are executed

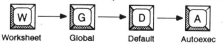

Insert rows or columns in worksheet

Deletes worksheet rows, columns, files, or sheets from memory

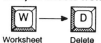

Alters width of a single column

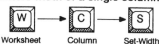

Hides a worksheet column

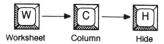

Alters width of a range of columns

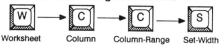

Erases worksheet even if worksheet has not been saved

Worksheet Commands

Sets and clears worksheet titles

Sets and clears worksheet windows

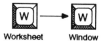

Adds page break at the cell pointer location

Range Commands

Assigns format to a range

Changes label alignment of a range of labels

Erases contents of a range

Creates and deletes range names

Applies entry in worksheet cell to the cell immediately to its right

Alters orientation of a range of entries

Allows you to search for an entry in a range

Copy Command

Copies worksheet entries and formats

Copy

Move Command

Moves worksheet entries

Move

File Commands

Retrieves file from disk

File Retrieve

Saves file to disk

File Save

Cancels save request

File Save Cancel

Tells 1-2-3 to replace disk file
with current contents of memory

File Save Replace

Creates .WK1 file and .BAK file

File Save Backup

Combines information from disk
with the current worksheet

File Combine

Saves part of a worksheet to disk

File Xtract

Erases a file on disk

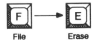

File Erase

File Commands

Creates list of files
in the current directory

File List

Imports data into worksheet

File Import

Changes current directory

File Directory

Refreshes links to external files

File Admin Link-Refresh

Print Commands

Directs print output to printer

Print Printer

Establishes range for printing

Print Printer Range

Advances one line

Print Printer Line

Advances one page

Print Printer Page

Allows you to enter a header line

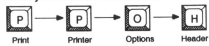

Print Printer Options Header

Allows you to enter a footer line

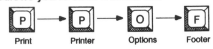

Print Printer Options Footer

Print Commands

Allows you to set top, bottom, right, left margins

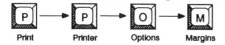

Allows you to establish border rows or columns

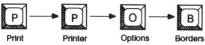

Allows you to enter a setup string to control print output

Allows you to set page length

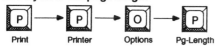

Provides access to other print settings

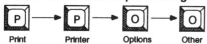

Quits the Print Options menu

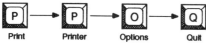

Clears print settings

Zeroes line count and tells
1-2-3 you're starting a new page

Starts printing

Allows you to print a graph

Directs print output to a disk file

Graph Commands

Allows you to select a graph type

Sets the X graph range

Sets the A graph range

Sets the B graph range

Sets the C graph range

Sets the D graph range

Sets the E graph range

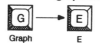

Sets the F graph range

Lets you view the graph

Saves the graph image file

Allows you to establish legends
for each graph data range

Graph Commands

Allows you to create graph titles

Allows you to establish and clear grid lines

Sets display to color

Sets display to black and white

Allows you to create and use graph names

Allows you to set all graph ranges with one command

Data Commands

Generates series of evenly spaced numbers

Specifies range for sorting

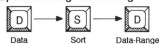

Specifies main sort key

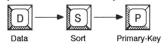

Specifies secondary sort key

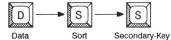

Sorts data

Data Commands

Specifies input range for query

Tells 1-2-3 which record to use

Specifies output range for query

Highlights matching records

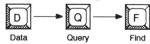

Extracts matching records

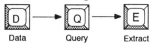

Allows you to create and edit a format line for parsing data

Defines input for data parse operation

Defines location for output of data parse

Splits long label according to definition and data parse format line

System Command

Temporarily exits to the operating system

System

Quit Command

**Quits 1-2-3 even if the worksheet
hasn't been saved**

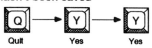

Quit   Yes   Yes

Add-In Commands

Loads an Add-In program into memory

Add-In   Attach

Removes an Add-In program from memory

Add-In   Detach

Activates an attached Add-In program

Add-In   Invoke

Clears all Add-In programs from memory

Add-In   Clear

Quits the Add-In menu

Add-In   Quit

You're important to us...

We'd like to know what you're interested in, what kinds of books you're looking for, and what you thought about this book in particular.

Please fill out the attached card and mail it in. We'll do our best to keep you informed about Osborne's newest books and special offers.

YES, SEND ME A FREE COLOR CATALOG
of all Osborne/McGraw-Hill computer books.

Name:_____ Title:_____

Company:_____

Address:_____

City:_____ State:_____ Zip:_____

I'M PARTICULARLY INTERESTED IN THE FOLLOWING*(Check all that apply)*

I use this software:
- ❏ Lotus 1-2-3
- ❏ Quattro
- ❏ dBASE
- ❏ WordPerfect
- ❏ Microsoft Word
- ❏ WordStar
- ❏ Others_____

I use this operating system:
- ❏ DOS
- ❏ OS/2
- ❏ UNIX
- ❏ Macintosh
- ❏ Others_____

I rate this book:
❏ Excellent   ❏ Good   ❏ Poor

I program in:
- ❏ C
- ❏ PASCAL
- ❏ BASIC
- ❏ Others_____

I chose this book because...
- ❏ Recognized author's name
- ❏ Osborne/McGraw-Hill's reputation
- ❏ Read book review
- ❏ Read Osborne catalog
- ❏ Saw advertisement in _____
- ❏ Found while browsing in store
- ❏ Found/recommended in library
- ❏ Required textbook
- ❏ Price
- ❏ Other_____

Comments_____
_____

Topics I would like to see covered in future books by Osborne/McGraw-Hill

include:_____
_____

ISBN# 554-1

BUSINESS REPLY MAIL

First Class   Permit NO. 3111 Berkeley, CA

Postage will be paid by addressee

Osborne **McGraw-Hill**

2600 Tenth Street
Berkeley, California 94710–9938